winterskills

The official handbook of
Mountain Training's winter schemes

Design and production

 REVISED EDITION

winterskills

Essential walking and climbing techniques

The official handbook of
Mountain Training's winter schemes

Written by **Andy Cunningham**
and **Allen Fyffe**

winterskills

The official handbook of
Mountain Training's winter schemes

Copyright © 2020   Andy Cunningham and Allen Fyffe

Published by Mountain Training United Kingdom and Ireland
www.mountain-training.org

All rights reserved. No part of this work covered by the copyright hereon may be reproduced or used in any form or by any means – graphic, electronic, or mechanised, including photocopying, recording, taping, or information storage and retrieval systems – without the written permission of the publisher.

First printed 2007
2nd Revised Edition printed 2011
3rd Revised Edition printed 2020
ISBN 978-0-9930337-1-1

Cover photo: Crossing the Ben Nevis plateau by Garry Smith

Designed, typeset and illustrated
by Vertebrate Publishing, Sheffield
www.v-publishing.co.uk

This product includes mapping data licensed from Ordnance Survey with the permission of the Controller of Her Majesty's Stationery Office. Copyright ©. All rights reserved. Licence reference 100040262

This product contains maps reproduced with the permission of Harvey, 12–16 Main Street, Doune FK16 6BJ.
www.harveymaps.co.uk

Printed and bound in China on behalf of Latitude Press Ltd.

While every attempt has been made to ensure that the instructions in this book cover the subject safely and in full detail, the authors and publishers cannot accept any responsibility for any accident, injury, loss or damage sustained while following any of the techniques described.

Contents

Authors' acknowledgements xii
Editor's note xiv
Foreword xv
   Dedication – Allister McQuoid xvi
Introduction xvii
ⓘ Participation statement xix

Part 1 The winter environment 1

1 Mountaineering equipment 3
  1.1 Clothing 4
    1.1.1 Base layer 4
ⓘ 1 Clothing 4
    1.1.2 Mid-layer 5
    1.1.3 Soft shell 5
    1.1.4 Outer shell 6
  1.2 The layering system 7
  1.3 Boots 7
    1.3.1 Leather boots 8
    1.3.2 Fabric boots 8
    1.3.3 Plastic boots 9
    1.3.4 Lacing 9
    1.3.5 Foot beds 9
  1.4 Gaiters 9
  1.5 Gloves 10
ⓘ 2 Gloves & hats 10
  1.6 Hat 11
  1.7 Rucksack 11
  1.8 Headtorch 12
  1.9 Goggles 12
  1.10 Bivvy bag 12
  1.11 Group shelter 13
  1.12 Walking poles 13
    1.12.1 Types of poles 14
    1.12.2 Use of poles 14
    1.12.3 Maintenance of poles 15
  1.13 Sunglasses 15
  1.14 Sun screen 15

2 Environmental issues 17
  2.1 Erosion 18
  2.2 Sanitation 19
  2.3 Litter 20
  2.4 Winter climbs 20
  2.5 Cairns 21
ⓘ 3 Environment issues 21

3 Winter weather 23
  3.1 Winter air masses and airflows 24
  3.2 Weather factors 26
    3.2.1 Precipitation 26
    3.2.2 Lapse rates 26
    3.2.3 Temperature 26
    3.2.4 Visibility 26
ⓘ 4 Wind 26
    3.2.5 Clouds 28
    3.2.6 Wind speeds 28
    3.2.7 Windchill 28
  3.3 Winter weather and weather forecasts 28

4 Winter navigation 31
  4.1 Problem winter conditions 32
    4.1.1 Freezing temperatures 32
    4.1.2 Snow cover 32
    4.1.3 Poor visibility 32
    4.1.4 Strong winds 33
    4.1.5 Whiteout 33
  4.2 Coping with the winter environment 33
    4.2.1 Map 33
    4.2.2 Compass 34
    4.2.3 Wristwatch 34
    4.2.4 Altimeter 35
    4.2.5 Clothing and equipment 35

4.3 Know where you are! 35
    4.3.1 Revise the basic skills .. 36
4.4 Winter navigation 38
    strategies
    4.4.1 The winter 38
        navigational leg
    4.4.2 Taking a bearing 38
    4.4.3 Sighting 39
    4.4.4 Sighting on your own . 39
    4.4.5 Sighting on a person .. 40
    4.4.6 Using footprints 40
    4.4.7 Measuring distance .. 41
    4.4.8 Estimating distance .. 41
    4.4.9 Map reading – 41
        the 'mental checklist'
4.5 Map reading 42
    considerations
    4.5.1 Short legs 42
    4.5.2 Use safe 42
        large-scale features
    4.5.3 Contours 42
    4.5.4 Route choice 42
    4.5.5 Slope changes 42
    4.5.6 On a slope 42
(i) 5 **Interpreting contours** **43**
    4.5.7 Aiming-off and 43
        attack points
    Route choice and tick-off ... **44**
    features
    4.5.8 Linear features 44
    4.5.9 Dog-leg 44
    4.5.10 Boxing 45
    4.5.11 Slope aspect 45
    4.5.12 What happens if...? .. 45
4.6 Observations 46
    4.6.1 Using the group 46
4.7 Dangers 48
4.8 Possible Errors 49
4.9 Using GPS in winter 49
(i) 5 **Navigation** **51**

Part 2 Basic winter skills **53**
5 Ice axe **55**
   5.1 The head 56
   5.2 The shaft 57
   5.3 The spike 57
   5.4 Leashes 57
(i) 6 **Carrying the axe** **58**
   5.5 Axe length 58
   5.6 Stowing the axe 58

6 Moving on snow **61**
   6.1 Carrying the axe 62
   6.2 Kicking steps 62
(i) 7 **Kicking steps directly** **63**
    up a slope
    6.2.1 Direct ascent 63
    6.2.2 Diagonal ascent 63
(i) 8 **Kicking diagonal steps** **64**
    6.2.3 Traversing 64
    6.2.4 Descending steps 64
(i) 9 **Walking through snow** **65**
   6.3 Cutting steps 65
    6.3.1 Cutting in snow 65
    6.3.2 Step patterns 66
    6.3.3 Types of steps 66
    6.3.4 Slash steps 66
    6.3.5 Side steps 68
    6.3.6 Slab steps 68
    6.3.7 Bucket steps 68
    6.3.8 Pigeonhole steps 69
    6.3.9 Steps in descent 69
(i) 10 **Cutting steps** **70**

7 Self-arrest **71**
   7.1 Slope selection 72
   7.2 Self-belay 72
   7.3 Self-arrest 73
    7.3.1 Preparation 73
    7.3.2 The basic self-arrest ... 74
        position

7.3.3 Sliding feet first on your back ... 75	9.5.1 Rounding ... 101
11 Basic self-arrest ... **76**	9.5.2 Faceting ... 102
7.3.4 Sliding head first, face down ... 76	9.5.3 Melt-freeze cycle ... 103
	9.5.4 Solar radiation ... 104
7.3.5 Sliding head first on your back ... 77	**9.6 Wind effects** ... **104**
	9.6.1 Wind features ... 104
12 Advanced self-arrest ... **79**	**9.7 Snow types and formations** ... **105**
7.4 Rolling and tumbling ... **79**	
7.5 Without the axe ... **79**	9.7.1 Dry loose snow ... 106
7.6 Other considerations ... **79**	9.7.2 Wind slab ... 106
7.7 Glissading ... **80**	9.7.3 Wet snow ... 107
13 Self-arrest teaching plan ... **81**	9.7.4 Cornices ... 107
	10 Avalanches ... **109**
8 Crampons ... **83**	**10.1 Types of avalanche** ... **110**
8.1 Crampon Types ... **84**	10.1.1 Loose snow avalanches ... 110
8.1.1 C1 flexible crampons ... 84	
8.1.2 C2 articulated crampons ... 84	10.1.2 Slab avalanches ... 111
	10.1.3 Wet snow avalanches ... 114
8.1.3 C3 rigid crampons ... 86	
8.1.4 Anti-balling plates ... 87	10.1.4 Avalanche size scale ... 114
8.2 Attachment ... **87**	**10.2 Avalanche awareness** ... **114**
8.3 Fit ... **87**	10.2.1 Sources of information ... 114
8.4 Carrying crampons ... **88**	
8.5 Care and maintenance ... **88**	**Avalanche sizes** ... **115**
8.5.1 Emergency repairs ... 89	**SAIS avalanche hazard forecasting** ... **116**
8.6 Putting on crampons ... **89**	
8.7 Considerations for use ... **90**	**15 BAA Trainer Pack** ... **117**
14 Crampon fitting ... **90**	10.2.2 Planning your trip ... 118
8.8 French technique ... **91**	10.2.3 The journey ... 118
8.9 Front-pointing ... **93**	10.2.4 Mountain features ... 119
8.10 Hybrid technique (Mixed ... 94 or American technique)	**10.3 Closer observations** ... **120**
	16 Snow pits in context ... **121**
	10.3.1 Snow pits ... 121
Part 3 Snow and avalanche ... **97**	10.3.2 Hardness ... 121
9 Snow structure ... **99**	10.3.3 Wetness tests ... 122
9.1 Snow in the air ... **100**	10.3.4 Crystal and grain size ... 122
9.2 Rime ice ... **100**	
9.3 Verglas ... **100**	10.3.5 Stability checks ... 122
9.4 Graupel ... **101**	**10.4 Hazard evaluation** ... **124**
9.5 Snow on the ground ... **101**	**10.5 Avalanche avoidance** ... **124**
	10.5.1 Route selection ... 124

Avalanche Checklist – 125
Top 10 Factors
   10.5.2 Personal 126
       preparations
   10.5.3 Belaying 126
   10.5.4 Action if caught 126
   10.5.5 Survival 127
   10.5.6 Rescue 128
   10.5.7 Organised searches 128
   10.5.8 Avalanche 129
       transceivers
   10.5.9 Recco® system 129
17 **Equipment** **129**

Part 4 Security on steep ground 131

11 Providing security in winter . . 133
  11.1 Winter steep ground 134
  11.2 Security without a rope .. 134
  11.3 Using a rope for security . 134
     11.3.1 Tying relevant knots .. 139
     11.3.2 Attaching to the 139
         rope
     11.3.3 Tying to anchors 139
     Tying to anchors – **140**
     Belaying using a distant anchor
     11.3.4 Controlling the rope .. 141
     Tying to anchors – **142**
     Positioning at stance
  11.4 Descent techniques 142
  11.5 Group organisation 142
     Tying to anchors – **143**
     Directly with the rope
     11.5.1 Briefing 143
     11.5.2 Communication 143
     Tying to anchors using a ... **144**
     sling and karabiner
     11.5.3 Keeping control 144
  11.6 A sense of urgency 145
  11.7 Problems in ascent 148
  11.8 The leader's safety 148
  11.9 Protecting near a 148
     corniced edge
  11.10 Confidence-roping 150

12 Basic winter anchors 153
& belays
  12.1 Snow anchors and 154
     belays
     12.1.1 Using snow belays ... 154
18 **Snow anchors** **155**
     12.1.2 General 155
        considerations
     12.1.3 Bucket seat 156
     12.1.4 The waist belay 157
     12.1.5 Stomper 157
     12.1.6 Snow bollard 158
     12.1.7 Buried axe 160
     12.1.8 Deadman 163
  12.2 Other snow anchors 165
     and belays
     12.2.1 Foot brake 166
     12.2.2 Vertical axe 167
  12.3 Improvised snow 167
     anchors
  12.4 Ice anchors and belays .. 167
  12.5 Ice bollard 168
  12.6 Other natural ice 168
     anchors
     12.6.1 Ice curtain thread ... 168
     12.6.2 Jammed axe 169
  12.7 Belaying on rock in 169
     winter
     12.7.1 Finding rock anchors .. 169

Part 5 Winter climbing 173

13 Climbing equipment 175
  13.1 Clothing 176
     13.1.1 Shell jacket 176
     13.1.2 Shell trousers 176
     13.1.3 Boots 176
     13.1.4 Gaiters 176

Climbing equipment **177**	14.2.10 Other 206
safety standards	considerations
13.1.5 Rucksack 177	14.3 Mixed climbing **207**
13.1.6 Contents of a 177	14.3.1 Axe techniques 207
rucksack	14.3.2 Crampons on rock .. 210
13.1.7 Hat 178	14.3.3 Vegetation (turf) 210
13.1.8 Gloves 178	14.3.4 Other considerations . 211
13.2 Technical equipment **178**	14.4 Leashless climbing 213
13.2.1 Climbing axes 178	14.5 Dry tooling 214
Wrist loop leash design ... **184**	14.6 Falling off 214
13.2.2 Technical crampons .. 185	14.7 Training for winter 215
13.2.3 Rope 187	climbing
13.2.4 Helmet 187	
13.2.5 Harness 188	**15 Winter anchors and belays** .. **217**
13.2.6 Belay device 188	15.1 Snow anchors and belays 218
Basic personal equipment .. **189**	15.1.1 Changeovers at 219
13.2.7 Karabiners 189	snow belays
13.2.8 Quickdraws 189	15.2 Ice anchors 219
Basic winter rack **190**	15.2.1 Ice screws 219
13.2.9 Slings 191	**Snow Anchors and Belays** .. **220**
14 Climbing techniques **193**	**Ice screws and their** **223**
14.1 Snow climbing 194	**placement**
14.1.1 Daggering 194	15.2.2 Ice drive-ins 226
Winter grades **195**	15.2.3 Ice hook (Bulldog®) .. 227
14.1.2 Classic overhead 196	15.2.4 Ice threads 227
swing	('V' threads or Abalakov
14.1.3 Resting.............. 197	threads)
14.1.4 Negotiating a 197	15.2.5 Accessories 228
cornice	15.3 Ice belays 229
14.2 Ice climbing 199	15.4 Rock anchors 230
14.2.1 The axe swing 199	15.4.1 Finding anchors 231
14.2.2 Reading the ice 201	15.4.2 Chocks.............. 231
14.2.3 Crampon 201	**Placing and removing** **232**
techniques	**pitons**
14.2.4 Moving on 202	15.4.3 Spring-loaded 232
steep ice	devices: Cams
14.2.5 Traversing 203	15.4.4 Pitons 232
14.2.6 Down climbing 203	15.4.5 Warthog (Turfie) 233
14.2.7 Ice formations 204	**Tying to anchors and** **234**
14.2.8 Thin ice 205	**linking anchors**
14.2.9 Ice bulges.......... 205	15.5 In-situ anchors 236

15.6 Linking anchors 236
15.7 Stance construction 236

16 Winter climbing strategies . . **239**
  16.1 Strategies on ice 240
    16.1.1 Stances on ice 241
  16.2 General strategies 242
    16.2.1 Preparation 242
    16.2.2 Approaching the 243
      climb
    16.2.3 Gearing up 243
    16.2.4 On the climb 243
    16.2.5 Stance management . 245
    16.2.6 Planning 246
  16.3 Descent 247
    16.3.1 Abseiling in winter . . 247
  16.4 Soloing 249
  16.5 Multi-pitch problem- 249
    solving (Improvised rescue)
  16.6 Nutrition – Food and 249
    Drink

17 Winter ridges:
    Rope techniques **251**
  17.1 General considerations . . 252
  17.2 Moving together: 252
    Long roping
    17.2.1 Tying on 253
    17.2.2 Descent 254
    17.2.3 Traversing 254
  17.3 Short-roping 254
    17.3.1 Tying on 254
    Taking chest coils **255**
    Definitions **257**

18 Teaching winter climbing . . . **259**
  18.1 Base 260
  18.2 Approach 260
    BMC Participation **260**
    Statement
  18.3 Teaching strategies 262

18.4 Guiding 262
  18.4.1 Rope systems 263
  18.4.2 Climbing in series . . 263
  18.4.3 Climbing in parallel . . 264
  18.4.4 Stance 264
    management
18.5 Teaching leading in 265
  winter
  18.5.1 General 265
  18.5.2 Soloing 265
  Stance management **266**
  18.5.3 Fixed rope 268
18.6 Descents 268
18.7 Technique training 269
  18.7.1 Ice and mixed 269
    bouldering, bottom-
    roping and indoor walls
  Abseiling with clients **270**

Part 6 Winter incidents **275**
19 Winter shelters **277**
  19.1 Tools 278
  19.2 Location and material . . . 279
  ⓘ 19 **Locating snow shelter** . . . **280**
    sites
  19.3 Cutting blocks 280
  19.4 Other considerations . . . 281
  19.5 Personal preparation . . . 281
  19.6 Finishing off 282
  19.7 Bivouac bags 282
  19.8 Environmental 282
    considerations
  19.9 Constructing 283
    emergency snow shelters
    19.9.1 Bivvy shelter 283
    19.9.2 Blocked hole 284
  ⓘ 20 **Unplanned bivouac** **285**
    Snow graves **286**
    19.9.3 Snow graves 286
    19.9.4 Shovel-ups or 287
    snow mounds

19.10 Constructing planned snow shelters	288
19.10.1 Snow holes and caves	288
19.10.2 Living in a snow hole	290
ⓘ 21 **Briefing notes for snow shelters**	**293**

| **20 Water hazards** | **295** |

21 Cold injuries	**297**
21.1 Hypothermia	298
ⓘ 22 **Prevention of hypothermia**	**298**
21.2 Frostbite	299
21.2.1 Superficial frostbite	299
21.2.2 Deep frostbite	300
21.3 Immersion foot	300
21.4 Snow blindness	301
21.5 Sunburn	301
21.6 Prevention	301
ⓘ 23 **Prevention of cold injuries**	**302**

Appendices	**305**
A1 Access legislation	306
A2 Mountain Training	308
A3 Useful contacts	310
A4 Index	312

Author's acknowledgements

Taking on the writing of this book in view of the success and high standard of the previous publications in this series, Hill Walking by Steve Long and Rock Climbing by Libby Peter, was a daunting task. To try and match the level of the books in both clarity of writing and technical explanation was always going to be extremely difficult. We can only hope we have at least approached the standards set by these two books.

Hill walking and rock climbing could be considered to be discrete activities, albeit with no real upper limit. They can be expanded into regions further afield such as walking in polar or desert regions or climbing big rock walls around the world. Both activities could be built on the foundations detailed in these books. To us however, winter walking and climbing seemed to present the problem of where to start and where to end. How much prior knowledge could we expect the reader to start with, and at the other end of the scale, how much was merely superfluous detail best learned by the participant honing their own skills in their own manner. We have tried to write this book so that it will stand alone without the need to refer to the first two books in the series, yet at the same time avoid labouring points which could well be familiar to some readers. We hope that individual readers can forgive this compromise and, if necessary, perhaps address any omission by reference to either Hill Walking or Rock Climbing.

Many people have contributed to the production of this book by offering suggestions, commenting on the text and supplying photographs. We would particularly like to pay tribute to the contribution to all the Mountain Training United Kingdom and Ireland publications played by the late Allister 'Waldo' McQuoid. John Cousins and Steve Long of Mountain Training United Kingdom and Ireland and Libby Peter were the main driving forces and major contributors, editors, advisors and, at times, diplomats. Others from the national Mountain Training organisations including Sue Doyle, Mal Creasey, Andy Say and Phill Thomas all contributed as did Blair Fyffe, Stuart MacAleese, George McEwan, Dave Hollinger, Alison McLure, North West Outdoor team of Lawrence Hughes and John Lavelle, Iain Peter, Olly Sanders, George Reid, Ian Taylor, Mike Turner, Brendan Whelan and Blyth Wright. The authors' thanks are also extended to all the winter walkers and climbers who we photographed and spoke with and all the clients and groups that we accompanied on the hills. Most of all however, we would like to thank all our climbing and walking companions over the years who taught us so much about the mountains in winter and ultimately provided the material to make this book possible.

Lastly, we are indebted to our families for their tolerance and understanding over the last eighteen months and we look forward to spending much more time in the mountains with them.

Andy Cunningham, Allen Fyffe
December 2006

Author's Acknowledgments for the Third Edition

It has been thirteen years since the first edition of Winter Skills and although the skills and techniques described in the first edition are as relevant now as they were in 2006, there are some changes and additions to this volume. In particular, Part 3; Snow and Avalanche has been updated and some 'modernising' of climbing techniques to align with current methods and equipment. Additionally, we have sourced new photographs and edited some existing diagrams where necessary.

It is generally accepted that climate change is influencing our winter weather patterns with more frequent warm spells leading to rapid thaws at times throughout the season and less reliable winter conditions. However, it is with great pleasure that we continue to witness an increase in winter mountain users and the enjoyment for all that winter provides, regardless of the conditions. Rest assured, we (the authors) also continue to experience the enjoyment of a grand day out in winter – despite being thirteen years older!

In addition to acknowledging all those who helped in the production of the first edition of Winter Skills, we would like to say a big thank you to the following who contributed to this edition, including and in particular; Nicola Jasieniecka of Mountain Training UK and Ireland who patiently waded through and edited text, photographs and diagrams; George McEwan of Mountain Training Scotland who proof read and commented on text and diagrams; Murdoch Jamieson for advice on modern hard mixed climbing and supplying photographs; Paul Noble and all those who supplied new photographs, whether ultimately used in the book or not; Mark Diggins, Coordinator Scottish Avalanche Information Service, John Cousins, MTUKI for advice and 'cracking the whip' when needed, Iain Peter of Mountain Training Publications and finally, Vertebrate Publishing.

Andy Cunningham, Allen Fyffe
December 2019

Editor's note

Thirteen winter seasons have passed since this book was first published and while the adventures and wonder haven't changed, technique, knowledge and equipment have certainly moved on. This third edition has been fully updated to reflect developments in winter walking and climbing including equipment, the theory behind teaching people about avalanche avoidance and rope work relevant for leaders and instructors, among other areas.

As with all our titles the illustrations and images used throughout the book are invaluable in providing a visual representation of the skills described. Thank you to Jane Beagley at Vertebrate Publishing for the refreshed style and design as well as Simon Norris for his work on the many illustrations. Huge thanks also to the following individuals for having their own winter adventures, training and assessing candidates in often challenging conditions and subsequently sharing their stunning photographs to bring this book to life: Bill Strachan, Dave Evans, Garry Smith, George McEwan, Giles Trussell, Jon Jones, Karl Midlane, Libby Peter, Lou Beetlestone, Mark Diggins, Matt Hawkins, Murdoch Jamieson, Paul Noble, Pete Hill, Rob Johnson and Sam Leary.

My thanks to Nicola Jasieniecka for managing the overall production of this edition, supported by Annette Greenwood and watched over by Iain Peter and Roger Ward. The authors and the Mountain Training Publications team have worked hard to maintain this book's position as the authoritative text on winter skills techniques and we hope it continues to support new and developing winter mountaineers for many years to come.

John Cousins
December 2019

Foreword

Our winter mountains provide a heightened challenge to walkers, climbers and mountaineers. Low temperatures, ice, snow, rain, avalanches, poor visibility and high winds are the norm, not the exception. It is these winter elements that give us our most demanding, rewarding and memorable days on hills of extravagant beauty.

This series of books was conceived by Mountain Training to support formal training. However, the books have done far more than expected and give even the most experienced amongst us food for thought, new ideas, and alternative methods of practice. This third volume in the series had to maintain the exceptional standards set in Hill Walking and Rock Climbing. It has been the most difficult and complex production yet, but the authors and Publications Working Group of Mountain Training United Kingdom and Ireland have succeeded in meeting the challenge.

Andy Cunningham and Allen Fyffe have a wealth of experience in the field. Allen is an IFMGA Mountain Guide and both he and Andy are Winter Mountaineering and Climbing Instructors. Andy Cunningham is a very experienced instructor and climber with a host of hard new routes to his name in the Cairngorms and North West Highlands. Allen has climbed throughout the world and has made significant first ascents in the Alps, Himalayas and in Scotland.

Both authors have spent virtually all of their adult lives living, climbing and working in the Scottish Highlands. They have brought their great talent and experience as mountaineers to the authorship of the book and share their skills in readily understandable terms. Supported by clear diagrams and photographs, this book deserves a place on every mountaineer's book shelf.

This edition is dedicated to the memory of Allister McQuoid

Allister was the chairman of Mountain Training Publications Ltd. when the idea of producing this series of books was first suggested. He had a vision of what was required and the business acumen and experience to ensure that the books were brought in on time and on budget. The standards set were high and have been justly rewarded with excellent reviews and good sales.

Throughout his time as Chair, Allister was very seriously ill. He showed astonishing resilience, drive and commitment to a project dear to his heart. He always gave his best, the rapier wit and intellect cutting to the quick, driving through the discussion, direct and to the point. An outstanding character, an inspiration to all who knew him, these books are fitting reminder of his love for the mountains, for mountaineers and for the craic that that is enjoyed when the two come together!

Iain Peter
Chair, Mountain Training Publications Working Group

This book is published by Mountain Training United Kingdom and Ireland, which is a registered charity. Revenue from the sale of books published by MTUKI is used for the continuation of its publishing programme and for charitable purposes associated with training leaders.

Introduction

Walking and climbing in winter are immensely rewarding and challenging activities. There is much to be learned about the winter environment and this is best done after a solid grounding of the basic skills has been gained in more amenable conditions. Equipment, basic movement, navigation, route finding, rope work, belaying and other skills can be adapted to the harsher conditions of winter rather than learned there for the first time. That is not to say that you must begin in summer, rather that tackling basic skills while dealing with cold, bad weather, poor visibility and difficult walking conditions is not the ideal learning situation. Even simple tasks take on another dimension when snow and ice coat your equipment and the wind is at gale force. Indeed, some would say that there is no such thing as winter walking – it is winter mountaineering, and the range of skills needed is wider than that required for summer conditions.

Similarly, a winter climb is not the best place to learn how to tie knots, find anchors and belay your companion. While in summer it is possible to be a rock climber and not a mountaineer by focusing on easily accessible crags, this is not an option in winter. To climb in winter, you require all the essential winter walking skills. Starting in winter means a steep learning curve leaving little spare to appreciate the other pleasures the mountains have to offer.

In winter, both rewards and risks are increased. While the mountains demand respect all year round, this must be greater when they are covered with snow and ice. Short daylight hours, physically demanding walking, more difficult route finding and navigation, and often inclement weather all make for greater challenges. However, the rewards can be greater than in summer, when on those memorable rare days, weather and snow conditions combine to produce a great day out and a day's winter walking or climbing can be truly unforgettable. Indeed, days like these have us coming back and accepting the more usual foul weather, indifferent snow, non-existent views, cold, wet, discomfort, apprehension and sometimes very real danger.

Almost everything in winter can take longer and presents more problems than at other times. The simplest of acts, such as looking at a map or putting a rope through a belay device can, in bad winter conditions, be a problem. Besides physical difficulties, the mental aspects of winter have greater significance. Not knowing exactly where you are when navigating in a blizzard requires concentration and belief in your abilities to cope with the situation. On a climb it may be necessary to go further than you feel comfortable without protection. Tackling a route where the rock is plastered in snow and ice and every piece of gear must be excavated can be daunting. Experience and knowledge are greater factors in winter and the variety of conditions means that experience takes longer to accumulate.

Winter conditions cannot be defined by the month of the year; you may experience summer conditions in January, yet snow can fall on the high tops in any month. Winter conditions can occur from October to May and good winter conditions can disappear overnight. Planning for winter is a difficult process and finding good conditions is becoming more difficult unless you can take advantage of them immediately. The danger of pressing on with your plans, because so much time and effort has been invested in the trip, has resulted in too many accidents. Knowing when to retreat is an essential part of the winter experience.

Leading groups in winter should not be undertaken lightly. It is essential that you have the relevant skills, techniques, knowledge and a realistic appreciation of your ability. You must be able to navigate to a higher standard than in summer, do this in bad weather and limited visibility and still be able to look after your group. There is little point in equipping a novice winter group with ice axe and crampons if you cannot instruct them on how to use them safely and efficiently. To a degree, a winter leader has to become a winter instructor.

There are several skills that must be mastered by any winter walker, and a number more with which a familiarity is required. These skills allow safe progress through winter mountains and should not be seen out of context. Self-arrest, for example, is needed if there is any danger of a slip turning into a slide. Its main purpose should not be forgotten as part of the whole, and ice axe braking turned into an activity for its own sake. If there is no firm snow to slide on and no danger of a slip becoming a slide, then why spend hours trying to develop a technique which is irrelevant on that occasion? The correct balance must be sought and the reason for doing things considered. In the ever-changing winter environment, the present and future weather and under-foot conditions influence activities.

Leaders must be flexible to get the most for their group. Realistic objectives and assessment of the group's abilities and aspirations are essential and it is these which should influence decisions, not a leader's needs or objectives. Sympathetic, inventive and imaginative leadership, rather than a rote-learning process, will give the greatest rewards in both walking and climbing situations.

> **Learning to lead**
> This book contains valuable information for those taking others walking and climbing whether as friends, fellow club members, leaders, instructors or guides; throughout the book information on looking after others is boxed separately and indicated by the symbol shown above.

> **Participation statement**
> **Mountain Training** recognises that climbing, hill walking and mountaineering are **activities with a danger of personal injury or death. Participants in these activities should be aware** of and accept these risks and be responsible for their own actions.
>
> Mountain Training has developed a range of training and assessment schemes and associated supporting literature to help leaders manage these risks and to enable new participants to have positive experiences while learning about their responsibilities.

VIEW ACROSS CARN MOR DEARG ARÊTE   *PHOTO // GILES TRUSSELL*

part 1

The winter environment

APPROACHING THE SUMMIT OF BUCHAILLE ETIVE BEAG   *PHOTO // DAVE EVANS*

1

Mountaineering equipment

Personal equipment in winter is basically an extension of that required for summer conditions.

Those venturing into winter from summer mountaineering should already have much of what is required. The basic clothing principles remain the same although boots will probably need to be upgraded and extra technical items purchased. It is usually a matter of extending what you have, rather than replacing it.

Clothing and equipment is continually evolving both in terms of materials and design. Magazines and online sources carry many articles on the latest gear, and no book can reflect this ever-changing picture. Only an outline of basic principles is covered here. While most mountaineering skills remain constant, the appropriate gear will vary with time.

1.1 Clothing

The basic principles of a good, wicking base layer worn next to the skin, an insulating mid-layer and a windproof, waterproof and breathable outer shell apply in winter but need to cope with a greater temperature range, wind strength, energy expenditure and forms of moisture than in summer. To be dry and comfortable in the rain at sea level and then to feel the same at over 1,000m in a blizzard puts huge demands on equipment. Not only is the range of external conditions much greater, but your personal state is also more variable. Carrying heavier loads in more demanding conditions means a greater energy output and consequently sweating and the wetting of clothing. Differences between moving and stopping are more pronounced. The transition from sweating to shivering can be extremely rapid. Getting it right in winter calls for more from your clothing and greater experimentation from its user.

1.1.1 Base layer

These garments should maintain a dry layer of air next to the skin and wick moisture away from the body. This ability to transfer moisture away from the body is extremely important and affects all other layers. Base layers are primarily made of synthetic materials although modern wool garments are also extremely effective and most fabrics employ various strategies to aid the transport and evaporation of moisture. These include

> **1 Clothing**
> Keeping the group at the right energy output is important. Once damp, it may be very difficult to dry out, so setting a good comfortable pace is vital. If necessary, get in front and slow the group down if they are walking too fast, or otherwise dictate the pace and any stops. Look back often to check how everyone is doing. Take the lead in suggesting clothing alterations and adjustment stops and don't simply ask the group to say if they are too hot or too cold, if the pace is too fast or if they need to have a drink or something to eat. Few group members like to appear as if they cannot keep up or need help to sort their gear and will feel more comfortable following the instructor's lead.

FIGURE 1.1 A GROUP IN WINDY CONDITIONS   *PHOTO // GILES TRUSSELL*

using different types of yarns and different diameters or chemical treatments. While these come in various weights, mid-weight seems most versatile. Closer fitting garments are generally warmer and reduce airflow and smoother fabrics enhance freedom of movement. While design features are often a matter of personal preference, zip openings at the neck and long tails are good features.

1.1.2 Mid-layer

These provide the bulk of the warmth by trapping insulating air close to the body. The majority of these garments are made from breathable synthetic materials, such as fleece or fibre pile, are good at shedding water and are quick-drying. Although normal fleeces offer little resistance to the wind, windproof ones reduce this problem. Mid-layers come in a variety of weights and in a bewildering choice of designs but several lighter layers give greater versatility than one heavy layer.

1.1.3 Soft shell

Also referred to as wind shell, this is basically windproof and water-resistant to varying degrees. There is an extensive range of materials and designs, such as windproof fleeces, fleece and micro-fibre combinations, enhanced fabrics and high-performance stretch fabrics. They do not eliminate the need for a waterproof outer layer but can be used as part of the overall layering system. Their soft flexible feel is comfortable and gives excellent freedom of movement. Some are exceptionally good at transferring moisture to the outer surface and then permitting rapid evaporation. These can even cope with a reasonable amount of precipitation while still maintaining dry conditions next to the skin. Some are worn next to the skin to enhance moisture transfer and can be very good in wet, cold conditions.

FIGURE 1.2 BELAYING IN COLD WEATHER   *PHOTO // LOU BEETLESTONE*

1.1.4 Outer shell

The outer or hard shell should keep out wind and water, but allow moisture to escape outwards. This is done using waterproof/breathable fabrics of which there are several different types. These generally perform best in dry, cold conditions, when warm moist air is more easily transferred out through the fabric. This driving effect is enhanced by a water-repellent coating on the outside that causes surface water to bead and roll off. A saturated outer fabric means a reduced rate of breathability. Unfortunately, this is exactly the type of problem liable to be encountered in poor winter conditions. On cold days, wearing thick insulation means that less body heat reaches the outer layers, so decreasing the driving effect pushing moisture out through the shell. Removing a layer may help to remove perspiration.

Outer shells come in a huge range of styles and designs. When combined with cost, most of these garments from reputable mountaineering equipment manufacturers have some plus and minus points. Good jacket design features include robust, protected zips providing adequate ventilation, a big stiffened hood to give protection for the face yet not hamper vision. The cuffs should give good seals and the jacket should have sufficient and convenient pockets which can be accessed when wearing a harness or rucksack.

In general, a jacket and over-trouser combination is most versatile. Over-trouser zips should be long enough to allow them to be put on easily when wearing boots and even crampons, and can also aid temperature control. Salopettes reduce the gap at the waist, but putting them on means removing your jacket. In winter, over-trousers or salopettes are often worn for the whole day. This reduces the weight to be carried and eliminates the need to wear a windproof layer on the legs.

FIGURE 1.3 A LIGHTWEIGHT RIGID WINTER BOOT   *PHOTO // GILES TRUSSELL*

This is particularly handy when climbing, as coming into contact with snow leads to wet legs.

1.2 The layering system

While this works well in theory, in practice there are some drawbacks. Damp, wet conditions may prevent efficient moisture transfer to the outer layer and wearing a rucksack often results in a wet back. Temperature regulation is critical to reduce dampness – changing a wet base layer in winter is unpleasant. Even removing an outer layer to put on more insulation can be a problem with the wind tugging at your clothing and snow wetting the new insulating layer. Nothing can be put down on the ground lest it blows away, and as soon as your insulation is exposed to the wind you lose heat rapidly.

Rather than remove anything to add layers, it is better to put on more insulation on top of the outer shell. Jackets and waistcoats of synthetic materials worn on top of the hard shell can improve warmth rapidly. Although they will probably get wet, the material is not too adversely affected, they dry out quickly with no ill effects and their slick nylon gives good freedom of movement. They are often sold as belay jackets *(see Figure 1.2)*.

1.3 Boots

Boots are probably the most important item of winter equipment. Good boots are essential for safety and comfort and should be chosen with care and an eye to their intended use. Boots for winter use are classed as 4-season boots and, for anything but occasional use, are essential. There is an extensive range of type and construction of boots, many of which are designed for specific types of mountaineering. With this specialisation, it is important to get boots that match their intended use and the conditions liable to be encountered. Any boot will, to some degree, be a compromise – one which is good for using with crampons on steep ice may be less comfortable for walking long distances, while a flexible and perhaps comfortable boot may be unsuitable for use with crampons. Other features can have drawbacks, for example, a totally waterproof boot will get damp through condensation and a very stiff ankle will make it difficult to perform certain crampon techniques.

It is worthwhile spending the time shopping around to get a pair of boots to suit your needs. Go to a knowledgeable supplier, try on different makes and types and get as much advice as possible before buying. The option of hiring different boots for short periods to try out can also be worthwhile.

A suitable winter boot has to be warm, waterproof, provide good ankle support and have a rigid sole. The sole itself should be of cleated rubber for good grip. Those with a solid inside edge below the toe are better for rock climbing but this is less important when crampons are worn. The sole may also have a slight curve along its length, the rocker, which makes for easier walking. The larger the boot the more likely it is that there will be some degree of flex along the length of the sole. A suitable boot will also have toe and heel counters, reinforced areas, which protect these parts, particularly when kicking steps. A good seal such as a bellows tongue is mandatory for winter boots.

Suitable boots are usually warm enough with one pair of good quality socks, but this is a matter of personal choice and circulation. Feet that are too warm will get wet from sweating, ultimately resulting in colder toes. A good fit is important and wearing extra socks may not be warmer if the boots are too tight and restrict circulation.

There are two main types of boot construction: leather and synthetic fabric. While the actual construction may use a combination of materials it is useful to use these categories. Advances in boot design and construction have led to an overlap in features, so any boot is likely to be made of several materials.

1.3.1 Leather boots

Leather is the traditional material for mountaineering boots and gives more 'feel' when climbing, especially on rock. They can be very comfortable when broken in, last for a long time and take more than one re-sole. However, there are compromises – a heavier leather boot will be more waterproof but less breathable. A boot with as few seams as possible is best, as seams are points of weakness and entry for water. Leather boots require maintenance and need cleaning and waterproofing on a regular basis. Some leather boots can be less comfortable until broken in to fit the shape of your foot.

1.3.2 Fabric boots

These were only generally used for two or three season boots but now some boots of materials such as nylon, Kevlar and breathable membranes are suitable for winter use *(see Figure 1.3)*. These tend to be rigid, lightweight and mainly for climbing of a higher standard, where their light weight is an advantage. However, they are likely to be less robust and warm than leather or plastic boots. Seams are likely to be points of wear and weakness with extended use.

1.3.3 Plastic boots

Whilst plastic boots are far less common, they may be available in some outlets and are therefore described here for completeness. These generally consist of a plastic outer shell and an inner boot which is usually constructed of materials such as leather, wool, felt or foam. The outer can either be of one or two piece construction with a hinge at the ankle. Plastic boots are waterproof, durable, require little maintenance, need no breaking in, are relatively warm and give good support. The downside is that they tend to be heavier, more cumbersome, have less 'feel' and the stiffness may make some crampon techniques more difficult. If they do not fit comfortably to begin with they are unlikely to improve with use. However, specialist shops can alter the shape of some boot shells.

1.3.4 Lacing

Boots with a pulley system rather than simple rings are easier to lace up firmly, particularly with plastic boots. For boots with simple rings, it will be easier to tighten if the lace is taken from below the ring then up through it. If the lace is taken downwards through the ring, they will tend to be self-locking. To lock the lace at a hook, take it from top down and over itself across to the next hook.

1.3.5 Foot beds

Instead of the insole supplied with the boot, a good quality or even a custom-made foot bed can increase comfort, improve your walking and climbing by holding the foot in a more natural position, provide extra insulation and solve some boot fitting problems. They last a long time, are usable with different boots and can be a huge bonus for those with foot or joint problems.

1.4 Gaiters

Gaiters are a must in winter. They stop snow and moisture from entering, protect the boot and provide extra insulation round the lower leg, which helps keep the feet warmer. They also provide protection from snagging on crampon points and so fulfil an important safety role. While many mountaineering pants and over-trousers have an integral gaiter, these may not be effective enough on their own, especially when walking through deep snow or breakable crust. However, these can be adequate in many situations if combined with short gaiters. Some modern boots, particularly those of leather or fabric construction, have a short outer gaiter built onto the boot. These, when combined with the gaiter on pants or overtrousers, are sufficient for most situations.

Full-length gaiters of a waterproof/breathable material with a full-length closure are best. Those of a stiff material stay up better and are less likely to get spiked by crampons. In warmer conditions the tops can be left open for more ventilation but still need some type of closure at the top. Front opening gaiters with a zip closure and a Velcro® flap are easiest to put on. The Velcro® is important, for should a zip fail, there is still some way of closing the gaiter. Wide Velcro® on its own is also an option and is quick and convenient and, since many people like to tighten their boots before climbing, these are easier to open to adjust the laces. Suitable gaiters have a good seal at the boot to stop snow getting pushed up inside and 'one-size-fits-all' styles generally do not give as good a fit as sized ones. The instep strap should be robust and replaceable, and buckles or similar fastenings should go on the outside of the foot to prevent them catching.

Supergaiters have a rubber rand round the whole boot and under the instep and provide greater protection, insulation and waterproofing. If using these with clip-on crampons ensure that they do not cover the heel and toe welts. With some types of boots, especially those with rounded toes, the rand tends to slip up and off at the front. A drop of glue usually cures this problem. If used on leather or fabric boots, do not leave supergaiters on when not in use for long periods as they tend to cause the boot toes to curl up.

1.5 Gloves

Gloves are among the most difficult items of equipment to get right for conditions in this country. Normally, as temperatures drop, wearing more clothing and thicker gloves will keep your hands warmer. However, wet, wind and cold conditions are difficult to combat and these, combined with the need to take your gloves off to perform certain tasks, make it difficult for gloves to operate totally effectively. Even in sub-zero conditions holding an ice axe and handling snow-covered items mean that wetness usually enters the equation, especially when climbing and handling ropes and equipment.

Whether mitts or gloves are chosen, there are certain desirable features. Cuffs should be long enough to make a good wrist seal. It is important to keep the wrist warm, as the blood supply to the fingers is very close to the surface of the skin and if it is cooled before it reaches the extremities, will result in cold fingers. Gauntlets with a long cuff need some sort of closure at the top and a strap or elastication at the wrist to give a neater fit, although this can snag in some situations. Removable

> **2 Gloves & hats**
> Ensuring that the group has plenty of spare mitts and gloves is essential. Novices often underestimate how cold their hands can get and over-estimate how good their gloves are. Having some spares is extremely handy as gloves do get lost with remarkable regularity, especially in windy conditions. It is also worth noting that one study showed that women's fingers were 3 to 4°C cooler than men's.

inners are handy for drying, but if the inner is pulled out accidentally, getting them back in can be a problem. It can also be difficult to get some gloves on if your hands are wet, especially if they are a tight fit. Loops of thin elastic or cord round the wrist are useful to prevent them being dropped when removed.

The problem with all gloves and mitts is that they get wet quite quickly and soon lose their insulating properties, and all have a large hole in them: the one you put your hand in! If you pull the cuff over your jacket sleeve, water will run down into the glove when your hands are low. If you pull your jacket sleeve over the wrist cuff, moisture can get up your sleeve when your hands are above your head. What you do will depend on how wide your jacket sleeve is and what sort of fastening it has at the cuff. Looking at the two together when buying gloves or mitts is useful.

While mitts are warmer than gloves, the extra warmth is gained at the cost of dexterity. Mitts are generally cheaper than gloves, however, and it may be possible to wear thin gloves underneath without restricting circulation. Mitts with a waterproof/breathable shell and fleece inners are good in foul weather but woollen mitts are cheap, long-lasting and remarkably warm when wet. Specialist winter climbing gloves, with a waterproof/breathable outer and a fleece inner, are good for all round use but can be expensive and can wear out quickly, especially when climbing.

Thin inner gloves, which can be worn under the main glove or mitt, are useful if they do not make the hand too bulky or restrict circulation. Wind block fleece gloves are great for milder conditions being fairly light and cheap. In wet or thawing conditions however, few gloves or mitts will stay dry and warm all day, so having several pairs to change into is often the only answer.

1.6 Hat

Some form of head covering is necessary, as up to a third of body heat can be lost through the head and neck. A wide range of hats is available in a variety of materials and designs, but they must stay on in high winds, and if a helmet is worn it should fit comfortably underneath. Having more than one piece of headgear for various conditions is sensible and a balaclava with a long neck which forms a seal with the rest of your insulation is often essential. A scarf or a fleece neck-gaiter to seal the neck area helps preserve body heat.

1.7 Rucksack

For winter, a rucksack with the features found on a summer rucksack is needed but with a larger volume of about 50 litres. It should be comfortable, with clean lines, good compression straps at the side and of a simple and straight-forward design. A flexible waist belt that can be fastened out of the way round the sack is handy when climbing. It is best not to carry anything on the outside of the sack, so extra straps and fastenings are unnecessary. Too many straps can be a hazard if the wind lashes them about your face. Zips and fastenings must be easy to use when wearing gloves or mitts. It should be large enough for all your kit to fit inside comfortably, so that all the contents can be accessed without unpacking. Similarly, the ability to bundle everything into the sack when the weather is bad is a great saving in time and effort. Some tasks such as changing gloves, opening food, even pouring a drink can be done with bare hands in the shelter of the sack. If excess volume is not needed then compression straps can reduce the rucksack's size.

1.8 Headtorch

A reliable headtorch is essential and now there is a torch to suit every situation. LED torches give incredible battery life and some have a beam which can be focused, while halogen bulbs are exceptionally bright. Headtorches which combine these features give the best of both worlds. LED's with red light and flashing modes may also be useful. Instead of carrying spare batteries and bulbs, a spare LED headtorch can be carried as a back-up. Whatever you carry, it has to work when you need it most, so don't let the batteries run out.

1.9 Goggles

With strong winds, blowing snow and especially with bright light, goggles protect the eyes, improve visibility and keep the face feeling warmer. Snow blowing onto the eyeballs can be very painful! The best goggles have double lenses, which are less prone to misting up, good ventilation and a good seal round the face. Low-profile goggles allow better peripheral vision and more flexible ones are less likely to crack. Suitable goggles should give 100% UV protection. Lenses that are yellow, light amber or rose-tinted give greater definition to the landscape, especially in poor or flat light, but in instructional situations, limit eye contact between client(s) and instructor.

To be effective, goggles must be put on before the face becomes wet, as this causes misting up. Put them on warm, for example, after being stored inside the jacket. Once on, leave them on and keep the inside dry to prevent misting. Pushing the goggles up onto the forehead is not recommended. If they do mist up, then holding a top edge open for a little while to let warm, moist air escape may help. Wiping the inside of the lens with washing up liquid can help reduce condensation.

A drawback to goggles is that they can give the wearer a feeling of isolation or separation from the environment, which is unhelpful in situations demanding full concentration. The reduction in peripheral vision can be noticeable when navigating or climbing.

1.10 Bivvy bag

A personal bivouac shelter such as a simple, heavy-duty polythene bag is cheap and convenient. A waterproof/breathable bivvy bag is more expensive but more pleasant to stay in and is a good investment if going to the Alps or other high mountains, or for planned bivouacs.

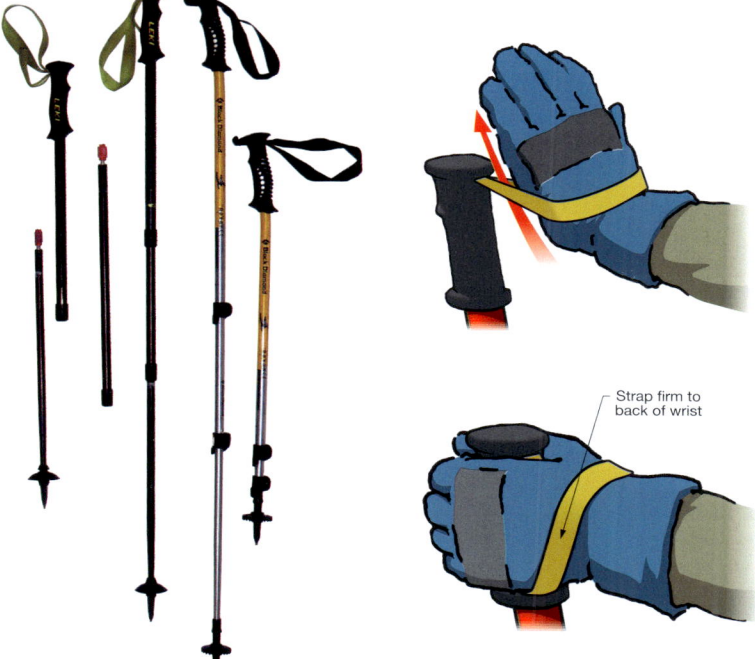

FIGURE 1.4 WALKING POLES WITH INTERNAL AND EXTERNAL LOCKING MECHANISMS

FIGURE 1.5 USING A WALKING POLE WRIST STRAP

1.11 Group shelter

This is a very useful piece of equipment for a leader or group. Basically, it is a large vented windproof and water-resistant nylon bag, under which several people can sit. They come in a variety of sizes and provide communal shelter. Its use needs to be well co-ordinated in windy conditions, normally with people sitting inside on its edge to provide a seal.

1.12 Walking poles

Walking or trekking poles provide a good aid to balance, may allow more efficient movement and take some of the load off the knees and hips. The worse the conditions for walking, the more of an aid they become, so when negotiating broken ground, crossing streams, carrying heavy packs or walking through unconsolidated snow, they can make a significant difference to effort and security. The disadvantage is the temptation to use them on inappropriate terrain or when navigating. When an ice axe is required they should be put away and the axe used. It is easy to continue too long with poles and become insecure in a position where it is difficult to deploy the axe. There is some evidence that misuse of poles can cause damage to the wrists or elbows. While one pole helps, using two gives more balance and stability.

FIGURE 1.6 USING POLES IN DEEP SNOW AND STRONG WINDS

1.12.1 Types of pole

Adjustable poles are the most convenient. This adjustment can be made by an expanding plug which is pushed to the appropriate position and screwed to lock the sections together, or by sprung pins or an external locking system. The disadvantage of the expanding plug is that it can slip, particularly if worn or if the pole gets wet or iced up. If this happens flexing the pole slightly when trying to lock it may help the plug to grip. External adjustment systems are generally the most reliable but can sometimes be accidentally knocked loose *(see Figure 1.4)*. To extend the pole, take the lower section to its stop marker and adjust the length using the top two sections.

Those that telescope to the shortest length are the handiest, especially in a climbing situation, where they can be stowed in the rucksack or in compression straps when not in use. Stow them point down as then the spikes are less likely to catch and this prevents water entering the joints where it can freeze and so make it difficult to extend the poles later. Taking the pole apart to store it in the rucksack is an option if they are easy to re-assemble. There are two main types of baskets. The normal ski type gives more support when on soft snow and can be used to clip the poles together and easily carried in one hand. The smaller, solid baskets catch less on vegetation and rocks, and take up less space.

1.12.2 Use of poles

Walking poles are a very natural aid. The wrist strap takes most of the strain and if used correctly means that you need not grip too tightly. The hand is taken up through the strap then down on top of it so that it supports the wrist *(see Figure 1.5)*. In situations where a slip or fall is possible, such as in high winds or in difficult terrain, then take the hands out of the loops *(see Figure 1.6)*. If you stumble, a jammed pole can be released before it can cause any damage. If using poles while walking in a group, then leave adequate space between people, for if a pole skates off the ground and flicks backwards, it could injure someone behind.

1.12.3 Maintenance of poles

If the pole does not have extra insulation below the handle, then taping it up is worthwhile, with the tape overlapping uppermost for a better grip. This means that the pole can be held there to shorten it, such as when traversing a slope, since adjusting the length for short sections is usually inconvenient. An aid to ensuring the adjustment works effectively is to take the poles apart and dry them out after use. This reduces corrosion inside the pole. If the adjustment becomes worn and slips, roughing up the plastic of the plug and scoring the interior or the pole's tubing can help to restore grip.

1.13 Sunglasses

Sunglasses are important in winter even in this country. On snow, sunglasses can be essential when ultra-violet rays from the sun that are not absorbed by the atmosphere are reflected into your eyes from below, and especially on partially cloudy days when the UV is trapped between the cloud and the snow, increasing its power. Generally any reasonable pair of sunglasses will suffice. However, a pair with comfortable frames and a close fit so that light cannot get in from the sides, above or below is best. Glacier glasses with side shields reduce light entry and prevent snow blowing behind the lens.

1.14 Sun screen

Sun-cream and lip salve may be required on bright days when there is full snow cover. This becomes more important as the season progresses and the sun gets higher in the sky. Sunburn under the nose or ears from reflected light is not uncommon on sunny days.

DESCENDING THROUGH THE REGENERATING BIRCH WOODLAND OF COIRE ARDAIR,
CREAG MEAGAIDH NATURE RESERVE   *PHOTO // GARRY SMITH*

Environmental issues

When the ground is covered with snow and ice, and visibility reduced to our immediate surroundings, it is easy to forget that we still affect the plants and animals of the mountain environment.

FIGURE 2.1 A PAIR OF PTARMIGAN   *PHOTO // GILES TRUSSELL*

In summer, environmental issues can contribute to our enjoyment but in winter they tend to be overlooked, as does our impact on them. Anyone venturing into the mountains should appreciate the problems of erosion and man's influence on the environment. Knowing what wildlife can be found and what effect we have on the mountain environment is the first step to minimising that impact *(see Figure 2.1)*.

2.1 Erosion

Erosion takes place all year and our contribution to this can be as great in winter as in summer. Heavier, stiffer boots with sharper edged soles do more damage to vegetation than lighter summer footwear. Wearing crampons on bare ground damages it and crampon marks are evident on many of our mountains, especially the rockier ridges and popular scrambles. While this hardly contributes to the wearing down of the hills, it is an indication of the passing of thousands of pairs of feet and the damage they can do on softer and more vulnerable ground. Walking poles also contribute to the process of erosion and the scarring of the landscape, particularly along the soft edges of footpaths.

Paths become covered in snow and ice, particularly those which are recessed and in which snow accumulates. When trodden on, this snow becomes compacted and icy giving a slippery walking surface. The temptation is then to walk on the verges, which leads to path widening through the destruction of vegetation and subsequent soil erosion *(see Figure 2.2)*. Parts of paths in popular areas show numerous small, parallel tracks which are the result of this or the path itself being hidden by snow. If this is a problem, then walking well away from the track may be the best way to reduce erosion. If a group spreads out, damage is not concentrated. During thaw conditions when the ground is waterlogged, the surface is more easily cut up by boots. In the worst cases of waterlogged

FIGURE 2.2 PATH WIDENING AND EROSION   *PHOTO // PAUL NOBLE*

soil lying on a still-frozen base, it can move in a wave with every footstep. The options for minimising our impact are limited but an appreciation of the problem and the damage we cause is a good starting point for making changes.

Another problem of erosion is the vegetation damage which occurs at the edges of snow patches. Often it is easier to walk round the edges of snow patches, and if this happens often enough, new tracks develop. Over time these can become better established and more pointless paths created. This is hastened on hard or steeper ground by boots kicked in on their edges to form steps. Good route planning and awareness helps to reduce this damage.

2.2 Sanitation

The same principles of sanitation apply all year round. Defecation and urination should be discreet and at least 50m from streams and paths and 200m from huts, bothies and crags. Excrement should be carried out or buried in a hole at least 15cm deep and if this is not possible, then spread as thinly as possible to help the natural breakdown. Toilet paper and sanitary items should be carried out. Burying excrement in the snow only hides the problem until the thaw, when there is more chance of it getting into streams which may not be obvious when the ground is snow-covered. The processes of natural breakdown are slowed down with the low temperatures, so the signs of your passing take longer to disappear in cold conditions.

2.3 Litter

This is very simple – nothing is left and everything is carried out. There is no reason for leaving any litter, including food scraps which take a long time to degrade. Leaving food in the hills in winter is analogous to putting your waste in the fridge in the kitchen rather than your bin. The limited type and number of local birds do not generally eat human food, but this does attract scavengers such as gulls and crows. These may then stay into the spring and then take the eggs of the indigenous birds contributing to the reduction in their numbers. Careful packaging of food using the fewest possible bags and wrappers will reduce the problem of litter blowing away.

2.4 Winter climbs

Winter routes, which are predominantly on snow and ice, are little affected by climbers, although places where belays or runners are regularly placed may become scarred, especially if pitons are used. However, this is now less of a problem as fewer routes require pitons. Snow and ice routes, which are often wet faults, are less pleasant than popular summer climbs and damage is often hidden away and less obvious.

Mixed buttress climbs do become scarred with crampon and axe marks. Modern buttress and face routes may be little protected by snow or ice and in some conditions this must be cleared to reveal the rock beneath, both for climbing and for protection. Here, tools can scratch and deface the rock, leaving unsightly scars which are even more obvious in summer *(see Figure 2.3)*. Hooking and particularly torquing can put great pressure on the edges of cracks, blocks and flakes causing rock damage, loosening and even the removal of the rock. Vegetation used for axe and crampon placements is easily damaged and eventually removed. This leaves bare soil, which quickly erodes, becomes unsightly and leads to dirt being washed down the climb. On some harder routes, the loss of vegetation can affect the grade of climbs, usually making them harder. The loss of a single patch of moss can make a huge difference to some harder routes as, once it is gone, there may be little to use in its place. These problems are exacerbated when the turf is not frozen. This happens not only during a thaw, but also when a layer of insulating snow protects the vegetation. If there is a heavy snowfall before the cliffs are frozen, the vegetation may remain soft and liable to be damaged for longer.

What constitutes good or even reasonable winter climbing conditions can be open to much debate, especially when global warming is making winters shorter, more variable and liable to rapid changes in conditions. It is however unacceptable to climb routes where obvious damage will occur bearing in mind that it is important for conservation reasons that vegetation is well frozen to minimise damage. Routes basically on rock rather than vegetation may be less unpleasant and less liable to damage in marginal conditions, but climbs with loose or blocky ground should be treated with care. Some climbs, which are perfectly safe when everything is held together with a hard freeze and a good cover of snow and ice, may be quite unstable when thawing, particularly when torquing

FIGURE 2.3 ROCK SCARRING

and hooking. While this rock damage is probably only an acceleration of the natural processes of erosion, we should attempt to keep the signs of our climbing to a minimum, especially on routes which are popular summer climbs. However, it is worth remembering that compared with how nature alters some climbs, our influence is minor and generally cosmetic.

2.5 Cairns

Whilst most cairns are useful as marker points, for example on mountain summits, or way-marking complicated navigation legs or at the top of descent routes, others are pointless and inappropriate. Lifting stones off or out of the ground to build or add to an existing cairn can leave the ground exposed to erosion and damage the surrounding vegetation, compounding the visual intrusion.

> ### 3 Environmental issues
> It is incumbent on leaders and instructors to educate groups on environmental issues, particularly local ones as they become apparent during an outing. For example, encourage people to carry a spare bag to remove any litter found out on the hill.

GOOD WEATHER IN TORRIDON, BUT APPROACHING FRONT TO THE WEST

Winter weather

The one constant factor of our winter weather is its changeability, and the speed and range of these changes seem to be increasing as climate change makes itself felt.

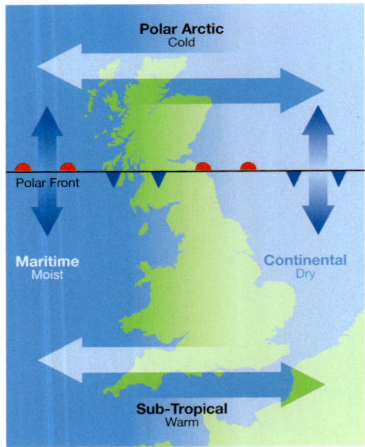

FIGURE 3.1 THE MAIN INFLUENCES ON OUR WINTER WEATHER

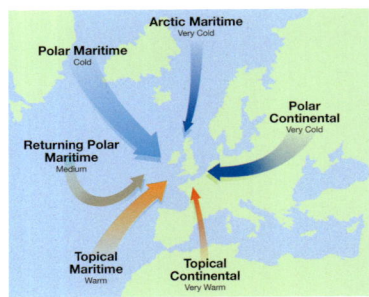

FIGURE 3.2 THE MAIN AIRSTREAMS AFFECTING THE BRITISH ISLES. THE WIDTH OF THE ARROW IS INDICATIVE OF THE FREQUENCY WITH WHICH THEY OCCUR

There is clear evidence that British winter weather is changing, not only seasonally, but also in the longer term. In February 2018, during a notable cold spell dubbed 'The Beast from the East', Cairngorm summit temperatures dipped to -14°C and in combination with a strong 'Siberian' easterly wind, wind chill temperatures approached -30°C; the lowest temperatures recorded in at least the previous 25 years. During the same month in 2019, Cairngorm summit temperatures peaked at +14°C with a total loss of snow cover in other mountain areas!

A basic understanding of weather is needed to venture into the mountains at any time, but in winter, knowledge of weather is vital to ensure appropriate decisions are made and to make the most of the conditions. A winter walker or climber must be able to interpret weather forecasts and identify the signs of weather change.

3.1 Winter air masses and airflows

There are two main influences controlling our winter weather patterns. Firstly, the 'polar front' is the boundary between cold arctic air to the north and a warm moist sub-tropical air to the south. There is also an east-west boundary between maritime air over the Atlantic and continental dry air to the east over continental Eurasia *(see Figure 3.1)*.

Britain lies near these two global climatic boundaries and the relative position of each will cause a different airstream to cover the country. However, it is the polar front that has the dominant effect on our winter weather. If it shifts its average position north of Britain, our main weather influence will be from milder airflows. If the front moves to the south, then we will enjoy a colder and drier airflow. If continental air masses extend from the east, we will have a spell of cold, dry weather.

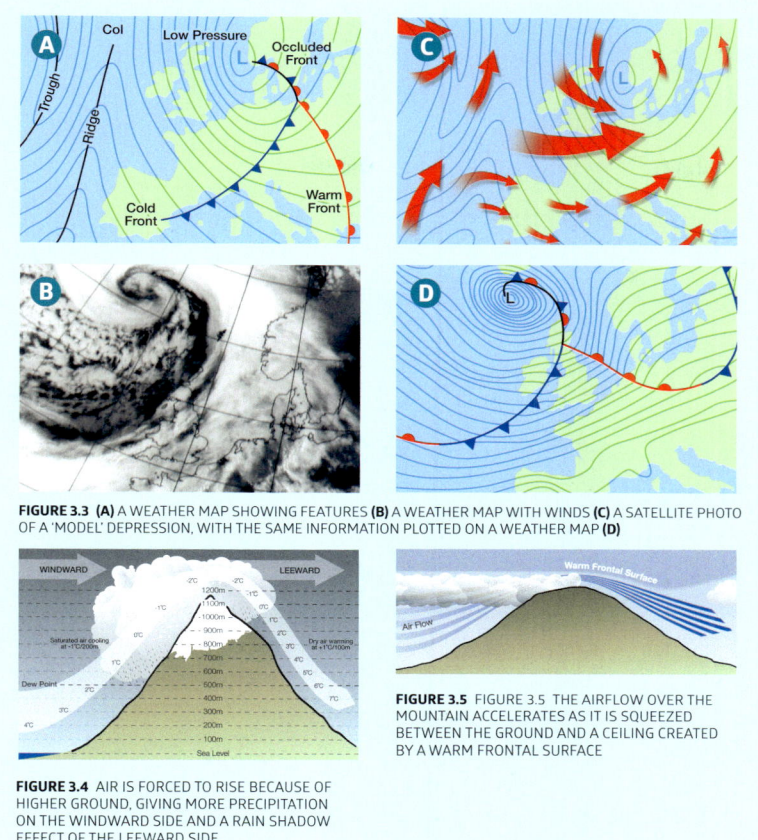

FIGURE 3.3 **(A)** A WEATHER MAP SHOWING FEATURES **(B)** A WEATHER MAP WITH WINDS **(C)** A SATELLITE PHOTO OF A 'MODEL' DEPRESSION, WITH THE SAME INFORMATION PLOTTED ON A WEATHER MAP **(D)**

FIGURE 3.4 AIR IS FORCED TO RISE BECAUSE OF HIGHER GROUND, GIVING MORE PRECIPITATION ON THE WINDWARD SIDE AND A RAIN SHADOW EFFECT OF THE LEEWARD SIDE

FIGURE 3.5 FIGURE 3.5 THE AIRFLOW OVER THE MOUNTAIN ACCELERATES AS IT IS SQUEEZED BETWEEN THE GROUND AND A CEILING CREATED BY A WARM FRONTAL SURFACE

There are six main air masses that affect us *(see Figure 3.2)*:

- Polar Maritime (PM) generally from the north-west;
- Returning Polar Maritime (rPM) from the west;
- Arctic Maritime (AM) from the north and north-east;
- Polar Continental (PC) from the east and north-east;
- Tropical Continental (TC) mainly from the south-east; and
- Tropical Maritime (TM) south to south-westerly.

Each airstream has a signature weather pattern derived mainly from its source region, with minor modification during its flow towards Britain. Knowing the origin of the air covering the country gives a general picture of the weather and conditions. We also have the influences from local warm, cold and occluded fronts associated with depressions and anticyclones (areas of low and high pressures) that generally track west to east across Britain *(see Figure 3.3)*. The ability to interpret a synoptic chart is an important skill for a winter mountaineer. Then there are very local weather influences, such as mountain barriers, rain shadow effects and orographic precipitation *(see Figures 3.4 and 3.5)*.

FIGURE 3.6 A CLOUD CAP FORMING ON LIATHACH, WITH A FRONT APPROACHING FROM THE WEST

3.2 Weather factors

With this basic information of general air masses and airflows (periodic), the effects of a frontal system (systematic) and local effects (topographic), it is possible, to an extent, to predict the weather pattern for the near future. There are several factors of direct concern to the winter mountaineer, who is seldom affected by only one of them. They are all interlinked and together form the weather.

3.2.1 Precipitation

In winter, rain, sleet, hail and snow can be encountered, often all in the course of one day or a single ascent of a hill. Knowing what is falling, where it is falling, how it is likely to change and the effect it will have on conditions are all vital for comfort and safety.

3.2.2 Lapse rates

This is the rate at which air cools with altitude. The dry air lapse rate for unsaturated air is 1°C per 100m and saturated air, essentially cloud, cools at 1°C per 200m. Dew point is the temperature at which visible droplets form. These figures can be used to estimate the temperature at any height on the mountain.

3.2.3 Temperature

The temperature at any altitude affects the snow pack, walking and climbing conditions, avalanche hazard and the form of any precipitation. In general, temperature drops with height gained except in an inversion when the opposite is the case. The freezing level, the altitude at which the temperature is 0°C, is a primary factor in decision-making, especially with regards to conditions. The best type of weather for creating firm snow is when the freezing level moves up and down producing a freeze/thaw cycle leading to good, consolidated snow. Snow can fall up to 300m

FIGURE 3.7 THE UNMISTAKABLE SHAPE OF LENTICULAR CLOUDS, INDICATING HIGH WINDS

below the freezing level (the 'wet bulb' freezing level), particularly associated with drier air conditions.

Besides air temperature, other factors are the strength and the amount of sunshine and as the year progresses these become more important. Some south-facing aspects are severely affected by the sun and may produce problems of thawing, melting snow and ice and collapsing cornices while other shaded areas may remain in good winter condition.

3.2.4 Visibility
Visibility is affected by length of day, cloud, precipitation and wind-blown snow. A lot of winter activity takes place in conditions of less than

> **4 Wind**
> Looking after a group in high winds can be difficult. The force of the wind in a gale can be terrifying and may constitute a serious risk of injury. People have been blown over and even picked off their feet by a severe gust. The effort involved in battling a strong wind can tire a group rapidly and it may not be possible to go anywhere but downwind.
>
> Communications can be difficult and may only be possible if the group is huddled closely together. Sometimes a lighter or weaker person may be confidence-roped or helped by linking arms in a small group, but above a certain force this is not an option. Listening to the sound of the wind can help, as a change in note may precede a stronger gust and when heard, crouching down or lying on the ground may be the best defence. In some places such as corries, the wind direction may not correspond to the prevailing wind and come from different directions as the shape of the ground deflects it. Also, cross loading, leading to localised avalanche conditions, should be anticipated in high winds and spindrift.

perfect visibility. Cloud over the tops is common in winter *(see Figure 3.6)*. For example, the top of Ben Nevis is only cloud-free for about 30% of the time. Even with clear skies, visibility can be poor as blowing snow obscures the ground and makes looking into it painful.

3.2.5 Clouds
The sequence of clouds heralding the arrival of warm, cold and occluded fronts should be recognisable. These can give a good indication of forthcoming changes in weather. It is important to anticipate their arrival, passing and effects on local mountain conditions. Also important are lenticular clouds and wave bars which usually indicate high winds, as does a cloud cap sitting over the tops *(see Figure 3.7)*.

3.2.6 Wind speeds
Wind has a tremendous effect on us as well as the snow pack and avalanche conditions. Its speed, direction and any changes in strength and direction should be monitored, not only throughout the day, but also before your mountain trip. Wind speeds on the tops can be two to three times those in the valley.

Depending on local topography, wind direction and atmospheric conditions, this increase can be even greater. The wind speed over some ridges and through cols may be greater as air is squeezed through a narrower space and consequently flows faster. Conversely there can be areas of relative calm in a gale where the ground shape creates an eddy. For example, slacker wind is sometimes found at the top of cliffs when the wind blowing directly onto them is forced upwards.

While factors such as snow and avalanche conditions can be anticipated and avoided, there is no escape from the wind, which can present a serious hazard. Physics dictates that a doubling in wind speed exerts four times as much force on an object and a tripling in speed exerts nine times as much. Walking in strong winds is unpleasant, physically demanding, affects your stability with the associated risk of injury, and increases the potential for losing equipment.

3.2.7 Windchill
Windchill is the combined cooling effect of wind and temperature. This effect increases rapidly at lower wind speeds, being most marked up to about 15mph or 25km/h. Although not so marked above these speeds, the effort involved in walking in such winds will increase, as will the effect of blowing snow or rain *(see Table 3.1 overleaf)*.

3.3 Winter weather and weather forecasts
The weather itself may not be a hazard, but how it affects the conditions on the ground, and the timing of its effect, can be. Timing is important, since if a weather event such as a front arrives sooner or later than predicted, it can have a significant effect. Fronts can increase the level of rivers through rain or snow melt. Likewise, past weather has a great impact on conditions. A strong wind during the night may not have an

immediate effect but this does not mean it can be ignored. For example, it can re-deposit snow and create an avalanche risk. Weather forecasts must be part of your preparations and you should be able to interpret national and regional forecasts for the weather in the mountains. Your own knowledge of weather is essential to being able to anticipate what is likely to happen.

Forecasts are available from a range of sources such as smart phone apps, internet, radio, television, newspapers, posted bulletins and it is likely that anyone who mountaineers regularly will have used these sources and have their own favourite source. Some internet forecasts are for very specific areas and for a variety of time scales.

	Temperature °C										
Wind speed mph	20°C	16°C	12°C	8°C	4°C	0°C	-4°C	-8°C	-12°C	-16°C	-20°C	-24°C
4 mph	18	14	9	7	0	-5	-6	-14	-18	-23	-28	-32
8 mph	17	12	7	2	-3	-8	-13	-18	-23	-28	-33	-38
12 mph	16	11	5	0	-5	-10	-16	-21	-26	-31	-37	-42
16 mph	15	10	4	-1	-7	-12	-18	-23	-29	-34	-40	-45
20 mph	15	9	3	-2	-8	-14	-19	-25	-31	-36	-42	-47
24 mph	14	8	3	-3	-9	-15	-20	-26	-32	-38	-44	-49
28 mph	14	8	2	-4	-10	-16	-21	-27	-33	-39	-45	-51
32 mph	14	8	2	-4	-10	-16	-22	-28	-34	-40	-46	-52
36 mph	13	7	1	-5	-11	-17	-23	-29	-35	-41	-47	-53
40 mph	13	7	1	-5	-11	-17	-23	-29	-35	-41	-48	-54
44 mph	13	7	1	-5	-11	-17	-23	-30	-36	-42	-48	-54
48 mph	13	7	1	-5	-11	-17	-24	-30	-36	-42	-48	-54
54 mph	13	7	1	-5	-11	-17	-23	-30	-36	-42	-48	-54

TABLE 3.1 WINDCHILL CHART

FIGURE 3.8 AN APPROACHING WARM FRONT, HERALDING THE ARRIVAL OF BAD WEATHER

TAKING A BEARING IN WINTER CONDITIONS   *PHOTO // ROB JOHNSON*

Winter navigation

The ability to navigate effectively and confidently through a winter storm is as demanding as mountain navigation gets. The penalties for an error can be serious and many winter accidents are the result of an initial navigational mistake.

Winter brings with it problems such as reduced visibility, shorter daylight hours and the absence of many summer navigational features. Other dangers include corniced edges, avalanche-prone slopes, ice-covered paths and the reduction in options of navigational features and safe routes. You must use all the techniques required to navigate in summer conditions, only better! However, there are extra skills and strategies to cope with winter conditions.

4.1 Problem winter conditions

4.1.1 Freezing temperatures
Freezing temperatures can have a major effect on performing such simple tasks as taking a bearing. Numb fingers and frozen gloves make it difficult to manipulate a map and compass. Riming *(see Rime ice, page 100)* may cause the compass to slip on the map and obscure details, eyelashes can become iced making it difficult to see clearly and zippers and buckles can freeze up making it difficult to access other equipment, such as that inside a rucksack.

4.1.2 Snow cover
Complete snow cover can dramatically reduce useable navigation features. Spot, linear and area features such as cairns, footpaths, streams (their junctions and intersections), lochans, scree slopes, boulder fields and small features, such as knolls and re-entrants, may be under snow and hidden or unrecognisable *(see Figure 4.1)*. Changes in slope angle may be obscured by deep snow, making ground shape and contours more difficult to interpret.

4.1.3 Poor visibility
Cloud reduces visibility and when combined with full snow cover, can produce difficult flat light conditions. This may cause a whiteout, with the loss of horizon, colours, shading or anything to focus on.

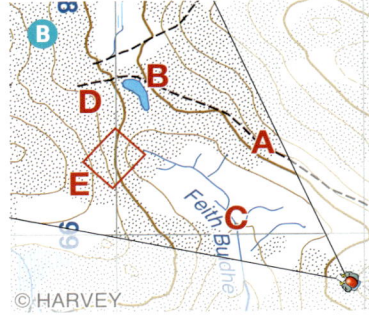

FIGURE 4.1 (A) **COMPLETE SNOW COVER OBSCURING FEATURES:** A FOOTPATH, B LOCHAN, C STREAMS, D BOULDERFIELD, E STEEP GROUND: OBVIOUS SLOPE CHANGE FEATURE (B) A MAP SHOWING THE SAME AREA AND FEATURES

FIGURE 4.2 WELL PREPARED FOR WINTER NAVIGATION   *PHOTO // SAM LEARY*

4.1.4 Strong winds

Strong winds can cause drifting off course and make it difficult to hold a map and compass steady. Spindrift can make seeing difficult and a headwind can slow you down. The strength and direction of the wind can influence direction of travel and navigation options. For instance, it may be unsafe to follow a corniced edge if the wind is blowing you towards it, or it may be impossible to walk into the wind.

4.1.5 Whiteout

In the worst case, the above conditions can produce a full whiteout where you may experience disorientation, affected concentration, numbness and loss of confidence. Prolonged exposure to such conditions can produce feelings such as nausea and problems with balance similar to seasickness. This is because there is nothing to focus on and some people can feel so bad they have to lie down to recover!

4.2 Coping with the winter environment

Be thoroughly prepared before you start out. General route planning, weather forecast and, if available, avalanche forecast, must be considered, but also ensure your clothing and equipment are appropriate *(see Figure 4.2)*.

4.2.1 Map

The map should be kept to hand and stored in an accessible pocket and not in your rucksack! It can also be modified:

- Fold or cut your map to a manageable size. Although cutting may seem drastic it is often easier to fold a cut-down map to the required area. If your route crosses a fold, then prepare the map so you do not

have to re-fold it on the hill. The hard covers of most maps can be removed so it can be folded more easily.
- Waterproof maps, although expensive, are useful. Home waterproofing is an option, such as laminating, sealing using a thin waterproof film, or simply putting the map into a tight-fitting sealed polythene bag.
- Some laminated maps are difficult to fold, but strong rubber bands can be used to hold the folded map conveniently. Maps from commercial PC software can be printed to size but need to be waterproofed.
- Some types of map cases can blow about and can be unmanageable in high winds or become stiff and brittle in the cold. The best are those of soft plastic which can be folded.
- Enlarging a map can help those with poor eyesight. A map with a scale of 1:50,000 can be enlarged to 1:25,000, while keeping the original map features. Generally, use the appropriate map scale for the situation. The usual scales of 1:50,000, 1:40,000 and 1:25,000 each have their pros and cons.

4.2.2 Compass

This should be accessible, preferably attached to the zipper of a jacket outer pocket and stored with the map. Avoid keeping the compass round your neck or attached to your wrist, as in high winds opening your jacket lets in snow and a compass hanging from your wrist can tangle. The following compass features are desirable:

- The length of attachment cord should allow ease of sighting: too short and it is difficult to sight with, too long and it may tangle.
- A long base plate enables longer distances to be measured and, when sighting, it 'points the way ahead' better.
- The housing must be large enough to be manipulated while wearing gloves.
- Luminous points marking the needle, orienting arrow and the direction of travel arrow help in the dark and whilst using a headtorch.
- A magnifying lens in the base plate can be used to show the finer contour details.
- Rubber feet on the base plate help hold the compass steady on the map or map case, particularly in wet or icy conditions.

4.2.3 Wristwatch

When timing is used to measure distance on the ground, a digital watch with a stopwatch, a large easily viewed face, easily manipulated function buttons and a backlight for night navigation is recommended. One that can be worn on the outside of the jacket or on a rucksack strap is convenient.

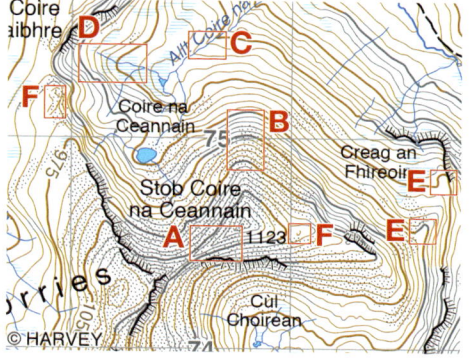

FIGURE 4.3 CONTOUR INTERPRETATION:
A SHARP CONTOURS INDICATING A PROMINENT RIDGE
B ROUNDED CONTOURS INDICATING A SHOULDER
C SHARP CONTOURS INDICATING A RE-ENTRANT AND PROMINENT STREAM LINE
D ROUNDED CONTOURS INDICATING A LARGE BOWL OR MINOR CORRIE
E 'AMOEBA'-SHAPED CONTOURS INDICATING A MINOR HIGH POINT ON A SPUR
F FORM LINE CONTOUR INDICATING A KNOLL

4.2.4 Altimeter

An altimeter can be a useful aid to navigation and is used as normal but in winter the speed with which the weather and air pressure alters is increased so an altimeter must be re-set regularly to be accurate.

4.2.5 Clothing and equipment

The metal of the axe, particularly the head, can affect the magnetic needle if held too close so keep it clear of the compass when following a bearing. Use crampons appropriately as they allow you to concentrate on the navigation rather than on what is underfoot.

A shell jacket with a spacious hood, a stiff-wired visor and a high main zipper will maintain the shape of the hood in strong winds and protect the face from spindrift. Occasional or removable hoods are not adequate. Cord attached to zip pulls allows easier use. The map pocket should be on the outside of the jacket and have easy access. The second option is a map pocket inside the main zip flap, but one inside the jacket is not recommended. Gloves are better than mitts for manipulating the map and compass, particularly when rimed up.

Goggles help when navigating into a headwind and spectacle-wearers may have no other option but to protect their eyes. It has even been known for contact lenses to be blown out by the wind! However, some people find they cannot use goggles for difficult tasks or in stressful situations. In winter, navigating in the dark is common. A powerful waterproof headtorch is recommended, with a strong beam that can penetrate spindrift and cloud cover. Snow or rime may coat the lens of a headtorch, reducing the strength of the beam so keep clearing the lens with a hand. Put poles in your rucksack, as you need both hands free to navigate effectively. Be aware that some metal poles may affect the compass.

4.3 Know where you are!

In winter, relocation is more difficult as there are fewer features to be found and major ones may be further apart. Some techniques such as resections have limited use, as for much of the time it is not possible to see and identify two or more features to take back bearings. Observation is continually required and the emphasis is on knowing where you are at

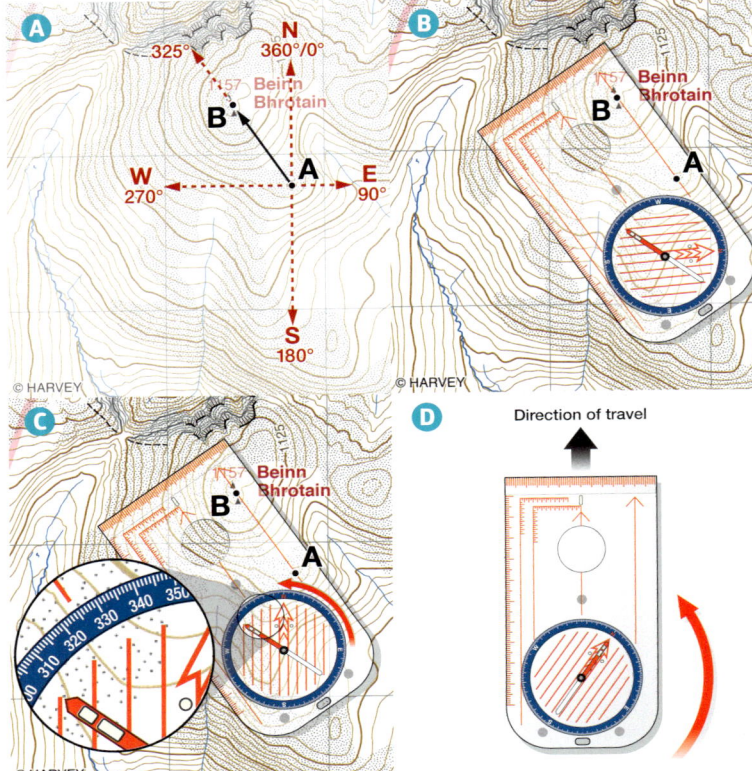

FIGURE 4.4 TAKING A BEARING WITH A COMPASS: **(A)** ESTIMATE THE ANGLE (GRID BEARING). TRAVELLING FROM A TO B, THE ANGLE IS JUST OVER HALF WAY BETWEEN 270° AND 360° – ROUGHLY 320° TO 330° **(B)** USING A LINE ON THE BASE PLATE, LINK POINTS A (WHERE YOU ARE) AND B (YOUR INTENDED DESTINATION) WITH THE DIRECTION OF TRAVEL ARROW POINTING FROM A TO B. **(C)** ROTATE THE COMPASS HOUSING TO ALIGN THE ORIENTING LINES WITH THE NORTH–SOUTH GRID LINES ON THE MAP, WITH THE ORIENTING ARROW POINTING NORTH. ROTATE THE COMPASS HOUSING TO COMPENSATE FOR MAGNETIC VARIATION **(D)** REMOVE THE COMPASS FROM THE MAP AND ROTATE THE COMPASS TO ALIGN THE NORTH (RED) END OF THE NEEDLE AND THE ORIENTING ARROW. KEEPING BOTH NEEDLE AND ARROW ALIGNED, FOLLOW THE DIRECTION OF TRAVEL ARROW.

all times. The speed with which weather and conditions change makes this more important than in summer and the option of being able to return to your last known point and start again must be kept open.

4.3.1 Revise the basic skills

All the skills and techniques of summer navigation such as map reading, contour interpretation, taking and following bearings and estimating distance should be learned and practised before venturing into the mountains in winter.

Map reading
Contour interpretation is a vital skill and even more critical when many features are hidden under snow and only the general shape of the ground can be seen. The basic rule that the closer the contours are, the steeper the ground is, allows the shape of the terrain to be interpreted from the lines on the map. Other contour observations include:

- Sharp bends in the contours represent 'sharp' ground features. Equally, round bends in the contours represent rounded features.
- Contours that bend to 'point' from low to high ground signify a depression feature. Where there are many contours, this signifies a glen or corrie and one or two contour lines signify a small-scale re-entrant feature. Conversely, contours that bend to 'point' downhill represent either a ridge (sharp bends) or a shoulder (rounded bends) on a large scale, or a spur on a small scale. On a 1:50,000 map for example, even a bend in a single contour represents a significant ground feature.
- Ring contours represent a knoll. Many knolls or high-point features are not shown by a ring contour on the map, because the feature is not high enough. Some maps show these by a hatched contour line and on others by a type of 'amoeba' shaped contour *(see Figure 4.3E)*.
- Some maps have dashed lines, form lines, between the solid contour lines. These show the shape of the ground which is not prominent enough to be seen otherwise.

Taking a bearing

To take a bearing, lay an edge of the compass base plate, or a line parallel to the edge, along a line from where you are to your destination, with the direction of travel arrow pointing to where you wish to go. Turn the compass housing until north on the housing points to north on the map and the orienting lines in the housing are parallel to the north-south grid lines. The grid bearing can be read off from the index line and the magnetic variation (taken from the map legend) is added to obtain the magnetic bearing, which is then followed *(see Figure 4.4D)*.

Following a bearing

Hold the compass in both hands at about waist level so that you can look down on the housing and the arrows. By using both hands, it is easier to sight straight ahead and prevent accidentally twisting the compass. However, in winter when an axe may need to be carried, hold the compass in one hand (fingers held along one edge, thumb along the other with the compass corner in your palm and elbow braced against your body) with the direction of travel arrow pointing directly ahead *(see Figure 4.4)*. Turn around until the compass needle lies above the orienting arrow. Sight along the direction of travel arrow to find an object to use as a marker and walk to that marker, repeating the process until you reach your objective. Try to have the next marker picked out before you reach the one aimed at, as this cuts down the need to stop and re-sight. Each sighting should be a slowing down rather than a complete halt.

Estimating distance

Accurate distance estimation is an essential skill. This can be by pacing or timing, and in bad conditions both may be used together. In poor visibility, distance estimation is used continually to aid map reading and compass work.

Pacing
Work out how many double paces are needed to cover 100m on various slope angles. This means going out and pacing a number of measured 100m legs. The average number of paces on the flat is about 65 but can rise to about 100 double paces ascending steep ground. Measure the distance on the map then pace this out in 100m blocks, adjusting the number of double paces for each 100m when the angle or the conditions underfoot vary.

Timing
In ideal conditions, use Naismith's Rule, which allows 5 kilometres per hour and 1 minute for each 10m of height gained. Any moderate descent is considered the same as travelling on the flat but steep descents take longer. The time for both horizontal distance and height gain can be altered to suit conditions and should not be considered to be absolutes.

4.4 Winter navigation strategies

In winter, the techniques available for navigation may be reduced, as some slopes can be too dangerous, or cliff and ridge edges too corniced to approach. Aiming off and attack points can be limited because of the snow cover. Convex slopes are more likely to be avalanche-prone, while concave slopes may have corniced tops. However, there are several variations on summer techniques that can be employed.

4.4.1 The winter navigational leg
Following a procedure can assist navigation by serving as a reminder and encouraging a clear process for the calculations. There is an assumption that you know where you are and that you have decided where to go to next: the navigational leg.

1. Magnetic Bearing
2. Measure Distance
3. Time or Pace Distance
4. Map Reading – 'Mental Checklist'
5. Dangers
6. Possible Errors

Although map reading underpins all aspects of navigation, the calculations of bearings and distances are made first and the interpretation of contour detail is then an ongoing process. However, very detailed map reading is less useful if smaller features are hidden under snow.

4.4.2 Taking a bearing
Roughly estimate the bearing as a simple way to check for major errors, such as using the wrong grid lines or turning the compass housing to point south instead of north. For example, if going roughly west your bearing should be about 270° and any answer greatly different from this

indicates an error. Set the compass to your estimate before you take the bearing. Assuming the estimate is correct, this means less movement of the housing and potentially reduces slippage while taking a bearing. Use the line on the base plate parallel to the compass edge to line up the two points, rather than the edge itself *(see Figure 4.4)*. This is more accurate since you can see clearly through the base plate that you are linking the two points. There may also be ruler lines along the edge obscuring the map. Light refraction through the edge can affect accuracy. Wipe the map and compass clear of any rime before taking a bearing. Since a bearing can be taken in any position (you do not need to orient the map), seek shelter or at least face downwind and a kneeling position will allow a knee to be used as a solid base for the map as illustrated in *Figure 4.2, page 33*.

4.4.3 Sighting
The procedure is the same whenever following a bearing, but in winter there may be fewer points to sight on. When you move to line up the magnetic needle in the orienting arrow, do so by turning your feet, keeping the compass square to your body, rather than twisting round to align the compass. Once the compass is set, maintain the alignment and move it out from your body to sight *(see Figure 4.5)*.

Usual sighting points such as rocks, boulders and distinctive vegetation can be hidden in winter. Even with a complete snow cover however, there may be other marks that can be used: old footsteps, different shapes or shades of snow, lumps of ice or pieces of blown vegetation, but this requires more practice. The worse the conditions and visibility, the more it is necessary to sight on closer features to follow a bearing accurately. The greater the snow cover the more difficult following a bearing becomes and in a white-out with mist, cloud or blowing snow and a total snow cover it can be extremely difficult.

Unfortunately, there is no real alternative to having something to sight on to follow a bearing accurately. Holding the magnetic needle steady in the orienting arrow and trying to keep them aligned while walking is unlikely to be sufficiently accurate for any realistic distance, particularly in bad weather when the wind and snow make walking difficult. With practice though, dead-reckoning (relying solely on the compass) over short distances is possible until something appears in sight.

4.4.4 Sighting on your own
In a white-out, you may be able to produce markers by throwing snowballs or kicking snow out. This needs fairly specific types of conditions to work and is time-consuming and laborious. Throwing anything else in front is more likely to result in lost equipment! More useful in poor visibility is using points not on your line of travel and estimating where the correct position is to the side of that point and re-adjusting accordingly.

FIGURE 4.5 FOLLOWING A BEARING: SIGHTING THROUGH A MARKER

4.4.5 Sighting on a person

In bad visibility it is possible to send someone, usually the second best navigator, out to the limit of visibility and use them as a sighting point. Before leaving they must know the bearing, the length of the leg and the feature you are seeking. A clear communication procedure must be established using signs or sounds, usually whistle blasts, and the person in front must not get out of sight of the compass user. Signals should include 'go', 'stop', 'go left', 'go right' and 'come back'. Although effective this is slow and the extra time may not be available. It produces a stop/start progress and is often used sooner than necessary by those not practiced in picking out sighting points in the snow. Slow navigation with a group can lead to group members getting cold and disinterested.

A variation is leapfrogging, where there are two navigators of equal competence and they alternate leads out to the limit of visibility, being directed from behind. When swapping leads, remain on the same side each time, otherwise you may 'crab' sideways off the bearing.

4.4.6 Using footprints

In certain types of whiteout, especially with soft snow, a person can be sent in front to leave steps which can be used as sighting points. The step-maker does not walk on the bearing, but rather in a wavy manner, crossing the bearing line. It is these steps when crossing the bearing that can be sighted on. The person in front needs to look back often and cross the bearing regularly. Communications must be established before starting. This does permit continuous movement, but the person making the track will walk further!

4.4.7 Measuring distance

The most convenient method to measure map distance is to use the Romer scale found on some compasses. This is particularly useful when the distance is less than 1km, although some clip-on Romers can measure greater distances. When using a Romer, it is possible to measure distances down to about 25m. For 1:50,000 maps the millimetre scale of the compass can be used: halve the number of millimetres measured and multiply by 100 to calculate hundreds of metres. For example, 17mm equals 850m. This allows accuracy to within about 25m (0.5mm).

4.4.8 Estimating distance

Whether timing, pacing or both is most appropriate will depend on distance, conditions underfoot, weather, accuracy required and how much communication is needed, as this can limit the usefulness of pacing, which requires counting and concentration. Either way, adjustments are made during the leg to compensate for alteration in the speed of walking or the paces required per 100m.

Timing can vary considerably from the basic rule and may be below 2km/h in deep snow with 2 or even 3 minutes for each 10m of height gained. Compensating for slow descents is common. Alternatively, on good firm névé, it is possible to walk faster and more comfortably than in summer. Timing works best for longer distances and the secret of accurate timing is to have practised enough so that you know what it feels like to walk at various speeds.

Pacing can be very accurate over shorter distances and even ground but a disadvantage is that you have to walk in a straight line, making it awkward to avoid difficulties without losing accuracy. With practice, you can adjust the pace count to compensate for any deviations and shortening of stride.

A small laminated timing chart attached to the compass cord, a 100m pace counter or system of sliding toggles on a cord attached to a jacket zipper, and a clear digital watch are helpful tools.

4.4.9 Map reading – the 'mental checklist'

Checking off features on the way is important confirmation that you are on the correct route. In winter there are fewer points for this, so less pronounced features can be used to confirm that you are on the correct route, such as vague depressions in the snow that can cover streams or less-pronounced slope angle changes, together with greater attention to distance estimation.

It is vital to be able to visualise the shape of the ground by interpreting contour detail. The leg is broken down into a checklist of mental tick-off points as you follow the bearing. You must be observant and aware of the shape of the ground whilst following a bearing to identify the points along the way. If the ground does not fit your interpretation or mental image, then you are not on the intended route, or you have missed something during the map reading. Either way, you must stop and re-assess the situation.

4.5 Map reading considerations

4.5.1 Short legs
Try to keep your navigational legs as short as possible, as this will reduce compounding any error made during either the calculations or while following a bearing. Since winter navigation can involve featureless terrain, it may be difficult to keep legs shorter than 1km between obvious features.

4.5.2 Use safe large-scale features
Navigating to and from large obvious features will aid poor weather navigation and in relocation should you need to reverse a leg.

4.5.3 Contours
Close inspection of the map is crucial for interpreting the finer contour detail. Every bend in a contour signifies something and depending on the scale, it may mean a change in aspect or a small feature. The better you are at interpreting contours the more tick-off features you will be able to use while following a bearing *(see Route choice and tick-off features)*. When interpreting contours, place the line on your compass baseplate on the map linking your location to your destination and look along the line in the direction of travel *(see Interpreting Contours)*. This allows accurate contour interpretation and means that tick-off features on the map on the right or left of the line will be on the same side on the ground as you follow the bearing. However, there is no point in interpreting the contours to the sides of your line of travel any further than visibility limit.

4.5.4 Route choice
Don't break a long leg into shorter sections unless there are features to tick-off, to aim for, or to use as attack points. Don't set yourself up with difficult navigation to a vague point purely to shorten the distance of a longer leg *(see Route choice and tick-off features)*.

4.5.5 Slope changes
Major slope changes such as defined edges are good features to use in winter. A flat spot on a broad shoulder, a saddle before a top, or small highpoint ('amoeba knoll') are less obvious features that can also be used. On a wide flat saddle or broad shoulder, navigate to a recognisable change in slope which would indicate that you are on one side of the feature rather than at a vague point near the middle. This positions you more accurately on the map.

4.5.6 On a slope
If you are ascending or descending a slope note your angle to the fall-line, relating it to the contours *(see Figure 4.6)*. Use your base plate line to link up the two points and check the angle this is to the contours: at 90°, you will be on the fall-line and if at an angle to the contours, note which side will be high and low ground as you are following the bearing up or down the slope. The most difficult bearing to follow is one which goes diagonally across a slope.

Interpreting contours

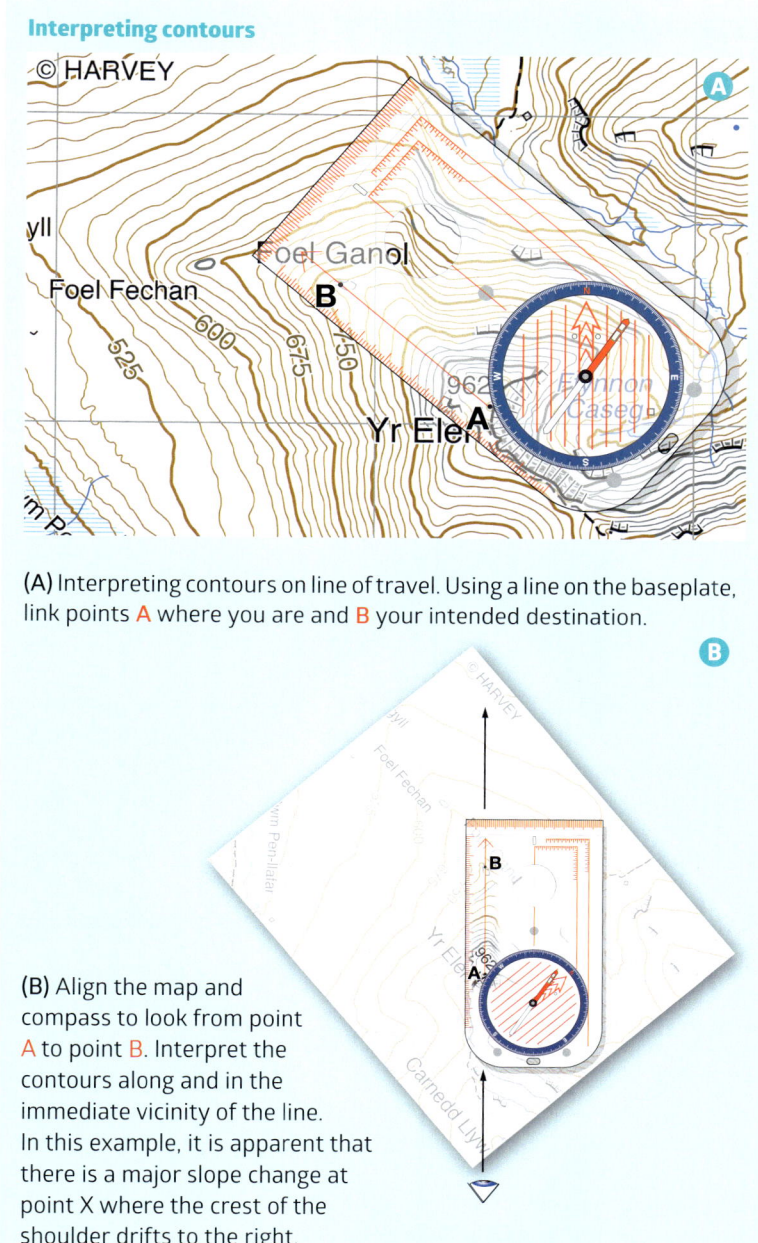

(A) Interpreting contours on line of travel. Using a line on the baseplate, link points **A** where you are and **B** your intended destination.

(B) Align the map and compass to look from point **A** to point **B**. Interpret the contours along and in the immediate vicinity of the line. In this example, it is apparent that there is a major slope change at point X where the crest of the shoulder drifts to the right.

4.5.7 Aiming-off and attack points

Use obvious features you know will be visible on the ground. Aiming-off onto large-scale linear contour features such as an obvious slope change is worthwhile, while trying to use a path could be a mistake *(see Figure 4.7)*.

Route choice and tick-off features

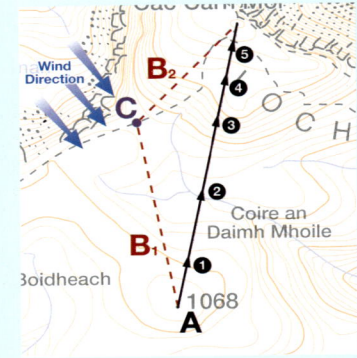

Although route **A** is a long leg at 1.5km (estimated 32 minutes), there are many tick-off features and it is the better route choice.

Route **B** is broken into two shorter legs, via the saddle at point **C**. It is less efficient than route **A** because it will take longer overall, it may prove difficult to locate point **C** in the middle of a broad saddle and in this example is more exposed to the wind.

Route Tick-off Points:
(1) A gentle descent (more or less on the fall line) from point 1068 leads into a wide depression on slightly steeper ground, with a broad spur on the right
(2) After 600m (7–8 mins), the lowest point of the leg is reached (the line of the stream) in an open area with ground descending slightly to the right
(3) The ground gradually steepens (concave slope and generally up the fall-line) to the steepest section of the leg at 350m (10 mins) from the lowest point
(4) The ground has significantly eased in angle into a traverse (high ground on the right) below a minor knoll ('amoeba' contour) and a vague re-entrant on the left. There may be a very slight descent into the re-entrant on the left
(5) A gentle, uniform slope up the fall-line leads to the open summit of Cac Carn Mor.

4.5.8 Linear features
Linear features may be used to follow or handrail, but take into account safety considerations, such as cornices, visibility and wind direction if following an edge *(see Figure 4.7)*. Consider convexities relating to avalanches if you use a slope change feature.

4.5.9 Dog-leg
Dog-leg is a common winter technique: go on one bearing for a set distance and then turn on to another bearing to walk a further distance to the objective. In fact, coming off Ben Nevis requires exactly this manoeuvre. Keep the first leg as short as possible as this reduces any error at the end. Select a point on the map and measure distance and bearing to it. This point may be a physical feature which may not be visible, such as a stream junction, or it could be a point which is only on the map, such as a grid line and contour intersection. Importantly, it is something you

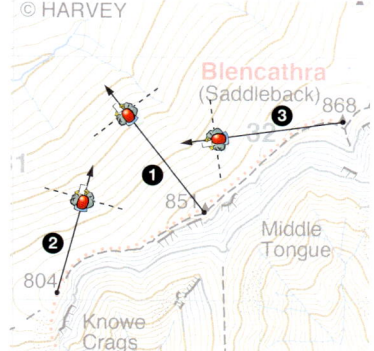

FIGURE 4.6 CONSIDER THE ANGLE OF THE BEARING TO THE FALL LINE: **(1)** THE BEARING LEADS DIRECTLY DOWN THE FALL-LINE WITH LEVEL GROUND ON EITHER SIDE (AT 90° TO THE BEARING) **(2)** THE BEARING LEADS TO THE RIGHT OF THE FALL-LINE. HIGH GROUND IS ON THE RIGHT-HAND SIDE AND LOW GROUND ON THE LEFT-HAND SIDE **(3)** THE BEARING LEADS TO THE LEFT OF THE FALL-LINE WITH GROUND RISING TO THE LEFT AND DESCENDING TO THE RIGHT.

can measure to and from when taking the distance and bearing *(see Figure 4.8A)*. When planning a dog-leg, remember it is easier to walk at right angles to the contours – the fall-line.

4.5.10 Boxing
Boxing is basically a double dog-leg and can be used in poor visibility to avoid a cliff edge with dangerous cornices or in-cuts such as gullies *(see Figure 4.8B)*. Alternatively, use either of the four compass points as appropriate (North, South, East or West) on the compass housing rather than adding or subtracting 90 degrees as this reduces the chance of error in the calculation. Similarly, to reverse a bearing use South on the dial to set the compass needle to.

4.5.11 Slope aspect
A slope has a direction that it faces: its aspect. It is simple to assess the general aspect of a slope, north, south, east, west, and relate it to a map visually. However for more accuracy, take a bearing down the fall-line, making sure that it is representative of the main slope. The fall-line implies that the bearing is at 90° to the contours. Next, relate the bearing to the contours. Subtract the current magnetic variation, and place the compass on the map in the area you are in. Move the compass until the orienting lines are parallel to the north—south grid lines. Keep the compass oriented in this direction and slide it across the map until the base plate line cuts the contours at 90°. You will be somewhere on this line.

This can be used at any time as a useful confirmation that you are on the correct course. Finding the fall-line in winter can be difficult under poor visibility, full snow cover and flat light. Rolling a snowball or using people to show the shape of the ground can help. Once you have worked out which slope you are on, then by working back to estimate how far onto the slope you are (near the top, bottom or in the middle, and slope angle and profile), you can get a reasonable fix of your location – a good technique for relocation *(see Figure 4.9)*.

4.5.12 What happens if...?
Interpret and visualise how the shape of the ground will differ if you travel off bearing or overshoot the objective. Is there a catching feature at the point you are heading to? *(See Figure 4.10)*

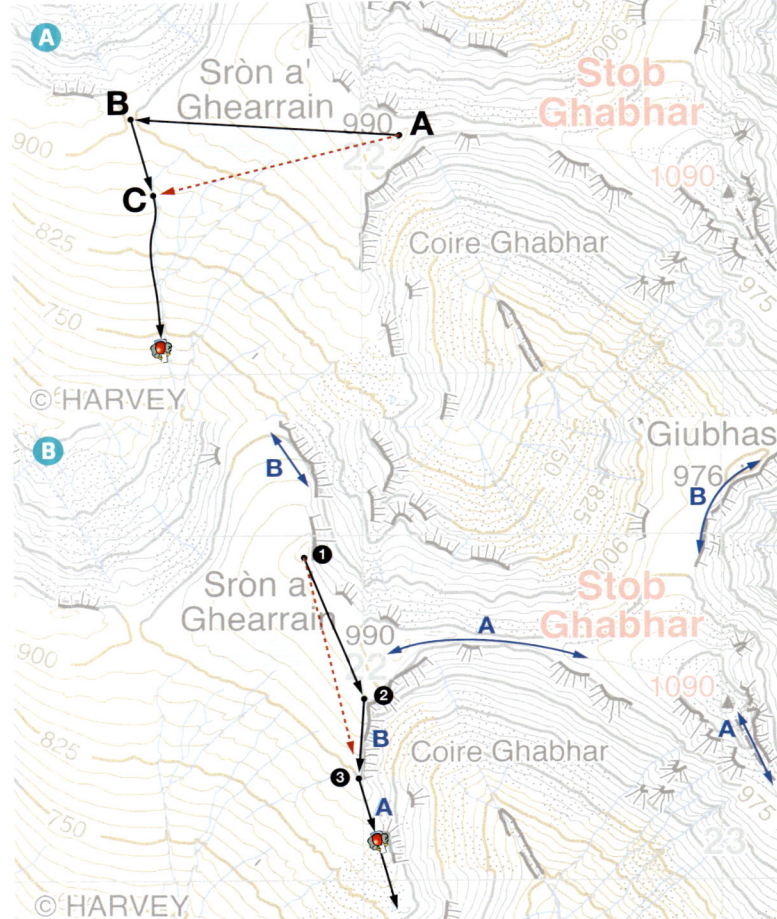

FIGURE 4.7 (A) AN ATTACK POINT: THE SADDLE AT POINT **B** IS USED AS AN ATTACK POINT TO LOCATE AND DESCEND A STREAM LINE FROM POINT **C**. THE NARROW SADDLE IS AN OBVIOUS LARGE SCALE FEATURE AND IS MUCH CLOSER TO POINT **C** THAN IS POINT **A**. **(B) AIMING OFF ONTO A LINEAR FEATURE:** INSTEAD OF TAKING A DIRECT BEARING FROM POINT **1** TO THE RIDGE AT POINT **3**, TO AVOID THE POSSIBILITY OF BEING DRAWN ONTO THE SLOPE ON THE RIGHT, A BEARING IS TAKEN TO POINT **2**, AIMING OFF TO THE LEFT OF THE DIRECT BEARING AND ON TO THE CORRIE EDGE. THE EDGE IS FOLLOWED DOWN TO POINT **3**. **LINEAR FEATURES: A** A RIDGE, **B** AN EDGE, **C** A STREAM LINE AS INDICATED ON UPPER MAP

4.6 Observations

Continually observing the ground and any features that can be distinguished is vital in poor conditions. There is no room for lapses of concentration. If the cloud lifts temporarily, stop and gather as much information about the terrain as possible and use it to confirm that you are on the correct line.

4.6.1 Using the group

Group members can be used to assist sighting while following a bearing or to show the shape of the ground. Placing people on the bearing on either side of the navigator gives an impression of slope angles. Keeping an eye on a group walking in line behind can reveal high or low points on the ground.

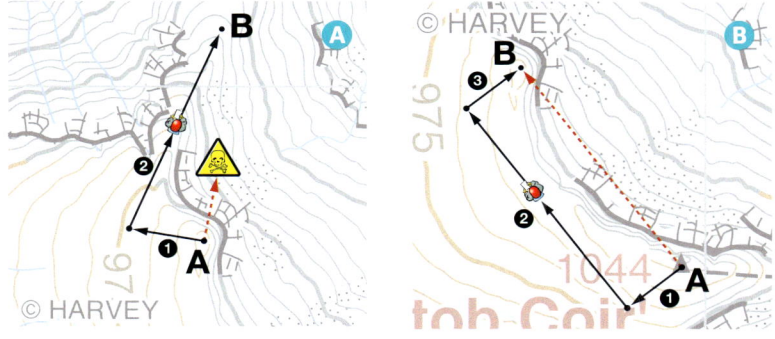

FIGURE 4.8 (A) A DOG-LEG: A DIRECT LINE FROM POINT A TO POINT B IS NOT POSSIBLE AND A DOG-LEG IS APPROPRIATE TO AVOID THE EDGE. LEG 1 IS A SHORT DISTANCE DOWN THE FALL-LINE TO A POINT THAT WILL ENABLE LEG 2 TO BE A DIRECT LINE DOWN THE RIDGE TO POINT **B**
(B) BOXING A CORRIE: A DIRECT LINE BETWEEN POINTS **A** AND **B** IS NOT POSSIBLE, AND TO AVOID THE EDGE, A SINGLE DOG-LEG IS CONSIDERED INAPPROPRIATE. TO BOX THE CORRIE, FIRST TAKE A DIRECT MAGNETIC BEARING FROM POINT **A** TO POINT **B** AND MEASURE THE DISTANCE BETWEEN THE TWO POINTS.
(1) SUBTRACT 90° FROM THE DIRECT BEARING AND ESTIMATE THE DISTANCE ON THE NEW BEARING NEEDED TO AVOID THE EDGE ON STAGE 2. FOLLOW THE BEARING FOR THE ESTIMATED DISTANCE
(2) ADD 90° TO REGAIN THE ORIGINAL MAGNETIC BEARING AND FOLLOW THIS FOR THE CALCULATED DISTANCE BETWEEN POINTS **A** AND **B (3)** ADD 90° AND PACE THE DISTANCE CALCULATED ON STAGE 1 UP TO POINT **B**. ALTERNATIVELY, USE EITHER OF THE FOUR COMPASS POINTS (NORTH, SOUTH, EAST OR WEST) AS APPROPRIATE ON THE COMPASS HOUSING RATHER THAN ADDING OR SUBTRACTING 90 DEGREES AS THIS REDUCES THE CHANCE OF ERROR IN THE CALCULATION. SIMILARLY, TO REVERSE A BEARING, ALIGN THE NEEDLE TO SOUTH ON THE DIAL AND FOLLOW THE BEARING AS NORMAL.

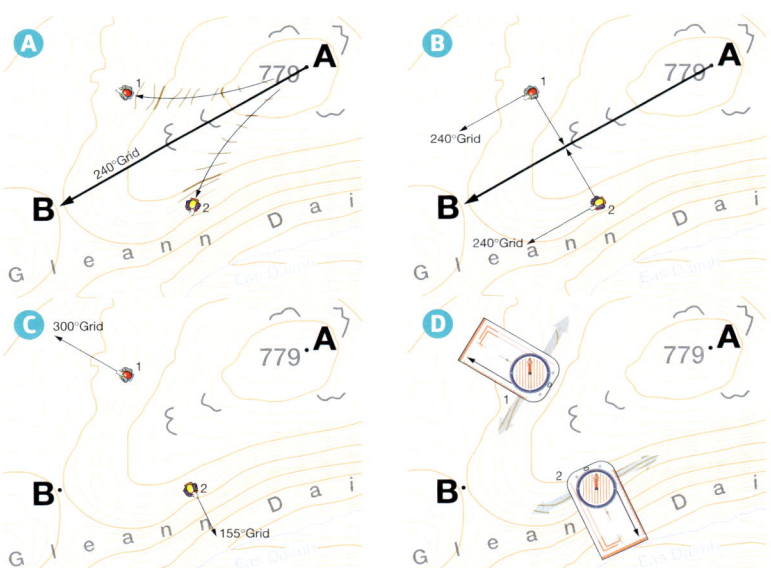

FIGURE 4.9 SLOPE ASPECT: (A) RELOCATING USING SLOPE ASPECT. THE NAVIGATOR HAS DRIFTED OFF COURSE ONTO A RELATIVELY STEEP SLOPE AND IS UNAWARE ON WHICH SIDE OF THE SHOULDER, EITHER AT POINT **1** OR POINT **2 (B)** BY ALIGNING THE COMPASS, IT IS APPARENT THAT THERE IS HIGH GROUND TO THE LEFT AT POINT **1** INDICATING A POSITION RIGHT OF THE INTENDED LINE WHILE AT POINT 2, HIGH GROUND IS TO THE RIGHT, INDICATING A POSITION LEFT OF THE INTENDED LINE **(C)** CALCULATE THE SLOPE ASPECT BY TAKING A MAGNETIC BEARING DOWN THE FALL-LINE AND CONVERT TO A GRID BEARING **(D)** KEEPING THE ORIENTING LINES PARALLEL TO GRID NORTH AND THE ORIENTING ARROW ALIGNED NORTH (NOT THE NEEDLE), MOVE THE COMPASS ACROSS THE MAP AROUND THE ESTIMATED POSITION UNTIL THE BASEPLATE LINE CUTS THE CONTOURS AT RIGHT-ANGLES

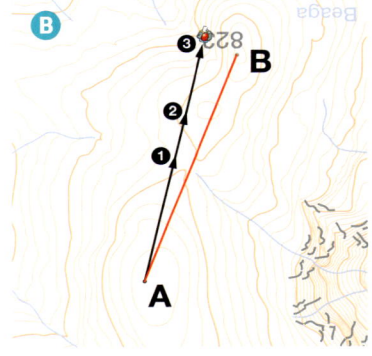
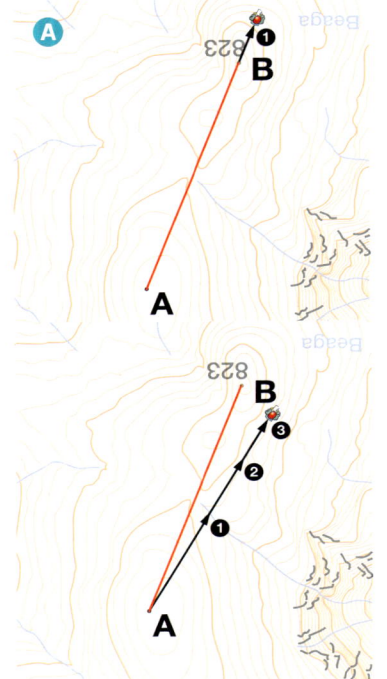

FIGURE 4.10 THE SHAPE OF THE GROUND – CONSIDER THE ALTERNATIVES: (A) OVERSHOOTING THE DESTINATION. CONTINUING ON THE BEARING AFTER POINT B, THE GROUND DESCENDS RELATIVELY STEEPLY – A GOOD CATCHING FEATURE: POINT **1** **(B)** TRAVELLING 10° LEFT OF THE BEARING. AT POINTS **1** AND **2**, THERE IS HIGH GROUND TO THE RIGHT WHEREAS THE CORRECT LINE TRAVELS ALONG THE CREST OF THE FEATURE. AT POINT **3**, THE LINE DESCENDS ONTO STEEP GROUND AT A RE-ENTRANT WITH STEEP HIGH GROUND ON THE RIGHT **(C)** TRAVELLING 10° RIGHT OF THE BEARING. THE LINE OF TRAVEL IMMEDIATELY LEAVES THE CREST AND DESCENDS TO A RE-ENTRANT AT POINT **1**, WITH GROUND RISING TO THE SADDLE ON THE LEFT. THEREAFTER, THE LINE RISES OUT OF THE RE-ENTRANT, TRAVERSES BELOW THE CREST AND KNOLL AT POINT **2** AND CONTINUES THE TRAVERSE TO POINT **3** WITH INCREASINGLY HIGH GROUND ON THE LEFT

A group sweep search can be useful but the leader must have complete confidence in the ability of those on the outside of the sweep. Placing inexperienced people out of sight in difficult conditions can have serious consequences. A thorough briefing is vital. Information such as the objective, the bearing and distance, and procedures when the objective is found are all important. If the objective is found on a sweep then the line stops and gathers together, individuals only moving in after the person on the outside is in sight. If the leader in the middle can see the outside people during the sweep, there is little to be gained *(see Figure 4.11)*.

4.7 Dangers

Dangers include avalanche-prone slopes, corniced edges, melting snow bridges, frozen lochans, iced-up paths and crags and cliffs with dangerous edges or convex lead-in slopes from above. Observations during the day, such as an increased volume of drifting snow or wet rock from a sudden rise in temperature, may indicate an increase in avalanche danger. Be aware of avalanche-prone aspects and use safe travel strategies as described in *10.5 Avalanche avoidance*, on page 124. It is easier to stray on to an avalanche-prone slope from above. When following a corniced edge, stay on or close to rocks or obvious solid ground back from the edge. There is also the option of using a rope to protect the navigator, as described in *11.9 Protecting near a corniced edge* on page 148.

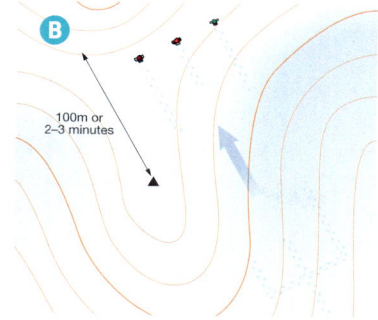
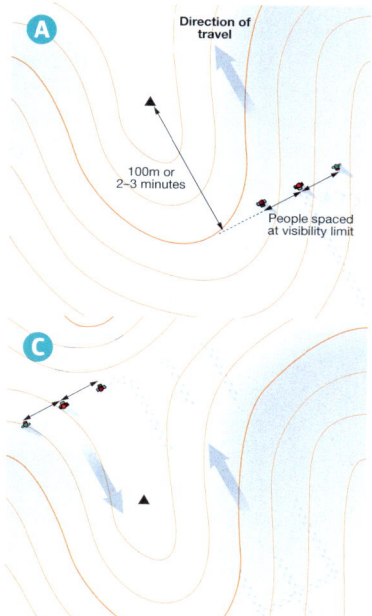

FIGURE 4.11 A SWEEP SEARCH: **(A)** STOP AN APPROPRIATE DISTANCE SHORT OF THE OBJECTIVE AND POSITION THE GROUP IN A LINE AT 90° TO THE BEARING **(B)** FOLLOW THE BEARING FOR THE ORIGINAL CALCULATED DISTANCE AND IF THE OBJECTIVE IS NOT FOUND, CONTINUE FOR AN APPROPRIATE DISTANCE. DURING THE SWEEP, INFORMATION REGARDING THE SHAPE OF THE GROUND IS GAINED FROM THE RELATIVE POSITIONS OF THE GROUP MEMBERS. **(C)** MOVE THE LINE ACROSS TO SWEEP BACK ON THE SIDE CALCULATED MOST LIKELY TO DISCOVER THE OBJECTIVE

4.8 Possible Errors

If you recognise possible errors, then take them into account and adjust for them. Be aware of time loss if you slow down because of the wind or conditions under foot. Similarly adjust for shortened paces such as when negotiating deep snow drifts. There is a tendency to drift downhill or to over-compensate the other way when traversing a slope and a side wind may blow you off course. Concentrate more on your sightings and choose obvious sight features to follow.

4.9 Using GPS in winter

A global positioning device is not a substitute for good navigational skills including use of map and compass. When using a GPS in winter, the same skills and techniques apply as using one in summer. For it to be operated efficiently and effectively, it must be properly set up, you must be completely familiar with its many functions and able to interpret the information given whether using it purely for location (relocating in an emergency), or as a primary navigational aid. GPS devices can also be used with digital mapping software to great effect. As well as dedicated handheld devices, GPS is found in smart phones (including downloadable apps) and watches, each with a particular form of antenna *(see Figure 4.12)*. Consider the following for winter use:
- Rugged construction, waterproof and a large bright display screen. Also, consider using a protective case for your device.
- Use fully charged batteries, whether they are built in to the device or rechargeable (low self-discharge Nickel Metal Hydride (NiMH)) or disposable. Disposable Lithium batteries operate best in cold conditions.

FIGURE 4.12 SELECTION OF GPS DEVICES **(A)** BASIC DEVICE, **(B)** ADVANCED DEVICE, **(C)** GPS WATCH, **(D)** MOBILE PHONE.

- Use a quadrifilar helix antenna over patch as the former is more sensitive, particularly in terrain where blocking due to mountain topography may be an issue.
- Touchscreens should be kept dry and both screen and push button devices should be able to be used with gloves.
- Keep the device handy in an accessible pocket or a pouch attached to your rucksack shoulder strap.
- It must be switched on and have a 'sky' view to be able to receive signals and track accurately.
- Use coordinates on the GPS that correspond to the 'paper' map you are using, for example British Grid format using Ordinance Survey map datum.
- Revise the basic skills of location, using waypoints, route setting and track back.

5 Navigation

Navigation in winter must be efficient, with few unnecessary stops. Continually stopping may lead to the group getting cold, with related complications and a loss of confidence in the leader. Practise walking on bearings with few stops. Keep checking the group to monitor their comfort and fitness. There is a tendency to walk too fast when a leader is concentrating on navigating, so slow down if necessary. Appointing a back-marker can help keep the group together and alert the leader to developing situations, but does not lessen the leader's responsibility to the group. The ability to navigate confidently at night is important.

Teaching navigation in winter

Assuming that most people will have previous navigation experience, a quick revision of basic skills may be productive. However, practical experience gained in the hills in winter is invaluable. Practise following bearings and accurate timing and pacing in difficult conditions. Practical navigation also highlights limitations in the student's clothing and equipment. Revise contour interpretation, being observant whilst navigating and let people adjust to limited contour features under winter conditions. Stress that there is little use interpreting contours outside visibility limit. Training should also include points that encourage visualisation skills (such as map memory exercises) and practice of night navigation. Teaching the use of GPS in winter is also a consideration.

GAINING CONFIDENCE ON GRADE I GROUND, BROAD GULLY, STOB COIRE NAN LOCHAN, GLENCOE
PHOTO // LIBBY PETER

Basic winter skills

THE NORTHEAST RIDGE OF STOB COIRE NAN LOCHAN, GLENCOE   *PHOTO // GARRY SMITH*

Ice axe

From the first beginnings as a metal-tipped pole to which was added a cutting blade at the top, the ice axe has developed in sophistication and shortened in length over the years to become today's highly designed and manufactured tool.

The ice axe is composed of a head, consisting of an adze and a pick at one end of the shaft, and a spike at the other *(see Figure 5.1)*. The axe is used for balance, cutting, probing, extra security on snow and ice, support, digging, as a hand-hold and as insurance should things go wrong. It is the indispensable winter tool, essential for travel on snow and ice.

Over the years axes have become more specialised but the basic parts remain the same, whether used for walking or climbing. Those used for mountaineering are called ice axes, while those specifically intended for climbing are referred to as ice or technical tools. Initially, walking and mountaineering axes will be considered here and technical tools in the section on climbing.

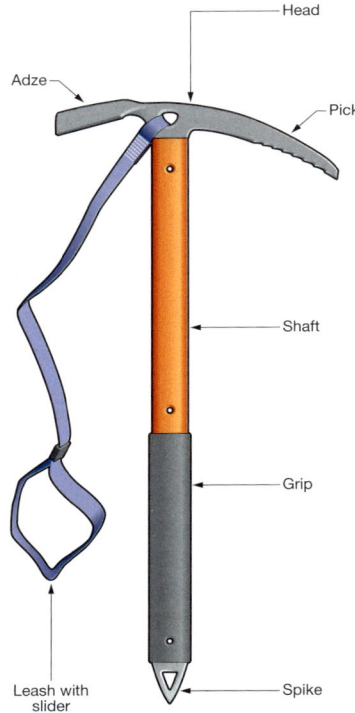

FIGURE 5.1 PARTS OF AN ICE AXE

5.1 The head

This consists of an adze and a curved pick. The first axes had straight picks which were designed for cutting ice, but since the 1970s the pick was curved to grip in snow and ice. The head is either of stamped and welded construction or forged. The former are generally cheaper to produce but are not as comfortable to hold as the forged heads. The head may also have a karabiner hole which can be used to attach the leash. Some heads have further lightening holes.

The curvature of the pick (the radius of its underside) influences the holding power of the axe, particularly when placed above the head and pulled on. If this radius is greater than the length of the shaft then the pick will tend to move outwards when pulled, while a shorter radius and steeper curve will tend to dig in deeper *(see Figure 5.2)*. On the underside of the pick is a set of teeth. These may only be at the front or extend the whole length and may increase in size towards the shaft. This helps increase the holding power but can make it less comfortable to carry.

The adze is primarily used for cutting and clearing snow and those that are relatively flat with a straight edge and minimal droop are best for this. Steeper angled adzes can be used for purchase in softer snow and ice, but are less efficient when cutting and less comfortable to hold.

The pick can have positive, negative or neutral clearance, depending on angle of the tip of the pick relative to the shaft. If the tip is parallel to the shaft, it is said to have neutral clearance, if angled towards the shaft it has negative and away from the shaft positive clearance *(see Figure 5.3)*. These make little if any difference in snow but in hard ice, a pick with

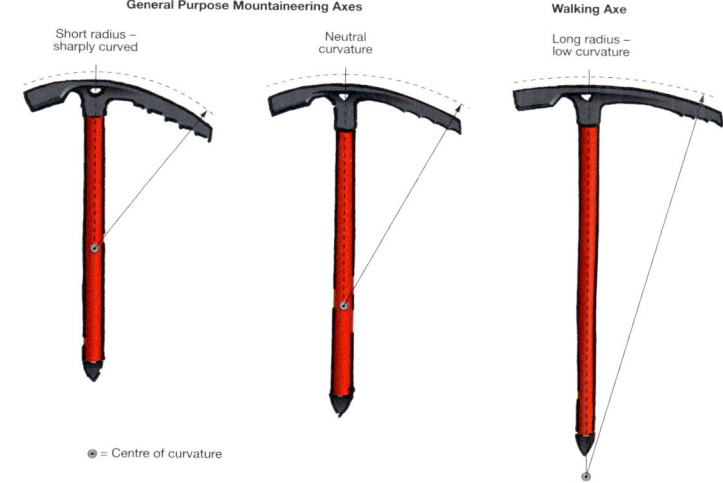

FIGURE 5.2 PICK CURVATURES

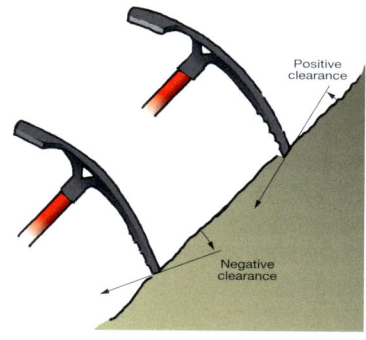

FIGURE 5.3 POSITIVE AND NEGATIVE CLEARANCE

positive clearance is less likely to bounce out when swung into the ice.

5.2 The shaft

The first axe shafts were made of wood but now almost all are made from oval cross-section aluminium tubing, which is light and strong. The majority of shafts have a rubber or similar coating to improve insulation, grip and vibration dampening. This may be on the bottom third of the shaft or extend the whole length. Some more specialised shafts are made from materials such as carbon fibre.

5.3 The spike

The main function of the spike is to provide a sharp point when the shaft is pushed into the snow and a simple symmetrical shape works best. The spike may be attached to the shaft by a ferrule and should join in a smooth tapered manner.

5.4 Leashes

Leashes or wrist loops have several uses. They prevent the axe being lost if dropped or when the hands need to be free for other tasks, and provide extra support if the axe is used as a hold or for cutting. Leashes can be useful when climbing, particularly when used above the head. The disadvantages are the need continually to change the leash over when zig-zagging up or down a slope and in a slide or fall they keep the axe with all its sharp bits near the body. On a mountaineering axe, the leash is usually attached to the head, normally through the karabiner hole.

> **6 Carrying the axe**
> Axes and crampons can be dangerous and those unused to carrying them can easily spike themselves and others, especially when in crowded areas such as in queues, car parks and on public transport. It may be better to carry the axe in the hand in these situations and have crampons packed in the rucksack. Axes and crampons should not be attached to rucksacks when in vehicles, but stowed away in the boot or under the seats. Rubber head and spike protectors should be removed before setting off so the axe is available for use immediately it is required.

It should have a loop with a slider to secure it round the wrist and be long enough so that the leash is tight when the axe is held near the bottom of the shaft. It is an advantage if the leash is easily detached and removed, such as with a lark's foot through the karabiner hole.

Letting the leash dangle from the axe when not in use is not an option, as it can get caught in a crampon or under the foot, causing a trip. In this situation it can either be removed or wrapped round the head, or shortened by putting the loop over the adze and cinching the slider tight round the top. This effectively halves the length of the leash but does leave a loop that may catch a crampon on steep ground.

5.5 Axe length

This is a crucial consideration and is primarily determined by the steepness of the terrain it is to be used on. A good guide for the length of a general purpose axe is that, when held with your arm straight by your side the spike is about the level of your boot top. An axe longer than this may be more comfortable to use as a walking stick and a shorter axe is more convenient for some other tasks. While personal height and preference will have some influence, a good general purpose length is 55–60cm. Those used primarily for walking can be a bit longer and those for climbing can be shorter. The weight and balance of the axe both influence how it feels and handles.

5.6 Stowing the axe

When not required, the axe can be carried on the rucksack. Most sacks provide ice axe attachments, but buckles are awkward in cold weather and when wearing gloves. Also, these attachments tend to make the axe hang back at an angle which can be a hazard when in a group. A better option is to push the axe down the side compression straps with the pick pointing back. It can be easily removed if needed, especially if using a buddy system, when one person can access the axe for a partner without removing sacks. Another option is to push it diagonally down the back between the shoulder straps with the pick pointing to the outside. This way it can be retrieved or put away easily, but remember to take it out before removing the sack or it will drop out and may be lost.

THE FINAL SNOW SLOPES OF AM BODACH, ABOVE GLENCOE   PHOTO // GARRY SMITH

Moving on snow

Snow can vary from being light and insubstantial to nearly as hard as ice, with a huge range of hardness in between, but from a mountaineer's point of view, the difference between snow and ice is that in snow, steps can be kicked but on ice this is not possible.

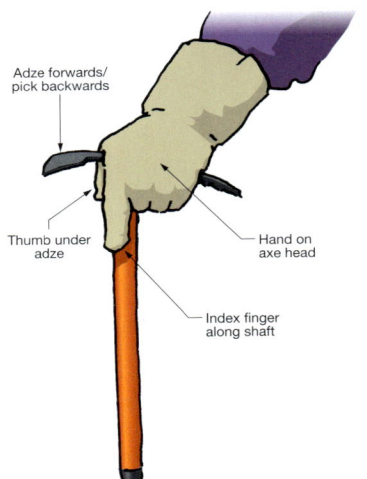

(ABOVE) **FIGURE 6.2** KICKING STEPS IN DIRECT ASCENT ON VERY HARD SNOW

(LEFT) **FIGURE 6.1** HOW TO CARRY THE ICE AXE

The way we move over snow depends on its type and hardness, the angle of the slope and the equipment being used. There is a progression in the amount of equipment necessary to move safely, from boots to the axe to crampons. In all cases, the axe is used as means of support and security and as insurance should a slip occur. Generally, the harder the snow the more likely it is that axe and crampons will be required, but other factors such as the size of the slope, the run-out, personal ability and experience can influence which method is used.

6.1 Carrying the axe

When walking on snow, where a slip or stumble could lead to a slide, the axe is held in the uphill hand with the adze facing forward and the pick back, the thumb under the adze, the index finger down the line of the shaft and the others below the pick *(see Figure 6.1)*. This is the basic position from which the ice axe braking position can easily be adopted. This is marginally easier to do when wearing gloves rather than mitts. How much it is used for support and balance will depend on the angle of the slope and the hardness of the snow. If moving horizontally or diagonally it is held in the uphill hand but if moving straight up or down a slope it is normally held in the stronger hand. When used for support, balance and assurance, it is moved when you are standing in a secure, stable position with both feet on good steps.

On flat ground when the axe is not needed, it can be carried horizontally with the spike facing forward and the pick down. This means there is less chance of spiking others in the group

6.2 Kicking steps

For step-kicking, stiff winter boots are necessary. They should have a square edge to the sole, deep treads and give good ankle support. Kicking steps for long periods in hard snow can be painful because of the jarring, so comfortable boots are essential.

> **ⓘ 7 Kicking steps directly up a slope**
>
> Going directly up the fall-line is the shortest way to ascend a slope, so the least number of steps is required. It is also the method of step-kicking that allows the steepest slopes to be ascended and can be done the same way if wearing crampons. The leader can make very positive steps and each person in the line can also kick to improve the step. Less confident group members are facing into the slope and with a positive, inward slanting step will feel more secure. However, direct ascent is more tiring on the calf muscles and if someone slips, they can dislodge others below.

6.2.1 Direct ascent

When ascending directly up a slope, the boot is used to make steps large enough to stand in securely, normally deep enough to take the front half of the boot. This is angled into the slope to give a positive hold *(see Figure 6.2)*.

This may take one or more kicks, with the leg swung vigorously, using the hips and the knee but most of the swing comes from the latter. The longer the swing of the leg, the more momentum can help; short, choppy kicks are more tiring.

FIGURE 6.3 IN DIAGONAL ASCENT WITH THE AXE IN THE UPHILL HAND USED FOR SUPPORT AND THE LEGS IN THE STABLE POSITION

The steeper the slope, the more the action comes from the knee as it becomes more difficult to take a big swing on higher-angled slopes. The size of the step will depend on the hardness of the snow, although the number of people who use the step may influence the depth. If the kicked steps are not secure, are slow to create or require too much effort, it is time to use a different method of progress.

An alternative is to hold the axe in both hands and drive it into the slope directly in front of you. This can be more secure and may be used on steeper slopes or when the snow is firmer. This method is slower, requires good balance and means that greater distance must be put between group members.

6.2.2 Diagonal ascent

The most comfortable way to kick steps up a slope is in diagonal, zig-zagging ascent. The usual angle of ascent is about 45° to the fall-line but the angle will depend on the slope – the steeper the slope, the lower the angle the steps take.

Steps are created with the edge of the boot and should be as long as the foot, about half a boot width and angled into the slope. They are made by kicking and scraping and use a sawing action with the edge of the sole. The uphill step is kicked with the outside of the boot, the lower step with the inner.

> **8 Kicking diagonal steps**
> Diagonal steps are the least tiring for a group to follow, but they can easily degrade and become less secure for those towards the back. Ensure each step is well formed, angled into the slope and big enough even for large boots. Have the group take extra care after changing direction, when some will be moving directly above others waiting to get on to the new diagonal.

When standing with the uphill foot above and ahead of the lower foot you are in a secure position with your weight distributed between both feet *(see Figure 6.3)*. It is in this stable position that the axe should be moved. With the next step, kicked by the outer foot, you are in a cross-legged position with most of your weight on the downhill or lower leg so mostly on one step and in a less secure stance.

When changing direction, the most secure way is to kick a platform with both feet so you are facing uphill. When secure, swap the axe to the new uphill hand and continue in the new direction. A quick but less secure method is to stand in the position of instability with the outer foot in the uphill position, swap hands on the axe, pivot on the upper foot and begin kicking the new diagonal with the new outer leg.

6.2.3 Traversing

If the snow is soft or the slope easy-angled, steps can be kicked when facing along the line of travel. This is less secure on steep slopes or firm snow, when it is best to face the slope and kick in to produce steps as for direct ascent. Each foot kicks its own step, moving them alternately together then apart. The supporting axe is moved when you are in a more stable position with the feet apart. It is better to plan the route to avoid traversing like this.

6.2.4 Descending steps

When descending diagonally, steps similar to those used in ascent can be kicked across the fall-line. When descending facing out, plunge steps are made with the heel of the boot. These feel a less natural way of moving as

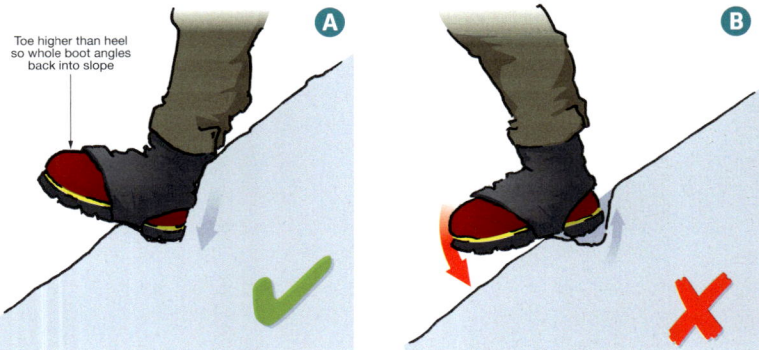

FIGURE 6.4 PLUNGE STEPS IN DESCENT **(A)** THE HEEL IN SECURELY IN THE PLUNGE STEP. **(B)** THE HEEL ROCKING OUT OF THE STEP

> **ⓘ 9 Walking through snow**
> Walking through soft, deep or crusty snow is tiring. Have the group in line and rotate the lead to spread this effort. Once the person at the front has finished their stint, they step to the side, let the next take their turn and join on the end of the line. Don't let anyone do too much and don't feel you need to do all the trail-breaking. Ask those with a longer stride to adjust their step for smaller members of the party. Part of learning about winter is appreciating the effort involved and conserving energy throughout the day, therefore good route choice over snow covered terrain is important. For example, depending on the nature of the snow, it may be best to avoid going near boulders, as the snow is often softer near them, so steps are more likely to break through. On the other hand, it may be easier to walk near the edge of snow patches where it isn't as deep.

you step forward and down, driving the heel into the slope. A full heel in the snow is a minimum to give good purchase. Use a positive, stiff-legged action with all your weight coming on the heel. A slight hop will put more force into the step. The toes are kept up in the air and care taken not to rock forward to bring the foot out of the step onto the slope where a slip could occur *(see Figure 6.4)*. The axe is held in the stronger hand, but it can be used for support by reaching down the slope and driving the axe into the snow. This makes it more difficult to put enough weight on the foot to produce a good step and feels less secure than standing upright.

Plunge steps are not effective or safe on hard snow, when it is better to face in and kick steps as for direct ascent but for going down. When descending, it is possible to make the steps further apart.

6.3 Cutting steps

When the slope is too steep or the snow too hard to move over it safely or comfortably, crampons are usually put on, but sometimes this is not the best option. For example, to cross a small patch of hard snow, it would be more time-consuming to stop, put on crampons then take them off a short time later. Even when wearing crampons, the extra security provided by cutting steps can be beneficial. Crampons can be forgotten, lost, broken or poorly fitted, or someone could be injured, ill, tired or lacking in confidence, with a line of steps can speed up progress and increase safety. On winter climbs a few steps provide a welcome rest for aching calf muscles.

6.3.1 Cutting in snow

The one basic principle of cutting in snow is that, after the first blow of the adze, always cut into that hole. This applies to cutting steps, stances or making belays and makes these tasks easier and more efficient. This usually means that the first cut is nearest to you and subsequent blows work away from the body.

6.3.2 Step patterns

Step patterns depend on their size and shape and the angle of the slope. A guide to the most efficient pattern is to imagine the tracks you would make if you walked up or down that slope. If the slope is steep enough to require hand-holds, then the steps would ascend ladder-fashion staggered left–right. However, a slope like this would be best tackled wearing crampons and using the axe as a climbing tool.

On a slope where there is a choice of line, steps are cut ascending diagonally and/or zig-zag. The angle of the line depends on the slope but generally will be at about 45° to 60° to the fall-line. On a line at more than 60°, steps are difficult to ascend comfortably while an angle below 45° involves more sideways movement. Before starting, work out the best line to reduce the effort involved. For example, most people are better and more comfortable cutting with their dominant hand so the majority of step-cutters will have a longer line of steps going left when they cut with their stronger right hand.

FIGURE 6.5 CUTTING SLASH STEPS IN DIAGONAL ASCENT

If the slope is not too steep, a single line of steps is the most energy efficient. On steeper slopes, it may be necessary to cut a double line with a step for each foot. While this requires more effort, it can feel more secure.

6.3.3 Types of steps

The type of step required depends on the hardness of the snow and the angle and shape of the slope as well as the competence of those using them. Steps must provide secure footing for all that use them, including those at the back of a group where the steps can become degraded. Steps should be positive, angled into the slope, a comfortable distance apart and cut in a positive manner using a combination of skill and strength, the former being the more important! The weight and momentum of the axe should do much of the work, but efficient cutting is the result of practice on a wide range of slopes and conditions.

6.3.4 Slash steps

These are the quickest and most efficient steps to cut and are used when going diagonally or zig-zagging up a slope. To cut these, face across the slope with the axe in the uphill hand. The axe is swung from the shoulder with the arm almost straight and the axe in a line with the arm *(see Figure 6.5)*. The other hand can be braced on either knee for stability. The adze cuts the step at the lower part of the arc of the swing *(see Figure 6.6)*

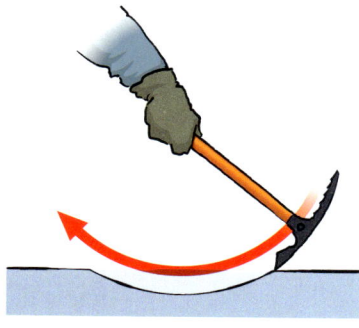

FIGURE 6.6 A SLASH STEP BEING CUT USING A PENDULUM ACTION WITH THE AXE

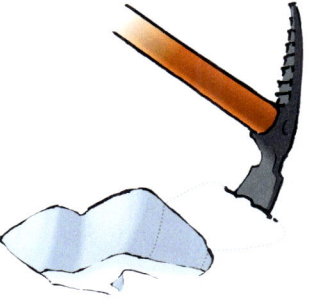

FIGURE 6.7 CUTTING A SIDE STEP: AFTER THE FIRST CUT, EACH SUBSEQUENT BLOW CUTS INTO THE EXISTING HOLE

entering and leaving the snow with a pendulum action, producing a step which is long enough for the boot, about as wide as the adze and angled slightly into the slope. The size of this arc depends on where the shaft is held, with fine adjustment achieved by raising or lowering the shoulder. If the swing is too short, the axe will miss the slope, if too long the adze will bury in the snow and stick.

In good snow and with practice, one swing should be enough to produce an adequate step, but often more are needed, especially if a larger step is required. A tight leash gives stability to the swing and takes some strain off the arm.

If the step is not angled sufficiently into the slope, tilt the wrist inwards to change the adze position so that it cuts at an angle *(see Figure 6.5)*. If the line of the diagonal is too shallow you have to reach far forward, which means that the axe cannot be swung properly and will either stick or produce a step which slopes backwards.

There are several different methods for changing direction. A simple and effective way is to cut a bucket step large enough for both feet. Move into this with both feet, face uphill and when secure, swap the axe hand, face the new direction and start the next line of steps. A more elegant method is to cut the first step on the next diagonal. This is above and behind the last step which is longer than usual. Step onto the middle of the last step with one foot, pivot on the toe to face the new direction and bring the other foot onto the step in the new direction to stand in the stable position. While turning, use the axe pushed vertically in the slope for support and swap hands at the same time. This is not the best method if several others are following the steps.

On steeper slopes a double line of steps may be better. In this case, two offset steps are cut before moving onto them with both feet before cutting the next pair. This means more cutting but you are always working from a secure and stable position. It is less efficient, however, to cut a double line of steps with the same pendulum action used to make a single line.

For those following a line of steps, the axe can be pushed into the slope for security and only moved when standing in a balanced position on two steps.

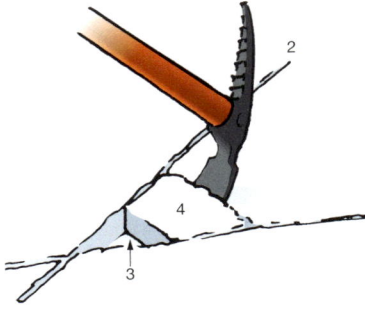

(ABOVE) **FIGURE 6.9** CUTTING A SLAB STEP: THE PICK MAKES THE INITIAL CUTS AND THE ADZE IS USED TO REMOVE THE SNOW BETWEEN THEM

(LEFT) **FIGURE 6.8** CUTTING A LETTERBOX STEP WHILE STANDING IN A BUCKET STEP

6.3.5 Side steps

These can be used in a diagonal pattern, on shallower diagonals or even traverses. The step is made by cutting vertically down with the adze initially to form a hole which angles into the slope. This is then enlarged to the length of the boot by chopping away from the first hole, cutting a horizontal step which goes from the heel to the toe *(see Figure 6.7)*. While these take more effort they can be enlarged to give a more secure step and can be cut in very hard snow or even ice, and can be cut with the downhill hand or even using both hands. When on a traverse, it is better to cut offset steps rather than have them in line. This gives a more secure footing.

Another form is the letterbox step where the initial hole is across the fall-line and at right-angles to the slope. Subsequent blows cut into this hole to form a step at right-angles to the slope. This provides a secure footing as the step's shape angles the boot into the slope *(see Figure 6.8)*.

6.3.6 Slab steps

These are for use in snow which is either crusty or slabby, liable to break up into blocks and not take your weight. Use the pick to cut two diagonal lines in the snow, with their intersection nearest to you. Then use the adze to remove the snow between them working from the heel to the toe *(see Figure 6.9)*. The lower edge of the step may then take your weight without collapsing.

6.3.7 Bucket steps

From bucket steps to bucket seats and stances, these are semi-circular holes angled into the slope to give positive ledges. Bucket steps vary in size depending on their purpose, and range from just big enough to take the front half of the boot to something large enough to stand in comfortably with both feet *(see Figure 6.8)*. As they are positive and feel

FIGURE 6.10 CUTTING SLASH STEPS IN DIRECT DESCENT: PREPARING TO STEP THE UPPER FOOT ONTO THE STEP JUST VACATED BY THE LOWER FOOT

FIGURE 6.11 SLASH STEPS IN DIAGONAL DESCENT: THE UPPER FOOT IS STEPPED THROUGH AND DOWN ONTO THE NEXT STEP, WHICH LIFTS THE OTHER FOOT UPWARDS

safe they are suitable for groups following or when conditions demand an extra degree of security. Although it is preferable to use both hands on the axe, they are still tiring and time-consuming to fashion.

Use the adze to make an initial hole, then enlarge by cutting into this. If a larger step is needed, after the initial blow dig away from this to produce a horizontal slot angled down into the slope as in a letterbox step. The snow above the initial slot is removed by chopping down into it. This is the best method for constructing a stance or enlarging into a bucket seat.

6.3.8 Pigeonhole steps

These are a smaller version of bucket steps but cut when handholds are needed for security. They are normally used in direct ascent and would only be used on steep or icy terrain, as they are tiring to make. The step is large enough to take the front part of the boot and is angled to have a lip which makes a positive hold. Cutting is done with the adze hacking down into the slope. Make as few steps as possible, with the distance between them near the maximum distance of one step. Cut above shoulder level where the axe can be swung efficiently and try to make at least two before moving up.

6.3.9 Steps in descent

Steps can only be cut going downhill if the slope is not too steep. If handholds are needed, an alternative method, such as abseiling, must be used. When cutting downhill, slash steps are used and are actually easier to cut this way because of the better body position. Face across the slope, drop the lower shoulder and cut with the downhill hand, usually the dominant one. From standing in two steps cut a lower one, step the lower foot onto it then the upper foot onto the step just vacated *(see Figure 6.10)*.

For balance, the uphill hand can rest on the slope on steeper ground or it can be braced against the upper or the lower knee. If on the latter the elbow can rest on the upper knee. It is also possible to step the upper foot behind the lower leg and onto the lower step but this is not as secure or stable.

An alternative is to cut a double line of steps, standing with the lower foot some way behind the upper one. Cut two offset steps, one for each foot and step down on them with one foot at a time. This is slightly more stable but requires more cutting.

If diagonal steps are required, then slash steps or side steps are used. Descent can still be lower foot/upper foot, or, from the stable position the upper foot can be stepped through, between the slope and the lower leg and down onto the step. The lower leg must be bent to do this and the weighted foot is rolled outwards when this happens and so is less secure *(see Figure 6.11)*. When cutting steps in descent keep checking the fall-line to ensure that the steps stay at 90° to it and you do not drift off line.

> **10 Cutting steps**
>
> While step-cutting may seem a somewhat old-fashioned technique there are many occasions when the ability to cut good, safe and efficient steps can be extremely useful. When a group is tired or someone injured, when crampons are broken, lost or do not fit well, when a short section of hard snow needs to be negotiated, then a few steps can increase security. This is a skill which should be in every leader's repertoire, but one that needs practice to maintain proficiency.
>
> Remember that, when cutting steps for others, they should be big enough to accommodate the largest boot size in the group, not just the leader's.

PRACTISING ICE AXE ARREST IN THE WHITE CORRIES, GLEN COE PHOTO // DAVE EVANS

Self-arrest

Mastery of basic movement skills is a priority in winter. As a form of essential insurance, everyone venturing onto snow slopes must also learn techniques which can prevent a slip becoming an uncontrolled slide. A trip on snow can turn into an unstoppable slide extremely rapidly and it is vital to regain control as soon as possible.

There are two main skills to be considered in self-arrest. There is self-belay, which should stop a slip developing into a slide and there is self-arrest or ice axe braking, which should stop a slide once started. These need to be practised so that they become instinctive and can be relied upon in an emergency.

7.1 Slope selection

Both techniques can be practised on the same type of slope, ideally a concave slope which levels off allowing a natural stop should the arresting technique be unsuccessful. There should be no protruding rocks or other obstructions. Obviously the slope should not be avalanche prone, but be aware of developing situations in heavy spindrift conditions, especially higher up the slope and in poor visibility. As a concave slope steepens uphill, then height and sliding speed can be increased as skills develop. While it is beneficial to work up to speeds approaching those reached in the case of a real slide, this depends on the nature of the snow as well as the slope. A good slope one day may be too slow or too fast the following day, or too cut up and uneven the next. The clothes worn while sliding should also be taken into account. Basically, the smoother the material, the faster the slide and within any group it is possible to have people who slide too fast and others too slow.

While it is not advocated that self-belaying and self-arrest practice take place on slopes with obstructions, sometimes a good slope is hard to find and there may be boulders to collide with. If it is possible for anyone to slide into them, they can be made a bit safer by padding them with ropes, rucksacks and the like.

7.2 Self-belay

This is used to stop a slip developing into a slide. The axe is carried in the uphill hand with the adze pointing forward and the shaft pushed vertically down into the slope and only moved when the feet are in a stable position *(see Figure 7.1/1)*. In the event of a slip the axe is pushed down into the snow to stop the slip and the feet are kicked into the slope at the same time. In soft snow the full shaft can be driven into the slope. For this to work the axe must be pushed into the snow immediately a slip happens and on harder snow, body weight must be applied over the axe head to push it down *(see Figure 7.1/2)*. If the snow is too hard for the shaft to penetrate sufficiently, the free hand is moved quickly to grasp the shaft just above the snow. This reduces the chance of it levering out *(see Figure 7.1/3)*. If done too late or with insufficient force then the axe will be at an angle and likely to pull out.

On very hard snow there is too much resistance for this to work. On steep hard snow, it is possible to use the pick. The axe is held with the pick forward and in a slip the pick is pushed into the snow. However, if you do not stop with the self-belay, it will take longer to get into the correct self-arrest position, as the axe needs to be turned in your hand. Likewise, if normal self-belay with the shaft fails, then it will take longer to start arresting.

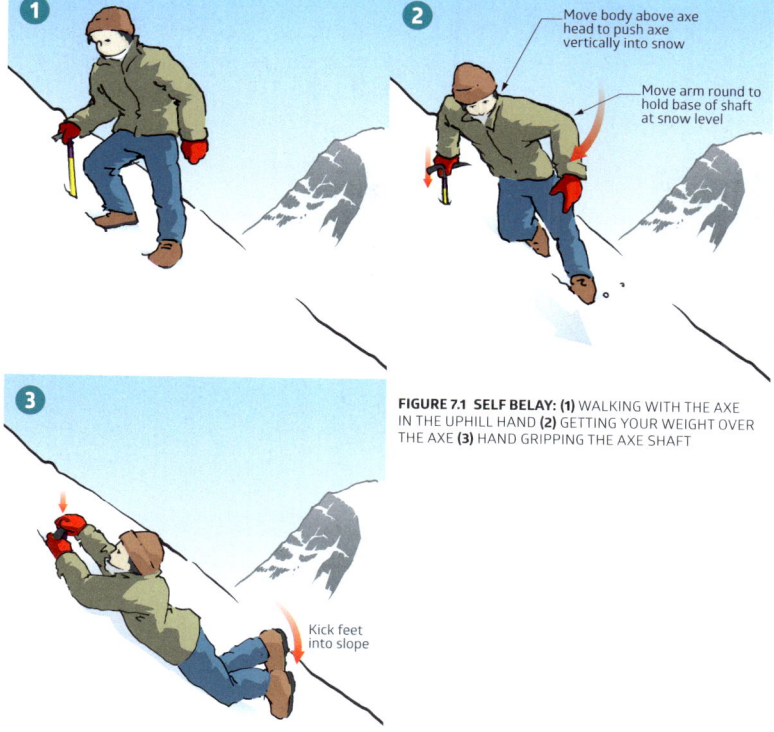

FIGURE 7.1 SELF BELAY: **(1)** WALKING WITH THE AXE IN THE UPHILL HAND **(2)** GETTING YOUR WEIGHT OVER THE AXE **(3)** HAND GRIPPING THE AXE SHAFT

7.3 Self-arrest

Any fall or slip on snow must be stopped as quickly as possible before too much speed and momentum build up. If self-belay is not possible or does not work, the next line of defence is self-arrest or ice axe braking. There is a logical and well-established progression of techniques and the method described has been tried and tested over many years.

7.3.1 Preparation

Self-arrest should never be practised wearing crampons. If the points touch the snow they can cause ankle and leg injuries and start tumbling falls. Helmets and full waterproofs should be worn and gloves are essential. Remove all items from pockets, for example mobile phones, cameras or car keys as they can cause injury during self-arrest. For some slides, tucking the jacket into the over-trousers prevents snow getting in at the waist and may permit a faster and smoother slide. Ice axe leashes or wrist loops should be removed or tied up out of the way. If control is lost on a slide and a leash is used, then the attached axe can cause injuries. It is unlikely that if the axe is lost in this situation that it will be brought under control again. Putting a rubber bung over the spike covers at least one sharp point and it may be worth putting tape over the edge of the adze. With adzes with sharp corners, it may be better to round them off slightly with a file.

7.3.2 The basic self-arrest position

No matter how a slide starts, the basic self-arrest position is the one which you must get into. In this position, body weight and pressure are used to push the pick into the snow to brake. While it is necessary to be able to self-arrest with either hand on the axe head, for clarity's sake the upper hand will refer to the hand holding the head and the lower hand the one holding the bottom of the shaft.

The starting point is the basic axe carrying position with the hand on the head of the axe, fingers curled under the adze and pick, and the pick pointing backwards. The axe is held diagonally across the chest with the lower hand on the bottom of the shaft, covering the spike and ferrule. The head of the axe is below the shoulder with the adze edge

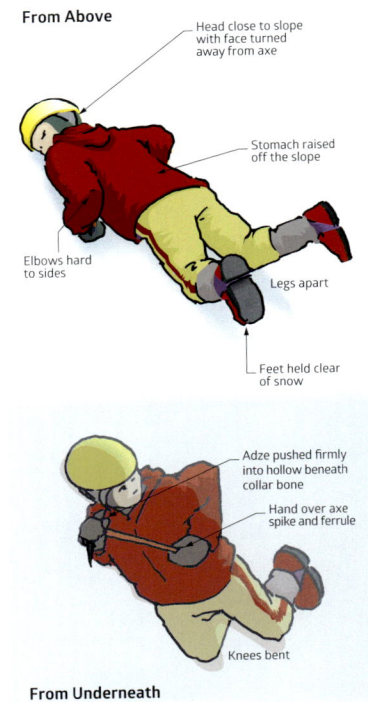

FIGURE 7.2 BASIC ICE AXE ARREST FROM ABOVE AND BELOW

tucked into the hollow just below the collarbone. When face down on the slope, the pick is pushed into the snow using the weight of the upper body. This is aided by pulling up on the lower end of the shaft so that the breastbone is used as the pivot point for the levering action and keeps the spike clear of the slope. The elbows are held tightly into the sides, as this is a strong position. The legs are splayed for stability; if kept together, the upper body, being heavier, tends to swing downhill so you end up sliding diagonally or sideways rather than facing up the slope. The feet are kept up as if you were wearing crampons, for if spikes were to touch the slope they could cause an injury. However, this is for practice. In a real fall, if crampons were not worn, then the toes could be used to assist braking.

To maximise the pressure on the axe head, most of your weight should be concentrated here. This is achieved by raising the stomach off the slope, so that you are sliding on your knees and the pick. Keep your head close to the slope and turn it to face away from the adze *(see Figure 7.2)*. This reduces the chance of injury should the axe hit an obstruction and bounce out. If you raise your head, then weight comes off the shoulder and the axe, so braking is less effective.

To begin, lie in this position with your weight on the pick. Arch your back to bring the pick out of the snow and start to slide, then bend forward and apply pressure to the axe head to stop. This is repeated with increasing speed. When pressure is applied to the axe it must be done in

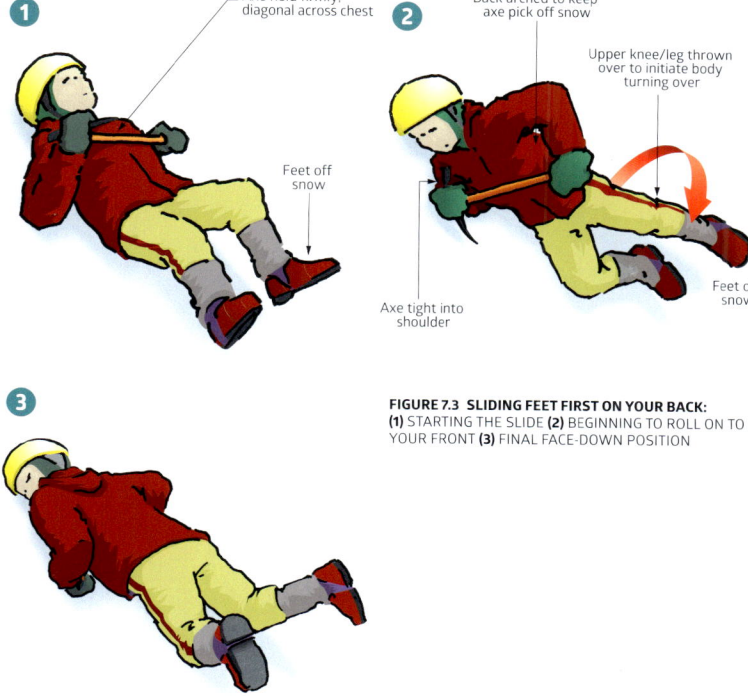

FIGURE 7.3 SLIDING FEET FIRST ON YOUR BACK:
(1) STARTING THE SLIDE **(2)** BEGINNING TO ROLL ON TO YOUR FRONT **(3)** FINAL FACE-DOWN POSITION

a progressive manner. If applied too quickly, the pick could stick and the axe be torn from your grasp or pulled from the correct position. If the adze is not under your shoulder, you cannot get enough force onto the axe to brake effectively. If this happens you must remove the pick from the snow, arch your back, place the adze in the correct position under the shoulder and start again.

7.3.3 Sliding feet first on your back

To get into the braking position when sliding feet first on your back, you must roll over onto your front. Roll over onto your front with the axe securely held diagonally across your body, with the adze tucked into the hollow below the shoulder and the pick facing forward. This is done towards the upper side where the head is held. If done the other way, towards the bottom of the axe, the spike can dig in and the axe can be wrenched from your grasp. Although the lower hand is held over the spike and ferrule to help prevent this happening, it is still a danger especially with longer axes. This roll takes you onto your front but your back stays arched to keep the axe off the slope. The knees are bent as rolling is initiated and the feet are held clear of the surface. This is the basic position. You can now move your shoulders down to apply increasing pressure to the axe head to start braking *(see Figure 7.3)*.

It is important to get right over onto your front in the braking position before applying pressure to the axe. If the pick touches the slope while

> **ⓘ 11 Basic self-arrest**
> Braking in the face-down position is basic, vital and must be well established before moving on to the next stage.
>
> Some things that help with assessment and self-assessment, besides whether the braking works or not, is what you can see when looking from above. If the edge of the adze is visible, insufficient pressure will be applied through the axe head. If the hollow below the collar-bone is not a bit sore after practice, then it is likely too little pressure has been used or braking has not been done correctly. Getting snow caught under the rim of the helmet is a good indication that the head is being held in the correct position close to the slope.

you are still rolling over and before full body weight can be applied, it can be pulled out of position or even ripped from your hands.

7.3.4 Sliding head first, face down

Achieving the braking position consists of two actions: first, getting in a feet-downhill position and second, the braking. When sliding head first the axe is held out to the side at about shoulder level with the upper hand holding the axe head and the lower the bottom of the shaft. Having a slight bend at the elbow is a stronger position than a totally straight arm *(see Figure 7.4/1)*. The pick is then dragged across the snow to create drag and the body swings round away from that side. The pick is not pushed into the snow but rather angled back uphill and dragged across the surface *(see Figure 7.4/2)*. If the pick points forward it can be forced into the snow by your momentum and torn from your grip. Turn and look to check you have the correct arm and axe positions.

With the pick dragged across the snow, that side of your body will slow down so this swinging action will happen naturally *(see Figure 7.4/3)*. When your feet are downhill, the pick is lifted up, the back arched and the axe put into the correct position with the adze under the shoulder *(see Figure 7.4/4)*. Progressive pressure is then applied to brake *(see Figure 7.4/5)*.

The further out to the side the pick, the greater the turning effect. This also takes the axe head with its cutting edges as far away from your face as possible. Never hold the axe directly downhill as it could bounce up into your face and cause injury. The faster the slide, the less the pick need be applied to produce a turning effect. It may be necessary to take the pick out before your feet are completely round, as once started, momentum may complete your turn, but the amount and length of pressure applied will depend on speed and the hardness of the snow. If the initial axe position is held for too long it is possible to swing through the fall-line into a diagonal position across the slope. It is even possible to turn into a feet down position without the axe by using your hand and the correct, curved body position.

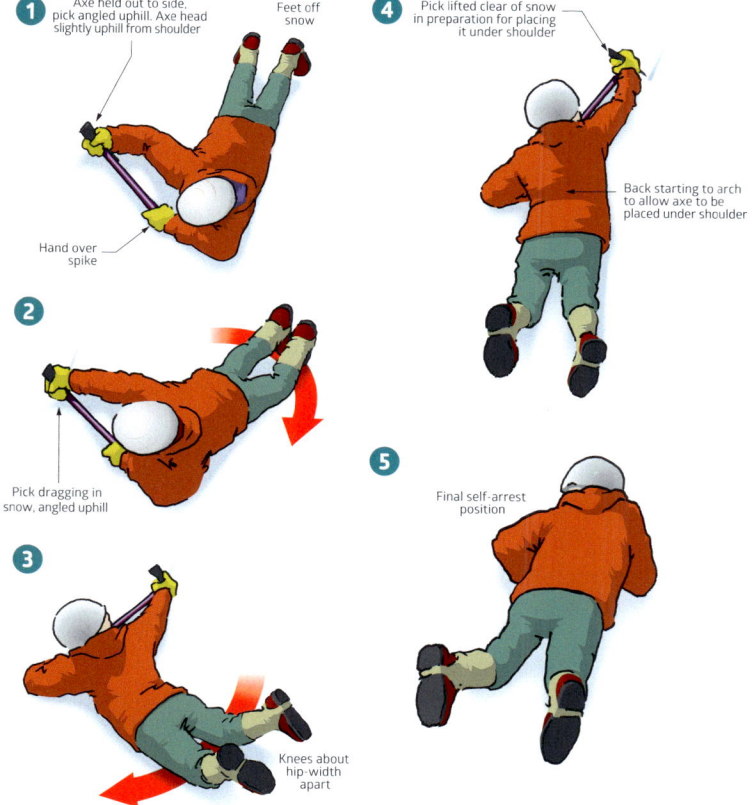

FIGURE 7.4 SLIDING HEAD FIRST, FACE DOWN: (1) STARTING THE SLIDE **(2)** BODY STARTING TO PIVOT AROUND, AWAY FROM THE AXE HEAD **(3)** ROTATION NEARLY COMPLETE **(4)** ROTATION COMPLETE **(5)** THE FINAL SELF-ARREST POSITION

The easiest way to start is from a slot cut across the slope above a stance. Get into the head down position by kneeling in the stance and lie flat with the toes in the slot and using the pick in the snow for support. When ready, put the axe out to the side and lift your feet out of the slot to start sliding. This type of fall is not uncommon when walking downhill facing out and snagging your crampons. This can mean a heavy, winding fall to begin with.

7.3.5 Sliding head first on your back

This initially feels more difficult, but there is more than one way to deal with it. The slower option is to roll onto your front and then use the previous procedure. The alternative is to get into the braking position in one movement.

When sliding on your back the pick is dragged through the snow at the side of your upper hand, at the level of your hip and a bit out to the side. Do not stab the pick into the snow as it may be wrenched out of your hand in hard snow conditions. The arm holding the head of the axe is straight *(see Figure 7.5/1)*. The resistance created by the pick allows you

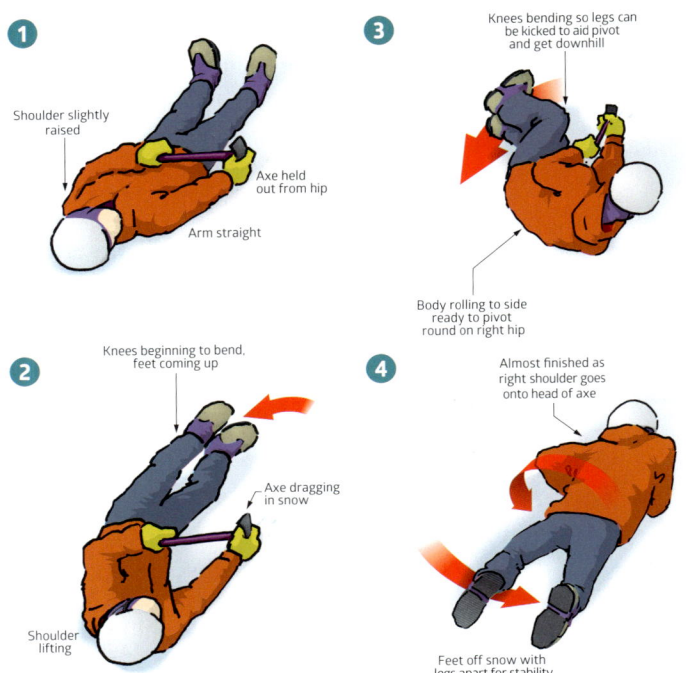

FIGURE 7.5 SLIDING HEAD FIRST ON YOUR BACK: (1) STARTING THE SLIDE **(2)** BEGINNING THE PIVOT **(3)** PIVOTING AROUND **(4)** THE FINAL SELF-ARREST POSITION

to pull your shoulders off the snow with the shoulder of the lower hand slightly higher. An alternative is to roll onto your hip first, which is a pivot point, and reach out and uphill with the axe. This forms a 'banana' body shape which naturally initiates the turn and is easier for those without strong abdominal muscles. At the same time the knees are bent and you are sliding on the hip at the axe side *(see Figure 7.5/2)*. From this position the feet are kicked to the side and downwards to initiate a rolling and turning action. This takes the body away from the axe and moves round so you are now on your front *(see Figure 7.5/3)*. If done correctly the axe remains in the snow and you move onto it with the upper shoulder going onto the adze *(see Figure 7.5/4)*. The feet should be kept clear of the slope.

To start sliding this way, cut a large but shallow bucket seat, sit in it and use the axe for support while you shuffle round so your feet are uphill. A slot for your heels or someone holding your ankles can help. You can then slide by lying back down and lifting out your axe.

From this position you need to be more active. If you only sit up and raise your knees you will end up sliding sideways or rolling down the hill. The action of the legs kicking out and down is essential to turn the body. However, while this may seem awkward at first, once learned it does feel quite natural.

> **ⓘ 12 Advanced self-arrest**
> When instructing, it may be necessary to help with the turning action. From lying on their back in the bucket seat, get the student to raise their shoulders, bend their knees and roll slightly onto the hip by the axe head. By holding their feet the action of kicking and turning can be assisted in a nearly static manner. This can be built on by sliding a bit to allow momentum to assist with turning. Finally a slight push on the feet may be all that is required to get the feeling of this action. Put hoods up to stop snow going down the back of necks.

7.4 Rolling and tumbling

Slides or falls may develop into rolls or tumbles which can knock your breath out and be disorientating. If this happens the first priority is to get stabilised in a sliding position from which the braking position can be accessed. To stop any tumbling, spread your arms and legs to form a star or spread-eagle shape. This also takes the axe as far away from the body as possible *(see Figure 7.6)*. From this position, with the axe head held in one hand well out to the side, the action of grasping the lower hand on the bottom of the shaft, 'collecting' the axe, must be practised. Focusing on the axe shaft whilst collecting the axe helps.

There is more chance of injury if things get out of control. It is vital to keep the axe away from the body until sliding in a stable position. For rolling, lie across the slope with the axe in one hand and the arms above the head. Again using a large bucket seat makes getting started easier. After a few rolls get into a star position to stop the roll and start sliding before making the moves to get into the braking position.

7.5 Without the axe

If the axe is not available or lost, it is still possible to get some control in a slide by getting your feet downslope and using your hands, single or doubled, as a substitute for the pick. Once round, push yourself up off the slope so that your weight is concentrated on your feet with your arms straight, as if finishing off a push-up *(see Figure 7.7)*. Some braking can then be done with the sides or the toes of the boots. If the toes are used, the ankles are flexed and the toes point uphill so that they will slide over anything firm and not cause a backward flip. Take care not to push too powerfully as it is possible to go over backwards.

This is an action of last resort, but it may give some control. If the snow is soft it may even be possible to use this with crampons on, if the toes point up the slope and the points dig in less. However, never practise this while wearing crampons.

7.6 Other considerations

Self-arrest is better done with an ice axe rather than a technical tool, especially those with bent shafts which are difficult to use. For self-belay, the shaft is important, but for braking, the head, and particularly the pick, are crucial. A steeply inclined pick is designed to stick and grip and if

FIGURE 7.6 THE STAR POSITION

FIGURE 7.7 BRAKING WITHOUT AN ICE AXE

Ankles flexed so toes are uphill from heels

used for braking this is what it will do with a greatly increased chance of being torn from your hands. Self-arrest is best learned using a curved pick before moving on to practising with an inclined pick. However, you need to be able to brake with the tool you normally carry, so practise using it. Pressure on the head needs to be applied in a very controlled manner to prevent it from grabbing.

If a slip does happen, then instant action is needed but there are liable to be other complications. If you are sliding on your back wearing a heavy rucksack then it may be difficult to roll onto your front because of the weight. A head-first slide with a sack will also be more difficult to control as the sack moves forward onto your head and restricts arm movement, especially if there is no waist belt. However, never give up even if the braking does not appear to be working. It will at least keep you sliding feet first and hopefully reduce the danger of head injury. If all else fails in a slide, try with your last big effort to hit obstacles feet first.

7.7 Glissading

Glissading is controlled sliding down a slope and can be an efficient and exhilarating way to descend snow. Unfortunately, it is not without its danger, so competence at self-arrest is mandatory. It is only possible in certain snow conditions and should only be done where there is a safe run-out, the whole descent can be seen and there are no rocks lurking close to the surface. Never glissade with crampons on and always wear gloves and, if possible, a helmet.

There are several methods which depend on ability and the nature of the slope and the snow. The best snow for glissading is firm but with a softer layer on top, conditions more often found in the spring and in the afternoon when the snow begins to soften. Be careful if going from areas of light into shadow with patches of both thawing and frozen snow.

There are three main forms of glissade:

Standing glissade

This is the most elegant, comfortable and most difficult but only possible in a limited range of conditions – basically, it is skiing without skis! Stand upright with your knees and ankles flexed and the axe held in the stronger hand with the arms out to the side to aid balance *(see Figure 7.8A)*. One foot is slightly ahead of the other with your weight over the balls of your

> **13 Self-arrest teaching plan**
> In general, self-arrest sessions should be constructive and enjoyable. Initially, some people feel quite daunted throwing themselves down a slope and this is not conducive to learning. Consider creating a comfortable stance to start from and/or have other people hold the feet until the person is ready to slide.
>
> There must be clear explanations and demonstrations, and slowing down demonstrations will help. Make each method relevant by explaining the situations under which a particular slide may occur.
>
> Students must be in a position to see and hear, not squinting into stinging spindrift. Have their backs to the wind which also gives the instructor some shelter. The instructor should also be able to see the student practise and provide constructive, on-the-spot feedback. The best place to stand is about three-quarters of the way up the run so that a view is possible looking down and feedback can be given as they return to the top.
>
> Keep the feedback simple and usually only one point to work on rather than overloading with too much information.
>
> Common faults include:
> - rolling to the wrong side,
> - keeping the feet down and/or the head up,
> - allowing the axe to move from under the shoulder,
> - the axe not far enough out to the side and not replacing it in the correct position under the shoulder when sliding head first.

feet and let them slide. Leaning too far forward causes the toes to catch, too far back and your feet will shoot out beneath you. Turns can be made by rotating the body and feet so that the boots are on their uphill edges. As in skiing, turns can be assisted by un-weighting: sink down slightly by bending the ankles and knees, then with an upward motion reduce the pressure on the boots and turn them at the same time. To slow down turn the feet across the slope or put more weight on the heels so they dig in more. On an easy angled slope a skating type of step can be made to progress.

Crouching glissade
In a low crouched position the weight is taken on the feet and the axe is held at one side of the body with the spike on the snow. The upper hand holds the head of the axe and the other grips the shaft above the ferrule so that the spike can be pushed down to control speed *(see Figure 7.8B)*. This is slower and more stable than the standing glissade, but you cannot use your boots to control direction or speed as efficiently.

FIGURE 7.8 THE THREE MAIN FORMS OF GLISSADE:
(A) STANDING GLISSADE **(B)** CROUCHING GLISSADE
(C) SITTING GLISSADE

Sitting glissade

This is sitting on the snow and sliding - also known as the 'bum slide'. The axe can be held to one side with the strong hand on the head, the weak hand on the shaft above the ferrule and the spike pushed into the snow to brake *(see Figure 7.8C)*. Alternatively, it can be in the self-arrest position in case things get too fast when you can roll onto your front to brake. Lying back and lifting the feet can increase speed, sitting up and using your feet can help to slow down. This works best in soft snow but be prepared to get wet in most conditions.

WALKING OFF BEINN BHAN ON BULLET HARD NÉVÉ   *PHOTO // JOHN COUSINS*

Crampons

Crampons were first developed in the Alps by shepherds and farmers for use on snow and for cutting hay on steep slopes. From these rudimentary beginnings using horseshoe nails on a crude frame the modern crampon has evolved.

Oscar Eckenstein is credited with redesigning crampons in 1909 to produce a ten-point crampon – one where all the points faced downwards. These were manufactured by Grivel, the blacksmith in Courmayeur in Italy and were an improvement on nailed boots for use on snow and ice, permitted safer travel and reduced the amount of step cutting required. In 1932 Laurent Grivel added two forward-facing points for use on steeper terrain.

These two types of crampons, ten or twelve points, gave rise to two differing techniques. French technique uses all the downward-facing points while Austrian or German technique also made use of the two forward-facing points. These techniques are still around today and while there is now a range of crampon types and designs, the basic roots are still evident. In the late 1970s binding systems using front bails and heel clips rather than straps were developed to speed up fitting and removal. In recent years manufacturers have worked to create specific boot/crampon combinations designed to give a better fit and increased stability.

8.1 Crampon Types

There are different types of crampon catering for a range of uses, but it is important that the crampon is matched to the boot with which it will be used. There are several combinations but basically non-rigid boots should be fitted with flexible or articulated crampons which can bend with the boot. With rigid boots either articulated or rigid crampons can be used. But due to the range of shapes, not all crampons can be fitted to all boots. Crampons can be divided into three main categories to provide guidance for the various combinations. Crampons can be categorised as C1, C2 and C3. These, combined with boots categories B1, B2 and B3, can be used to assess the suitability of various combinations *(see Tables 8.1, 8.2 and 8.3)*.

8.1.1 C1 flexible crampons

These are designed to fit flexible boots for walking on moderately angled snow and ice. They normally have ten or twelve points but may not have any forward-facing front points. The front and heel sections are connected by a flexible metal strip and use a strapping arrangement for attachment.

8.1.2 C2 articulated crampons

Also called mountaineering, general purpose or twelve-point crampons, these usually have ten downward-facing, two forward-facing points and are hinged below the instep, although some technical climbing crampons are also hinged. They normally have eight points on the forward section and four below the heel. The connection between the two sections can either be a hinged bar or metal strip and this permits some movement in the crampons, making them easier to walk with, allows their use with some non-rigid boots and decreases the chance of crampon breakage due to stress. They are generally symmetrical in shape and have horizontal or vertically aligned front points which can be either curved or angled

Boot category	Description	Suitable crampon types
B0	A flexible 3-season walking boot (generally with thin leather or fabric uppers) intended for summer or light year round hillwalking with the emphasis on comfort. Use of crampons not recommended as the boot does not provide a sufficiently stable platform, leading to the danger of the crampon becoming detached in use.	None
B1	Four season hillwalking boots with a semi-stiffened midsole and a more supportive and durable leather upper. This allows the use of crampons for walking on short sections of easy snow and ice.	C1
B2	An almost fully stiffened 4-season mountain boot with a thicker upper, higher ankle profile and usually the facility for crampons with heel clip bindings to be fitted. Suitable for general walking, glacial terrain and easy/mid grade mountaineering and climbing.	C2, (C1)
B3	A totally rigid technical mountain boot, allowing the use of crampons with heel clips and wire toe bails. For everything from walking to technical and high-altitude mountaineering or hard ice/mixed climbing, depending on design.	C3, (C2, C1)

TABLE 8.1 BOOT CATEGORIES, DESCRIPTIONS AND CRAMPON COMPATIBILITIES (WITH THANKS TO BRIAN HALL & SCARPA)

Crampon type	Binding type	Boot type required features
C1	Fully strapped or flexible plastic cradle/strap combination	B1 – None apart from a good fit to the crampon
C2	Cradle/strap or (more commonly) cradle/heel-clip combination	B2 – Adequate heel welt and thick upper around the ankle if heel-clip binding
C3	Heel-clip with any toe attachment	B3 – Adequate heel and toe welts, thick uppers throughout

TABLE 8.2 SUMMARY OF COMMONLY USED CRAMPON BINDING TYPES

Crampon usage	C1	C2	C3
Walking on easy-angled terrain	B1 – Good B2 – Good B3 – Good	B2 – Acceptable B3 – Acceptable	B3 – Poor*
Steep/rough walking, scrambling or mid-angled snow and ice slopes	B1 – Not recommended B2 – Acceptable B3 – Acceptable	B2 – Good B3 – Acceptable	B3 – Acceptable
Steep (up to vertical) snow and ice and mid-grade climbing	B1 – No! B2 – Acceptable B3 – Acceptable	B2 – Acceptable B3 – Good	B3 – Good
Vertical or overhanging rock & ice climbing	B1 – No! B2 – No! B3 – Poor	B2 – Poor B3 – Acceptable	B3 – Good

TABLE 8.3 CHOICE OF CRAMPONS FOR INTENDED USAGE

Notes: *C3 crampons are prone to damage or failure when used for walking or scrambling, due to metal fatigue. They will also be more susceptible to balling up, particularly if used without anti-balling plates – *see Figure 8.5*.

downwards. The first pair of downward-facing points, the secondary points, are generally near vertical or slightly raked forward. This design has been around for a long time and is a good all-round choice, performing well over a wide range of conditions.

Lightweight aluminium alloy crampons are for occasional or emergency use. They are not particularly robust or durable and not really suitable for normal winter use.

8.1.3 C3 rigid crampons

Also known as technical crampons, these are of a rigid construction and designed for use on steep terrain, particularly ice. When combined with a stiff-soled boot, they give a stable platform and reduced vibration but are generally heavier and less comfortable for walking on moderate or rocky terrain. The frame is often aligned at 90° to the sole for greater rigidity. The number of points may vary but the emphasis is on the front and secondary points, for which there is a range of designs, including double and mono front points.

While rigid crampons are better on specific types of climbs they are less versatile. They tend to ball-up more, are less comfortable for walking and should not be used on non-rigid boots.

8.1.4 Anti-balling plates

Anti-balling or 'antibot' plates are designed to prevent snow collecting and compacting in the base of crampons – 'balling-up' *(see Figure 8.5, page 90)*. They are made of plastic or latex which retains its elasticity in cold conditions, and clip into the base and over the central bar of the crampon, normally in a separate front and heel section. Anti-balling plates are considered an essential part of a crampon and almost all come with a pair included, but can be bought separately or replaced should they become damaged.

8.2 Attachment

There are two attachment methods, strapping or clip-on. Straps are traditional, have some advantages and are most likely found on flexible or articulated crampons but are seldom seen on modern crampons. Good straps are secure and can be used on non-rigid boots or on boots with insufficient welt at the toe and heel for clip-ons.

Take care that the straps are not too tight and restrict circulation – more of a problem with boots that have a soft upper.

'French style' fastening, in which the front posts are connected by straps and a ring or a plastic toe cradle through which the front strap is threaded *(see Figure 8.1)* is faster and less likely to restrict circulation than a full strapping system.

Clip-on crampons are more convenient and are now the norm, particularly with technical crampons and rigid boots. They are quick, secure and do not affect circulation. There are several types which basically use a rear lever system which rests on the heel welt and forces the boot forward into either a metal bail, toe straps or cradle *(see Figure 8.2)*. The lever has a strapping system which either goes round the ankle or runs through the front of the crampon, helps secure it in place and acts as a safety strap should the crampon come off. The safety strap will have some closure system such as D rings or buckles. Some plastic closures can be knocked loose or become brittle when very cold, but D rings can ice up making them difficult to unfasten.

8.3 Fit

Crampons should fit closely to the boot sole with no movement between them. Some crampons are adjustable for length and breadth and can be altered to fit the boot exactly. Others can only be adjusted lengthwise. Clip-on crampons may have adjustment for the position of the heel level and a finer adjustment on the heel lever itself. Both can alter the forward pressure. The heel lever should snap securely into the heel welt but not be excessively tight, as this can be uncomfortable, especially with leather boots. There may be a number of adjustment options with the heel lever to optimise the fit *(see Figure 8.3)*.

Crampons with toe bails and heel levers should be a neat fit. The fit of the toe bail is critical and should match the curve of the toe welt. French straps or cradles are not so critical, but the front posts must be tight against the sides of the boot. The rear crampon points should lie directly below the heel.

FIGURE 8.1 FRENCH STRAPPING WITH TOE RING

FIGURE 8.2 CLIP-ON CRAMPON
PHOTO // GEORGE McEWAN

Fitting problems with clip-on crampons are not limited to boots without sufficient welts. With variations in the size and shape of different soles, toe and heel profiles and sole thickness, not all crampons fit all boots. If there is too much space between the boot and crampon at any point, then the fit will not be sufficiently secure.

Vertical posts at the toe and heel should be in contact with the sides of the sole and should provide enough pressure to hold the crampon firmly to the boot so that it stays in place if the boot is lifted up. Other side posts should also fit neatly.

For those with smaller feet, adjustment may be needed to fit some crampons. The hinge bar on some articulated crampons may need to be shortened and even some fully adjustable crampons may require some alterations. Larger boots might also have problems requiring an extension bar.

8.4 Carrying crampons

Many rucksacks have reinforcing and straps for carrying crampons, but crampons attached to the rucksack are more liable to get snagged. These straps and buckles are slower and less convenient, especially in bad weather and it is not unknown for crampons to drop off. As most crampons come with a crampon bag, it is better to carry them in the bag, or similar, inside the rucksack. Some articulated crampons fold at the hinge and fit into a climbing helmet which will also protect the sack and contents. Rubber point protectors are easy to remove but are less convenient when stowing crampons again and are practically of little use, particularly if using a crampon bag.

8.5 Care and maintenance

Crampons are subject to a lot of stress and require checking on a regular basis. Look closely at any stress points such as around holes, sharp bends or square inside corners, the instep bar on articulated crampons and near the front points. A magnifying glass can be used to search for cracks which, if found, mean that the crampon is no longer safe. Other points of weakness are near bolts or adjustment holes. Screws and nuts may need

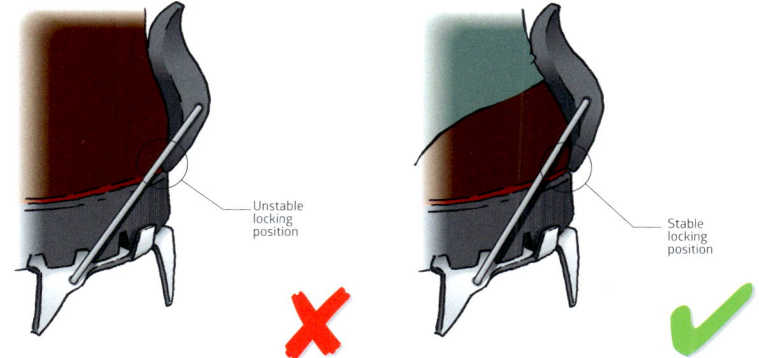

FIGURE 8.3 HEEL CLIP FITTING

to be tightened and some may benefit from a touch of glue. Frayed nylon straps should be tidied as loose fibres become iced up and can jam in buckles and/or rings. A flame can be used to melt and tidy these threads. Straps and their attachments, such as rivets, should be regularly inspected.

When crampons become blunt they should be sharpened with a hand file, not a grinder which could over-heat the metal and damage the temper. Flat front points should be sharpened like a chisel, from the top downwards so the cutting edge is on the bottom. Vertical front points are sharpened from the sides. Downward facing points are sharpened along the narrow edges to maintain their thickness. Sharpen before points get too rounded as this means considerable shortening to reform the point.

Dry them out after use, and at the end of the season, clean and lightly lubricate them to keep them rust-free. They should not be stored with rubber protectors on the points, for if there is any dampness, they can rust.

8.5.1 Emergency repairs

Breaking a crampon can vary from a minor inconvenience to a major problem so having an emergency repair kit is sensible. This can be simple, consisting of a long strap and buckle, spare rivets, nuts, bolts and screws, some thin wire, cable ties and tape. A screwdriver, Allen keys and light pliers should allow most repairs to be carried out.

8.6 Putting on crampons

Crampons should be put on before they are required, but after gear such as over-trousers or harness. Plan ahead and try to anticipate what you are going to encounter and when crampons will be needed. Find somewhere level or not too steep where there is a firm surface; boulder fields often provide good gearing-up spots. Alternatively, on snow, cut a good comfortable stance or stamp out a platform. Face uphill, place one crampon securely on the slope (if the snow is firm or on another firm surface) remembering buckles always go to the outside of the crampon (see Figure 8.4). If the snow is very soft you can use your rucksack as a platform to place your crampon on.

FIGURE 8.4 PUTTING ON CRAMPONS ON A SLOPE
PHOTO // SAM LEARY

FIGURE 8.5 BALLING-UP

Clear any snow off the boot by tapping it on a rock or with the axe. Ensure that the welts are clear of snow and place the foot on the crampon. With clip-ons, the toe is first placed under the wire bail or toe strap. With strap-on crampons, the heel or the toe can go in first but ensure that the side posts are firm against the sides and not underneath the sole. Check that the boot sole is flat on the crampon and the posts are snug on the sides of the boot. Do up the heel lever or fasten the straps, then tuck any excess strapping out of the way. On flat ground crampons can be put on in a kneeling position.

Some crampon straps cannot be fastened easily when wearing gloves and may require bare hands. It is easiest and safest to put on crampons standing up and facing uphill. Sitting down and putting the crampon on by holding it onto the sole is awkward and often leads to improper fitting.

8.7 Considerations for use

Crampons, with all their points, can be a hazard and you must always remember that you are wearing them. They can snag clothing or equipment, so be as neat and tidy as possible. Baggy trousers or over-trousers should be tucked into gaiters, and straps and laces tucked out of the way. To minimise the chance of spiking yourself, have your feet wider apart than normal. Walk with your legs at about hip width apart and be aware of how you move your boots, especially if making any feet or leg crossing movements.

> **14 Crampon fitting**
>
> Putting on and taking off crampons is something that beginners may be slow at. While checking crampons before going out and practising putting them on will help, there is no real short-cut to proficiency. Time spent putting crampons on, taking them off and re-fastening them in the course of a day should be seen as part of the learning process and not necessarily something to avoid doing. The best way to get good at crampon fitting is to do it a lot!

FIGURE 8.6 FLAT FOOTING, FEET POINTING AHEAD

FIGURE 8.7 FLAT FOOTING, FEET ANGLED

When the snow is soft or sticky it adheres to the crampon masking the points, making them ineffective and adding weight to the foot. This is called balling-up *(see Figure 8.5)*. Rigid crampons and those of the 'cookie cutter' design, where the frame is at 90° to the sole of the boot, are most affected. Articulated crampons ball-up less because they flex. Although most crampons have, or can be fitted with, anti-balling plates, they may still ball-up. Some plastic plates become less effective as they get scratched and snow sticks to them more easily. A coating of ski wax or similar can help alleviate this problem.

If your crampons do ball-up then tapping them with the axe shaft or knocking the foot against a rock can clear them. The former method can damage the axe shaft and the latter is not very good for the crampons, especially if you have sharp points.

While crampons are primarily used for snow and ice they are also remarkably good on frozen vegetation and can also be used on bare or rocky ground, although they will damage vegetation and scar bare ground. When walking on bare ground however, you are standing higher on the points so are less stable, especially in windy conditions, and it is easy to turn an ankle or trip over the points. The difficulty of walking on rocky ground, over boulder fields or similar should not be underestimated and becomes part of the whole decision-making process: when is it quicker and safer to leave crampons on and when to take them off? The issue of environmental damage also needs to be considered.

8.8 French technique

Also known as flat-footing, this technique uses the crampon's downward-facing points. When walking on flat, firm snow or even ice, this is the method which would naturally be adopted. All the downward points are pushed into the surface by your weight. With an increase in slope angle the crampons are still kept flat but the ankles are flexed to do this.

If walking straight up a slope, flat-footing becomes impractical at quite low angles so it is better to go diagonally. On moderate slopes your feet can point in the direction of travel but the ankles must be flexed.

FIGURE 8.8 FLAT FOOTING IN DESCENT

FIGURE 8.9 FLAT FOOTING, CROSSED LEGS

It is easier to flex the lower ankle which bends outwards than the upper ankle which must bend inwards. Body weight is kept directly over the feet and the knees and ankles are rolled outward to maintain this position *(see Figure 8.6)*. As the slope becomes steeper, flexing becomes more difficult so the toes are pointed slightly down the slope, although the body continues to face the direction of travel *(see Figure 8.7)*. The steeper the slope, the more the toes must point downhill and the more the body must also move round. The steepest slopes that can be ascended with this technique are with the toes pointing downhill, as this allows maximum ankle flexion, and the body facing the same way. This is the same body position and action adopted when descending a slope using French technique *(see Figure 8.8)*.

In French technique, it is important to use all the downward points. Keeping the feet level and using only the points under the edges of the boots is unsafe, as the points can shear out of snow or fail to grip on ice. Leaning in towards the slope also makes the points break out. When on steeper or harder slopes, a little more pressure may be required and a slight stamping action can be used.

When on a moderate to steep slope, the axe can be used for support and security. When in a position of balance and stability with the lower foot below the upper and weight mostly on the lower leg, the axe is held in the upper hand for support. Weight is then transferred to the upper foot, the lower foot is stepped above and forward of the weighted leg and placed securely *(see Figure 8.9)*. Weight is then transferred and the upper leg is moved up and through, back in the position of stability. The axe is then moved up and forward for the next two steps. The steeper the slope, the greater the care required as the crampon points are moved past the weighted leg.

When changing direction, stand in the balance position with the axe securely in the snow and turn to face directly uphill. Bring the upper foot round to face the new direction of travel. Weight the leg in the new direction, change hands on the axe and move the un-weighted foot around and through to face the new direction in the position of balance

 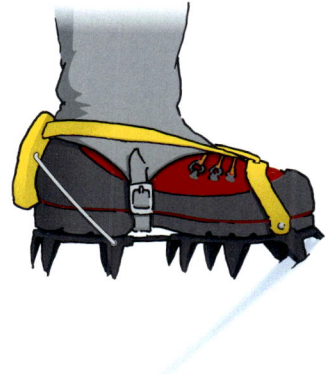

FIGURE 8.10 FLAT FOOTING, CHANGE OF DIRECTION   **FIGURE 8.11** FRONT POINTING

(see Figure 8.10). This requires a degree of flexibility. Alternatively move into front-pointing with both feet, then into flat-footing facing the new direction. Looking ahead for easier angled sections and planning your route to take advantage of these makes direction changes easier.

8.9 Front-pointing

This is the normal way to climb steep snow or ice, although it is tiring on the calf muscles. The body is held vertically, not leaning in, and the axe can be used for support and balance. The two forward-facing points and often the secondary points are tapped into the slope for support *(see Figure 8.11)*. The degree of penetration depends on the hardness of the snow or ice and the amount the secondary points are used depends on the angle and the design of the crampon.

When front-pointing, the angle of the crampon to the slope is very important and the points should go in with the foot about horizontal. If the heel is too high or too low the points can lever out. If the boots, crampons or combination is not stiff enough, then the points do not make a secure platform. It is also difficult to judge the correct angle and with a non-stiffened boot the heel may be level, but the points levered out by the flex of the sole.

When on hard snow, the action of kicking the toes and the points into the slope is very natural and similar to kicking steps straight up a slope. The feet are kept at about horizontal, around hip-width apart for stability and square to the slope so the front points go straight in *(see Figure 8.12)*. As the slope becomes harder or steeper, a little more force may be needed. However, even on ice, a gentle tap should be sufficient. Kick too hard and the crampons bounce back out and your toes get bruised.

Front-pointing works best in straight ascent. When going diagonally, the action is slightly less natural, as care must be taken to keep the feet square to the slope. When traversing, face the slope and move sideways with the feet taken apart then together in the direction of travel. When descending using front points, then face in and descend backwards.

FIGURE 8.12 FRONT POINTING

FIGURE 8.13 HYBRID TECHNIQUE

8.10 Hybrid technique (Mixed or American technique)

This is where the upper foot is front-pointing and the lower is flat-footing, the lower ankle being the easier to flex *(see Figure 8.13)*. The axe is held normally for support. This can be used in straight ascent or steep zig-zag, but is less natural on a diagonal, as care has to be taken to place the front points square to the slope and not angle them in the direction of travel. This technique allows some rest for the lower leg from the strain of front-pointing. Swapping the role of the legs gives some respite.

AVALANCHE DEBRIS IN OBSERVATORY GULLY, BEN NEVIS   *PHOTO // SAIS*

part 3
Snow and avalanche

BLOWING SNOW ON GLAS MAOL IN THE SOUTHERN CAIRNGORMS, ACCUMULATING AS UNSTABLE WIND SLAB IN THE LEE OF THE RIDGE   *PHOTO // PAUL NOBLE*

Snow structure

Snow and avalanches are complex subjects but the main concepts are relatively simple.

While research into snow structures and the mechanisms of avalanche release and behaviour continues to increase our understanding, the basics should be learned by all who encounter snow in the mountains. Snow is an incredibly variable substance where old packed snow can be 50,000 times harder than fresh dry loose snow. This is one of the factors which makes winter mountaineering so challenging. An understanding of how snow behaves and how and why avalanches occur will increase your enjoyment and safety. It helps you assess where to find the best walking and climbing conditions and which areas are liable to present an avalanche hazard.

FIGURE 9.1 SNOW CRYSTALS **(A)** STELLAR CRYSTALS MIXED WITH BROKEN AND RIMED CRYSTALS, **(B)** NEEDLE CRYSTALS

9.1 Snow in the air

Snow forms in the atmosphere where super-cooled water droplets condense around microscopic particles such as dust or plant spores. As water vapour freezes around these nuclei, snow crystals are formed. These are generally hexagonal but can also be plates, columns and needles *(see Figure 9.1)*. As these fall through the air they can grow in size and become more complex. Further growth can be due to water vapour deposited on the crystals (sublimation) or by water droplets freezing onto them (riming). The shape and form of the crystals are largely determined by the temperature and humidity at their formation and on the journey through the atmosphere. Generally, the lightest and driest snow is formed in moderately cold, calm conditions while the higher the temperature, the heavier and wetter the snow, with larger, more complex snowflakes.

While new snow is falling or being blown about, it can be modified, mostly by the wind breaking up the crystals and snowflakes. In the mountains it is likely that most snow is of this type.

9.2 Rime ice

This is the white crust which builds up on the windward side of exposed objects such as boulders and cliffs. Rime differs from snow as it forms when tiny super-cooled water droplets freeze on contact with a surface. Rime always grows into the wind showing the previous wind directions and can vary in form from delicate, feathery flakes to much harder, icy encrustations *(see Figure 9.2)*.

9.3 Verglas

This is the thin layer of usually clear ice that forms when water or water vapour comes into contact with a surface below 0°C. An extensive coating

FIGURE 9.2 RIME FORMING ON THE WINDWARD SIDE OF A BOULDER

FIGURE 9.3 GRAUPEL

of verglas can make walking and climbing dangerous and precarious. It may be difficult to see and, if it is covered by a fall of snow, it can be treacherous.

9.4 Graupel

One type of snow, which is altered on its journey down through the atmosphere, is graupel or soft hail and is formed by riming onto snowflakes. It is associated with turbulent conditions, when crystals may fall then ascend in updrafts several times, each time picking up more riming and becoming rounded *(see Figure 9.3)*. This typically occurs in cumulo-nimbus clouds associated with cold front showers. Graupel on the ground appears as small white spheres which can roll and flow when disturbed. Although this may show as a layer, because of the ease with which it moves, it is more often found as deeper deposits at the foot of slopes and collecting features such as gullies and crag aprons. Because of their size and already rounded shape, graupel can last unchanged in the snow pack for a considerable time.

9.5 Snow on the ground

Once on the ground, the snow pack continues to change (metamorphose) under the influence of a number of processes. These changes take place even though the surrounding conditions do not alter.

9.5.1 Rounding

Previously known as dry-snow or equi-temperature metamorphism, this takes place in any cold or non-thawing snow pack. Over time complex, branched crystals become rounded as water sublimates – changes from solid to vapour and back to solid, from points to hollows *(see Figure 9.4)*. Grains become more rounded and gradually attach themselves to neighbours, forming a stronger structure. Fresh snow with its light, interlocked crystals and huge air content becomes a series of better-bonded, more spherical crystals *(see Figure 9.5)*. This process is known as

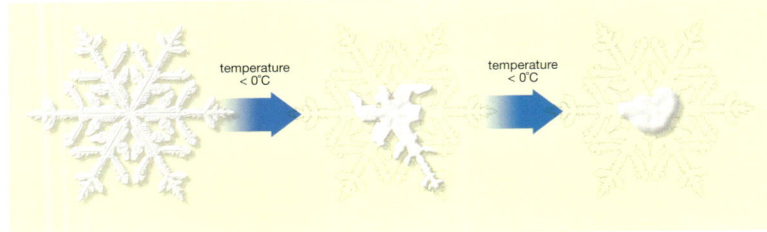

FIGURE 9.4 CRYSTAL ROUNDING – SINGLE CRYSTAL

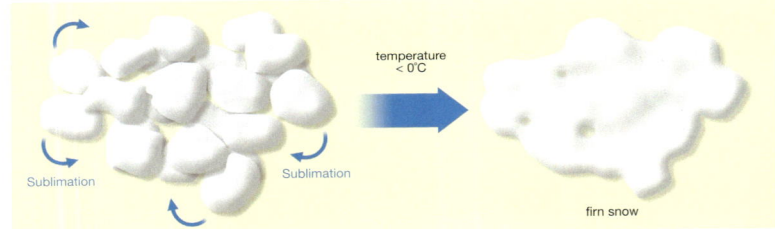

FIGURE 9.5 CRYSTAL ROUNDING – MULTIPLE CRYSTALS

sintering as the bonds or necks between crystals become stronger. This eventually leads to the formation of firn snow where all the grains are interlocked. This process occurs more rapidly near 0°C and ceases altogether at −40°C.

9.5.2 Faceting

Under snow, the ground is generally at about 0°C but the surface temperature may be much lower. In this situation the temperature through the snow pack varies, producing a temperature gradient. This is the difference between the temperature at the bottom and the top of the snow pack and is measured in °C per cm. If there is a big difference between the bottom and top then the temperature gradient is said to be strong and if the snow pack is shallow, it can be even more pronounced *(see Figure 9.7)*.

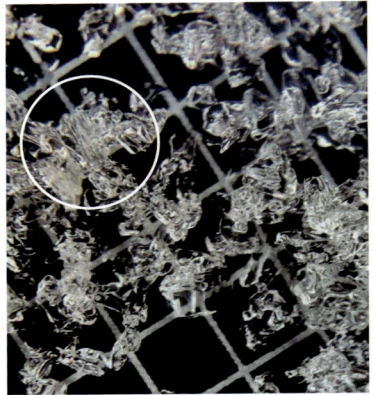

FIGURE 9.6 SQUARE EDGED FACETED CRYSTALS ON A PLATE WITH SIZE 3MM SQUARES. LARGER STRIATED CRYSTALS OF DEPTH HOAR HIGHLIGHTED
PHOTO // MARK DIGGINS, SAIS

With a strong temperature gradient, greater than 1°C/10cm, a process known as kinetic growth becomes dominant, as water vapour migrates vertically up through the snow pack and can lead to the development of a weak layer of fragile or poorly bonded, faceted crystals *(see Figure 9.6)*. Facets usually form in a less dense layer and near a distinct change within the snow pack such as a buried crust layer. The crystals have a distinctive angular 'sugary' appearance with stepped or striated faces and can form very quickly. During long periods of low temperatures, faceted crystals can remain in the snow pack becoming a persistent weak layer, and with

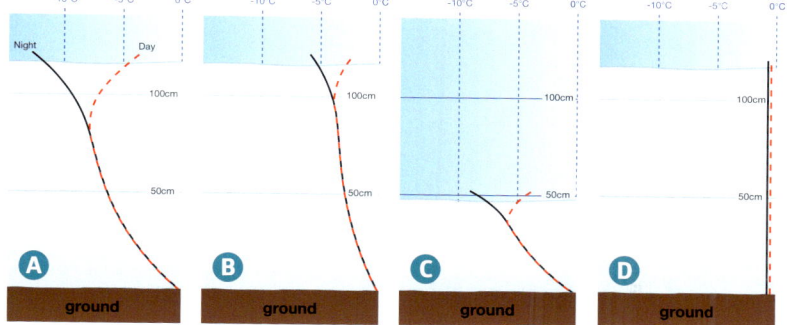

FIGURE 9.7 TEMPERATURE THROUGH THE SNOW PACK: (A) STRONG TEMPERATURE GRADIENT, **(B)** WEAK TEMPERATURE GRADIENT, **(C)** VERY STRONG TEMPERATURE GRADIENT, **(D)** ISOTHERMIC (EQUI-TEMPERATURE) SNOWPACK UNDER THAW CONDITIONS

FIGURE 9.8 A LAYER OF DEPTH HOAR NEAR THE BOTTOM OF THE SNOW PACK

FIGURE 9.9 SURFACE HOAR SHOWING TYPICAL FEATHERY CRYSTALS

continuing low temperatures, can further develop into **depth hoar** *(Figure 9.8)*. Depth hoar crystals typically display stepped or striated faces, can be large, fragile and poorly bonded to each other and adjacent layers. The most distinctive form of depth hoar is cup crystals.

Surface hoar is deposited on the top of the snow and takes the form of brittle plates, *(see Figure 9.9)* most likely seen after cold, still nights and can become a weakness in the snow pack if buried by subsequent snowfall.

9.5.3 Melt-freeze cycle

This occurs when the snow pack is exposed to temperatures which alternate above and below freezing point. The crystals become surrounded by a film of water when thawing and this freezes when the temperature drops to form a strong, icy bond between crystals, quickly leading to a hard, rigid material and a generally stable snow pack. Most melting is produced by warm, wet winds and rainfall penetrating the snow. A number of melt-freeze cycles lead to a very strong, stable snow type often referred to as névé which gives the best snow for walking or climbing on.

FIGURE 9.10A WIND-TRANSPORTED SNOW ACCUMULATING AT THE FOOT OF A CLIFF

FIGURE 9.10B SPINDRIFT. WALKER APPROACHING THE RIDGE IS HIGHLIGHTED

9.5.4 Solar radiation

Later in the season, when the sun is higher in the sky, solar heating of the surface layer may occur, particularly on southerly aspects exposed to direct sunlight, leading to surface wet snow instabilities as the bonding between the snow crystals weaken. Single point releases leading to the production of 'roller-balls' or 'sun-wheels' are indicative of surface instability and they may combine (channelled) to produce a more significant avalanche.

9.6 Wind effects

Wind has a huge effect on the snow pack in our mountains and is usually the major influence. Crystals are moved and damaged by the wind as snow is moved and deposited in accumulation zones. These are areas, such as lee slopes, where the wind decelerates and can no longer transport the broken crystals *(see Figure 9.10A and B)*. Much of this wind-transported snow is carried in the first metre above the ground. The same snow can be moved several times with changes in wind strength and direction. While in general terms, erosion occurs on windward slopes and deposition on lee slopes, pockets of accumulation can occur on just about any aspect, especially in areas of complex topography such as the top of gullies. Cross-loading occurs where wind blows across a slope, generally scouring exposed areas and depositing localised drifts on the lee side. This can often affect features such as buttresses and gullies.

9.6.1 Wind features

One very distinctive erosion feature is sastrugi *(see Figure 9.12)*. These are wind-carved ridges which can vary in size from little ripples to larger ridges which can make difficult going. They run parallel to the direction of the wind that created them, with the steep V shaped erosion face pointing into the wind. Another feature is raised footsteps which are formed when initially soft snow is compressed by boots and made harder. If the wind then removes the surrounding soft snow these are left upstanding, indicating the slope they are on has been scoured *(see Figure*

FIGURE 9.11 CROSS LOADING: TYPICAL 'HAZY' SCENE AS SPINDRIFT IS BLOWN ACROSS THE SLOPE. WIND SLAB WILL ACCUMULATE IN THE GULLY AND OTHER LOCALISED SHELTERED AREAS

FIGURE 9.12 SASTRUGI

9.13). Raised footsteps and sastrugi indicate snow movement and the important question is where the transported snow has been deposited.

9.7 Snow types and formations

Snow on the ground is subject to a number of processes. These alter the snow pack and can lead to some fairly easily recognised snow types. Different snow formations may also be produced.

FIGURE 9.13 RAISED FOOTSTEPS WITH RIME FORMED ON THE WINDWARD SIDE

9.7.1 Dry loose snow

Unconsolidated snow, formed from crystals falling in sub-zero temperatures and light winds, usually referred to as 'powder snow'.

9.7.2 Wind slab

Wind slab is formed by the breaking and packing of snow crystals. The wind breaks up crystals by turbulence in the air or by blowing them along the ground. When these broken crystals are re-deposited, the resultant snow pack is known as wind slab. The hardness of wind slab is extremely variable depending on the strength of the wind, temperature and humidity when it formed. Generally it is divided into two classes – hard or soft slab. Soft slab is produced by lighter winds while hard slab is produced by strong winds. These can vary from snow in which you sink up to your knees to hard enough to require the use of crampons. Because of the weather conditions in this country, wind slab is extremely common and can even be formed when there is no snowfall. Wind slab can be deposited extremely quickly and be very unstable. A deposition rate of more than 3cm per hour is considered to be dangerously high and drifting can produce values of ten times this or more. Once settled, wind slab is subject to the changes outlined previously.

Wind slab may often be recognised by its characteristic dull colour and chalky appearance, especially when compared with other snow types, and its fine, smooth texture *(see Figure 9.10A)*. It may be apparent as whiter layers if lying on top of old snow, which usually has a greyer, and more textured surface. It may give a squeaky noise when walked on or when an axe shaft is pushed in.

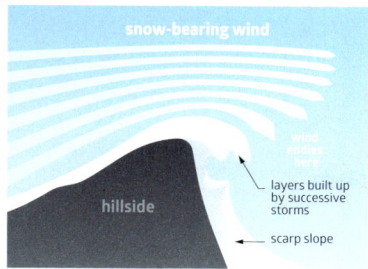
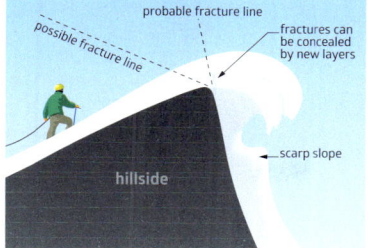

FIGURE 9.14 CORNICE

FIGURE 9.15 CORNICE BREAK-OFF

9.7.3 Wet snow

Wet snow forms where the temperature is above freezing, but there are many variations in consistency. These are related to crystal size, the prevailing weather pattern, and drainage. Bright sun has less effect on snow than you would suppose, but warm rain rapidly affects the snow pack. Large, rounded crystals, such as found in the spring are less affected by thawing, as water may be able to drain freely through them. Younger snow with less-developed crystals becomes slushy and water-logged sooner.

9.7.4 Cornices

Cornices are overhanging masses of snow, usually found on the lee side of sharp changes in slope angle such as on ridges or plateau edges. These are created by a cylindrical eddy that forms as the wind blows over the edge. Wind strength and direction, availability of snow and actual shape of the ground are the main contributory factors to the cornice's size and shape. Below the cornice on the lee slope, more snow is deposited. This is known as a scarp slope and the snow here can build up to high angles and can often be unstable wind slab *(see Figure 9.14)*.

It is often difficult to establish the extent of a cornice from above and the break-off point may be much further back from the edge than anticipated *(see Figure 9.15)*. Freshly formed or thawing cornices are the most unstable and liable to present the greatest hazard, collapsing spontaneously *(see Figure 10.16A on page 124)*. Very occasionally a change in wind direction can produce a double cornice on a narrow ridge. These are difficult to deal with safely.

HUMAN TRIGGERED SLAB AVALANCHE ABOVE THE SADDLE, STRATH NETHY, CAIRNGORM *PHOTO // SAIS*

10

Avalanches

In very simple terms an avalanche will occur when the force of gravity acting on the snow pack exceeds the strength of the anchors keeping the snow in place on the slope.

When an avalanche occurs a mass of snow will move downhill, typically at speed and originating from a **start zone**, travelling via the **avalanche track**, to a deposition or **runout zone** *(see Figure 10.1)*. Some avalanches will travel considerable distances, but even a small one may have serious consequences for the winter mountaineer. Avalanches may occur each season in locations with the same start zones and avalanche tracks. There are several factors used to describe avalanches.

Type of release:
- loose snow (single point) or slab

Position of sliding surface:
- full or partial depth

Humidity of the snow:
- dry or wet

Form of the track:
- confined or unconfined and distance travelled

Type of movement:
- airborne or surface
- type of trigger: natural (spontaneous), cornice or human
- size of avalanche

FIGURE 10.1 AVALANCHE CHARACTERISTICS

While there are several methods of classifying avalanches, the simple system described here is sufficient to describe the basic types of avalanche, bearing in mind that intermediate types are common *(see Figure 10.2)*.

10.1 Types of avalanche

10.1.1 Loose snow avalanches

When snow falls in conditions of very light or no wind, then loose snow or powder avalanches may occur, typically single point release. The greater the snowfall and the more rapid the accumulation of snow, the greater the danger, with falls of more than 3cm per hour and accumulations of more than 40cm representing high risks. Loose snow avalanches can occur when the weight of snow becomes greater than the strength of the bonds

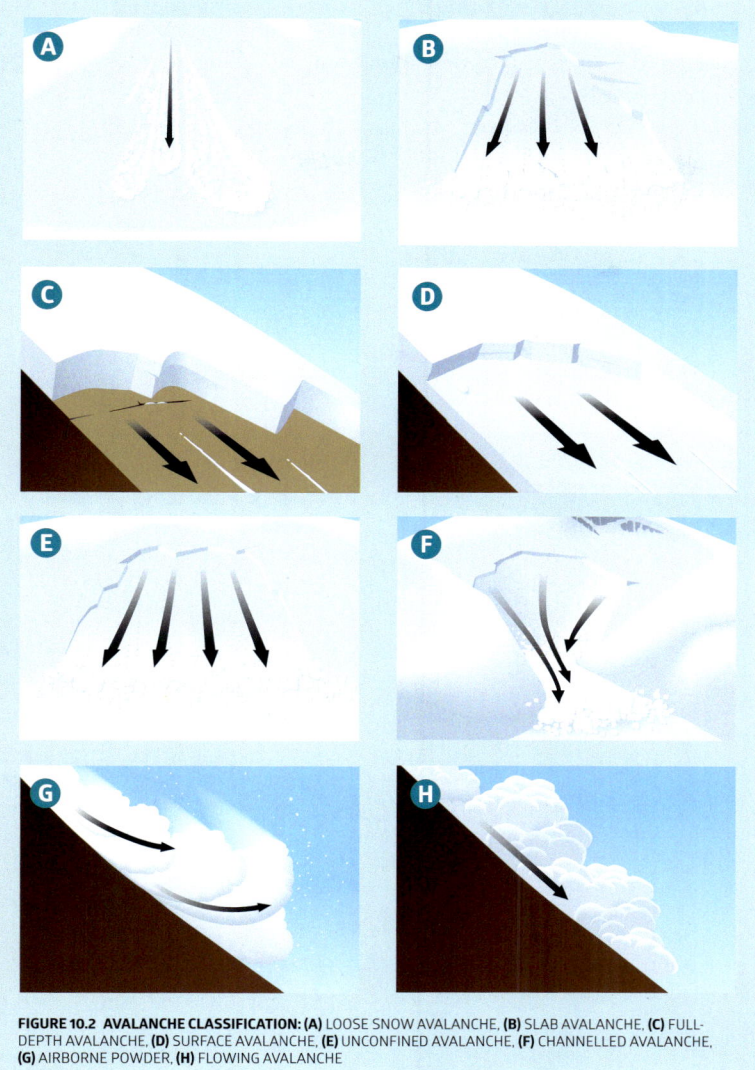

FIGURE 10.2 AVALANCHE CLASSIFICATION: (A) LOOSE SNOW AVALANCHE, **(B)** SLAB AVALANCHE, **(C)** FULL-DEPTH AVALANCHE, **(D)** SURFACE AVALANCHE, **(E)** UNCONFINED AVALANCHE, **(F)** CHANNELLED AVALANCHE, **(G)** AIRBORNE POWDER, **(H)** FLOWING AVALANCHE

within the snow pack. These are relatively uncommon in this country. They are more likely during snow-fall or in the 24 hours afterwards, but the danger will persist longer if the temperatures remain low and the processes of rounding and melt-freeze slow down. Small slides or sloughs, commonly known as a spindrift avalanche, are more common and are usually associated with wind-transported snow *(see Figure 10.3)*.

10.1.2 Slab avalanches

These are the most common and the most dangerous type of avalanche in this country. They occur when a discrete area of snow detaches from the surrounding snow pack and then rapidly breaks up into a mosaic of smaller blocks as it slides downhill *(see Figure 10.4)*. Depending on the

FIGURE 10.3 SNOW SLOUGH

FIGURE 10.4 SLAB BLOCKS FROM ABOVE

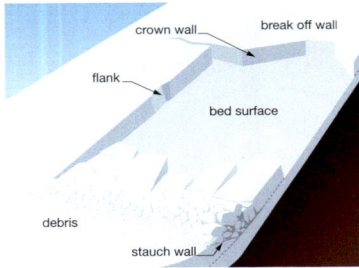

FIGURE 10.5 SLAB AVALANCHE

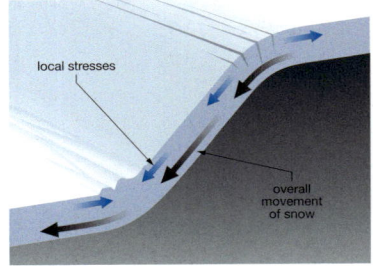

FIGURE 10.6 CONCAVE/CONVEX TENSION

FIGURE 10.7 PARTIAL DEPTH SLAB AVALANCHE ON A SCARP SLOPE BELOW A CORNICE

FIGURE 10.8 FULL-DEPTH SLAB AVALANCHE

hardness of the slab, these blocks may still be recognisable in the avalanche debris or have completely lost all form.

Slab avalanches can either be full depth, when the complete snow cover slides, or partial depth, when only the surface layer or layers slide. The surface which the slab slides on is called the bed surface and can be the ground, most likely a smooth layer such as rock slabs or vegetation such as grass, or another layer of snow. The break-off feature left at the top of a slab avalanche is the crown wall and its lower edge, which is much less defined and often obliterated, is the stauchwall *(see Figure 10.5)*. The bed surface is by far the most important in providing the strength of the slab's anchors and is therefore critical in an avalanche.

While slab avalanches can occur on slopes between 20° and 55°, most occur between 30° and 45°, with the mean figure at 37°. Below about 20° the slopes are generally too gentle although very well lubricated and heavy wet snow avalanches have occurred on even lower slope angles. Above about 45° snow tends not to accumulate in sufficient depths to form large avalanches but will usually slough off before dangerous amounts have built up. However, these can still be big enough to dislodge a walker or climber. The scarp slope directly below a cornice can have soft slab of 50° and greater.

FIGURE 10.9 GLIDE CRACKS

On uniform slopes, the tension within the snow pack will also be uniform. However, the snow pack is rarely uniform in depth and layering, which may lead to marked local variations in mechanical stability - spatial variability. On a convex slope there will be areas of tension and on a concave slope, areas of compression *(see Figure 10.6)*. Because of the tension at the top of a convex slope, avalanches are more likely to release from the top of these slopes.

Slab avalanches occur when the bonds anchoring the slab to the underlying layers (or the ground) fail *(see Figure 10.7)*. This can be due to a decrease in the strength of the bonds or an increase in the load. The trigger which sets the avalanche off can be internal – the weakening of bonds, such as the collapse of a fragile layer, or changes of snow pack properties due to temperature change. External triggers can be further snowfall, rain, melt-water or a sharp rise in temperature increasing the weight of the slab, cornice collapse or people on the slope. Large parties in particular apply a considerable extra load to the anchors securing a slab.

This failure of a weak layer can either be within the snow pack or at the surface of the ground. Sometimes this weak layer can be fragile crystals, such as facets, graupel or surface hoar buried by subsequent snowfall. If hard slab is deposited on top of softer snow, the softer snow can settle and leave the hard slab poised over empty space. If slab is laid on an old icy layer, the bonding can be very weak; in a thaw, meltwater can trickle over the hard layer weakening the bonds and providing lubrication. This also happens when the slab lies on a hard, impervious surface such as rock slabs, which is common in full depth wet slab avalanches *(see Figure 10.8)*.

Sometimes the reason for a slab sliding is not at all obvious and may be due to subtle differences in the slab caused by small variations in wind strength and direction, leading to differences in broken crystal size and shape as the slab was being deposited. These differing layers may only be seen after the avalanche has occurred.

A tension release fracture may propagate at speed across a slope (shooting cracks), typically where a slab is in tension on a convexity (roll-over) but the slab does not release because the internal bonding or ground anchors are sufficient to hold it in place.

10.1.3 Wet snow avalanches
These occur when the temperature is above zero. The snow pack becomes heavier and the bonds are weakened and lubricated by meltwater. These can be extremely destructive because of the weight of wet snow, but they are easier to anticipate with signs such as saturated snow, melting cornices and running water. Glide cracks can open up where the snow pack fractures due to the extra weight. However, it is very difficult to predict the time of their release release *(see Figure 10.9)*. Many wet snow avalanches occur within the first hour of the onset of rainfall.

10.1.4 Avalanche size scale
Avalanches are categorised on an ascending size scale of 1 – 5 *(see Figure 10.10)* relating to their typical dimensions, distance travelled, run-out and potential damage. However, a small avalanche of size 1, could seriously injure a person if they are knocked over on steep, exposed rocky terrain.

10.2 Avalanche awareness
The ability to assess the safety of snow covered terrain is challenging, but is paramount for anyone travelling in the mountains in winter. Good judgement makes journeys safer and this knowledge goes hand in hand with finding the best walking, climbing and skiing conditions and maintaining a low exposure to avalanche terrain and hazard. This ability takes time and experience and is part of the larger picture of winter walking and climbing. Avalanche awareness is composed of a number of factors, but the decision-making process should start long before any snow slope is reached. You should have a good idea of what conditions are like and where any hazards are likely to be found beforehand. This will be refined by your continual observations and assessments during your journey on the hill and modified if necessary, particularly in poor visibility. Importantly, ensure you have a flexible plan and are open to modify your journey when conditions dictate.

10.2.1 Sources of information
Scottish Avalanche Information Service (SAIS) – *www.sais.gov.uk*. During the winter season, the SAIS publishes on its website daily reports and blogs of observed and forecast avalanche, snow, and mountain conditions for a number of popular areas in Scotland *(Figure 10.11)*. Also

Avalanche sizes
(Based on the European Avalanche Warning Services (EAWS) avalanche size classification)

Size 1 (Small avalanche)
Potential impact: Could injure a person, or be potentially fatal, especially in steep rocky terrain. Unlikely to bury a person except in terrain trap run-out zones
Run-out: Typically stops on relatively steep terrain
Typical dimensions: Length; 10-30m, Volume; 100m^3

Size 2 (Medium avalanche)
Potential impact: Could injure or bury a person. Potentially fatal, especially in steep rocky terrain
Run-out: Can reach the end of the slope
Typical dimensions: Length; 50-200m, Volume; 1000m^3

Size 3 (Large avalanche)
Potential impact: Could damage or bury a car or trees
Run-out: Can cross flat terrain (well below 30°) over a distance of less than 50m
Typical dimensions: Length; several hundred metres, Volume; 10,000m^3

Size 4 (Very large avalanche)
Potential impact: Could destroy or bury a building or a truck or railway locomotive
Run-out: Crosses flat terrain (well below 30°) over a distance of more than 50m. Can reach the valley floor
Typical dimensions: Length; 1-2Km, Volume; 100,000m^3

Size 5 (Extremely large avalanche)
Potential impact: Could destroy a village or large forest. Can devastate the landscape and has catastrophic destructive potential
Run-out: Reaches the valley floor. Largest known avalanche
Typical dimensions: Length; approx 3Km, Volume; >100,000m^3

Note: In the UK, small and medium sized avalanches (size 1 and 2) are relatively common and due to the nature of steep and exposed rocky terrain, often combined with the existence of isolated areas of snow pack instability, smaller sized avalanches can have a significant impact on the winter mountain user.

FIGURE 10.10 AVALANCHE SIZES

available is a smart phone app for both iOS and Android devices, social media outlets including a YouTube channel for short video clips and a host of other educational information including the 'Be Avalanche Aware' initiative and an archive of all avalanche forecasts since 1993. The website and blogs are interactive and allow feedback. Using an online form, the SAIS encourages reporting an avalanche, especially if witnessed, which can provide useful information for all mountain users and which

SAIS avalanche hazard forecasting

During February and March 2018, prolonged cold spells produced strong temperature gradients in the snow pack in all SAIS forecasting areas. This led to the development of faceted crystals *(see Figure 9.6, page 102)* and depth hoar, which notably became a persistent weak layer (PWL) in most forecast areas. In the Northern Cairngorms area, natural avalanches up to size 4 were recorded during this time. The SAIS forecasters followed the development of the PWL and recorded this on the SAIS website, including in the relevant reports (Avalanche Hazard Forecast, Snow Profile and Observed Avalanche Hazard pages), in the blogs and in short video clips.

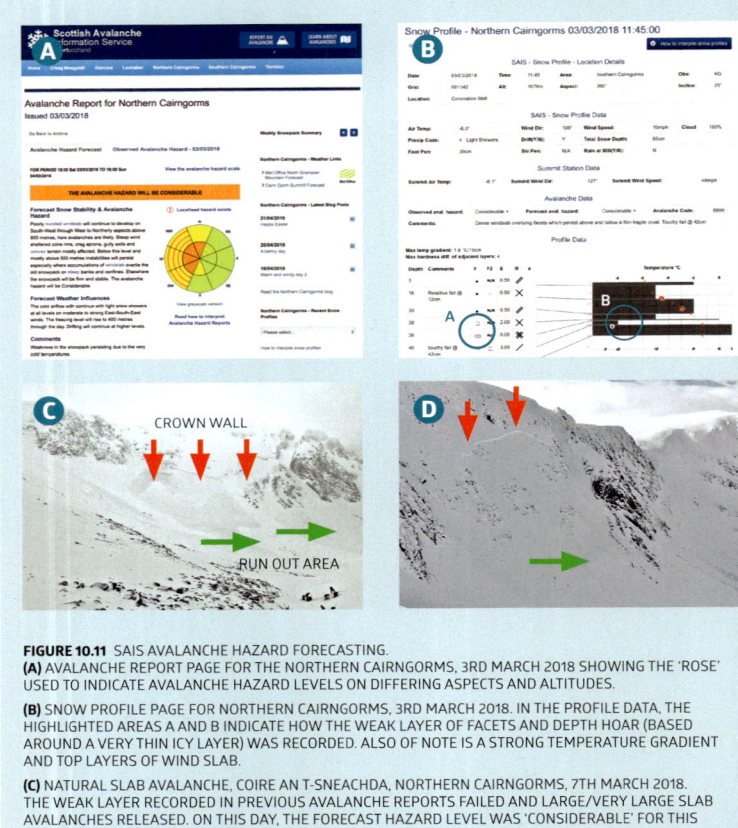

FIGURE 10.11 SAIS AVALANCHE HAZARD FORECASTING.
(A) AVALANCHE REPORT PAGE FOR THE NORTHERN CAIRNGORMS, 3RD MARCH 2018 SHOWING THE 'ROSE' USED TO INDICATE AVALANCHE HAZARD LEVELS ON DIFFERING ASPECTS AND ALTITUDES.
(B) SNOW PROFILE PAGE FOR NORTHERN CAIRNGORMS, 3RD MARCH 2018. IN THE PROFILE DATA, THE HIGHLIGHTED AREAS A AND B INDICATE HOW THE WEAK LAYER OF FACETS AND DEPTH HOAR (BASED AROUND A VERY THIN ICY LAYER) WAS RECORDED. ALSO OF NOTE IS A STRONG TEMPERATURE GRADIENT AND TOP LAYERS OF WIND SLAB.
(C) NATURAL SLAB AVALANCHE, COIRE AN T-SNEACHDA, NORTHERN CAIRNGORMS, 7TH MARCH 2018. THE WEAK LAYER RECORDED IN PREVIOUS AVALANCHE REPORTS FAILED AND LARGE/VERY LARGE SLAB AVALANCHES RELEASED. ON THIS DAY, THE FORECAST HAZARD LEVEL WAS 'CONSIDERABLE' FOR THIS ASPECT AND ALTITUDE.
(D) NATURAL SLAB AVALANCHE IN SAME LOCATION AS C, 8TH MARCH 2018. FURTHER WIND BLOWN SNOW DEPOSITION OCCURRED OVERNIGHT AND A SECOND LARGE SLAB AVALANCHE RELEASED HIGHER ON THE SAME SLOPE. THE AVALANCHE HAZARD LEVEL REMAINED 'CONSIDERABLE'.

also provides essential data for avalanche research. The avalanche reports may also be posted at key access points to mountainous areas and in local information points such as climbing shops and ski areas.

Other sources of information include climbing and walking guidebooks which may give some indication of where avalanche risks are most common and internet blog sites such as UKC (ukclimbing.com) which may have reports of current avalanche activity.

FIGURE 10.12 BAA TRAINER PACK

FIGURE 10.13 SLAB BREAKING UP BELOW FOOTSTEPS: A DANGER SIGN

'Be Avalanche Aware' (BAA)
In 2011, the BAA initiative was developed following collaboration between many agencies and groups from throughout the UK and further afield with the objective of addressing the 'avalanche situation' in Scotland. Organised by the Snow and Avalanche Foundation of Scotland (SAFOS) and managed by the SAIS, a BAA leaflet was introduced in the winter of 2013, later followed by the BAA app. The BAA guidelines outline a decision making process for winter mountain users, based on fundamental considerations of assessing avalanche hazard and essentially offering good advice for winter mountain users.

Any decision that is made in the winter mountains concerning avalanche awareness and hazard evaluation is based around three fundamental factors: 1 Weather, mountain conditions and the avalanche hazard; 2 Your (and your party's) skills and experience; 3 The mountain terrain and landscape you intend to visit. Additionally, these factors in turn should be considered and evaluated during each of three phases leading up to and during your trip: A Planning; B Throughout your journey in the mountains; C Key places and times during your journey.

The planning phase is by far the most important, starting at home over the long term by keeping up to date with snowpack and avalanche information updates throughout the winter, modified in the short term with avalanche/weather forecasts and current information on the amount of snow you expect in the mountains. Check that your skill and experience levels match the trip you are planning, such as ice axe and crampon skills, winter navigation and that you have the appropriate clothing and equipment for the expected weather and conditions.

15 BAA Trainer Pack
Consider using the 'Be Avalanche Aware' Trainer Pack *(Figure 10.12)*. It is a useful teaching resource which encourages a process of avalanche hazard evaluation and decision making, using information gathered at base and cue cards during the journey on the hill.

10.2.2 Planning your trip

The map
The map is important to give an initial picture of the mountain landscape you intend to visit and is crucial at the planning stage as a source of information. Some idea of slope angles, the location of features such as windward and lee slopes, safer routes such as ridges and more suspect slopes can all be gained from studying the map and considering the weather patterns.

Past weather
Weather conditions in the period (weeks to hours beforehand) leading up to a trip into the mountains will have great bearing on evaluating the avalanche hazard. Follow the weather and avalanche reports to form some idea of what is happening in the hills. Important factors are precipitation, particularly snow amounts and where it is lying, wind strength and direction, and freezing levels. Note that wind speeds of greater than 15mph will transport snow and form unstable wind slab. If appropriate, check recently published SAIS avalanche reports for both where and what level of hazard exists and it also includes a detailed weather forecast.

Preparation
If the terrain is likely to be steep and complex, you will require good mountain skills. Check that your equipment is in good working order and that your clothing will be appropriate for the trip. Are you fit enough to cope with long days, travelling in deep snow packs and navigating in severe weather conditions? Can you use axe and crampons effectively?

10.2.3 The journey

Present weather
What is happening on the approach to the mountains will give you clues about to what to expect. The weather may not fit particularly well with the forecast conditions, especially as weather systems move faster or slower than predicted and are affected locally by the mountains. On the walk-in and during the journey, the nature of the snow on the ground and any snow in the air should be noted. Wind strength and direction are crucial information and any signs of spindrift (snow redistribution) are a sure sign that wind slab is forming and avalanche conditions need to be kept in mind. The nature of the ground underfoot is equally telling and whether it is thawing or freezing. Signs of snow erosion such as raised footprints or sastrugi can indicate deposition elsewhere. Signs of deposition such as wind slab and cornices must be noted.

The rate of precipitation is important if it is snowing, but it must be considered along with the wind strength and direction. Low levels of accumulation in one area may translate into a rapid build-up where the terrain encourages accumulation, for example, at the top of depressions such as stream-beds, gullies and gully exits. Consider the effects of cross-loading.

Thawing conditions can also lead to an increased avalanche risk but rising temperature may not always be obvious and can be masked by factors like strong wind or how cold you feel (wind chill). However, higher temperatures are generally fairly obvious with signs such as slushy snow, running water and snow, ice and rime falling from rocks which become dark with water. The presence of roller-balls also indicates rising temperature; these are wheels of snow which have rolled down the slope, often starting from exposed rocks. Note should be taken of any cornices or cracks forming in the snow pack, such as glide cracks and tension release cracks, particularly on convex areas.

Most importantly, any rapid accumulation of snow or evidence of recent avalanche activity should never be ignored.

The snow below your feet
Walking on or through snow can also provide clues as to the stability of the snow pack. Whether the snow is hard or soft, icy or damp, consistent or crusty provides more information. Snow breaking away below your feet, particularly as blocks, or a squeaky noise consistent with wind slab are signs to note *(see Figure 10.13)*. Also by slowly pushing your ice axe shaft into the snow and feeling the resistance as it penetrates can give clues about any major differences in hardness.

10.2.4 Mountain features

Past and present weather conditions must always be considered in conjunction with the terrain itself. On easy-angled slopes, there may be no danger, even if many of these conditions are present. But on steep complex terrain with poor run-outs there may be a considerable hazard with only a few subtle indications. A few puffs of spindrift may be all that shows of dangerous accumulations in localised sheltered bowls hidden amongst rocks or below cornices. Slope angles are important, not just the ones that you are on but also the ones above you. Likewise the shape of the slope; convex slopes are more likely to be an avalanche risk but concave slopes are more likely to be corniced.

While slope angles are notoriously difficult to estimate, there are some angles which are easy to find. Use shafts of equal lengths, such as axes or poles, and with one placed vertically on the surface, slide the other at right-angles until it spans the gap between slope and vertical. For half height, the slope is about 30°, while from the top of the vertical, the measurement is obviously 45°. Other angles can be better estimated from these base lines which are also the range of common slope angles most likely to avalanche. If standing facing the slope you can rest a hand on it, then this is roughly 60°. Most smart phones will have an inclinometer (or able to download an app) which can be used to give slope angle by placing it on an ice axe shaft or pole lying on the snow surface.

FIGURE 10.14 COLLECTING SNOW PACK DATA FROM A SNOW PIT *PHOTO // JON JONES*

Terrain traps
The actual depth of an avalanche tip in the run-out zone will depend on the nature of the ground it runs onto. If the debris all collects in a hollow, then this may be out of all proportion to the actual size of the avalanche, as all the snow is funnelled into a limited area. These terrain traps can turn innocuous snow slides into death-traps. They can be found in many places such as changes in angles in gullies, in stream-beds, below rock outcrops or any natural depression.

Human factors – heuristic traps
It is accepted that human factors can play a significant part in avalanche accidents. We all use simple rules or heuristics when faced with complex decisions. A heuristic which leads to a decision making error is called a heuristic trap. In the winter mountains, common 'traps' may be related to – familiarity; 'we did this before so it will be ok again' (going to the same place and doing the same activity regardless), commitment; 'we planned for ages to do this and travelled a long way' (continuing with an objective even in bad weather/conditions), social evidence; 'other folk have done it/are doing it, so it must be ok' (a perceived 'expert' must know what they are doing), scarcity; 'the conditions are perfect this weekend and I'm fit enough' (a rare opportunity is presented). Smaller groups (2-3 people) and/or groups with an experienced leader are often safer because communicating, agreeing objectives and making decisions is easier than in larger groups.

Be aware that these heuristic traps exist so that they are recognised in your decision making processes.

10.3 Closer observations

While most observations are made from prior knowledge, during the journey and on the approach to steeper ground, when intending to move onto steep snow slopes, then a closer examination of the snow can provide further useful information. There are a number of methods used to examine the nature of the layers of snow comprising the snow pack.

However, they should never be used in isolation to evaluate a slope for an avalanche risk.

10.3.1 Snow pit
A snow pit is a hole in the snow, roughly one metre wide, dug to give a vertical back wall providing a snow profile in which the layers making up the snow pack can be seen. It can be dug with a shovel or an axe before the back wall is smoothed off so the layers can be identified and examined. It is normally dug down to the ground but if there is a sufficiently hard

> **ⓘ 16 Snow pits in context**
> Snow pits and stability checks should not be demonstrated or encouraged for general use as a means of avalanche hazard evaluation. They should be considered as a teaching aid; as an introduction to how a snowpack develops throughout the season and how the bonding of differing layers within the snowpack affects its stability. However, if a snow pit is used, the information collected can always be put to good use for other aspects of winter walking and climbing such as constructing belays and snow anchors or making emergency shelters.

and stable layer, then this will be deep enough *(see Figure 10.14)*.

Normally a snow pit is dug at a safe location in a protected site at the edge of the slope or on a smaller slope at the same altitude and aspect as the one to be investigated. Effort can be saved if the pit is dug in a shallow part of the snow pack. While this will show a similar stratification of the snow pack, the layers will vary in thickness and typically, the layers near the foot of a slope can be thinner than those at the top. A thin and almost insignificant layer near the bottom of a slope, particularly the top layer, may actually be much deeper near the top of the slope. This is often the case on the scarp slope below a cornice such as at the top of a gully.

Next, square the side walls and smooth off the back wall with the adze or shovel blade, not a hand as this will smudge any visible layering. Once smoothed off, the snow layers can be examined on the back wall of the pit for a number of different properties. As a simplification, the more the layers of the snow pack are alike the more stable it is likely to be and the greater the difference between adjacent layers, the greater the instability. The first task is to examine the stratification for visible differences between layers. These layers may be differentiated by gently prodding with the finger at intervals, from the top down through the snow pack or scraping with the edge of something hard such as a laminated card or a compass to feel for differences in resistance. Then, if appropriate, a series of checks can be done to highlight the properties of the snow layers. Examination of the layers is conducted at the edge of the back wall, leaving an undisturbed middle area for a stability check if necessary, and done prior to further investigation. A more detailed examination of a snow profile would be used as part of a formal avalanche assessment including temperature, crystal type, grain size and snow density.

10.3.2 Hardness

The hardness of a layer can be assessed by what object can be pushed into it and each hardness given a number between 1 and 5.

1. Gloved fist
2. Gloved fingers
3. Single finger
4. Pencil or ice axe spike
5. Knife or ice axe pick

10.3.3 Wetness tests

The wetness of a snow layer has a bearing on its weight and strength and again can be tested on a scale of 1 to 5 depending on how easy it is form a snowball.

1. Does not form a snowball (dry snow)
2. Forms a snowball (moist snow)
3. Snowball forms easily with a drop of water when squeezed (wet snow)
4. Water can be easily squeezed out (very wet snow)
5. Continuous stream of water (slush)

The information gained is used to help distinguish differences between layers, the hardness test being the most useful. While digging the snow pit, note should be made of features such as failures (clean shears as one layer slides on an adjacent layer) that occur when digging, layers which are particularly weak or hollow, any icy layers or crusts which could form sliding surfaces.

10.3.4 Crystal and grain size

This can be examined by eye (on a dark background such as a jacket sleeve) or with the use of a hand lens. In basic terms, new snow will exhibit snowflake form, wind slab shows broken crystals and the larger and more rounded the crystal, the older it is likely to be. Features such as faceting, buried surface hoar and graupel may show up in this crystal examination. Sometimes these very weak layers may show when digging a pit, such as by a very hollow layer or by graupel flowing out from the face, but often these layers are too thin to test. Visual examination however, can often highlight these dangers.

10.3.5 Stability checks

If there is a large difference between adjacent layers or an obvious weakness in the snow pack, then it may be appropriate to conduct a further check to identify any instabilities.

Shovel or hand test

This test is most useful when looking at the layers near the surface, particularly thin layers. First, isolate a block of snow about 30cm by 30cm using a snow saw or more usually the axe shaft. This is cut down to the level of the first suspect layer and simulates the release of all tension in the snow pack, it being held in place only by the bonding between the layers. Then the shovel or flat hands are carefully put down the back of the test block and forward pressure gently applied *(Figure 10.15)*. If using a shovel, it is important to avoid levering but to ensure a steady pull parallel to the snow surface. The force required to release any layers gives an indication of the strength of the bonds between layers and the stability of the snow pack only in the immediate area. After testing the upper layer, this procedure can be repeated on lower layers to ground level or until a hard stable layer is reached. This test is very subjective regarding the actual amount of force required to make a failure, but any very easy fails will indicate an obvious instability. However, as the area of each test is very small and the slope will not normally be homogeneous, it cannot be used in isolation to make a decision on the wider snow pack stability. To build up a fuller picture a check can be repeated at other locations and the information gained used in conjunction with wider snow pack observations.

FIGURE 10.15 DOING A HAND SHEAR TEST AFTER EXAMINATION OF THE BACK WALL OF A SNOW PIT

A degree of objectivity can be gained by using the hand shear test with the following scale in order of increasing load on the test block:

1 The block fails while isolating it
Kneel with straight arms parallel to the snow surface:
2 Fails when gently placing the hands down the back slot
3 Fails with a cock of the wrist (the load is applied across the block by spreading the fingers)
4 Fails with a gentle rock back onto the heels
5 Fails with a hard pull back
6 Does not fail

In very general terms, when the block fails at Stage 1 and 2 there is a major weakness in the test block, at Stage 3 and 4 there is a significant weakness, Stage 5 there is a weakness and Stage 6 the layers are well bonded. It is also worth inspecting the shear planes or surfaces of the test block. If it is a clean smooth shear, there is a weak layer or poor bonding between layers, and if there is a ragged uneven shear, there is unlikely to be a weakness.

Shovel tap (Compression) test
Isolate a column of snow about 90cm wide and 30cm deep and lay the shovel head on the top of this at one end. The shovel is then given a series of taps to see where and how easily the column fails. Firstly, give ten taps with fingers swung from the wrist, then ten with the knuckles swung from the elbow and finally ten swings from the shoulder. The ease with which any fails occur gives some indication of the snow pack stability, but the nature of the shear plane should also be examined. Any smooth shear is likely to be more significant than one which is ragged. Also, note if the failure propagated across the column and the rate of propagation. A partial propagation would not indicate as great an instability as one travelling at speed across the full 90cm.

Axe test
The axe shaft can be pushed down into the snow pack and the differences in resistance noted. If this is done with an action applying the same

FIGURE 10.16A SIZE 2 SOFT SLAB AVALANCHE. START ZONE: AT 900M, BELOW SUMMIT RIDGE. TRIGGER: SPONTANEOUS CORNICE COLLAPSE AFTER RAPID OVERNIGHT GROWTH. TRACK: INITIALLY OPEN SLOPE BUT BECAME CHANNELLED. RUN-OUT: AT 550M CROSSING NORMAL ROUTE INTO CORRIE!

FIGURE 10.16B KEEPING TO THE CREST OF A ROUNDED RIDGE TO AVOID THE MORE EXTENSIVE SNOW SLOPES ON EITHER SIDE

pressure to the spike each time, variations in hardness can be detected. This is also a useful way of continually monitoring a slope after a snow pit has been dug gaining further information on the local snow pack. Any changes in depth or hardness of the top layers should be apparent.

Boot test
Another quick test to perform when the snow underfoot is obviously slabby is gently to stamp out a ledge in the snow about two boot-lengths long. Step above the ledge about 20cm and apply weight gradually until a shear occurs. These tests can be done quickly when on the move and if they indicate any instability, then further evaluation of the avalanche hazard should be carried out.

10.4 Hazard evaluation

The purpose of these observations is to build up as accurate as possible a picture of the snow pack and therefore the avalanche risk of the slopes encountered. Observation and experience are vital for avalanche assessment. If there are signs of any avalanche activity anywhere in the mountains, this is a warning sign of existing instability.

10.5 Avalanche avoidance

10.5.1 Route selection

When travelling in snow-covered terrain, the risk of avalanches from the slopes you are on, possible hazard from slopes overlooking your proposed route, and general avalanche terrain exposure should be guarded against. If the assessment has been made that there is a hazard, then the first option is to avoid that terrain. At the start of the day, this will almost always be the best option when a different route or even retreat are still possible. At the end of the day, it may not be so easy with the pressures of time and maybe worsening weather to contend with. Then slope stability and route selection can be a matter of life or death and all available

Avalanche Checklist – Top 10 Factors

1. Visible avalanche activity: if you see avalanche activity in an area where you intend to go, go somewhere else.
2. New snow build-up; more than 3cm/h and more than 40cm continuous build-up is regarded as very hazardous. The majority of avalanches occur during snow storms and up to 48hrs after.
3. Slab lying on ice or névé, with or without aggravating factors such as thaw.
4. Discontinuity between layers, such as loose graupel pellets or air space.
5. Sudden temperature rise. The nearer this brings the snow temperature to 0°C, the higher the hazard, even if thaw does not occur.
6. Slope angle – most large slab avalanches run on slopes between 30° and 45°.
7. Slope profile – convex slopes are generally more hazardous than uniform or concave slopes. The point of maximum convexity is a frequent site of tension fractures, with the release of slab avalanches.
8. The cornice factor – soft slab scarp slopes are notoriously unstable. Collapsing cornices frequently trigger slab avalanches on the slopes below.
9. Avalanches can happen to you – around 90% of avalanches involving people are triggered by their victims.
10. Feels unsafe – the 'seat of the pants' feeling of an experienced person deserves respect.

information must be used to make your decision. Again the first thing to consider is avoiding the slope. Route selection and hazard evaluation can never be made in isolation from other factors, such as the state of the party, their experience, the whole range of snow and weather conditions, time and equipment, all of which will affect the choices you may have (Figure 10.16).

If suspect slopes have to be dealt with, there are some precautions which can improve the safety margin. While this may be the last and least favoured option, there are times when there may be no choice.

- Move between islands of safety such as rock outcrops. Stay at the sides of gullies, next to the rock, rather than in the middle.
- Travel one at a time and avoid having the whole party on the same suspect slope.
- Wait in a safe location when moving one at a time.
- Go straight up or straight down a slope rather than going diagonally.
- If on a suspect slope, look at the possible run-out and terrain traps below.
- If a slope must be crossed, traverse it high up so that if an avalanche occurs, you are on top of the slide rather than being buried from above.
- Avoid areas of tension if a convex slope must be crossed.
- Follow in the first set of tracks.
- Look out for cornices, not just straight above but also any which could be funnelled onto your route, such as down subsidiary gullies.

- Watch for increase in depth of surface slab accumulations, particularly when in ascent.
- Remember that just because one or even several people have moved safely, that does not mean that the slope is safe and will not then avalanche.
- Propagating a tension fracture or feeling a slope 'settling' (often accompanied by a 'whoomp' sound) are major signs of instability. Re-asses your route selection.
- Take extra care in descent, particularly at the top of slopes where you can quickly become exposed to avalanche hazard. Similarly in poor visibility and inclement weather.

10.5.2 Personal preparations

If you must move into a hazardous area then these few preparations can be helpful.

- As many avalanche fatalities are due to asphyxiation, cover the mouth and nose with clothing such as a scarf, balaclava or hood.
- Put on warm clothing in case of burial and cover any gaps.
- Take your hands out of axe leashes or walking pole straps.
- Rucksacks, especially heavy ones, are best worn with the waist strap undone and the shoulder straps loose or even with one off so that the sack can be jettisoned if a slide occurs. A heavy sack is more likely to pull the wearer into a head downhill and face down position in an avalanche. It is more likely that the sack will be ripped off by the avalanche than that you will have the time to remove it if caught.

10.5.3 Belaying

Using a rope to belay party members is only an option if the slope is narrow, such as a suspect gully. While this may prevent the person on the rope being swept away if the slope goes, there is a chance of injury due to the weight of snow crushing them. Another danger is that they can be pulled under by the action of the rope, so there is a chance of deeper burial should the avalanche not totally pass over them. There may even be a chance of belay failure. Unfortunately, there are many uncertainties in using a rope and each case needs to be examined on its own merits.

10.5.4 Action if caught

If caught in an avalanche there are some defensive actions which can improve the odds. While variables such as the type of avalanche, be it powder, slab or wet snow, can affect the effectiveness of these strategies, they, or improvisations on them, have had helpful results.

- Delay your departure for as long as possible so that you are nearer the top of the slide and less likely to be deeply buried. Use the axe as in the self-belay or even to self-arrest in the bed surface.
- If near the fracture line, make a big effort to get some purchase on the other side of it.

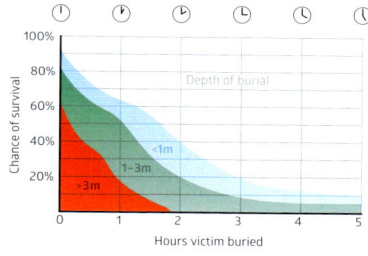
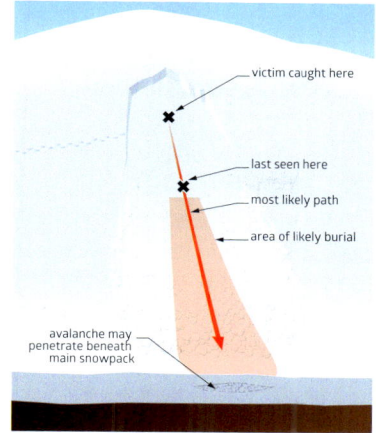

(ABOVE) **FIGURE 10.17** PROBABILITY OF SURVIVAL RELATED TO TIME AND DEPTH OF BURIAL

(RIGHT) **FIGURE 10.18** LIKELY BURIAL PLACES

- Before you go, try to see where the avalanche edges are and shout to attract attention of other group members so they can track your position.
- Try to roll diagonally towards the nearest edge.
- Make every attempt to stay near the surface of the avalanche by 'swimming'. Head up with your back to the slide seems to be the best position.
- If on hard slab try to stay on top of a block and ride it down.
- As the avalanche slows down, further actions can improve your chances of survival. Note that most avalanches stop quickly!
- Make a concentrated and concerted effort at this stage.
- Make a huge effort to get to the surface or at least get a limb free.
- Keep a hand in front of your mouth and nose to avoid snow blocking the airways.
- Try to establish an airspace in front of your face as the snow settles.
- If totally buried, try not to panic and use up precious oxygen and don't shout as this will not be heard on the surface.
- If possible try to start digging in front of your face. This may be impossible, particularly with damp snow which may solidify extremely rapidly when the avalanche has come to rest.

10.5.5 Survival

From previous accident statistics in Scotland it would appear that in about 70% of parties carried down in avalanches, someone is injured or killed. Of those carried down about 30% are injured or killed with 7% carried down killed and 24% injured. 12% of those carried down in avalanches are buried. In the case of fatalities around 50% die through asphyxiation and the rest through trauma, usually by hitting something.

The deeper and longer the burial, the less the chance of survival. If the victim is uninjured by the avalanche and they are rescued in less than 15 minutes they have a greater than 90% chance of survival but this falls dramatically up to about 45 minutes after which the decline is less rapid *(see Figure 10.17)*.

10.5.6 Rescue

While avoidance is paramount, knowing what to do in the event of someone being caught in an avalanche can save lives. The first consideration however, must be your own safety. Firstly, check that no further avalanches are likely, either from the slopes that you are on or from above. This is particularly the case where there are branching gully systems.

If you see someone being avalanched then watch carefully, follow their path and mark where the avalanche hit them and where they were last seen. These points should be physically marked with spare equipment. The victim should be somewhere close to the line running downhill from there to where the avalanche stops *(Figure 10.18)*. Speed is now vital but try to attract the attention of anyone else who can assist. If more than one person was involved in the avalanche then the same should be done for each one if at all possible. If it was your own party involved, check the numbers missing.

A visual search of the debris should be carried out immediately, looking for anything protruding through the snow: clothing, equipment or blood may give clues to the burial site. If this is not successful then the avalanche debris must be probed. This is best done with avalanche probes but if these are not available then poles with the baskets removed, tent poles or ice axes can be used although these are likely to be too short for anything but a very shallow burial. First, the area of maximum accumulation is probed then any other areas where a person could be buried on the avalanche track are searched. These could be terrain traps such as hollows, stream-beds or amongst large boulders.

Only if there is a large number of people available should someone be sent for help at this point. Immediate searching is vital and the first 30 minutes is the crucial period for finding a live victim. Help may be summoned by mobile phone in some areas. The rescue services will need full details of the accident including a six-figure grid reference, description of the site with particular reference to any routes and perhaps compass bearings to significant landmarks, the number involved in the accident, the number of rescuers and the equipment available.

Once located, the victim should be dug out immediately. The first priority is to free their head, clear the nose and mouth and remove any snow constricting their chest. If the victim is not breathing then clear the airway and start artificial resuscitation straight away. When recovering a victim, a shovel makes a huge difference compared with using the hands and ice axe, especially as the snow in an avalanche tip may be quite firm and compacted.

Anyone who has been involved in an avalanche is quite likely to have sustained major injuries and should be handled accordingly. Take care to avoid trauma, especially when digging out a victim, and remember anyone buried for any time is likely to be hypothermic.

10.5.7 Organised searches

If the victim is not found initially, then a full search will be needed. Avalanche dogs are very effective at searching for buried victims but they and their handlers are only likely to be available some time after the incident. Bad weather, compact and icy snow and other distracting smells will hamper the dogs' ability to scent a buried victim. Avalanche dogs and their handlers are trained and organised by the Search and Rescue Dog Association (SARDA) and will usually work in conjunction with a mountain rescue team. If dogs are to be used do not eat, smoke or urinate near the avalanche as this could affect the dogs' sense of smell.

Should a dog not be available or fail to find the victim, then the avalanche debris will need to be probed. This is a time-consuming and labour- intensive process that requires a lot of people and organisation. A probing team of about 20 under a controller and backed up by a shovel party stand in line. Each person has an avalanche probe about 3m in length and stands elbow to elbow. On command the probe is pushed into the snow between the feet down to about waist level. On command the probe is removed, the line moves forward one pace (70cm) and probes again. If anyone feels anything, the probe is left in place and the shovel team gets to work while a new probe is given to the searcher. This is called a coarse probe and has a 75% chance of locating a buried body. With a fine probe, the probes are put in between the feet and also in front of each foot. The probe line moves forward a half step (30cm) each time. This has a 100% chance of finding a body but is very slow.

10.5.8 Avalanche transceivers

Avalanche transceivers are the most effective means of finding a buried avalanche victim and are considered to be normal equipment for activities such as ski touring, particularly in Alpine areas. While used by some organised groups in this country, their use by walkers and climbers is not widespread. However, if transceivers are used they must be worn on the body, their use must be practised and certain checks carried out each day they are used. The availability of transceivers should never be used as a justification for venturing into hazardous avalanche terrain and avoiding normal safety precautions.

10.5.9 Recco® system

This two-part global system works on a radar technology signal basis, comprising a small lightweight reflector and a detector. Although originally developed for skiing, it is becoming more common in mountaineering. The reflector is a small piece of material which is carried or integrated into clothing and equipment and the detector can be hand held or search and rescue (SAR) helicopter mounted and is used by many rescue teams for locating buried avalanche victims. Since the reflector is very small, more than one can be used. If you are using Recco®, let someone know!

> **17 Equipment**
> Whilst there is no prescribed list of equipment that must be carried, in addition to an ice axe, Winter Mountain Leaders and Instructors may choose to carry other equipment such as walking poles, shovel, or probe which could be used to aid the rescue of someone buried by an avalanche.

WINTER MOUNTAIN LEADER TRAINING, CONFIDENCE ROPING ON THE NORTH EAST SIDE FIACAILL COIRE AN T-SNEACHDA *PHOTO // LOU BEETLESTONE*

part 4

Security on steep ground

WINTER MOUNTAIN LEADER TRAINING, CONFIDENCE ROPING ON THE NORTH EAST SIDE FIACAILL COIRE AN T-SNEACHDA PHOTO // GILES TRUSSELL

Providing security in winter

It may occasionally be necessary to provide unplanned security for one another, both as members of a party and for leaders and instructors in formal group situations.

A high level of competence and experience on difficult, steep or exposed ground is paramount so that attention can be focused on decision-making and using appropriate techniques, rather than worrying about the terrain, exposure and the consequences of a slip. In winter, additional factors, particularly environmental, complicate the situation and can turn a seemingly controlled scenario into an epic where good judgement, technical efficiency and quick decisions are required.

The skills required for providing security on steep ground in summer, using rock anchors and belays, can be adapted for winter and additionally include snow and ice anchors. While the techniques can be used in emergency situations, they are also the basis for anchors, belays and rope work when climbing.

11.1 Winter steep ground

Steep ground is a variable concept, is not the sole preserve of the winter climber and can refer to sections of open slope and terrain that in summer are quite benign, but in winter will require techniques not normally associated with walking. It is not only the angle and length of a slope which are important, but the type of ground, the quality of snow, the nature of the run-out and the consequences of a slip.

11.2 Security without a rope

Feeling vulnerable on steep open slopes, on little icy steps or on exposed mixed terrain can affect the confidence of less-experienced walkers. Security methods, actual or psychological, without the rope are similar to those used in summer.

Empathy and recognising signs of nervousness and loss of confidence are important. Simple methods of bolstering confidence such as encouragement, good communication, briefing and strategic positioning will help. If necessary, seek permission to use manual support, particularly if your actions could be in any way misconstrued. Sympathetic route choice such as keeping close to the edge of a steep snow slope can alleviate feelings of exposure. Also, stopping and cutting stances for rests may help, as can using crampons for security, particularly if the snow is hard and confidence is waning. Equally, on short exposed sections of snow, cutting steps to easier ground is an option. Often, planning ahead and anticipating likely problems can avoid situations developing.

In winter, be very cautious when using spotting techniques, as the consequences of inappropriate positioning can be serious if a fall or slip occurs. Be particularly aware of crampons and ice axes causing injury. Stay close to the person being assisted so that a slip can be stopped immediately. Offering assistance from above may be possible by presenting the ice axe for support from a stable stance above, the head of the axe being offered as a hold or hooked onto with another axe.

11.3 Using a rope for security

Using the rope is a last resort and is best avoided through planning, route choice, effective navigation and, for leaders, good party management. But

Tape knot

For joining two ends of tape, to make a sling, for example. It is vital to tighten up as much as possible and leave long tails (at least 10cm) as this knot can creep along the tape over time.

Overhand knot on a bight

The overhand knot on a bight may be tied anywhere in the rope. The closed loop is used to attach to an anchor or attach a person to the rope.

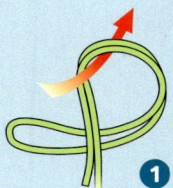

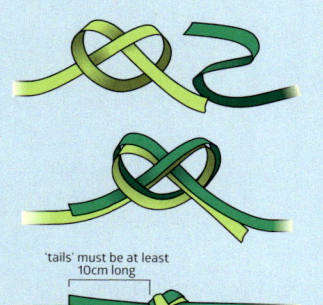

Overhand knot to join two ropes

An overhand knot is the quickest way to join two ropes and is very effective as long as the knot is pulled tight and has tails at least 60cm long. It is slightly less prone to jamming in cracks when being retrieved from an abseil.

Overhand knot

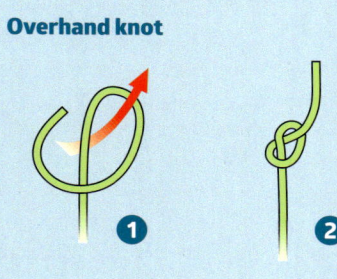

simple solutions such as using the rope or sling for confidence to give psychological rather than actual support can sometimes be appropriate. It should be obvious if a whole group needs roped security, such as when the terrain is beyond the technical abilities of the group members and a slip cannot be safeguarded otherwise. Strategies for coping with these situations should be thought through and alternatives considered before deploying the rope. For example, in ascent, it is probably easier to descend and go elsewhere!

Finding winter anchors and belays, assessing their strength and using them effectively are important skills for leaders and mountaineers alike. Anchors and belays can be made with a rope and a small amount of technical equipment. The same rope can be used as in summer, however longer sections where security is required are more common in winter. Since there is a compromise between weight and effective length, a longer thinner rope is preferable to a shorter, large diameter one: it should be at

Figure of 8

The figure of eight is one of the most popular knots because it is versatile and simple to learn. It is easy to see if it's been tied correctly as it looks like an 8 and is safe because making an error results in an overhand knot or a figure of nine, both safe knots in their own right. A figure of eight has many variations, it can be tied in a single strand of rope or in a bight of rope to create a loop (Figure of eight on a bight). A loop can also be formed by re-tracing a single figure of eight (Re-threaded figure of eight).

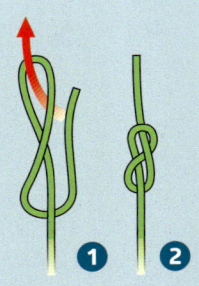

Figure of 8 on a bight

The figure of 8 on a bight may be tied anywhere in the rope. The closed loop is used to attach to an anchor or attach a person to the rope.

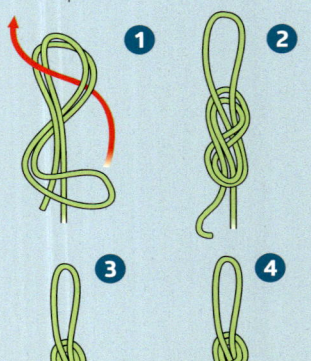

Rethreaded figure of 8

The rethreaded figure of 8 is commonly used for tying on to the end of the rope or threading anchors. A stopper knot is normally added, or leave a tail at least 25cm long.

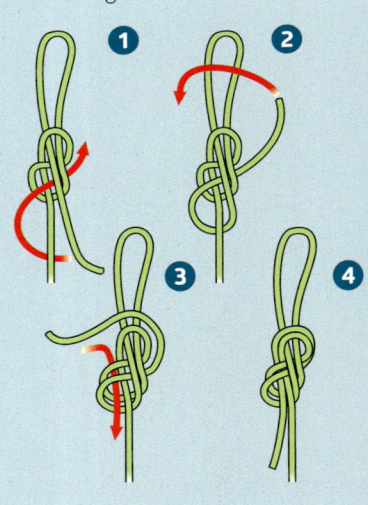

Bowline

A popular knot used for tying on to the end of the rope as it is quick to tie, easily adjusted and relatively easily untied after it has been loaded. It must always be secured with a stopper knot.

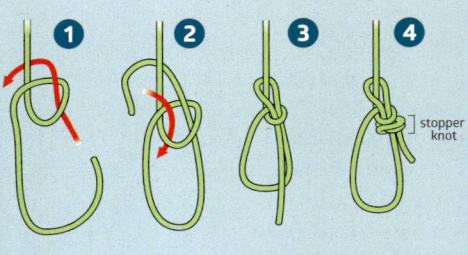

Stopper knot

Used to secure the rope end of other knots, normally the figure of 8 or the bowline.

Clove hitch

Very useful for tying onto anchor karabiners due to its simplicity and adjustability. The load rope should be positioned next to the back bar of the karabiner.

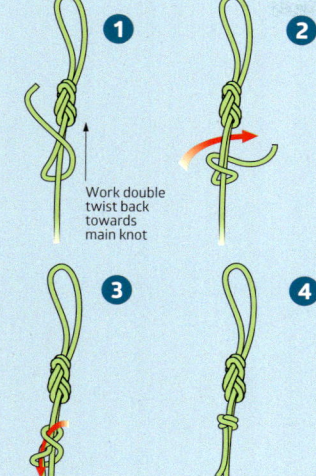

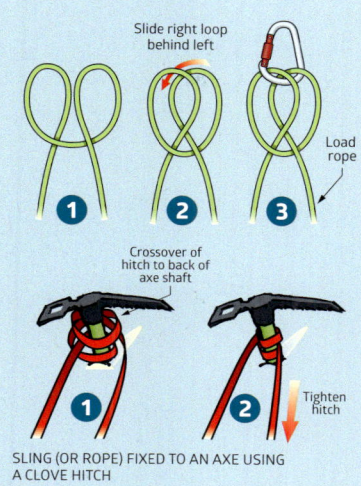

SLING (OR ROPE) FIXED TO AN AXE USING A CLOVE HITCH

Stoppered slipknot

1 The preferred method of attaching people in quick succession as...
2 its size is easily adjusted.
3 Initially judge the size of the waist loop relative to own size.

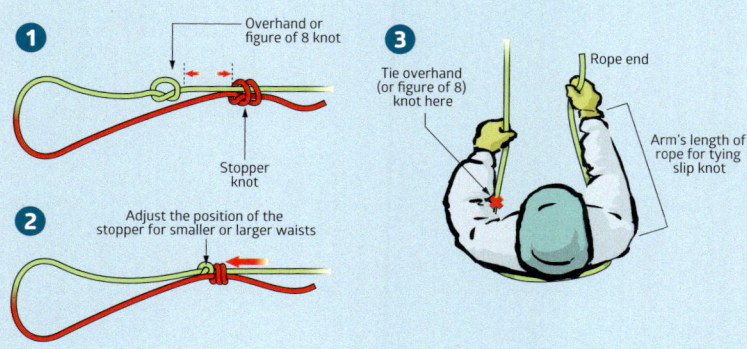

least 30m long and around 8mm in diameter.

Other emergency equipment includes a long nylon, Aramid or Dyneema® sling (120cm minimum) and a large HMS (pear-shaped) screwgate karabiner with a large gate opening which easily accommodates the rope and allows manipulation when wearing gloves. The rope, sling and karabiner can be stored in a stuff sack carried in the rucksack.

Note: Equipment carried outside of the rucksack may become wet and/or iced up and difficult to use and ropes, knots in slings and karabiner

gates may become frozen during legitimate use. Try re-warming frozen equipment by using heat from your breath and warm hands, then manipulating knots by pushing the strands through the knot to loosen them off. Frozen karabiner gates may be gently tapped with the axe to break an icy seal and weighting a screwgate karabiner whilst trying to unscrew the sleeve may also help.

When using the rope in an emergency, the same considerations apply as in summer. The following key rope-handling skills should be familiar:

11.3.1 Tying relevant knots
These include: the overhand and figure of eight knots which can be used singly, on a bight, re-threaded and tied-back versions; the bowline; clove hitch and tie-back using two half hitches; the stopper knot; the Italian hitch (used with an HMS screwgate karabiner) and the lark's foot.

11.3.2 Attaching to the rope
To tie on to the rope, the figure of eight and overhand knots (using re-threaded and bight versions) and the bowline can be used; the bowline being the easiest to adjust. The stoppered slipknot is useful when the rope is used for several people in succession as it is easily adjusted, but it can pull open if loaded on the waist loop. A bowline on a bight (improvised sit harness) or a bowline on a coil can be used where the load is spread more around the waist rather than concentrated in a single loop, and a sling and screwgate karabiner can be used to make a sit sling *(see Figure 11.1)*.

When attaching to a rope end, the tie-on loop is judged tight enough when a gloved hand can just fit between the rope and the waist, remembering that the loop will stretch under load and as clothing compresses. Methods of attaching an additional person include using an isolation loop if they are in-line or, less commonly, a 'Y' hang if they are side by side *(see Figure 11.7 and 11.8 on page 149)*. Both allow control of each person simultaneously rather than only the person closest to the belayer, as would be the case if they were tied directly to the rope and in-line.

11.3.3 Tying to anchors
Most belays use a stance, such as a bucket seat with a snow anchor and the belayer tied to the end of the rope. It is important that the belayer is tight to the anchor. There are then several options:

- If the anchor is within reach then the rope can be tied directly to it. For example, a figure of eight on a bight looped over a block or spike, or a clove hitch tied to a screwgate karabiner, which is easier to adjust to the correct length.
- An anchor that is out of reach requires the rope to be tied off at the belayer using a figure of eight on a bight tie-back through the waist loop or a clove hitch on a screwgate karabiner clipped to the waist loop.

Lark's foot
Useful to attach a sling to a person for confidence roping or from a harness to an anchor for personal safety. Not to be used in shock-loading situations.

Tying to anchors – Belaying using a distant anchor

1 Attach rope to anchor and move down to stance
2 Face anchor and kneel down to tie figure of eight tie-back, as a sitting stance is required with a low anchor

3 Keep anchor ropes taut as figure of 8 is tied
4 Tighten figure of 8 by pulling the tail of the knot towards the anchor

5 A clove hitch tie-back into a screwgate clipped to the waist loop is much easier to adjust than the figure of 8. Orientate karabiner so that the back bar faces up to prevent the moving waist belay rope inadvertently opening the karabiner

6 Turn around and move knot to the back, under your rucksack, if you are wearing one. Waist belay rope runs above anchor ropes and may run around rucksack for comfort

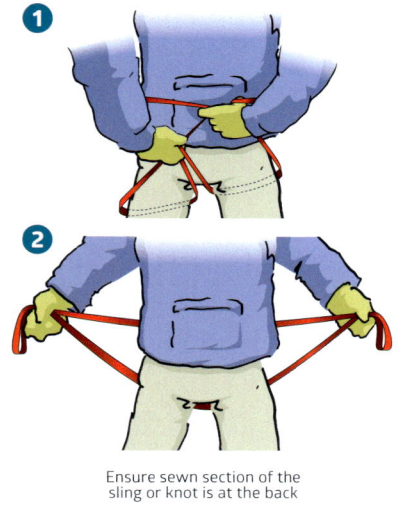

Ensure sewn section of the sling or knot is at the back

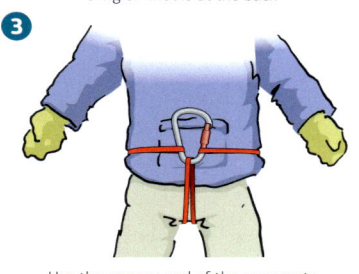

Use the narrow end of the screwgate to clip the loops

FIGURE 11.1 THE SIT SLING IS AN IMPROVISED HARNESS THAT MUST BE USED APPROPRIATELY, AS IT HAS A LOW CENTRE OF GRAVITY

Examples include a screwgate karabiner that is out of reach, or when the rope is round a snow bollard or large block anchor.

Attaching a sling and screwgate karabiner to the anchor, although it adds more links to the belay chain and uses extra equipment, simplifies the process of tying to buried axes, threads, spikes, blocks or ice bollards.

When tying into an anchor from a bucket seat, kneel at the back of the stance facing the anchor and clove hitch or tie back as appropriate. Leaning forward slightly when tying back with the figure of eight on a bight will take up small amounts of slack. The anchor rope will be tight when you are in the belay position *(see Figure 11.2)*. Although time-consuming, tying the end of the rope to the anchor then stepping into a waist loop positioned at the stance saves on rope. However, stepping into a loop on a steep slope has its dangers when wearing crampons or in windy weather. On a standing stance, small amounts of slack in the anchor rope can be taken up by lowering the stance by scraping away the snow floor of the stance using your feet.

11.3.4 Controlling the rope

Controlling the rope, whether loaded or not, is done using friction. This is created either by running the rope around the belayer's body, by using a friction hitch through a screwgate karabiner, or by direct friction around the anchor. The belayer can create friction around the body by using the waist belay *(see Figure 11.3)* or a shoulder belay used with the stomper *(see Figure 12.3 on page 157)*. The Italian hitch is the most commonly used friction hitch *(see Italian hitch on page 138)*. In some situations a simple twist around the screwgate karabiner gives enough control. A rock anchor may be used directly to create enough friction to control a loaded rope *(see Figure 11.5)*. A waist belay can be used as well to give more control when using direct anchors. Ice will not generate enough friction for a direct anchor and a loaded rope running over snow, such as around a snow bollard, will cut through the snow.

Tying to anchors – Positioning at stance

Anchor ropes tight and in-line vertically with belayer and expected load.
A High anchor: belayer may stand or sit
B Low anchor: belayer must sit to bring anchor in line with expected load
C Adopt the middle position where anchor, belayer and expected load are all in line, both vertically and horizontally

11.4 Descent techniques

Unless down-climbing is comfortably within the ability of the belayer, the rope will also be required to safeguard descent. Careful anchor selection is essential if the rope is to be retrieved and no equipment left behind. The rope is doubled around a snow or ice bollard or a rock anchor that allows a free-running rope so that it can be retrieved, but this halves the distance that can be rope-protected.

There are three main descending techniques: 'angel's wings' and the classic and South African abseils *(see Figure 11.6)*.

11.5 Group organisation

The group should be in a safe area away from danger before being attached to the rope. On a slope, this may mean digging comfortable stances, self-belayed with axes. If exposed to the weather as on a descent over an edge, a group shelter may be used to advantage, but be careful that it does not blow away, especially when there are few people in it. Individuals can be called to a collecting area where they can be tied on safely.

Tying to anchors – Directly with the rope

A The most efficient method (easier to adjust tight) is to tie back from anchor to waist tie-on loop
B If a spike or block anchor is close to the stance, a rope loop (overhand or figure of 8 on a bight) may be attached to the anchor
C The end of the rope is tied to the anchor and belayer attaches to a rope loop at the stance – difficult to adjust tight to the anchor but uses the least amount of rope

D The rope end is attached to a thread or chockstone using a re-threaded figure of 8 or a bowline
E An alternative method to D is to untie from the rope, thread the anchor, tie back on, move to the stance and tie off at waist

11.5.1 Briefing

A thorough briefing of the situation and procedures to be used should be given in a calm, clear and confident manner. Usually in an emergency situation, the weather will be bad and any form of communication can be very difficult. It is essential that the briefing includes everything that needs to be known as it may be impossible to communicate clearly later.

11.5.2 Communication

Keeping contact may be difficult, so it is vital that some form of communication is maintained. Visual communication works best when combined with some form of hand or arm signals. Verbal instructions are acceptable when someone is near, but can be impossible in bad weather, particularly if the person is out of sight. Rope-tugging signals can work well if kept simple, but whatever method is used, it must be made clear during the briefing.

Tying to anchors using a sling and karabiner

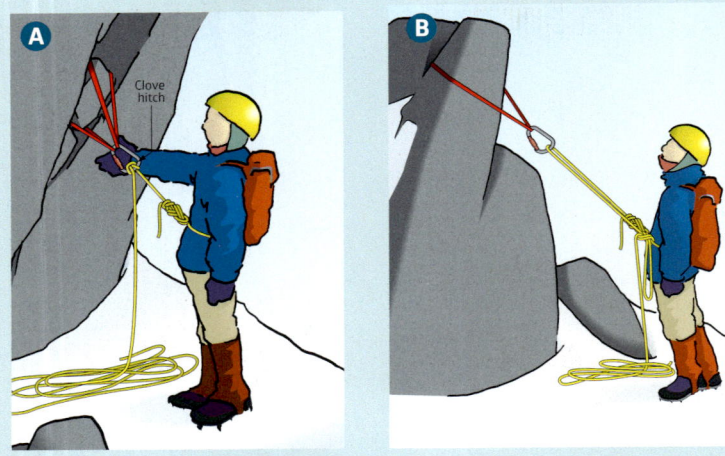

Note: Use a locking karabiner on single-point anchors
A Karabiner within reach: clove hitch
B Karabiner out of reach: clip in rope and lock the gate, move to the stance and tie off at the waist

11.5.3 Keeping control

When the rope is used in descent, for example over a cornice onto a steep slope, how to maintain control once over the edge must be considered. Who is going first, how far down the slope the descent will be and how the lower collecting zone is to be prepared need to be decided. Normally, sending a well-briefed experienced party member first is the best option. Techniques for descending may include reversing down with the person's weight taken by the rope, or sliding down a snow slope under the leader's control. This can be efficient, but may be more daunting, so the time saved may be minimal compared with reversing down. Also, beware of crampons snagging in the snow.

FIGURE 11.2 TYING OFF AT A BUCKET SEAT STANCE

Descending over a corniced edge is safer if it is first inspected and prepared. Choose the safest and easiest section of cornice and approach it using the anchored rope for security. The cornice can then be chopped down or a slot cut through. Do not have people hanging free, or at the very most, only for a very short time. Some weight may be taken off the waist of the person being lowered by tying a hand-hold loop in the rope within reach.

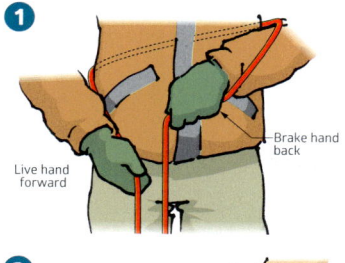
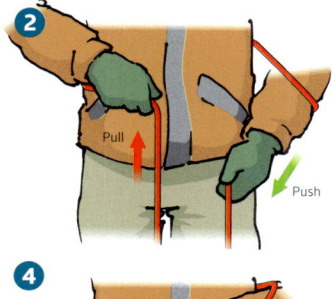
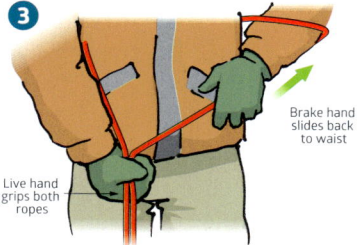
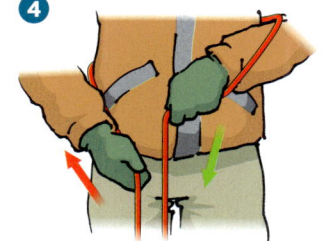

Waist belay in operation – Taking in

1 Take in live rope hand over hand until tight onto second. Flick a large rope loop overhead (and rucksack, if you are wearing one) to position around waist. The live hand grips forward and a rope twist is taken around brake hand arm
2 Slack is taken in with a push-and-pull action
3 Slide live hand down rope and grip both ropes in front of dead hand
4 Live hand releases grip on dead rope and repeat process
Braking and locking off
5 Braking and locking off

FIGURE 11.3 WAIST BELAY OPERATION

Controlling the length of descent is done by locking off the rope, so that the person being safeguarded stops and cannot go any further. They then dig a stance to the side of the descent line, stand in it and remove the rope carefully, particularly if wearing crampons and stepping out of a loop. It is preferable to remove the rope by untying a knot such as a bowline.

11.6 A sense of urgency

In an emergency situation, there will be a sense of urgency, particularly as weather and conditions are likely to be poor. Being able to find anchors, set up belays and manage the rope efficiently is vital, and good judgement will allow quick and appropriate decisions to be made. It is possible, with a good belay, to safeguard two people at a time in descent, although this

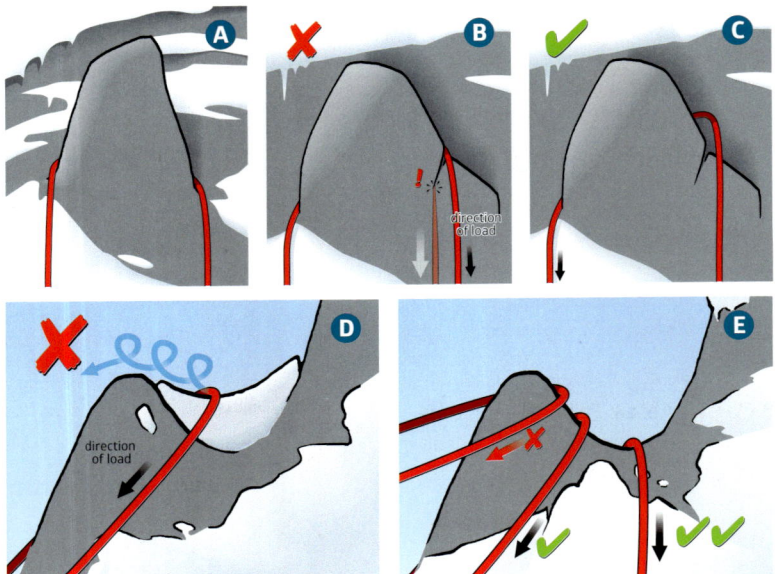

FIGURE 11.4 DIRECT BELAY – ROCK ANCHORS: (A) COMPLETELY REMOVE SNOW AND ICE FROM BEHIND BLOCK/SPIKE AND THOROUGHLY TEST FOR ITS SECURITY **(B)** ROPE MAY JAM IN CRACK **(C)** SPIKE MAY BE IMPROVED BY REVERSING THE ROPE AND HOLDING THE 'DEAD' SIDE CLEAR OF THE CRACK **(D)** ICE AND SNOW LEFT BEHIND SPIKE CAN ALLOW ROPE TO ROLL OFF **(E)** CLEARED OF SNOW, THE SPIKE CAN BE IMPROVED BY A DOWNWARD LOAD, BUT IT WILL BE WORSENED BY AN OUTWARD LOAD

FIGURE 11.5 DIRECT BELAY – ROCK ANCHORS: KEEP TENSION ON THE ROPE WHEN USING A DIRECT BELAY TO PREVENT A SHOCK LOAD IN THE EVENT OF THE SECOND SLIPPING. USE A PUSH–PULL ACTION, SIMILAR TO THE WAIST BELAY, TO MOVE THE ROPE AROUND THE ANCHOR. LOWER ON MODERATE GROUND BY USING BOTH HANDS ON THE DEAD ROPE, OR FOR GREATER CONTROL ON STEEPER DESCENTS, FACE THE ANCHOR AND USE A WAIST BELAY ON THE DEAD ROPE

reduces the amount of useable rope. Consider the weight and the length of the descent.

Tie one person onto the end of the rope, either directly or using a stoppered slipknot. The next person is tied on using an overhand isolation loop further up the rope *(see Figure 11.7)*. This distance depends on the steepness of the ground, as there must not be any contact between people during the descent, particularly when wearing crampons. The less steep, the closer together they can be. Safeguarding two at a time in line is

A Angel's Wings: This method is only suitable for low-angled descents. The rope runs around the back to create friction and both hands grip the rope. Friction is increased by taking a twist of rope around the lower arm.

B Classic Abseil: This technique is notoriously painful and is difficult to control on very steep ground. Turn sideways so that the rope does not cut directly into the groin for a slightly less painful descent. Classic abseil may be used with a single strand of rope.

C South African Abseil: Requires two strands of rope. Begin by stepping between the ropes and pass them under the arms. Each rope can be held individually or both ropes held in one hand, which allows the free hand to aid stability and fend off obstacles

FIGURE 11.6 DESCENT TECHNIQUES

initially difficult, particularly with a steep drop-off, regardless of whether a waist or a direct belay is used. The difficulty is keeping the rope on belay and tight to the person tied into the end of the rope (albeit only a very short distance) until the second person starts the descent on belay. This can be overcome by having the most competent person on the end of the rope and by initially keeping the rope hand tight. Safeguarding two in a Y-hang is another option since the weight of both is taken simultaneously by the belay *(see Figure 11.8)*.

11.7 Problems in ascent

It is unusual to need to use the rope in ascent while walking as retreat is the preferred option. Should it be absolutely necessary, then beware of problems with communication and control. In a group situation, a major difficulty is getting the rope back to the others after the first person is up. Usually, the weakest person is tied on first before the leader leaves the stance and the most experienced member ascends last and may be able to assist the others. Throwing the rope back down accurately can be difficult or even impossible in windy conditions and on longer sections of ascent. When throwing the rope, it must be flaked out so it runs freely and sufficient hand coils taken to provide some weight. Another option is to use the 'rope bomb' *(see Figure 16.7 on page 247)*. On exposed ground it may be necessary to brief people not to move off their stance to retrieve the rope in the event of an inaccurate throw. A good briefing and a clear demonstration of how to attach to the rope is necessary. Try to avoid having to descend and re-ascend after attaching each person to the rope.

11.8 The leader's safety

The leader's safety is paramount. Attach to anchors on exposed stances, rope up near corniced edges and protect steep descents. If abseiling over a cornice once the group is down, then a snow bollard is the ideal anchor, as no equipment needs to be left. Whichever abseil method is used, it is important to stay low when negotiating the edge to ensure that the pull is downwards on the anchor. Slide sideways over the edge until below the anchor then continue as normal. On less steep slopes, descending hand over hand or 'angel's wings' style can be quick and efficient.

To release a stuck abseil rope, undo twists and lessen the angle of pull and friction over the edge by moving out if possible. In secure locations, employ group members to add pulling weight.

11.9 Protecting near a corniced edge

Avoiding corniced edges is best, but there may be occasions when it is necessary to approach or follow one, for example, when looking for a descent route or using an edge as a handrail when navigating in bad visibility. When handrailing an edge, others must walk inside (away from the edge) of the leader's line. If the cornice must be approached, then the rope can be anchored back from the edge and used for security. Security can also be gained by being roped to others, but a clear briefing and good preparation, anticipation and communications are vital.

The leader ties on directly with a figure of eight on a bight, a bowline, or an improvised rope harness. This depends on the size and nature of the cornice and any likely break-off. If the leader could end up hanging free below the cornice, then an improvised harness or wider tie-on loop must be considered. The others are tied onto the rope about 10m from the leader, well away from the cornice. At least two experienced (particularly in ice axe arrest) 'heavyweights' are needed as a counterbalance should the leader fall (three or four group members are recommended), and tied in about 2m intervals *(see Figure 11.9)*. The rope must be kept taut between

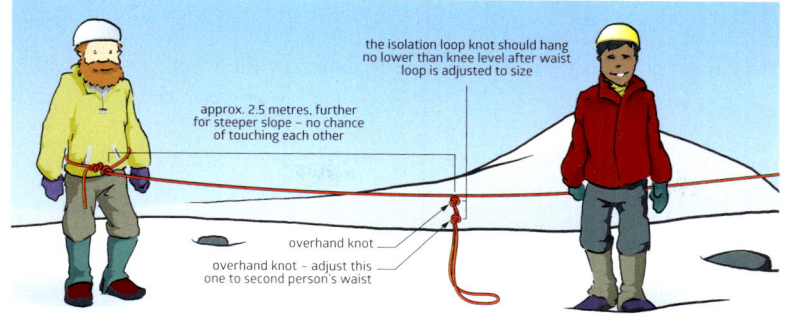

FIGURE 11.7 ATTACHMENT FOR TWO PEOPLE – IN LINE

A In-line: Lowering in-line using an Italian hitch and direct belay

B Y-hang: This method may be awkward on steep ground for those being safeguarded as there is a tendency to knock together. A longer extension from the knot enables more independence for each person.

FIGURE 11.8 SAFEGUARDING TWO PEOPLE ON A ROPE: BOTH METHODS REQUIRE A SOLID BELAY, GOOD CO-OPERATION BETWEEN THOSE BEING SAFEGUARDED AND IS NORMALLY USED ON TERRAIN WHERE THEY CAN SUPPORT MUCH OF THEIR OWN WEIGHT

the leader and the others and it is appropriate to have them tied on in line and direct to the rope. Overhand bights may be tied into the rope between the leader and the first person. These dig into the snow if a cornice collapses and help slow down the leader in the event of a fall. However, this shortens the available rope and takes more time to prepare. The first loop is within reach of the leader so it can be used as a handhold to aid in re-ascent or to take some weight off the waist tie-on should they be briefly free-hanging.

Fewer people may be used as counterbalance if the slope runs up to the cornice and more needed if there is a descent towards the edge. Communication that allows the group to move efficiently with tight ropes, towards, away from, or parallel to an edge and also to stop and go needs to be developed. Hand or arm signals work well if there is good enough visibility. Briefing on what to do in the event of the leader disappearing from sight is important as they could be hanging in space

FIGURE 11.9 PROTECTING TRAVEL NEAR AN EDGE

FIGURE 11.10 CONFIDENCE ROPING: CLEAR AND CONCISE DIRECTIONS ARE OFFERED TO ENCOURAGE CONFIDENT TRAVEL

and need lowering onto the slope below before being helped out.

11.10 Confidence-roping

Confidence-roping should only be used on ground where a slip will not have serious consequences. Physical support may be given by the leader, who can prevent a slip or a stumble developing into a fall, but it is primarily a confidence-boosting, one-to-one technique. In a group situation, the others have to be considered and monitored as well. Since winter conditions vary so much, ground that gives no problems one day may be treacherous the next, such as when wet snow freezes overnight. The situation and conditions need to be continually assessed and decisions made regarding the appropriateness of the technique. Confidence-roping is most likely in descent, where the most efficient line is straight down the fall-line or in steep zig-zags. Beware that the rucksack may interfere with the rope or sling. On a uniform snow slope where there are no difficult steps to negotiate, confidence-roping is straightforward. However, on mixed ground the principles are the same as those used in summer.

In most situations on a uniform slope, a long sling can be used. It can be attached round the other's waist by tying an overhand loop and it must be under the rucksack. The leader holds the end of the sling in the open loop or back over their wrist as in a walking pole grip. If more length is required the sling can be attached to a secure point on the rucksack using a karabiner or a lark's foot. Make sure that buckles are strong enough if attaching to a waist belt or shoulder strap. Long waist belt or shoulder strap tails may be tied back or together to reinforce the buckles.

Changing direction – Confidence roping and short roping:
1 Stop and make secure
2 Face downhill and place axe under arm
3 Swap rope over
4 Take axe and place it securely in snow
5 Turn to face new direction and safeguard other/s as they change directions

FIGURE 11.11 CHANGING DIRECTION

If the rope is used, then pull a few metres from the rucksack and attach directly to the person's waist. A knot can be tied in the rope for improved grip. Sometimes it is convenient to hold the waist loop for security, so a stoppered slipknot is inappropriate. There must be enough rope to allow full arm extension yet not so much slack that it could tangle or trip you. If a little extra rope is required periodically to negotiate small obstacles and steepenings, then when not in use, the excess can be tucked under a shoulder strap or waist belt, or a few small hand coils carried.

For security, the rope or sling is held tight, with the leader directly above the person, the distance between is as close as manageable without contact being made and the axe is carried in the uphill hand with the rope or sling in the downhill. Tension is maintained by dynamic body positioning and the leader's arm is bent in a strong position, with the elbow acting as a shock absorber and secondary tension adjuster *(see Figure 11.10)*. If there is any significant diagonal between the persons, then a slip could lead to a pendulum swing which may be impossible to hold. This may mean that if moving diagonally, or traversing, both people follow the same line but at different levels.

In a traverse or zig-zag ascent through soft snow, it may be more efficient to have the person follow footsteps rather than remain directly below. When changing direction, facing downhill makes swapping over axe hands easier. First, stop and have those on the rope secure themselves with good steps and their axe. Facing downhill, place the shaft of the ice axe under an arm, swap the rope over to the other hand, take the axe with the new free hand, place it securely in the snow and turn around to face the new direction *(see Figure 11.11)*

CONSTRUCTION OF A SNOW BOLLARD BELAY

Basic winter anchors & belays

Snow is generally considered to be the weakest medium for anchors, ice is stronger but the strongest anchors are rock. It is the strength of the snow that determines which type of anchor is used.

12.1 Snow anchors and belays

Snow varies enormously in hardness and can vary from place to place, even within a small area. The more consolidated and uniform the snowpack is, the greater the choice of anchor and in hard, consolidated snow, an anchor can be very strong. Information about the snowpack can be gained from the snow profile (you may have already dug a pit to assess the snowpack structure), or simply by pushing your axe shaft into the snow to gain a 'feel' for the layering within.

There are four basic principles that apply to indirect belays:

1 The belayer is tied tight to the anchor to reduce the shock if loaded.
2 The anchor, belayer and load rope must be in line. If the belayer is out of line, they will be pulled to a position in line with the anchor and the force.
3 The anchor should be above the level of the belayer's waist so any load pulls downwards rather than out.
4 The belayer is in a position to see and communicate with the person being safeguarded.

Imagine what will happen to your belay if it is loaded and position your stance accordingly.

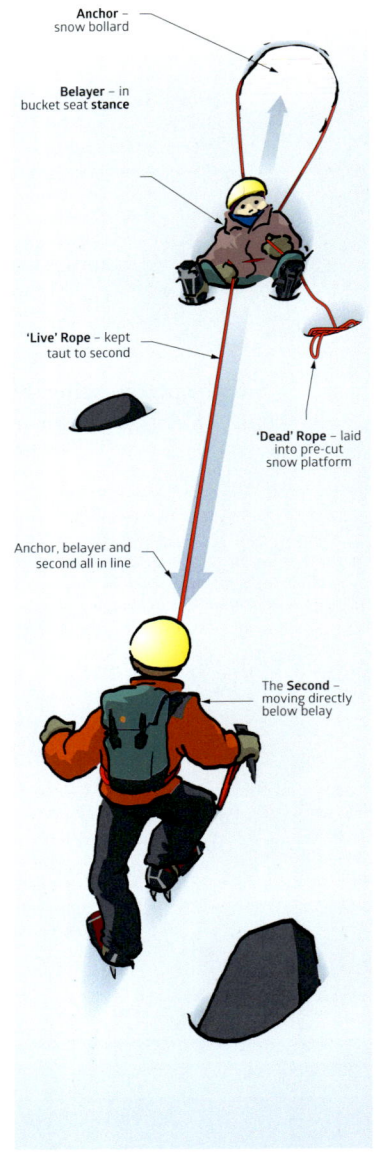

FIGURE 12.1 ELEMENTS OF A SNOW BELAY

12.1.1 Using snow belays

Snow belays can range from a simple solid stance such as a bucket seat, to a full belay which uses three elements: the stance, the snow anchor and the rope. The rope is used to attach the belayer to the anchor and a waist belay, to provide security for the climber by the rope running around the body for friction. Snow belays can be used to hold a fall in a lead climbing situation using the waist belay, or simply to provide security where the

> **ⓘ 18 Snow anchors**
> Since it can be difficult to assess the strength of snow anchors, the more experience gained in placing them and setting up belays, the better your judgement will become. Practise placing various anchors in different situations and test them for strength. If they fail, try to work out why, and how they may be improved, or try another type of anchor in a similar situation. Choose a safe practice slope and fill in holes after use. If testing an anchor by pulling on a rope, leave a long tail end which can be held (or secured) from above to prevent the anchor being pulled out violently and causing injury. Use a knot that unties easily after being loaded, such as a clove hitch or locked-off Italian hitch.

belay is above the person being safeguarded and the rope used for support *(see Figure 12.1)*. A bombproof snow anchor may be used directly if it is not going to be shock-loaded. If the snowpack is less than perfect, or in a lead climbing situation, a full snow belay is required to ensure that the anticipated load can be controlled indirectly using the waist belay where the belayer takes part or most of the strain.

12.1.2 General considerations

There are several different types of snow anchors and there are some general considerations applying to them all:

- Assess the snowpack carefully and use the strongest snow layer. The harder the snow is, the more load bearing it will be – the anchor is only as strong as the snow in which it is buried. Easy to dig soft snow will present the greatest challenge in which to construct a sound snow anchor.
- Choose an undisturbed area in which to make the anchor and try to disturb the snow around the anchor as little as possible both during and after construction. However, in certain conditions, for example soft wet snow, the anchor can be strengthened by compacting the snow by stamping down an area and placing the anchor at the top of, behind or around the compacted snow.
- Be neat, tidy and thorough with your anchor and belay construction. There is usually some urgency, so be as efficient as possible.
- The anchor, stance and expected direction of load should be straight down the fall-line *(see Figure 12.1)*.
- The pull on the anchor must always be down into the slope. Therefore, the shallower the slope angle, the greater the distance must be between the anchor and the stance to permit this.
- The rope is flaked in its own stance and away from the working area and cramponed boots where there is the possibility of tripping or spiking the rope. This is cut or stamped out beforehand close to the belay and on the dead-hand side.
- If necessary, remove your rucksack but ensure that it is well secured.

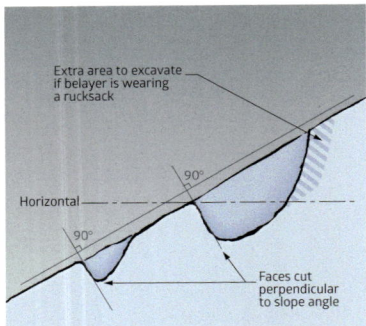 

FIGURE 12.2 BUCKET SEAT CONSTRUCTION: THE SEAT MUST NOT BE TOO DEEP OR THE LEGS WILL BE PUSHED TOWARDS THE CHEST AND COMPROMISE THE OPERATION AND CONTROL OF THE WAIST BELAY. THE BACK OF THE SEAT MUST NOT BE TOO HIGH OR IT WILL IMPEDE THE ANCHOR ROPE. A RUCKSACK WILL OBSTRUCT THE ANCHOR ROPES IF THE STANCE IS TOO DEEP AND THE TIE-ON LOOP MAY RIDE UP THE CHEST

- Tie into the end of the rope first, before attaching to anchors or other people. Tie to the bottom end of the flaked rope when descending and the top end in ascent.
- In a non-lead climbing situation, keep the live rope firm between the belayer and person being safeguarded. The less shock-load on the anchor, the safer it will be.
- If the axe is used for the anchor, fashion stances for belayer and rope before the axe is deployed.

12.1.3 Bucket seat

The bucket seat can be a simple and effective anchor if used appropriately with a waist belay, but it is critical that no shock-loading occurs in the event of a slip. However, the bucket seat alone should be used with caution and never on its own to belay a leader.

Cut a horizontal slot across the fall-line at least hip-width in length, angled down into the slope and work back, cutting and clearing with the adze in a semi-circular shape, whilst maintaining the depth. A double-handed cutting action from a secure position below the stance is most effective. Keep a smooth front face to the seat at 90° to the slope and keep removing the debris to maintain the depth and the right-angled front face. If it is too shallow, or less than 90° to the slope, there is less support and a chance that the belayer will be pulled from the seat under load. In soft snow, the angle of the front face of the seat may be steeper. The seat should be large enough to be comfortable when sitting and with enough space at the back for your rucksack, if necessary. It should be deep enough so that the backs of your thighs are in contact with the whole of the seat, as this provides the support if loaded. However, if the seat is too deep, it restricts arm movement when using the waist belay. Finally, if the snow is hard, cut two slots for your heels, or in soft snow, kick in your heels from a sitting position. Your heels may take part of the load if these steps are effective *(see Figure 12.2)*.

12.1.4 The waist belay

The belay rope is taken over the head and down round the waist; flick a large loop over your head to avoid snagging on the rucksack. The rope should run below the sack and around your hips rather than higher on the back. If the sack is fairly empty the rope can run across its back for extra padding. If it is full, undo the waist belt so the rope can be taken over the top then underneath the sack. The belay rope must lie above the rope from your waist to the anchor. If it is taken up from below instead of over your head, it could be pulled out from underneath the hips when loaded. Screwgate karabiners clipped to the waist loop for the anchor tie-back should be turned gate down to prevent the possibility of the moving rope opening it. If a bucket seat alone is used as your belay, do not allow the rope to ride too low on the hips, where again it could be pulled from under your body if loaded. Take a twist of the rope around the arm on the dead-hand side to increase the friction and take the dead arm across your body to increase friction and control further *(see Figure 11.3 on page 145)*.

12.1.5 Stomper

The stomper is simple, effective, quick to construct and can be used on moderate slopes or flat ground. However, it is not a complete belay system

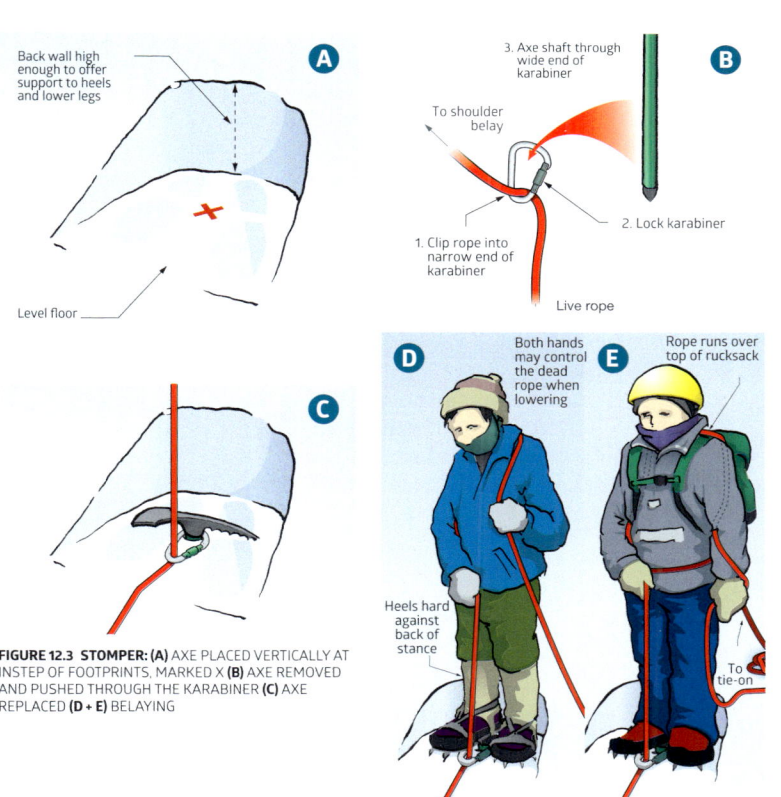

FIGURE 12.3 STOMPER: (A) AXE PLACED VERTICALLY AT INSTEP OF FOOTPRINTS, MARKED X **(B)** AXE REMOVED AND PUSHED THROUGH THE KARABINER **(C)** AXE REPLACED **(D + E)** BELAYING

and should be used with caution. It is only used from above to safeguard someone in ascent or descent and cannot be used to protect a lead climber. The depth of snow once the stance is cut limits its use, since it must be at least the depth of your axe. Very hard snow may make it impossible for the axe to penetrate. As the stomper is used standing up, the stability of the belayer must be considered if it is windy or the slope is steep.

A horizontal slot and ledge, wide enough for both feet, is cut into the slope, and should be deep enough for the back wall to provide support for the heels and calves and braced against for extra stability. This requires more digging on shallow slopes. However, in calm conditions or on the flat, this may not be necessary. Face out and downslope and, with feet together, kick each heel into the back of the ledge. Step to the side and where the boot instep prints are, push the axe vertically down as a mark. Remove the axe and slide an HMS screwgate karabiner up the shaft. Clip the rope through with the live rope running out beneath the narrow end of the screwgate karabiner, lock the gate and replace the axe up to its head with the pick and adze across the fall-line. Stand on top of the axe with your boot insteps on the pick and the adze. If the adze and pick are very curved it may be necessary to dig a slot for the head so your feet are level. Wearing crampons may provide extra purchase.

Once secure, use a waist belay, but with the rope running over the top of the rucksack. With enough bulk in the rucksack, this forms a platform to keep the rope in place, allows a twist to be taken round the dead arm and provides comfortable and easily used friction with any load acting down through the body *(see Figure 12.3)*. An alternative is to use a shoulder belay by bringing the rope under the arm of the live side and over the shoulder on the dead side. With this method however, you cannot take a twist in the dead rope, since it tends to roll off the shoulder.

If the snow is hard and it is difficult to place the axe, it can be rocked back and forward as pressure is applied, or stamped gently on the head to help drive it into place. However, if wearing crampons, use the heel to stamp with and not the instep, which can be damaged. If you do not have a screwgate karabiner big enough to slip over the shaft it may be possible to clip it through the hole in the head. This should be done so the karabiner sits horizontally under the adze. It can even be clipped to the tie-on loop of the leash if this is suitably attached.

12.1.6 Snow bollard

The snow bollard is a horseshoe shaped slot in the snow with the open-ended 'legs' running downhill, in the direction of the stance or expected load. The size depends on the hardness of the snow and the depth of the slot is dictated by the strength of any layers in the snowpack. It is critical that the rope lies on the hardest layer where there is less possibility of it cutting through. Correctly constructed, the snow bollard is a very effective anchor and can be used in a number of situations, including lead climbing. It is often used at the top of climbs and is particularly useful in a shallow but consolidated snow pack. It can be used as an abseil anchor without abandoning any gear *(see Figure 12.4 A/B)*.

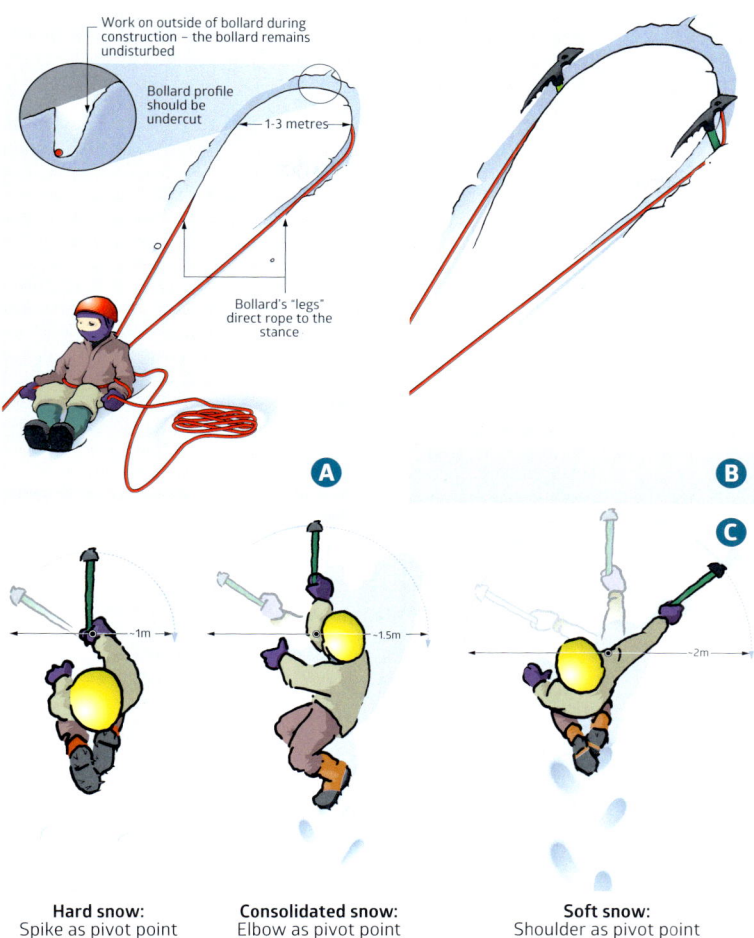

FIGURE 12.4 SNOW BOLLARD: (A) THE PROFILE OF THE SNOW BOLLARD **(B)** REINFORCED SNOW BOLLARD WITH 2 ICE AXES. A HAMMER OR SKI POLES CAN BE USED **(C)** THE SIZE OF THE BOLLARD

Decide on the size of the bollard: in hard snow it can be around 1m in diameter but up to about 3m diameter in soft snow. Scribe the shape on the snow using the pick of the axe ensuring that it is uniform with no bulges that could concentrate pressure if loaded. Start with the adze and cut out the initial shape. Work from the bottom of the legs up to the middle so you are clearing out as you cut. Stand on the outside of the shape to avoid disturbing the snow of the bollard itself. The slot should be deepest at the back, tapering to the surface at the bottom of the legs, angled inwards or have a lip and be wide enough to work in freely. Finish the slot by scraping the adze or the gloved hand round it to form a groove to keep the rope in place.

Use the shape of the ground to your advantage. A bollard cut around a bulge or convex slope is more secure, as there is more snow in the anchor and the rope pulls down into the slope. A reasonable improvised template for scribing the size and shape uses the length of the axe and your arm.

When facing the slope with a 50cm to 60cm axe hold the spike on the snow and use it as a pivot point to scribe the pick around in a semi-circle. This will form the basis for a bollard about 1m in diameter. For a bollard of about 1.5m in diameter, use your elbow as a pivot point and for one of about 2m in diameter, lean forward and use your extended straight arm and axe, your shoulder being the central point *(see Figure 12.4 C)*.

Continually remove debris from the slot while cutting as this helps to maintain the bollard's shape and depth. The legs should not join up to form an isolated 'tear drop' shape which is weaker. In soft snow an increase in diameter will make it stronger but to stop the rope from cutting through the snow, the back and 'shoulders' (the widest point) can be reinforced. Padding the slot with spare clothing, bivvy bag, rucksack or similar will help. Alternatively, two axes, one on either side at the shoulders, can be placed vertically and flush with the inner edge. If only one axe is available then it is best placed centrally at the back.

To use as a direct belay, the end of the rope is tied around the bollard using a bowline, the legs directing the rope to the knot. A figure of eight or overhand on a bight can be tied further down the rope and an HMS screwgate karabiner attached for use with an Italian hitch. This reduces the side-loading of the bowline when belaying from the main loop. Alternatively, a large figure of eight or overhand loop may be dropped over the bollard, but this is slower to set up. If the belayer is tied into the rope end and needs security whilst belaying, after feeding the rope around the bollard, tie an overhand on a bight in both ropes at the stance. The belayer will then be anchored and the double overhand loops will be the anchor point for the direct belay.

Bollards are commonly used for abseil anchors, particularly when negotiating cornices. If it has been used previously as a belay anchor, then the 'legs' have to be straightened to direct the ropes in a line wider apart for the abseil. To aid retrieval of the rope if it freezes in place, lightly saw it around the bollard to break any seal. Make sure that the rope isn't going to cut deeply into the edge and create a lot of friction. If appropriate, have someone below pull one end of the rope to check for ease of release before setting off. It helps to reduce the size of a cornice before descending and even cut a channel to make the start easier. The bollard should be used to protect any initial work close to the edge. A bollard far back from the edge may hinder rope retrieval by creating a lot of friction across the snow and limits the length of usable rope.

12.1.7 Buried axe

The buried axe is used in a number of situations, in descent and ascent and commonly on winter climbs where there are few alternatives. The axe is buried in a slot cut horizontally across the fall-line and a long sling is attached to the shaft to belay from *(see Figure 12.5)*. The rope can be tied directly to the axe if a sling is unavailable *(see Figure 12.6 on page 162)* but this is awkward. Take care not to disturb the snow in front of the buried axe.

Directly above a previously prepared stance, cut a slot 8–10cm wide across the fall line, a bit longer than the axe length and vertically down into the snow, or even angled back from the vertical towards the slope. To help, first mark a line to judge the length and angle of the slot. In softer conditions, widen the slot to 15cm to allow removal of snow by hand and smoothing of the front face. The distance between the slot and stance depends on the slope angle but should be such that the pull is always down into the slope. On a moderately steep slope this is approximately 2m above the back of the stance where any load pulls the axe down, not outwards.

Cut the slot vertically down to the required depth, keeping the front face smooth for the horizontal axe to brace against, and a flat base so that the axe is not hung up at its ends. In hard snow, use the pick to score the front face regularly during construction, and in softer snow, the back of a hand can be used to smooth off.

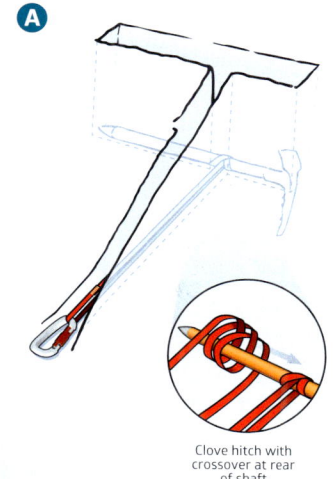

Clove hitch with crossover at rear of shaft

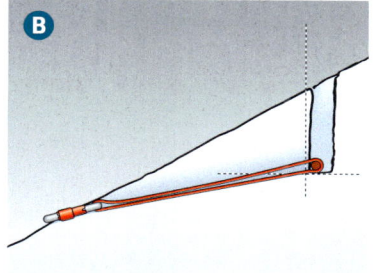

FIGURE 12.5 BURIED AXE: IT IS IMPORTANT TO MAINTAIN CLEAN, SQUARE ANGLES. ALWAYS USE THE ROPE TO TIE INTO THE SCREWGATE KARABINER.

Normally the slot should be about 40cm deep but should make use of any harder layers of snow. However, the minimum depth of the slot is such that the whole axe is in contact with the snow and the adze will not show after being placed. A shallow placement is possible in hard snow or when there is a hard layer at the surface.

Next, prepare a vertical slot for the sling or rope attachment, but first locate the point of attachment on the shaft. The sling is tied so that it is half way along the axe in terms of surface area so any loading is distributed equally, decreasing the chance of the axe pivoting out. The attachment point is roughly the balance point – about two-thirds the length of the shaft towards the head in most axes. Balance the axe across your hand side-on, to find this point. Replace the axe in the slot briefly and mark this point on the snow. Move below, and mark the line of the slot for the sling by lightly pulling the pick straight down the fall-line. This should be excavated so that it runs in a direct line, tapering from the bottom of the horizontal slot to the surface about 1.5m lower down, roughly where the screwgate karabiner to rest in. For the complete belay, from the bucket seat, use the rope to tie into the screwgate karabiner *(Figure 12.2, page 156)*. The sling is not clipped direct into your waist loop as the short distance from you and the snow anchor will exert an outward pull rather

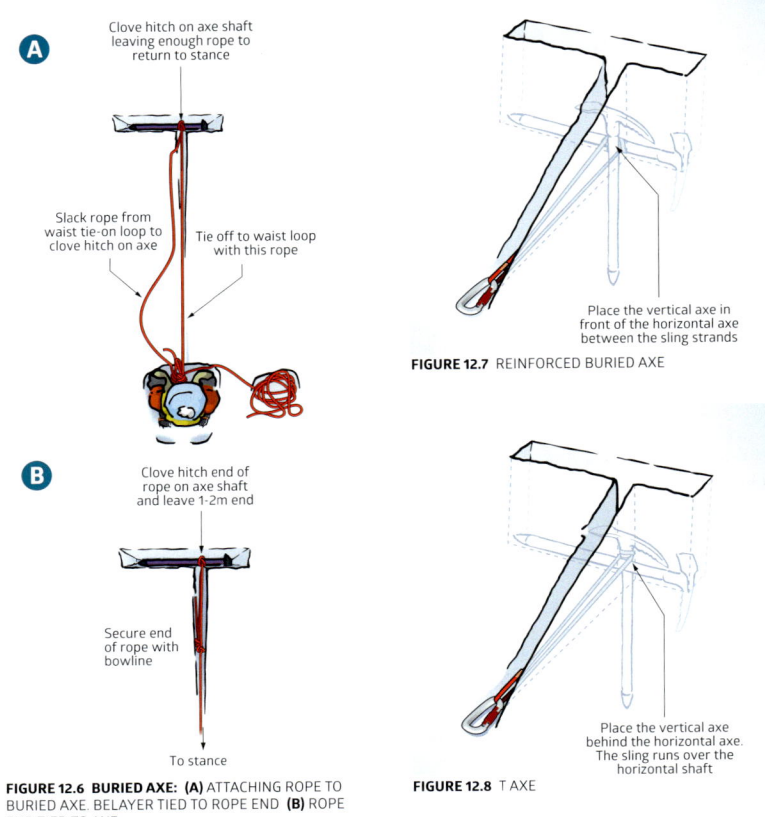

FIGURE 12.6 BURIED AXE: (A) ATTACHING ROPE TO BURIED AXE. BELAYER TIED TO ROPE END **(B)** ROPE END TIED TO AXE

FIGURE 12.7 REINFORCED BURIED AXE

FIGURE 12.8 T AXE

than a pull down into the slope. Generally, the more snow between the anchor and belayer, the stronger the belay.

Cut the vertical slot to remove as little snow as possible. Use a combination of the pick and the spike, using the narrow profile of the shaft. Work from bottom to top when excavating so that debris runs out of the bottom of the slot. Attach the long sling to the axe with a clove hitch, making sure that the cross-over of the hitch is at the back of the shaft so it will tighten up if loaded *(see Figure 12.5 (A) on page 161)*. Finally, place the axe pick down in the bottom of the horizontal slot. Ensure that the sling is in the vertical slot and running in a straight line with the sewn section (or knot) of the sling at the bottom by the karabiner and not jammed in the slot. A hollow can be fashioned for the screwgate karabiner to rest in. For the complete belay, from the bucket seat, use the rope to tie into the screwgate karabiner (*Figure 12.2, page 156*). The sling is not clipped direct into your waist loop as the short distance from you and the snow anchor will exert an outward pull rather than a pull down into the slope. Generally, the more snow between the anchor and belayer, the stronger the belay.

It is possible to attach the rope directly to the axe shaft. From the stance, clove-hitch the rope from your waist to the axe, but leave a little slack. Take the main rope through your waist loop and use a figure of eight tie-back to tighten to the anchor, or clove-hitch into a screw-gate karabiner clipped to your waist loop *(see Figure 12.6 and Figure 11.2 on page 144)*. If the rope end is clove-hitched to the axe, the hitch must be tied off to reduce slippage and the chance of it coming undone. One method is to leave a long end of rope on the clove hitch and use this to tie a bowline.

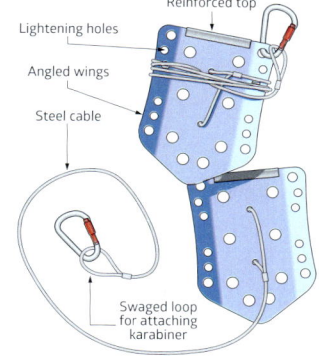

FIGURE 12.9 DEADMAN, AND PREPARED FOR CARRYING

Reinforced buried axe

If another axe is available, it can be used to reinforce the buried axe by pushing it in vertically, immediately in front of the horizontal axe. It should go between the two strands of the sling. The vertical axe must be flush with the front face of the slot so that there is no pivoting of the horizontal axe which should remain braced against the front face. In soft snow, it is easy to use the wide profile of the vertical shaft, and the pick and adze can seat easily. In harder snow, the narrow profile of the shaft is used, the pick running down the sling slot and the adze over the top of the horizontal axe. This saves the need for disturbing the front face *(see Figure 12.7)*.

T axe

This is a variation on the buried axe, but works on a different principle. It can be used in snow that has a number of thin, hard layers too shallow to place a buried axe in, such as multiple buried icy layers of variable consistency. Horizontal and vertical slots are dug, as for a buried axe, but the vertical axe, with a sling clove-hitched around the very top of the shaft, is pushed vertically into the snow behind the horizontal axe *(see Figure 12.8)*. When a load is applied to the top of the axe, the resistance to levering upwards of the vertical shaft gives the anchor its strength. The horizontal axe, or anything else, such as a pole or shovel handle provides the pivot point. The pull on the anchor must be down and not outwards. Due to the narrower range of acceptable conditions for this kind of anchor, more careful judgement is needed.

12.1.8 Deadman

This is a spade-shaped aluminium alloy plate, roughly 20cm x 25cm, pointed at the base and with a reinforced top so it may be hammered. A 2m-long steel cable is attached to its centre with a swaged loop for clipping into. It may have lightening holes and angled wings to improve stability *(see Figure 12.9)*. It is specifically designed as a snow anchor and can be used in a wide range of conditions but the harder the snow the stronger the anchor. It is particularly useful in less consolidated snow where other anchors are less secure. Climbers may carry a deadman if

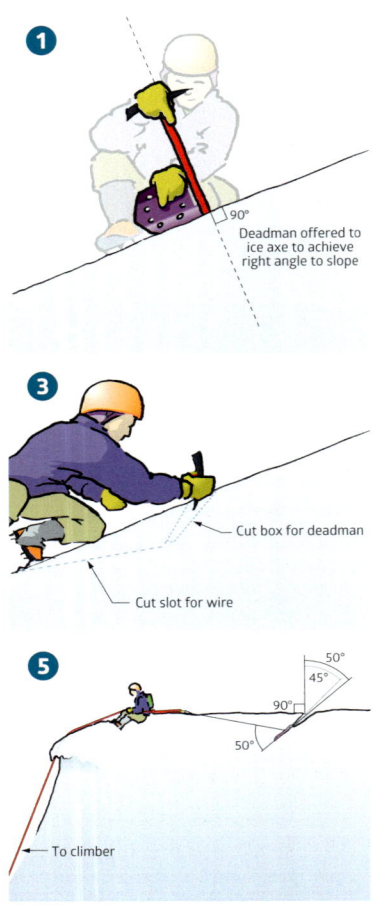
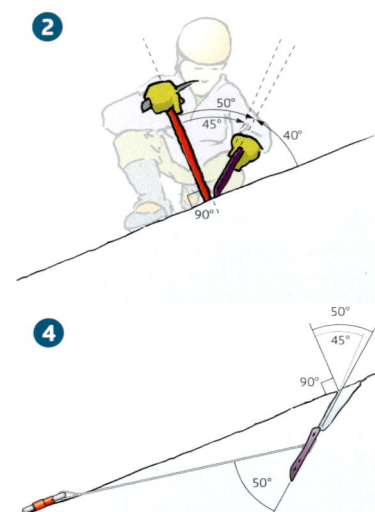

Placing a deadman:
1 Place axe at 90° to snow surface
2 Bisect the angle with the deadman and tilt it back 5°
3 Using the deadman as a guide, cut a slot at the same angle and mark the cable slot down the fall line
4 Seat the deadman down the front face of the angled slot. Test it making sure the cable runs in a straight line from the deadman to the snow surface
5 The deadman placed on level ground

FIGURE 12.10 PLACING A DEADMAN

going onto extensive snow slopes where two would be carried; one for each belay.

It is crucial that the deadman is placed at the correct angle, where it not only resists a force but, in soft snow, cuts down when loaded and increases its holding power. It is placed at 40° to the snow surface. If necessary, clear away loose snow to reveal any harder layers and the true angle of the slope. Place the spike of the axe in the snow so the shaft is 90° to the slope, using the edge of the deadman as a square if necessary. Looking from the side, place the deadman so it bisects the right angle and tilt it back another 5°: that is, very slightly! Maintaining the angle, push the deadman into the snow at right angles to the fall-line to act as a template.

Move to the side to get an accurate view, look along the edge of the deadman as a guide and cut a slot with the pick across the fall-line at 40°

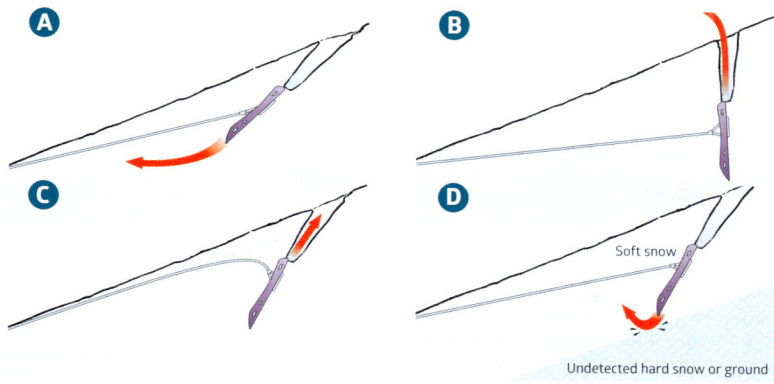

FIGURE 12.11 PROBLEMS PLACING A DEADMAN: (A) TOO SHALLOW AN ANGLE **(B)** TOO STEEP AN ANGLE **(C)** A BEND IN THE WIRE **(D)** THE DEADMAN MAY DEFLECT OFF HARD SNOW OR GROUND

to the slope. This slot should be at least pick depth, but can also be cut with the adze, as snow removed from behind where the plate goes is irrelevant to the strength of the anchor. Use the pick to scribe a line for the vertical slot from the middle of the deadman slot. Work back uphill clearing the wire slot, trying to remove as little snow as possible by using the pick or the narrow profile of the shaft. The slot should be at least as long as the wire and snow disturbance kept to a minimum.

Put the deadman into the prepared slots and, keeping it hard against the 40° face, push it into the snow. Tap the deadman in further using the axe shaft, and with the free hand, keep the wire taut so that it maintains the critical 40° angle. As the plate goes deeper keep the wire slot clear of snow so it is running in a straight line from the deadman, appearing at the surface 2m down-slope *(see Figure 12.10)*. When in place, it may be bedded more firmly by using the axe through the screwgate karabiner attached to the wire loop end to lever or tug the wire progressively until the plate is firm. The force should be applied down the surface of the slope and not outwards. The distance from the end of the cable to the stance should be around 1m, but it is important that the stance is below the level of the plate and the load is pulling down into the slope. If the deadman is placed incorrectly it will be less secure *(see Figure 12.11)*.

An advantage of the deadman is that the axe is free to use for personal safety and for cutting a stance in the correct location after it has been placed. The rope can be clipped into the deadman for security when the stance is being cut. It can be carried by wrapping the cable round the plate (there are normally retaining notches in the edge) and finished by taking a few turns of the wire around itself then clipping it to a corner lightening hole *(see Figure 12.9)*. It may be clipped to the bottom of rucksack shoulder straps, keeping it out of the way, but within reach.

12.2 Other snow anchors and belays

These either require the use of specialised equipment such as snow stakes, or are not an improvement on the methods described. However, one extra snow belay is worth considering.

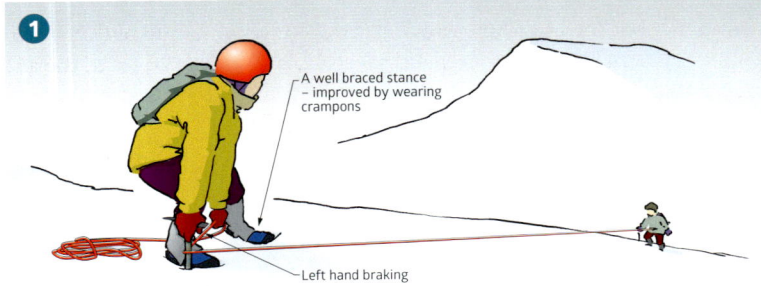

Foot brake

1. For a controlled descent, allow the rope to run smoothly, reducing grip or increasing friction around boot as appropriate
2. Taking in
3. Holding a load
4. Shallow or hard snowpack where axe cannot fully penetrate

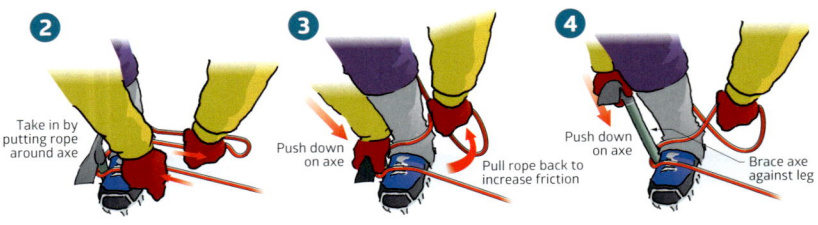

FIGURE 12.12 FOOT BRAKE

12.2.1 Foot brake

Often called the New Zealand foot brake or the boot axe belay, this is a quick and effective method of controlling static loads on moderately angled slopes. It should not be used in a shock-loading, lead climbing situation, but it can be a dynamic belay where the rope is allowed to run and braking is applied as a gradual increase in friction in a controlled manner. This does require a lot of practice to use safely. It is also useful in shallow snow packs, but it helps to be wearing crampons on harder snow.

Stamp, scrape or quickly cut a small ledge large enough for a boot to be placed across the slope. Ideally make a small lip on the front edge for further foot support. Push the axe vertically into the snow at the back of the ledge and, facing across the slope, stamp your uphill boot directly against the shaft so it is braced by the middle of the foot. The lower leg can also be braced downhill forming a stable stance and can also have a ledge. The live rope is run over the top of the boot, around the shaft (lift the axe up slightly to enable this) and back over the boot. The pick should be braced against the lower leg and the adze pointing forward across the slope *(see Figure 12.12)*.

Friction is increased by holding the dead rope with the downhill braking hand and pulling the rope back against the ankle. Taking in requires the uphill hand to pull the rope around the boot, the lower hand pulling on the live rope. The more the rope is wrapped around the ankle, the more friction will be generated. When loaded, the rope pulls the axe against the boot and the upper hand exerts downward pressure on the axe head. If the snow is too hard for the axe to be pushed in it can be stamped in or the axe head braced against the lower leg. The rope should be flaked on a ledge behind the belayer so that it is freely running between the legs.

12.2.2 Vertical axe

At one time this was the only type of axe anchor but it is notoriously unreliable, particularly when used with wooden shafted axes, and now almost totally abandoned. However, in very hard snow it may still be useful. The axe is driven vertically into the snow, but for it to be effective, it would require a lot of stamping or hammering which is not good for the axe. It can provide a quick anchor to safeguard an individual as a self-belay, rather than used in a more involved belay.

12.3 Improvised snow anchors

The main requirement of a snow anchor is that it provides resistance to a force. Anything that can be buried can be used in an emergency. In hard snow a number of possible anchors such as helmets, walking poles or even suitably shaped rocks can be used. The main requirement is that they are roughly flat and the rope can be attached to them. Even mitts have been used as demonstration anchors in very hard snow. In soft snow the object providing resistance must be larger, but a rucksack can be buried in a hole and be quite effective. Another versatile anchor is a stuff sack filled with snow and tied around its middle.

A common feature in winter after a thaw and in springtime is a Randkluft – the gap between rock and snow caused by the melt back from heat radiated by the rock. By using the gap in the snow, a quick buried axe or snow bollard can be constructed. Walking poles can be used in place of a buried axe. In the case of reinforcing a buried axe, if another axe is available and the snow is not deep enough to take a vertical axe, stacked axes are an option. These are placed horizontally, pick down with the heads near the middle and spikes pointing away from each other for greatest length. The sling is clove-hitched in the balance point of both axes.

12.4 Ice anchors and belays

Natural ice anchors are less common and usually require more work than snow or rock anchors, but can be very strong. The type of ice should be taken into account; snow ice is the easiest to work as it is softer than water ice. The ice colour can reflect its strength and reliability: opaque or white ice will have more air and snow mixed in, while blue or clear ice is denser, generally stronger but more brittle. Hollow ice may be detached from the underlying rock, but if sound, be readily adapted. The shape of the ice is a consideration: using an ice bulge is an advantage when cutting an ice bollard. This means there is more ice in the anchor and that the load is directed down into the ice. Freezing temperatures are desirable so that the ice keeps its strength. Thaws can cause melting from the rock, forming unusable hollow ice. Ice with a significant amount of snow mixed in or visible air pockets is usually too weak for anchors.

12.5 Ice bollard

Very occasionally, natural ice bollards are found, but they usually need to be created. Ice bollards are effective but can be time-consuming to make. Making them requires some practice, but they may be used for a belay or abseil anchor. Use the ice to your advantage and reduce the effort by creating a bollard round a natural bulge or convexity, such as where the ice drops back in angle on an icy step. An ice bollard is the same horseshoe shape as a snow bollard, but with smaller dimensions of 30–50cm across and 10–15cm deep and must have a pronounced lip to keep the sling or rope in place *(see Figure 12.13)*.

First mark out the shape on the ice with the pick and cut around this using the adze. Cut from the shape of the bollard outwards and away from the bollard itself. Once there is a rough outline, the final shaping and forming is done with the pick. A curved pick works better as it forms a natural curving lip in the ice. Scraping with the teeth of the pick like a saw rather than cutting is far more effective, particularly on harder ice which has a tendency to fracture. It is important that the pull on the ice bollard is downwards as there is less chance of the rope or sling sliding off. Before use, check for fractures or shattered areas that may weaken the ice. Opaque areas in otherwise clear ice may indicate fracturing. If necessary, remove the shattered areas, assess whether the strength of the anchor has been compromised and if not, reshape the bollard.

12.6 Other natural ice anchors

Commonly, these are found in the vicinity of rocky outcrops and bluffs where sheets or curtains of water ice drain down the rock and can form icicles and pillars. Ice bosses may form below icicles and after a small amount of adapting, can be used as ice bollards. Solid pillars of ice can also be adapted for anchors and slings, or the rope placed around them. It is crucial that you check that the pillar is securely connected at the base. A certain amount of careful clearing may be necessary before judging whether the pillar is suitable or not. Always ensure that the pull on such a feature comes down and not out. Ice curtains formed over a bulge or overhang can offer a number of options if there is a gap behind:

12.6.1 Ice curtain thread

Carefully chip one or two holes in the curtain, taking care not to create fracture lines and thread a long sling or rope through *(see Figure 12.14)*. Stiff Aramid slings are useful for this.

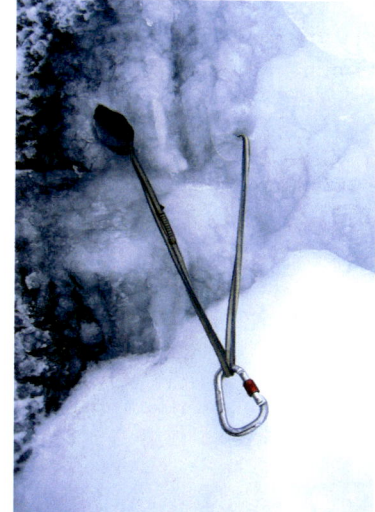

FIGURE 12.13 ICE BOLLARD

FIGURE 12.14 ICE CURTAIN THREAD

12.6.2 Jammed axe

If the gap is wide enough to reach an arm behind, then a hole is chipped in the ice. A long sling is clove-hitched to the axe shaft, which is placed horizontally behind the curtain and the sling taken out through the hole. This can also be done behind two large icicles.

12.7 Belaying on rock in winter

When belaying on rock in winter, the same principles apply as in summer, whether the belay is direct or indirect. Assuming a minimum of equipment, winter rock anchors will be natural rock features such as blocks, threads, spikes or chockstones around which the rope or a sling can be used.

12.7.1 Finding rock anchors

Where and how long to look in any situation is important, as time is always a consideration. Quick decisions about how long to spend searching for rock anchors and when to move on are needed. However, in some conditions such as during or after a thaw, the rock may be as clearly exposed as in summer. If there are no obvious anchors, then they may have to be uncovered. The ease with which this is done depends on the depth and hardness of the snow.

Soft snow can be brushed off with a gloved hand, but using the whole forearm allows greater areas to be cleared with one sweep. When the snow is firmer, the axe must be used: the shaft on softer snow, the adze on harder snow. This can be time-consuming, so be sure you are in a productive area and be careful not to blunt the adze or scar the rock.

Not only are natural rock anchors usually harder to find in winter, but they have to be treated with greater care. With spikes, blocks and flakes, it is essential to establish that they are part of the bedrock and not detached. Clear all around the feature to see that it is solid. Remove the snow from the base to ensure there are no cracks indicating a loose block. Apply body weight from a safe direction or thump the block with the hand (or hit with the axe) and feel for vibrations which could indicate looseness. If there is doubt or the snow is so deep or hard that these tests are not feasible, then the axe shaft can be used as a lever to test the block. This needs to be done with care both for the sake of the axe shaft and to avoid dislodging the block.

In other circumstances, a block may be securely frozen in place and provide a good anchor. Thorough testing is required. Sometimes an ice-covered block can be improved by chipping a channel in the ice around the sides and importantly, the back of the block. Forming a lip on the ice will hold a sling or the rope in place.

Threads between two blocks also provide good natural anchors. Sometimes a little excavation around blocks can reveal a good thread after establishing that the blocks are secure. Chockstones need to be thoroughly tested to establish that they are solid and mechanically sound. A chockstone that is iced in place may be acceptable after testing.

Another simple anchor, used in a situation of moderate loading, is the braced boulder belay. This is made by sitting down behind a secure boulder, bracing the feet against it and using a waist belay.

MURDOCH JAMIESON ON PITCH 1 OF *UNICORN*, VIII, 8, STOB COIRE NAN LOCHAN, GLENCOE
PHOTO // NICK BULLOCK

part 5

Winter climbing

PLACING AN ICE SCREW ON THE LEAD   *PHOTO // GEORGE McEWAN*

Climbing equipment

The first step towards efficient climbing is to have effective, appropriate clothing and equipment.

13.1 Clothing

The same clothing systems and basic principles apply to both winter walking and climbing but there are additional design features to consider.

13.1.1 Shell jacket

This must withstand much wear, especially on mixed routes. Heavier abrasion-resistant breathable material lasts longer than lightweight shells but at some cost in terms of flexibility. Reinforcing in exposed areas such as shoulders and arms helps. Soft shell, although ideal in terms of weight, fitting and breathability, lacks insulation when inactive: at belays, for example, where an extra outer layer, such as a belay jacket, will provide warmth. A climbing jacket will be about hip length, but long enough to tuck below the harness waist belt. It should not lift up when arms are raised and be close-fitting without being restrictive. Stretch side panels allow high arm movements. The visored hood must fit over the helmet without restricting head movement but not get in the way when not in use. Detachable hoods are not recommended. Ventilation pockets or zips will reduce overheating and excessive perspiration. Accessible external pockets should be clear of the harness or rucksack waist belt. Zips that can be operated with gloves or mittens and Velcro® on other closures work better than poppers which easily ice up.

13.1.2 Shell trousers

Salopettes, or trousers with braces, keep them from working down and a full length two-way leg zip allows them to be put on over crampons, used for ventilation and to drop the seat. The braces attachment points must be forward of the zips to allow this. One drawback is that trousers with braces have to be put on under a jacket, but large quick release buckles allow them to be removed without removing the jacket. These high-waisted designs are warmer and eliminate any gaps around the middle. Extra reinforcing for the knees, seat and inside lower leg (reducing crampon tears) will prolong their life, and stretch panels or gussets at the knees increase mobility.

13.1.3 Boots

There is little difference between winter mountaineering and climbing boots, although some of the more specialist climbing boots are lighter but need to be a good fit to perform well. Tightening the cuff for climbing provides greater ankle support and gives a more positive and relaxed foot placement, but this may be too tight for comfortable walking, so slackening the laces can be beneficial, especially with stiff boots. This also stops the possibility of bruising the lower shin, which is very painful if not checked in time and can last for days before the bruising heals.

13.1.4 Gaiters

Close-fitting gaiters are best for climbing, giving a clear view of foot placements and reducing the chance of a crampon snagging. Super-

> **Climbing equipment safety standards**
>
> Manufacturers are required by European law (PPE – Personal Protective Equipment directive) to meet specific, stringent standards in various categories of climbing equipment. It should meet the EN (European Norm) standards which have the CE (Communauté Européenne) or UIAA (Union Internationale des Associations d'Alpinisme) mark. Take note of the date of manufacture and purchase, as some equipment, such as climbing helmets and ropes, have a useable life after which they should be retired. Read the manufacturer's information leaflet which is supplied with each item of climbing equipment for further relevant details. Beware of purchasing or using non CE marked climbing equipment. They may be counterfeited copies and will not meet CE approved safety standards.

gaiters are less necessary in this country. They can obstruct the welt of the boot, making crampons fit less securely and their bulk increases the chance of crampons snagging. However, those with poor circulation may feel the extra insulation is worth these drawbacks.

13.1.5 Rucksack

A climbing rucksack should be uncomplicated and adjusted to be body-hugging without restricting movement. A single compartment sack will lie snugly on your back and the base should lie level with the top of your harness. Waist belts and buckles should allow access to your harness and not restrict vision of its gear loops and tie-on points. Gear loops on the rucksack waist belt are convenient for carrying a small amount of equipment. Otherwise, the waist belt can be conveniently fastened around the back of your sack. Excess straps and cord can snag when climbing and open pockets and pouches fill with snow. The main compartment should be sealable to stop spindrift entering. When climbing, it should feel balanced and part of your body: use the side compression straps to pull it together to keep its shape and distribute the load evenly. A few basic essentials can be kept in the lid for convenience and most sacks are fairly light when the rope and climbing equipment are in use.

13.1.6 Contents of a rucksack

Ideally you should carry enough to suit the weather and conditions on the day. On the climb, your sack should contain some food and drink (most of which is consumed to re-hydrate before starting) and a small amount of emergency equipment: personal bivvy bag, spare hat and gloves, emergency food, spare fleece/belay jacket for colder days and a first aid kit. A map and compass and a repairs kit are essential and a guide-book and mobile phone are sensible extras. Some of the above can be shared.

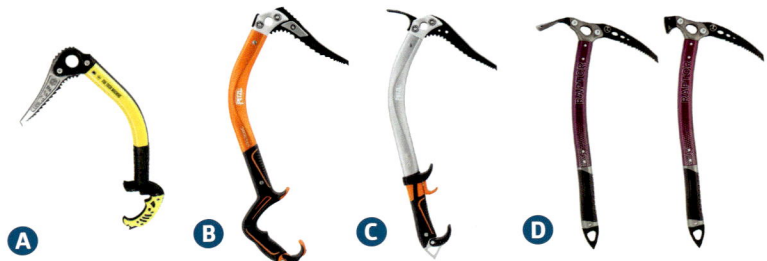

FIGURE 13.1 AXES: (A) SPECIALISED LEASHLESS TOOL **(B)** T-RATED MODULAR TOOL WITH HAMMER HEAD **(C)** T RATED MODULAR TOOL WITH WITH ADZE AND ATTACHED POMMEL AND FINGER REST **(D)** MATCHING PAIR OF T RATED MODULAR CLASSIC MOUNTAINEERING AXES

13.1.7 Hat

Hats should fit comfortably under a helmet without interfering with its fitting and adjustment. Thin thermal, power-stretch micro-fleece or silk helmet liners are ideal. Thin balaclavas of the same material are great for bad days as they protect the neck and form a seal into the top of clothing.

13.1.8 Gloves

Gloves, rather than mitts, are better for climbing as they allow easier manipulation of ropes, gear and the rock. The compromise is between enough insulation and waterproofness to keep your hands warm, and not being too bulky to lose feel and dexterity. Long-wristed gauntlets can give a good seal between glove and jacket. Beware of long draw-cords as they may snag. Mitts are great to change into at belays (have them accessible) along with your belay jacket. Thin gloves are worthwhile for dry days or hard mixed leads but offer less in the way of insulation. Thin waterproof or neoprene gloves can be effective in warm wet conditions. Since gloves inevitably wear, particularly on mixed climbs, it is often better to have several cheaper pairs.

13.2 Technical equipment

Innovations in climbing equipment are often driven by feedback from climbers and field-testing by experts, where small improvements become the norm. Specialisation in winter climbing means there is now a greater range of equipment and clothing, and choosing the correct tool or garment seems to have become more difficult. However, there is now much more up-to-date information available in magazines, brochures and on-line that helps to make informed choices. Retail staff are often well-informed and can give good advice based on research, staff training and sometimes practical use.

13.2.1 Climbing axes

There are two categories of climbing axe: mountaineering and technical *(see Figure 13.1)*, and components are the same for both. Mountaineering axes can be used singly on easier climbs or in pairs for moderately graded routes. For harder routes (around Grade IV and above), two technical tools are more appropriate, usually of the same design, length and manufacturer. This means that the weight, balance and swing of the tools

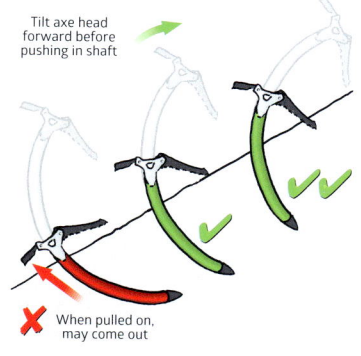

FIGURE 13.2 BENT SHAFTS

are similar, permitting more efficient climbing. One has an adze for chopping and clearing and the other a hammer head to place pitons and ice protection. Both can be torqued or wedged into cracks. Which tool goes in which hand is normally a matter of personal preference but will be influenced by the likely task ahead, like placing a piton or clearing snow.

Many mountaineering axes and all technical tools are modular, so that components can be replaced as necessary. This system allows you to purchase two shafts of the same design and add picks, adze, hammer head and leashes as needed. Specialised forms of climbing may use leashless tools without an adze and hammer head which saves weight. These tools are also safer in tenuous hooking situations where injury can occur if the pick skates off a hold. For the majority of UK winter climbs, however, an adze and hammer head remain essential parts of the tool.

Shaft

Shaft lengths are normally 50–55 cm and can either be straight or bent. They are roughly oval sectioned, tubular and normally made from a strong lightweight aluminium alloy. Carbon fibre or titanium shafts are lighter without losing strength, but are more expensive and require a good design to be well balanced.

Shafts may have an upper or lower bend or a regular continuous (compound) bend. A well-designed bent shaft offers protection for hands against hitting protrusions during the swing, provides clearance when reaching over ice bulges or rock ledges and allows a well-balanced swing for accurate placement. This is largely determined by how much weight there is forward of or behind the centre of gravity of the axe. Severely bent shafts force the centre of gravity behind the line of the shaft, compromising the balance of the tool. Mountaineering axes are either straight-shafted or have a slight bend which offers a small amount of clearance. A bent shaft may be more difficult to use in some situations such as cutting a stance or placing a piton.

When the shaft is pushed vertically into the snow, radical bends will impede penetration in consolidated snow. Shafts with moderate compound bends can still be used effectively by modifying the angle at which the axe is placed by anticipating the line of travel through the snow pack *(see Figure 13.2)*. The same criteria apply to both straight- and bent-shafted axes when using a horizontal buried axe anchor: the shaft must be in contact with the most consolidated layer of snow and the sling or rope tie-on at the point of equal surface area.

A rubber compound grip material covers at least the lower third of the shaft, but it is preferable if the grip extends the full length when your hand is used higher up. Stretchy sticky tape (specifically designed or improvised with plumber's tape or similar) may be used to improve grip. Tape from axe head down the shaft so the overlaps are uppermost. Technical tools will have a moulded handle, pommels or finger rests for added support, particularly useful on steep climbs, providing a more secure grip. Again, the disadvantage is that the shaft is virtually impossible to push into consolidated snow.

FIGURE 13.3 ICE PICKS: (A) ICE PICK **(B)** MIXED PICK **(C)** DROOPED PICK **(D)** TRADITIONAL CURVED

Axe head
This is the point of attachment of the shaft, pick, hammer or adze and it is usually made from cast aluminium alloy. Being lighter but not as strong as forged steel, it may not withstand hammering the axe into hard snow. The head is attached to the shaft with one or two rivets; a one-rivet attachment may wear more quickly making the head less secure. The head should have smooth lines and feel comfortable when holding the top of the axe.

Picks
The pick is probably the most important part of a climbing tool and is also the factor that most affects performance. It must penetrate all types of ice, hold in snow or vegetation, be able to be hooked on to edges or in cracks, torqued, wedged and hammered and even able to save you in the event of a life-threatening slide!

There are three main designs of pick: curved, straight-drooped and re-curved (or banana) *(see Figure 13.3)*. The most commonly used is the re-curved for technical tools, and a curved pick for mountaineering axes. Forged steel picks are generally stronger than those stamped and welded from flat plate and are smoother to grip. Rough and sharp edges on stamped picks and heads may need to be filed smooth.

Most technical picks have 'positive clearance' *(see Figure 5.3 on page 57)* designed for easy penetration and removal in ice. Teeth on the lower edge of the pick give holding power and extend from close to the tip back to the shaft with an assortment of shapes and sizes. Teeth set close to the shaft help with holding in crusty snow or hollow ice, but tend to damage gloves when the axe is held by the head. Sometimes the pick is 'factory tuned' by the manufacturer, with rounded teeth, the lower and upper

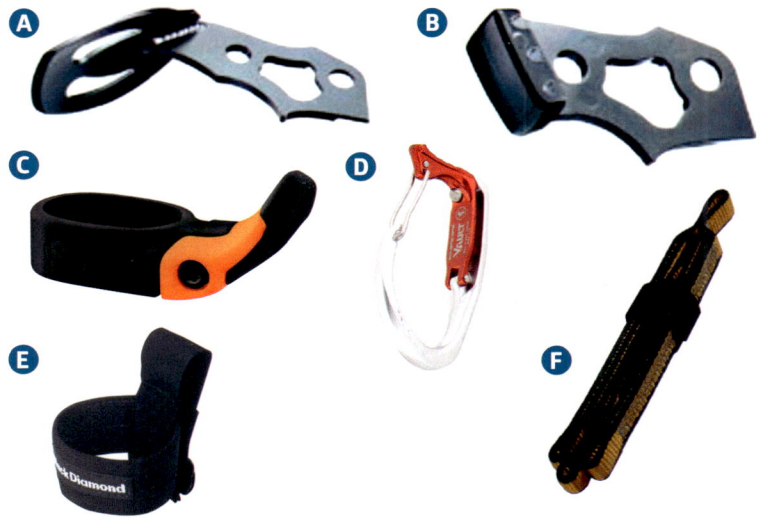

FIGURE 13.4 ACCESSORIES : (A) ADZE HEAD **(B)** HAMMER HEAD **(C)** AXE FINGER REST **(D)** CLIP HOLDER **(E)** HOLSTER **(F)** SCREAMER

edges bevelled and the whole pick may be taper-ground towards the tip by up to 1mm. This greatly assists in pick placement and removal.

Axe shafts and picks can be T- or B-rated. A T-rated component means that it has passed the most stringent tests. A B-rated pick may be of thinner steel than a stronger T-rated pick (3mm or less at the tip) and therefore more of an advantage on ice climbs, penetrating hard brittle ice with less fracturing. T-rated picks (4mm) are recommended for types of climbing that produce great strain on the metal, such as hooking and torquing, although some manufacturers consider torquing beyond the design specifications of their tools.

Fine-tuning your pick

If your picks are not factory-tuned, then some modification may be required. First, check the pick has positive clearance, since it will penetrate deeper in ice, hold better when weighted, is less likely to bounce off the ice when swung, and also concentrates the weight onto the point during hook moves on rock. Sharpen the top edge and bevel the teeth inward, both sides (except the point or first tooth) to between 30° and 45°, which helps with pick removal. Make a ramp behind the point to give a secure hooking hold in thin ice and rock edges. Finally, make the tip razor sharp, if you intend to climb hard ice. Less effort is needed to tune your pick for mixed routes, as the first hit against rock will fold over a sharp point!

Sharpen with a medium or fine flat hand-file, not a power grinder as this risks overheating the metal, thus weakening the pick by altering the temper. Work only one way with the file using firm strokes away from your body. Use an appropriately sized round file to re-shape the teeth, as a flat file will create sharp corners (stress points) which could also weaken your pick.

Adze
The adze is used for chopping, clearing, climbing and even hammering. It should be wide enough for efficient snow clearing when looking for anchor placements and fashioning stances. It should have a chisel-shaped edge for cutting steps on hard snow or small foot ledges on ice. Some adzes on technical tools are shaped to permit wedging or torquing into cracks. Sometimes it is useful to hammer gently with the adze, such as tapping the other tool to seat the pick into a crack or vegetation. Drooped adzes can be good in consolidated snow or cruddy soft ice, where the pick would pull through. However, an adze with too steep a droop is not efficient for cutting with. Maintain the adze by filing off burrs and keep the edge sharp enough to cut hard snow effectively.

Hammer head
The hammer head should be effective for hammering! Some bent-shafted tools make it awkward or nearly impossible to use it properly. It must extend forward and clear of the shaft and be set at an angle that is square to the swing of the tool. Beware of hammer heads that extend far forward of the shaft with thin necks as this can be a point of weakness. Most heads are shaped so that they can be wedged or torqued into cracks *(see Figure 13.4)*.

Spike
The spike is used to help the shaft penetrate the snow. It should be a regular symmetrical shape with a sharp point and have a smooth transition into the shaft through the ferrule. Most mountaineering axes have an effective spike, but technical tools with pommels, finger rests and moulded grips do not. Some spikes are angled forward to help protect knuckles and used as another point of contact with the ice or rock. On low-angled soft ice or névé, the pick and forward-raked spike can be punched into the ice by holding the shaft just above mid-point, most effective with a bent-shafted axe. With two tools, this allows a rapid way of climbing easier terrain. Most spikes also have a clip-in hole – useful for attaching lanyard leashes.

Pommels and finger rests
These give added hand support, particularly on steep ground, where the little finger rests against the pommel. They can either be permanent or removable and can be bought as an accessory. Finger rests can be adjusted so any finger can be used but many find using the index finger gives the greatest support.

Care and maintenance
Maintaining and tuning your tools is important for them to perform well. Read the manufacturer's specifications and follow their instructions and recommendations. Regularly clean, dry and inspect them for damage and store in a dry place when not in use. When stored, remove rubber protectors as condensation may form inside leading to corrosion. Ensure

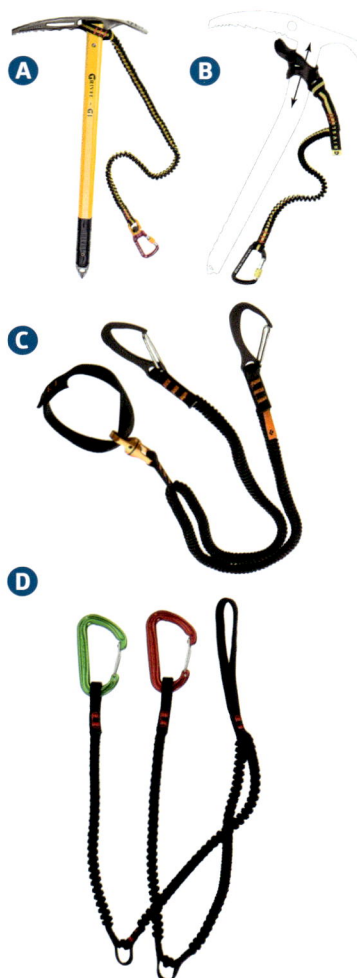

FIGURE 13.5 LANYARD LEASHES: (A) BASIC **(B)** SLIDER **(C)** WITH SWIVEL **(D)** WITH PULL-UP LOOP

that nuts and bolts are tightened properly and check frequently for loosening (a spot of Loctite® will help).

Degradation is not normally a problem with axes and any failures tend to be catastrophic, usually as a result of abuse, misuse or neglect! Check for burrs, knocks or signs of bending on the shaft or pick and for any tiny cracks around the teeth or lightening holes. With modular tools, check the bolt area for undue wear and cracks around the attachment holes. Fractures usually emanate from sharp corners, hairline cracks, machining marks or sudden changes in section – stress concentrators. Check for these before you buy your tools. If you find a fault, either change the component or seek the manufacturer's advice.

Lanyard leashes

As many technical tools have moulded handles which give a much more secure grip than a bent or vertical shaft, wrist loop leashes designed to take some of the load off your hands are no longer necessary. Also, not being attached to the tool in leashless climbing means that a greater range of moves are possible; it is easy to swap hands on a tool such as when traversing or going diagonally or use both hands on one tool *(see Chapter 14.4, page 213)*. The one big disadvantage is that it is possible to drop a tool and to this end lanyard leashes are useful. These are cords which attach to the tools and the climber. They can be home-made from suitably sized cord or purchased specifically for the job – these often have some sort of elasticated system to allow full stretch and retract, thus varying the length and reducing tangles. A full range of arm movement is necessary and water resistant materials are best to reduce the chance of the leashes freezing up. The lanyard is attached to the tools by small karabiners clipped into the hole in the spike, are usually lark's footed or clipped to the harness belay loop and may have some type of swivel at the end which goes to the harness to reduce tangling *(see Figure 13.5)*. One problem is that the karabiner can detach from the spike during use due

Wrist loop leash design
Clipper leash
Normally has a wide detachable lock-down wrist loop. The clip may be a sprung loaded catch and stud type or snap-link into a permanently attached wire loop which sits proud of the shaft for ease of clipping.

Clipper leashes can detach themselves unexpectedly. The stud type may twist off when the leash is pulled away from the shaft. Ensure that the attachments mate properly when re-clipping, but the wire may get abraded.

Lock-down wrist loop
The most effective method of opening and closing a wrist loop. When weighted, it will automatically lock around the wrist.

To exit the wrist loop, hook the accessory loop over the adze or hammer head and pull down – the wrist loop slides open. A small sliding stopper buckle determines how tightly the wrist loop locks.

D-ring or buckled wrist loop
The sling of the fixed leash must be pulled through locking rings or buckles to adjust the wrist loop size. The other hand or teeth must be used to pull the tabs to open the buckles or rings to exit the wrist loop.

Slider leash
A simple small plastic or metal tube slides along the fixed leash to lock or open the wrist loop. The other hand or teeth are used to pull the tab to move the slider, which can also move in normal use, making the leash feel insecure.

This is more prone to icing up than other designs of wrist loop adjustments.

---

to the metal twisting against metal. Tying a small loop of cord through the spike and linking to that reduces this danger by adding flexibility to the attachment and should be of the same load rating as the lanyard; purchased lanyards will normally have a load rating of around 2 to 3kN. On easier angled ground, for example when daggering or moving up high on a placement, care is necessary not to step or trip on the lanyard. A slider lanyard will allow the axe shaft and spike to be used without hindrance.

Wrist loop leashes
Although wrist loops have largely been superseded by lanyards for use in leashless climbing, they continue to be used and are still available from retail outlets. A wrist loop leash or wrist loop is used to keep your axe attached and to hang from when climbing. It should take strain from your hand gripping the axe, so reducing forearm fatigue. Wrist loops are either supplied with the axe or can be bought separately.

A wide wrist loop spreads the load comfortably and should have a system which closes securely yet allows easy opening. Extra-wide loops (stiffened to keep open) may dig uncomfortably into your lower arm, especially for people with small hands. Wrist loop leashes are adjusted so that your hand grips the base of the shaft. The axe is designed to be swung from this point and a choked-up grip (the shaft gripped higher up) from a poorly adjusted leash affects the swing detrimentally. Your little finger should be immediately above the ferrule. Wear your climbing gloves when adjusting leashes to the correct length.

Leashes are either fixed (permanently attached to your axe), or clipped and removable. Mountaineering axes generally have a fixed leash attached to the head through the 'karabiner' hole. Technical tools often have removable leashes which allow them to be detached to free your hand for other tasks.

Another consideration is how the axe hangs from your wrist. The hang point of most fixed leashes is from the axe head, so it will hang the full length of the leash, spike down. This makes it awkward to collect the axe, particularly on steep ground when hanging from the other tool. An accurate throw and catch is required! Having a lower hang point, as in clip-leashed tools, will let the axe hang head-down with the grip close to hand. This also means that the wrist loop is pulling closer to the line of the shaft making a more comfortable and mechanically sound grip. Hanging tools inevitably tangle with ropes or gear, although hanging full length creates fewer tangles. Fine adjustment of the hang point is required to have the shaft close to hand yet allow your hand onto the axe head when needed. Improvisation with fixed leashes, such as a jubilee clip (sharp edges taped) or a strong rubber ring (cut from car inner tubes) can be used for this adjustment.

Although it is much safer to clip direct to the tool if it is used to bear a load, if the leash must be used as a clip-in point, make sure that it is securely attached, and that the leash clip-in point is strong enough to bear a load. Leashes that are attached to the shaft are preferable in this situation, as a head-attached leash may twist the pick under load. Be aware that icing-up of moving parts, such as locking buckles and clippers, can pose problems in their use. Although it is usual to have similar leashes on each tool, a system using one fixed and one detachable leash can be convenient in some situations.

13.2.2 Technical crampons

Generally, footwear and route preference, (snow, ice or mixed) will influence your choice of crampon/binding combination. However, the more specialised crampons are, the better they will be on specific route types but may have disadvantages on others *(see Figure 13.6)*.

A solid connection between crampon and boot greatly improves performance. With secure binding systems enabling a good positive fit, there is a move away from the heavier rigid type for steep ice towards a two-piece crampon with interchangeable heel and front sections that can be changed from ice to mixed points. Choose your crampons to suit your

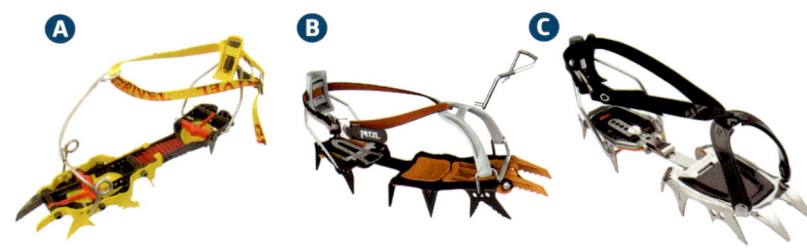

FIGURE 13.6 CRAMPONS: (A) MODULAR RIGID C3 CRAMPONS **(B)** MODULAR ARTICULATED C2 TECHNICAL CRAMPONS **(C)** C2 ARTICULATED MOUNTAINEERING CRAMPONS. ALL ARE SUPPLIED WITH ANTI-BALLING PLATES

level of climbing and be aware of their limitations. If you enjoy a range of route styles, then you either accept that your crampons will not be so effective on one style of climb, or that you have several pairs of crampons or even several crampon and boot combinations. However, a combination of a C2 or C3 crampon securely clipped to a rigid-soled B3 boot with anti-balling plates will be adequate on all but the most specialised type of climb.

There are a few general features of technical crampon to note:

- Vertically oriented front points, with teeth on the lower edge, provide easier penetration in hard ice than horizontally oriented ones, but less support in softer conditions. Some vertical front points are 'T' sectioned to hold better in softer conditions.
- A single front point (mono point) has advantages on steep technical terrain: they offer easy penetration on hard ice, can be used on small rock holds and in cracks and allow the foot to be pivoted on the single point. However, a mono point is more likely to shear through soft ice, snow and some vegetation.
- Modular construction allows the configuration, length and number of front points to be altered. For example, a mono point may be set at different positions along the front bar.
- Secondary points are often steeply raked forward for soft ice and snow. The closer they are to vertical, the better for mixed climbing. Backward-pointing third points, instep and heel spurs, and points under the ball of the foot assist techniques such as heel-hooking, back-stepping, 'egyptianing' or smearing!
- Asymmetrically shaped crampons can be fitted to the boot sole with the side points directly below the edge. This allows the points to be precisely placed and creates less leverage. For more precise placement, the mono point can also be situated below the big toe, rather than the centre of the foot.

Attachment
Technical crampons are fitted with an appropriate binding system for each boot/crampon combination and replacement parts are generally available. Front bails should have a metal or nylon retaining strap to prevent crampon loss if it is accidentally knocked from the welt. This can

happen when mixed or buttress climbing, or if the crampon is not correctly adjusted to the boot.

Fit
Technical crampons have many types of fine adjustments both to the crampon and the binding system to make a perfect fit to your boot. There should be no reason why your crampon and boot combination does not perform as one secure unit.

FIGURE 13.7 WINTER CLIMBING HELMET

13.2.3 Rope
For technical winter climbs, double-rope technique with two half ropes is recommended. They will normally be 8.5mm to 9mm in diameter and 50m to 60m in length. Half ropes, thinner than 8.5mm diameter, although lighter, are more difficult to manage, particularly when iced up, and are less durable. Longer ropes permit longer pitches so faster climbing overall and double ropes allow longer abseils. A single rope may be first choice for those starting out on lower grade climbs and are also used in guiding and instructing situations and range from around 9mm to 10.5mm diameter and 50m to 60m in length. The small diameter and lighter weight single ropes can also be used as a double rope.

Dry ropes are waterproofed through treatment with a hydrophobic solution. They handle better, weigh less, are stronger than a saturated rope and reduce the risk of icing. However, they are more expensive and normally lose their waterproofing over time. Ropes with a middle mark or pattern change at the half-way point are handy, but taped-on markers can jam in a belay or abseil device.

Regularly inspect ropes for damage, wash them if dirty and avoid standing on them, especially if the rope is lying on rock. There is usually less rope wear in winter as it will normally be running over less abrasive snow, ice or verglased rock. Follow the manufacturers' recommendations for the life of a rope and discard if it gets damaged.

13.2.4 Helmet
A helmet is essential for winter climbing and scrambling. There is a likelihood of debris falling from above, either knocked off by your own picks, from your partner, or even from a party ahead. Icicles and stones fall naturally during times of thaw and windy conditions.

A helmet of thick plastic shell construction (polycarbonate) either with an internal cradle or extruded foam padding is the best choice of weight versus strength. Most helmets are ergonomically shaped to cover the sides and back of the head partially without compromising peripheral vision *(see Figure 13.7)*. This offers some protection from side impacts, such as in a fall or from deflected debris. Other considerations include ease of adjustment, particularly whilst wearing gloves, space to accommodate a hat, and it must have an attachment for a headtorch. Ventilation holes are two-way and allow rain and spindrift in, so detachable plugs are useful, or alternatively, tape them over. It is important to adjust your helmet to a good fit as recommended by the manufacturer.

Visors or face guards offer protection against shards of ice or knocks from your tools. They are worth considering for indoor use (recommended for indoor dry tooling facilities) or bouldering outside, but restrict your vision on a winter climb in all but the best weather and conditions.

13.2.5 Harness

Adjustable leg loops for easy fitting when wearing crampons and a buckle system that can be fitted and adjusted when wearing gloves is recommended. A winter harness does not need to be heavily padded since extra clothing provides this. If a rucksack is worn, it may make stiffened padding dig into your back. A drop-seat harness will allow clothing changes at belays while staying attached at the waist belt.

At least four gear loops are ideal as an option for carrying gear on the harness as well as on a bandolier. Gear loops near the front are more accessible when wearing a rucksack. Some harnesses have fittings for attaching tool holders. A large obvious central loop (the 'belay loop') should be easily visible and can be used for abseiling. Lightweight alpine harnesses with 'nappy' style pull-through leg loops are also convenient. If there is no central loop, then use a maillon that allows multi-directional loading as the central point. Holsters can be handy for carrying some shorter axes when not in use and can be attached to your harness. Otherwise, an axe can be carried in a specific tool holding or racking karabiner (Caritool), preferably metal, or through a gear loop or wide karabiner.

13.2.6 Belay device

A standard or passive 'tube' style belay device is appropriate and is used as normal. Recognise its characteristics, such as whether it is slick or grabby for a given rope diameter, if it can be used with half and single ropes, or designed for thin or standard half ropes, and its ability to cope with iced up ropes when wearing gloves or mitts. For greatest safety the belay device should be matched to the diameter of the rope. Some devices offer a two-way operation that generates more or less friction, such as having cleats on one side giving greater control of snowed-up, iced or thin ropes. It should also be usable as an abseil device.

A device with an auto-blocking facility is convenient for belaying one or two seconds on a direct belay as in guiding situations. Thorough practice is required in its use, especially its operation when under load and when releasing a loaded rope to lower. Figure of eight descenders and auto-locking devices are not recommended for winter use. All belay devices should be used with a large locking karabiner (HMS) that can be easily manipulated when wearing gloves.

> **Basic personal equipment**
>
> Single or half rope, harness, one ice axe, or ice axe and hammer, crampons, helmet, belay device on HMS screwgate karabiner, spare large screwgate karabiner, one long sling (8mm–10mm, 120cm) with large screwgate karabiner.
>
> Also consider prusik and knife and abseil material (7mm cord), stored in the top lid of rucksack or in a pocket if you are not carrying a rucksack on the climb.

13.2.7 Karabiners

Large size, offset 'D' shaped with a wide gate opening are recommended for ease of use. A wired gate (bent stainless-steel 'paperclip') is lighter, easier to operate and less susceptible to freezing up. Solid gates are either straight or bent (which allows easier clipping and wider gate opening), and are best with a keyhole latch (a non-pin and hooked notch closure) which is easier for clipping and unclipping and less likely to snag. Minimum strengths should be 20kN major axis, 7kN minor axis (cross-loading) but check for 7kN as an important gate open loading.

Locking karabiners
These are used where it is important that the gate remains closed, such as on anchors and belay devices. Screwgate karabiners are the simplest and most reliable. They are less prone to icing or jamming with grit, are easier to operate when wearing gloves than auto-locking models and can be clipped and locked or unlocked single-handed. Avoid over-tightening screwgate karabiners as they may be difficult to undo. HMS screwgate karabiners are versatile and designed for use with an Italian hitch.

If a screwgate jams closed, then a few gentle taps of the locking sleeve against a hard object may break an icy seal, or weight the karabiner along its major axis (hang on it) and try to unscrew whilst weighted. If it is frozen closed you can warm it with your breath, in your hand or next to your body.

Care and maintenance
Although dropping karabiners from a height evidently does not affect their strength, check and retire any karabiner that has deep indentations, is bent or if the gate does not operate smoothly. Lubricate moving parts during maintenance and carefully remove any small burrs with a file and/or fine sandpaper.

13.2.8 Quickdraws

Quickdraws consist of a short tape sling of varying length (around 15cm for winter use) with a karabiner at either end. The bottom karabiner is usually captive, held in one position with gate opening down and out for ease of clipping in the rope. They are used to extend runners to reduce rope drag and lessen the chance of them lifting out. Quickdraws should not be used on anchors as there is usually no need to extend them, thus introducing two redundant links in the belay chain.

Energy-absorbing quickdraws ('Screamers')
These can be used on suspect runners and are sometimes used with ice-screw protection. The tearing of the stitching in the sling absorbs some of the energy and reduces the load on the runner. They are made in different sizes and shock-absorption capacities. If the stitches do not fully rip in a fall, the remaining stitching still has some shock-absorbing capability left *(see Figure 13.4F on page 181).*

Basic winter rack

The following is a rough guide and assumes average conditions and individual competence at each climbing grade, and should be modified accordingly. The rock type will also influence a mixed/buttress rack especially in the upper grades.

- 1 set of wired nuts, split 1–6 and 7–10 on two carrying karabiners.
- 3 hexcentrics (hexes) in larger sizes 6,7,8. Best on wire and carried on a karabiner.
- 3 flexible camming devices, Friend 1,2,3 or equivalent size, each on a karabiner.
- 4 quickdraws of medium length.
- 2 short slings each with two karabiners.

This rack is appropriate for climbs up to Grade II, snow and mixed. For pure snow climbs, consider adding two deadmen with large screwgate karabiners. For pure ice climbs, or mixed with a significant amount of ice, from Grade III to IV add: 4 to 8 ice screws plus carriers; 4 quickdraws (2 short, 1 medium, 1 long); 4 to 6 rock pitons (selection of sizes from knifeblade to angle) split between two karabiners.

For mixed or buttress climbs of Grade IV to VI consider adding: set of wired nuts; 3 flexible camming devices in the 1⁄2 sizes – 1⁄2, 11⁄2, 21⁄2 each on a karabiner; 6 quickdraws (4 short, 1 medium, 1 large); 6 rock pitons (1 knifeblade, 1 thin kingpin, 4 angles/leepers up to size 3⁄4 inch); 1–2 'turfies' if frozen turf or vegetation is expected; Bulldog® or smaller and thinner Terrier® for iced up cracks, frozen turf or quick ice placement, 1 short sling (knotted) with 2 karabiners.

For pure ice at Grade V and above, consider adding a 'screamer', or mixed and buttress above VI; micro nuts and micro cams - but you should know by now!

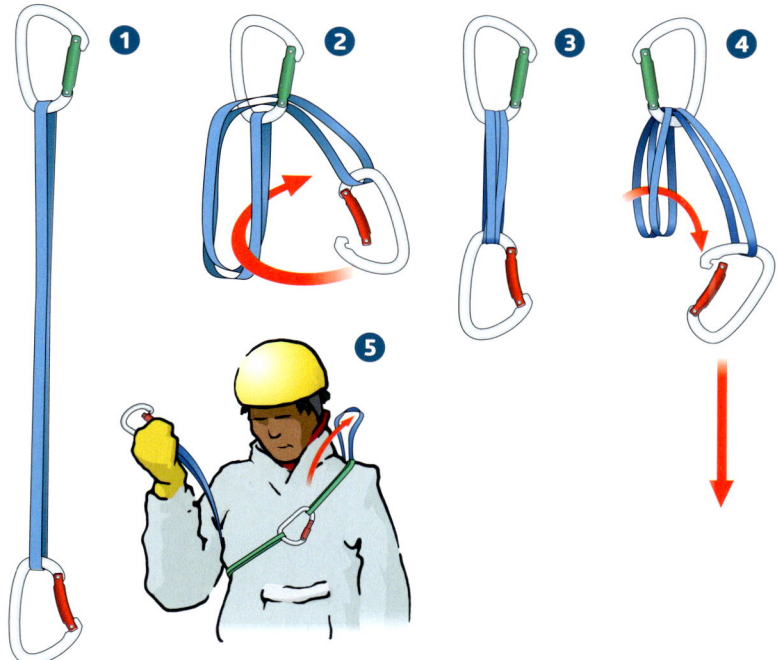

FIGURE 13.8 SLINGS: (1–3) CONVERT A SHORT SLING INTO A QUICKDRAW **(4)** EXTEND QUICKDRAW SLING **(5)** CARRY A LONG SLING AND SCREWGATE OVER THE SHOULDER. REMOVE SLING BY UNCLIPPING AND PULLING AROUND FROM BACK

13.2.9 Slings

Sewn slings can be used in a number of situations, such as extending runners, linking anchors to a central point and around natural anchors. Slings can be made from nylon Dyneema®, or Aramide and are either 60cm (short sling), 120cm (long sling or belay sling) or extra long at 240cm for using on large block anchors or linking anchors that are a long way apart *(see Figure 13.8)*. Daisy chains are long slings with a number of sewn sections along their length that are used either as a personal safety sling for clipping into anchors or to centralise two anchors, otherwise their use is limited. Do not clip a karabiner around the sewn section's stitching as this is usually only designed to take body weight loading. A knotted sling (tape knot) can be conveniently untied and used for abseil material. Do not sew or tape the ends of the sling as a loose knot can work along the sling (rather than undo), the strength of which will then rely on the taped or sewn ends! Check all slings regularly for damage and loose knots. Excessively 'furred-up' slings (indicating many broken individual fibres) should be regarded as damaged and retired, as this wear severely compromises the strength of the sling.

TIM NEILL ON THOLL GATE, VI, 6, FUARR THOLL, NORTH WEST HIGHLANDS   *PHOTO // DAVE EVANS*

Climbing techniques

There is much in common between each climbing style specific to snow, ice and mixed and there is usually a combination of all used on a single route.

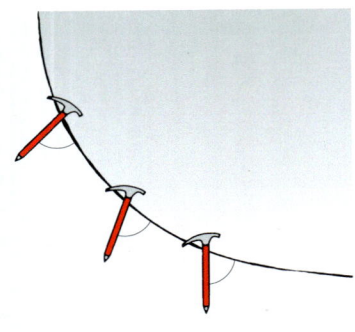 

FIGURE 14.1 AXE PLACEMENT AND SLOPE ANGLES

FIGURE 14.2 CHOKING THE AXE

There is a direct relationship between rock climbing and mixed or buttress climbing techniques. While some skills are new, others such as using equipment and belaying, are adapted from rock climbing.

14.1 Snow climbing

Snow climbs form a sound basis for all winter climbing, and learning the necessary skills on Grade I and II routes can take the winter mountaineer into some spectacular terrain and beautiful mountain scenery.

Using axe and crampons on a snow climb should be adapted to suit the varying snow conditions and slope angle. On easier ground, zig-zagging French technique is appropriate with steeper sections tackled by front-pointing. Hybrid technique is used on moderately steep ground to relieve your calves. A single axe is sufficient for straightforward climbs. A second axe, or hammer, can be useful for steeper sections and can be stowed on the rucksack or down between your sack and back when not required.

In moderately angled soft snow, plunge the axe vertically up to the head and kick in with both feet. As the slope steepens, the axe is driven in at a higher angle and on the steepest of slopes, about 45° to the surface for maximum support *(see Figure 14.1)*. Weight is spread between your feet forming a stable stance. Try not to pull on the axe too much in soft snow as it may lever out. If the snow is soft and deep then climb by plunging your axe and arms into the snow and create a trough with a wallowing action, compressing the snow with your feet and knees. Aim to get as much into the snow as you can to create the maximum amount of resistance to pull against. If the axe does not penetrate fully, the shaft can be held at the level of the snow to reduce leverage: 'choking' the axe *(see Figure 14.2)*. This can also be done with one hand on the axe head and the other on the shaft. On harder snow, another method used for balance when moving diagonally or traversing short sections relies on support from the spike pushed into the snow at waist level. The lower hand rests on the spike, the upper holds the axe head *(see Figure 14.3)*.

14.1.1 Daggering

Steep, hard snow may feel off balance if you hold the axe in the normal vertical manner. While front-pointing, the axe can be used for support

Winter grades

Climbs are graded using an open-ended two-tier system, similar to the UK rock climbing grading system. The overall difficulty of a route is indicated by the Roman numeral while the technical grades, Arabic numbers, apply to the hardest move or crux sequence. In this way, a V,4 is normally a serious ice route and V,5 would be a classic ice route with adequate protection, V,6 would be a classic mixed route and V,7 would indicate a technically difficult but well-protected mixed route. Each climb has the same overall difficulty but with varying degrees of seriousness and technical difficulty. The hardest winter routes may now be Grade X but few have had this grade confirmed. Winter grades can vary considerably with conditions but are graded for average conditions (which may be difficult to find!). Occasionally climbs have split grades, for example Grade II/ III when they are known to vary considerably with conditions such as build-up of snow.

Grade I
Uncomplicated, average-angled snow climbs normally having no defined pitches. However, they may have cornice difficulties or dangerous run-outs.

Grade II
Gullies which contain either individual or minor pitches, or high-angled snow with difficult cornice exits. The easiest buttresses or ridges under winter conditions.

Grade III
Gullies which contain ice in quantity, where there will normally be at least one substantial pitch and possibly several lesser ones. Sustained buttress and mixed climbs, but only technical in short sections.

Grade IV
Steeper and more technical with vertical sections found on ice climbs. Mixed routes will require a good repertoire of techniques.

Grade V
Climbs which are difficult, sustained and serious. If on ice, long sustained ice pitches are to be expected, while mixed routes will require a degree of rock climbing ability and the use of axe torquing and hooking and other winter techniques.

Grade VI
Thin and tenuous ice routes or those with long vertical sections. Mixed routes will include all that is defined above, but more of it.

Grade VII
Usually mixed routes which are very sustained or technically extreme. Also sustained routes on thin or vertical ice.

Grade VIII
Very hard and sustained mixed routes.

Grade IX and above
Extremely difficult in all aspects and likely to be very serious.

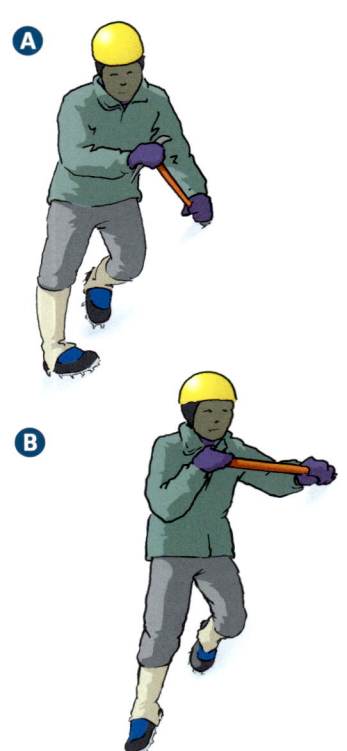

FIGURE 14.3 USING THE SPIKE FOR BALANCE: **(A)** MODERATELY ANGLED SLOPES – PUSH DOWN ON THE SPIKE FOR SUPPORT **(B)** STEEP SLOPES – THE SPIKE IS USED FOR BALANCE MORE THAN SUPPORT

and balance by pushing the pick into the snow at waist or hip level and directly below your shoulder. Use the palm of your hand to push down on the adze and use your weight, rather than muscle power, to force the pick into the snow *(see Figure 14.4)*. The curved or inclined shape of the pick assists this process. Front point (three small steps, feet square to the snow, horizontal and at least hip width apart) up to a level where your arm is near straight and replace the pick at waist level. Move your axe when in a stable stance with both feet at the same height. Your spare hand is braced on the snow for support, or your second axe is used in the same manner. When using two axes, the most efficient method is an alternate and diagonal pick–crampon action, or one at a time for most security. With practice, it can feel like 'running' up the slope. Daggering can be used in reverse to descend slopes. Traversing steep snow is similar with the axe in the same position at waist level and, with two axes, they are taken apart and placed together in the direction of travel.

Another method used on short sections of steep snow is to use two hands on a single axe. The axe is daggered into the snow at shoulder height with the stronger hand over the axe head and the other gripping the base of the shaft which is angled at a slight diagonal *(see Figure 14.5)*. This method can be used in ascent, descent and traverse. The same technique may be used for an axe that is swung into the snow.

14.1.2 Classic overhead swing

When the snow is too hard or awkward for daggering, a swing of the axe drives the pick into the snow. Hold the shaft above the ferrule and swing the axe in an arc from behind your head *(see Figure 14.6)*. If used, the wrist loop leash is adjusted to give support for the hand. Gain the maximum height from each placement as this technique is slower and more strenuous than others. As you ascend, slide your hand up the shaft until it is resting on the head. The leash must be adjusted to allow this. The free hand is braced on the snow, or a second axe may be used in the same fashion or daggered.

FIGURE 14.4 DAGGERING: PUSH DOWN, PALM ON THE ADZE FOR SUPPORT – THE OTHER HAND IS PLACED ON THE SNOW FOR BALANCE

FIGURE 14.5 DAGGERING – BOTH HANDS ON THE AXE

FIGURE 14.6 THE CLASSIC OVERHEAD SWING: (1 & 2) FROM A BALANCED STANCE, FOCUS ON A POINT IN THE SNOW OR ICE AND SWING THE AXE IN A NATURAL ARC TO PLACE THE PICK WITH A NEAR EXTENDED ARM **(3)** FOCUSING ON CRAMPONS, TAKE SMALL STEPS, KICKING WITH A SWING FROM THE KNEES. KEEP HEELS LOW AND FEET SQUARE TO THE SNOW OR ICE **(4)** GAIN MOST HEIGHT FROM A SINGLE PLACEMENT BY MOVING THE HAND UP THE SHAFT (LIKE USING A BANISTER RAIL) ONTO THE AXE HEAD

Descending steep snow using the axe swing is awkward. It is difficult to swing the axe in a low position to get a good placement and this means short descents between each placement. Descending too far on to a straight arm may make it difficult to remove the pick. On steep ground, it should feel like you are kicking up into the snow to keep the heels low for a good crampon placement.

14.1.3 Resting

On steep or hard snow, cut a foot ledge or small stance to rest on if your legs tire. To rest effectively it is important to get support for the heel, so a step as long as the boot is best. Otherwise, rest with the lower leg straight and the foot flat across the slope and the upper crampon on front points: mixed crampon technique. The knee of the upper leg can be braced against the snow. The pick is pushed into the snow with the palm resting on the axe head for support.

14.1.4 Negotiating a cornice

A large cornice is often the crux of a route. Some can be unclimbable, forcing a retreat. Large cornices are best avoided, especially during periods of thaw or heavy build-up. The steep scarp slope below a cornice is notoriously avalanche-prone under the wrong conditions. Tackle the cornice at the narrowest point where the least effort is required, usually at one side of a gully where rock protection may be available, or where there is a projection such as a ridge or buttress although this may mean a long traverse *(see Figure 14.7)*. Agree a communication system beforehand if you expect the belay to be back from the edge or in poor weather.

Caution is required with a large soft cornice – it must be stable. Check the run-out and consequences of a fall and work from a solid belay or runner – a deadman runner may be effective. The belayer should be off to the side and out of the line of fire of debris or cornice collapse. The closer the belay is to the cornice, the more rope will be available for the belay above, especially if the anchors are a long way back from the edge. Use any previously cut slots and follow footsteps made by others – disturbed and compressed snow is more consolidated and secure. Cutting through large cornices is strenuous, tiring and uncomfortable, especially if spindrift and debris is re-circulating in the wind.

It may be possible to climb smaller cornices directly. A soft edge can be chopped with the adze or knocked down with the axe head swung sideways, or use a shovel! If the snow is firmer and deeper, cut a shoulder-width slot directly through the cornice. For larger overhanging cornices, work diagonally until it is possible to finish direct by cutting steps through a slot. For right-handed climbers, move diagonally rightwards into the cornice (and vice versa for left-handers), chopping large steps until it is possible to tackle the cornice directly from a stable stance. Handholds can be fashioned for balance or the second axe driven in for support.

The exit, usually strenuous, is helped by being able to pull on a good axe placement. Use a vertical shaft in soft snow (difficult if using curved tools with handles) or the pick or adze in harder conditions. It is

FIGURE 14.7 AVOIDING A HUGE CORNICE OVERHANGING A GULLY: A BELAY AWAY FROM THE CORNICE, USING THE ROCKS TO THE RIGHT, IS A SAFER OPTION

FIGURE 14.8 THE AXE SWING

sometimes necessary to use your knees for the final move. Tunnelling a cornice should only be considered as a last resort since it is very time-consuming, tiring and wetting. Tunnelling or even cutting a deep slot may cause a cornice to collapse. This is very serious as the huge weight of snow can sweep climbers off and even cause belay failures. It is vital that the belayer is not threatened by possible cornice collapse. Solid icy cornices can be climbed like an ice bulge, with protection placed in the cornice and possibly even aid used.

14.2 Ice climbing

Ice climbing in the UK has a world-wide reputation, not because of its pure ice quality nor its easy, sunny approaches, but in the variety, history, unpredictability and changeability of the climbing set in an impressive and often harsh environment.

The same single axe techniques for snow climbing are used for low-angled ice. The classic axe swing and front-point technique is used when the snow-ice becomes hard for daggering. As the angle steepens, it becomes more difficult to remove a single axe without losing balance so an ice tool for each hand is necessary.

14.2.1 The axe swing

With specialised equipment, the classic swing is adapted. Different shafts and pick shapes require subtly different swings. The full swing is a natural arc, using the weight and balance of the tool, forward from behind your head into the ice *(see Figure 14.8)*.

Load: lift the tool up and straight back to behind your head;
Aim: by focusing on the target point on the ice;
Fire: swing the tool forward in an arc by releasing your arm at the shoulder and elbow;
Flick: finish with a flick of the wrist forward to lock again just as the pick engages the ice. Without the flick there is a chance of hitting your knuckles.

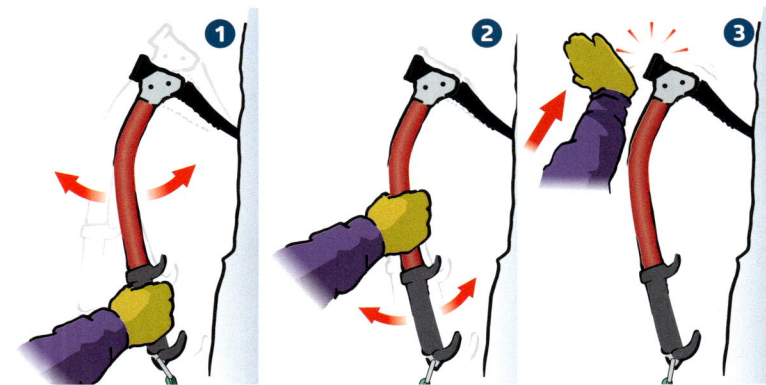

FIGURE 14.9 REMOVING THE AXE: (1 & 2) PUSH UP ON THE AXE AT THE SAME TIME AS MOVING THE SHAFT **(2)** USING A HIGHER GRIP WITH SMALLER SHAFT MOVEMENTS CAN HELP **(3)** STUBBORN PLACEMENTS CAN BE LOOSENED BY HITTING THE HAND ON THE UNDERSIDE OF THE HEAD

This swing is used for re-curved picks and works with bent or straight shafts. The curved pick has a similar swing without the final flick. The straight drooped pick requires a pull down on the elbow instead of a flick to hook into the ice. The grip remains constant throughout to stop the tool twisting as it hits the ice, and the arm is swung in a vertical plane square to the ice. For soft ice, the grip is released momentarily at the very end of the swing as the pick engages, as this saves energy.

A good placement does not wobble, has a solid sound with vibrations running down the shaft, and should finish parallel to the ice, with your hand just off its surface if using relatively straight shafts. For moulded grips, the handle can then be braced on the ice or a forward-pointing spike in contact with the ice for support and stability. A good placement will hold your weight if your crampons break out of the ice: your tools are your anchors! Test the pick placement by giving a sharp tug down whilst taking weight on your other tool. The judgement is to get a good placement without overdriving the tool as time and energy is wasted removing a stuck pick. The type and thickness of the ice can require modifications to the basic swing. A short swing may be sufficient for soft ice or where the pick does not need to be driven in, such as enhancing a hook and several short accurate blows ('pecking') may be required on thin ice.

To remove the pick, pull out on the shaft, push it back towards the ice a little, lift and push the axe up and out *(see Figure 14.9)*. If it does not release, try again several times and lift out. Moving your hand up the shaft and hitting on the underside of the head with your hand can loosen stubborn placements. If this loosens it, lift it out with your hand relocated on the grip. Twisting the pick from side to side gently may help, but too much twisting can damage or even break the pick. Keep your head away from the tool when removing it, as a sudden release can hit you in the face. A well-tuned pick will aid removal.

14.2.2 Reading the ice

Typically, there is a variety of ice on a route and an experienced climber will identify where the easiest and most secure placements are. Reading the ice saves time and energy. White, opaque ice is softer, either because it is mixed with snow or has air bubbles and pockets. This gives easier placements than clear brittle water ice (the freezing of a watercourse or free-draining melt-water) which is more likely to shatter. A frozen watercourse will also produce icicles, columns, shrouds (where wind blowing up the fall forms ice into an overhanging hood) and pillars which may require more delicate and subtle placements. Ice that has undergone a mild thaw gives the easiest placements and is often referred to as plastic ice. If the thaw continues, ice will become rotten and detached from the underlying rock as melt-water flows behind. If it then re-freezes, it can become brittle hollow ice.

'Eggshell' is another form of hollow ice formed by water dropping and freezing onto snow making an icy shield. This can be disconcerting as it breaks away on the underlying snow when it is weighted. Snow-ice, or névé, is the end form of snow freeze-thaw cycles and is one of the best mediums to climb on. There can be good placements at the top of steepenings or over bulges where the ice meets the snow. Convexities in the ice (areas of tension), such as on bulges, shatter more easily than small depressions and hollows.

Dinner-plating is where the ice shatters around a pick placement in the shape of a plate of various sizes and usually dislodges. If this happens, hit again in the same spot for a good placement. Starring is when cracks radiate from the pick but the ice does not dislodge and may still be a useable placement but usually precedes dinner-plating. Unless it is safe to clear the fractured ice, try again somewhere else. Falling ice is a very real danger if there are others below, especially your belayer. If you leave a dinner-plate, try not to crampon it as it could break out. Following other teams up an ice climb is not recommended – even the best ice climbers will create a falling debris hazard! To quote a well-known experienced ice climber, 'If the first rule of ice climbing is, "Don't fall off" then surely the second is, "Don't stand where you can get hit with falling ice."'

14.2.3 Crampon techniques

Initially, look for natural foot-holds or ones left by previous parties and focus on each crampon placement. On steep ice, lean out a little for a clearer view. Keep your feet at equal height, square to the ice surface, horizontal and about hip width apart before moving your tools. An amount of ankle flex will unlock your knees. This gives a stable platform, distributes your weight evenly and maintains balance *(see Figure 14.10)*. Use small steps as they are less strenuous than stepping high. In soft ice, one kick is all that is needed. On more brittle ice two or three short sharp kicks may be required to seat the points. On fluted ice, with dual point crampons, check that front points are in the ice and not either side of an icicle. Bridging positions take strain off your arms and provide a rest *(see Figure 14.11)*.

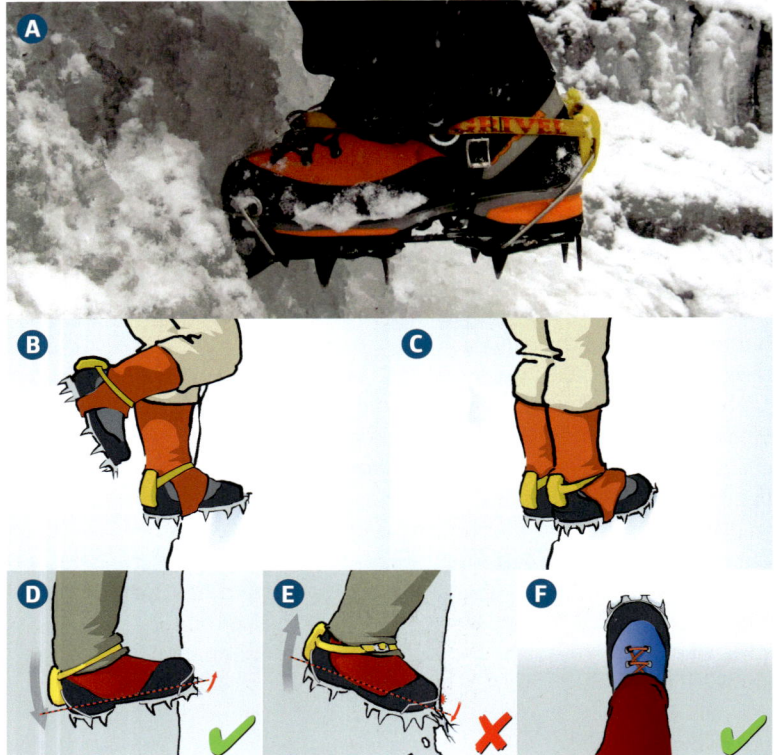

FIGURE 14.10 CRAMPONS ON STEEP ICE: (A) A STABLE PLATFORM IS FORMED BY THE FRONT AND SECOND SET OF POINTS – KEEP THE HEELS LOW WITH A DEGREE OF ANKLE AND KNEE FLEX **(B&C)** KICK INTO THE ICE BY SWINGING FROM THE KNEE. ON STEEP ICE, FEEL AS THOUGH YOU ARE KICKING UP ON THE FINAL PART OF THE SWING – LIKE 'TOE-BASHING' A FOOTBALL **(D)** ON STEEP ICE, DROPPING THE HEEL SLIGHTLY ENGAGES THE SECOND SET OF POINTS **(E)** HEEL LIFT ENCOURAGES THE FRONT POINTS TO SHEAR OUT OF THE ICE **(F)** KEEP YOUR FEET SQUARE TO THE ICE FOR THE MOST EFFECTIVE FRONT POINT PLACEMENT   PHOTO // GEORGE McEWAN

14.2.4 Moving on steep ice

Front-pointing is the most efficient method, keeping three points of contact and moving from a stable position. From this stance move one tool and place it at a comfortable distance above your head without over-reaching and at shoulder width. Follow this with the second tool at the same level. Look down and move your feet up in two or three small steps to another stable position and repeat the process *(see Figure 14.12)*. This is the basic and most secure feeling technique. Over-reaching placements encourage heel lift, risking the points levering out and make it difficult to lean out to check your crampon placements or remove the tool if necessary for a better placement. Moving up, share your weight between your tool placements and maintain a steady pull down as pulling out could unseat your picks. Pick placements too close together, particularly in brittle ice, can induce horizontal fracturing or dinner-plating which may cause both to fail.

A more effective method uses a different configuration of tool position – 'staggering'. From the same stance, with tools initially in front, place the first directly above your head and hold straight-armed. Move your feet up to equal height so that they and the upper tool form a stable triangle of contact points. As you move up, pull out on the lower tool to start releasing its pick. Remove the lower tool and replace it above the first placement and slightly off line roughly 50cm higher *(see Figure 14.13)*. Hang from it straight-armed, shift your body weight slightly to directly below the high tool, again forming a stable triangle. Step up, loosen the lower tool and repeat the process.

FIGURE 14.11 BRIDGING ON STEEP ICE

Staggering is more energy-efficient as there are fewer placements and lock-offs and with more chance to hang straight-armed. It allows a faster, more fluid movement as the lower tool moves from a position where it is easier to release the pick. In brittle ice, there is less chance of fracturing between your picks. There is however, the possibility of knocking ice onto your head from placements directly above and you are pulling on one tool at a time. Staggering your feet is a less balanced form of movement, but is a good technique to use with staggered tools for moving fast on 'comfortable' ground. In good ice and with confidence it is even more efficient to place the upper tool more directly above the lower one which permits even distance between placements.

14.2.5 Traversing

There are occasions that require a traverse or diagonal ascent, for example weaving around ice bulges. Traversing requires small movements with many tool and crampon placements, but on steep ice there is more opportunity to use straight arms. Reach comfortably to the side and place the leading tool vertically. Move your feet across until under the placement and place the trailing tool at an angle nearby. Crossing feet can be efficient on easier-angled ice but is awkward on steep ground. Lean off (layaway) the trailing tool without twisting the pick and repeat the sequence. Using the pick hole for the trailing tool that was made by the leading one saves time, energy and reduces dinner-plating. When moving diagonally or traversing, leashless tools are a real advantage. Place one tool in the direction of travel, move onto it, swap hands on the tool and place the next tool where you want to go. The tool not in use can be hooked over the shoulder using the pick to hold it in place *(see 14.4 Leashless climbing)*.

14.2.6 Down climbing

The sequence is the reverse of ascending except it is difficult to swing your tool below shoulder height to get a good placement. Use pick holes made in ascent to save energy, and move down in small steps, lean out and kick slightly up into the ice to seat the crampons. Move down until almost straight-armed and repeat, testing each placement more than you would in ascent. When down climbing steep ice, alternately place the

FIGURE 14.12 MOVING ON ICE: FROM A STABLE POSITION **(1)** REPLACE TOOLS AT A COMFORTABLE DISTANCE ABOVE **(2)** MOVE THE LEAST SECURE TOOL FIRST AND RESET WITH A SECURE PLACEMENT. THE SECOND TOOL MAY BE PLACED LESS SECURELY, WHICH WOULD THEN BE THE FIRST TOOL TO MOVE IN THE NEXT SEQUENCE. **(3)** FOCUS ON CRAMPON PLACEMENTS WHEN MOVING UP TO THE NEXT STABLE POSITION WITH FEET AT SIMILAR HEIGHT **(4&5)** WHEN MOVING ONTO AN EASING IN ANGLE, GAIN AS MUCH POSSIBLE FROM THE AXE PLACEMENTS

tools diagonally out to the side and slightly above waist height as this enables a more powerful swing and secure placement. Down climbing should only be for short sections and it is better to have overhead protection to safeguard the descent. If there are longer sections of down climbing, consider lowering off or abseiling, the latter option putting less load on the anchor point.

14.2.7 Ice formations

Ice rarely forms a single smooth sheet at a uniform angle. Use ice formations and adapt your positions to rest or take some strain off your arms. Rest calves by flat footing on ledges, flattenings or less steep sections. Leaning a shoulder or hip against an ice pillar or corner (body bracing or scumming), bridging and back-stepping are forms of resting.

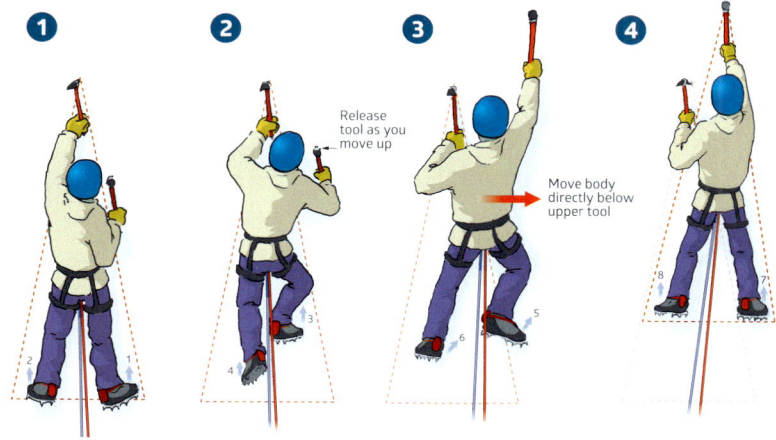

FIGURE 14.13 STAGGERING – MOVING FROM STABLE TRIANGLES OF CONTACT POINTS

Twist locking, cross-overs, underclings, sidepulls and heel hooks are rock climbing techniques that are possible when climbing steep, featured ice.

14.2.8 Thin ice

Ice that does not accept ice screw protection or a good depth pick placement is regarded as thin: around 8cm depth. It can form a sheet or it may be short sections of blobs or dribbles on small ledges and is relatively common on mixed climbs. Soft ice (around 0°C) is the most favourable for thin ice. Hollow, brittle thin ice may shatter off the rock. Thin ice requires a steadiness and good weight distribution, gentle placements with the crampons and the axe swung from the wrist. For very thin ice, peck with the pick by pulling down making a hole to hook into. Similarly, chip with the crampon points to create a hold. Weighting the points on an ice blob is sometimes all that is required, or chipping an edge with the pick for your foothold. Climb verglas by using your tools and crampons on underlying rock holds and take advantage of the occasional thicker ice such as in corners, grooves or cracks. Another technique is to scrape a slot in the ice with the pick to form a placement; this prevents the pick from bouncing out if it hits the rock beneath. It is not possible to reach as high as when swinging, therefore more placements like this are generally needed.

14.2.9 Ice bulges

Pulling over a sharp change in angle such as at the top of a steep section requires thoughtful crampon placements and an effort to keep your heels low. Firstly, arrange protection below the bulge and work your tools up and over the edge onto the easier angle. Placing your tools in the lip of the bulge can cause dinner-plating. Swinging your tool over the bulge is awkward, but bent shafts help as does an extreme wrist flick. Move your feet up high with small steps (lean out to see) and, from a good stable position, replace a tool further back. Continue stepping up and over onto the easing with the aid of a mantle onto your tools. It is vital to keep your

FIGURE 14.14 CLIMBING MODERATE ICE BULGES:
(1) FROM GOOD AXE PLACEMENTS **(2)** PULL OVER THE CHANGE IN ANGLE AND FOCUS ON KEEPING HEELS LOW, PARTICULARLY THE LOWER FOOT **(3)** A HIGH STEP ONTO THE LOWER ANGLED ICE MAY BE NECESSARY

centre of gravity above your feet and avoid leaning in *(see Figure 14.14)*. The last moves onto easier ground are often done with the crampons flat-footing as trying to front-point tips you forward too much.

14.2.10 Other considerations

It is often possible to hook into placements left by the leader or previous parties and on popular climbs they may be climbed totally on existing placements. The second can also use less well-driven placements in the interest of speed and conserving energy. If you are climbing using a line of old footholds, a good tool placement is often found at the back of the footprint. Old steps in snow are often more consolidated after compression and give better placements.

It is more comfortable and less strenuous to place protection before the start of steep sections *(see Ice screws and their placement on page 223)*. Place tools thoughtfully on steep fluted water ice to prevent shattering. Hooking, layaways and underclings can be used between ice flutes and icicles. It may be possible to peck a hooking hole with the pick in thinner ice between icicles for a good placement. Wet spots in the ice can indicate soft ice and a good placement. Beware of water spurting if it is running behind the ice!

To rest on steep uniform ice, hang straight-armed and relax your grip to save strength, which also means warmer hands. Using leashless tools, you can 'shake out' by alternately letting each arm hang and shake to release tension in the hand and arm. Stay relaxed and keep your weight on your feet. The 'monkey hang' uses this position, then step your feet up to bent knees. Pull up to a locked-off arm position and replace your tools

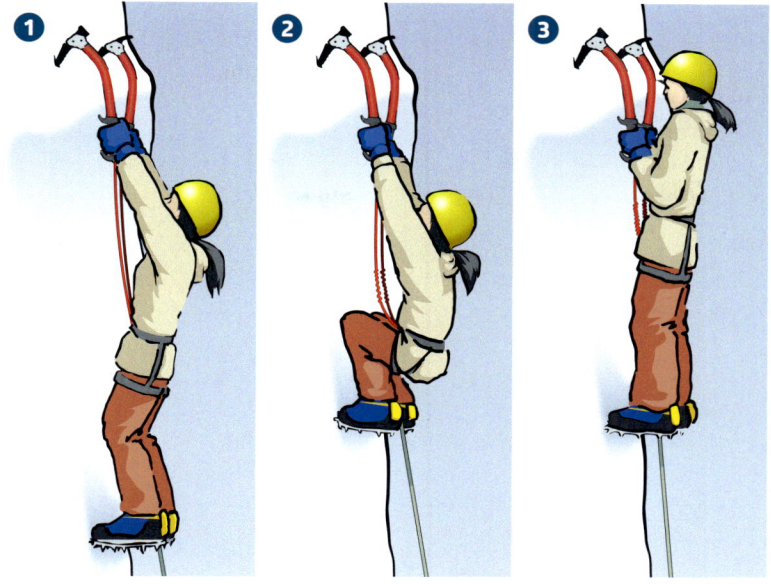

FIGURE 14.15 THE MONKEY HANG: ON STEEP ICE, THE MONKEY HANG TECHNIQUE RELIES ON STRENGTH-SAVING STRAIGHT-ARMED HANGS AND LOCK-OFFS FOR PROGRESS **(1)** WITH HIGH PLACEMENTS **(2)** MOVE YOUR FEET UP TO A BENT-KNEE, STRAIGHT-ARMED POSITION **(3)** IF NECESSARY LOOSEN ONE PICK PLACEMENT, PULL UP TO A LOCK OFF AND QUICKLY MOVE THE LOOSENED, OR LEAST SECURE PLACEMENT TO A HIGHER STRAIGHT-ARMED POSITION. TRANSFER YOUR WEIGHT TO THE HIGH TOOL AND REPLACE THE LOWER TOOL TO A STRAIGHT-ARMED HANG

to a higher straight-armed hang *(see Figure 14.15)*. Sometimes the ice deteriorates at the top of a steep section as it angles into snow. The last good placement is often at the junction of the ice and snow. Above, use the adze in the snow if it is too soft for the pick or use the shafts driven in vertically and the shaft 'choked' at snow level to reduce leverage if not in fully. The aim is to use whatever has the greatest surface area and so holding power. Sometimes chopping a deep slot in the snow may reveal an ice or turf placement or a hook on a rock. Stacking tools or 'T' stack is where one pick is hooked sideways over the pick of another in a good placement. It can be a good use of limited amounts of ice or to save strength on steep ground where a hook and pull to a lock-off enables the second higher placement. It helps to be dynamic with this move.

14.3 Mixed climbing

This requires a combination of rock, snow and ice techniques and the ability to rock climb while wearing crampons. Virtually every rock climbing technique has to be used, including using your hands on the rock. It is arguably the most satisfying of all forms of winter climbing, and sometimes the most frustrating!

14.3.1 Axe techniques

The ability to use the widest variety of placements is the key to mixed climbing success. Use your imagination and creativity! Laybacking, layaways, underclings, sharing on holds and cross-over moves are used. Experience and decision-making are probably more important on mixed climbs than on ice as routes will vary considerably according to weather

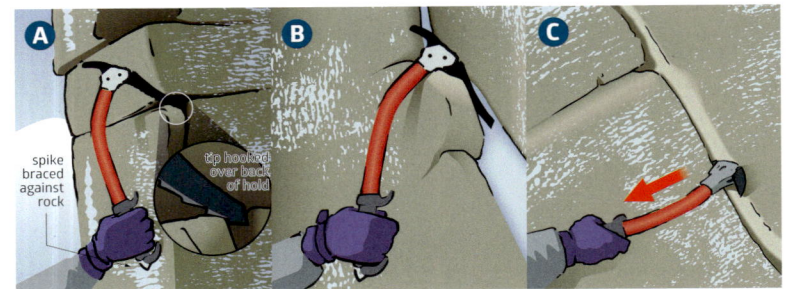

FIGURE 14.16 HOOKING: (A) PICK HOOK ON AN EDGE **(B)** PICK HOOKED OVER A FLAKE **(C)** PICK HOOKED ON A CRACK EDGE FOR A LAYAWAY MOVE

and conditions. For example, decisions are required concerning the amount of clearing of snow or ice from the rock to uncover holds or protection, or whether it can be used for placements. Blind tool placements are common on heavily snowed-up climbs and ice-filled cracks are good for pick placements but awkward to protect.

Hooking
This is the simplest type of pick placement and works best with re-curved or straight droop picks. It can be used on big holds or the smallest of edges, over chockstones or narrowings in cracks and in turf *(see Figure 14.16)*. The pick is used like a skyhook, with the point placed on or behind a suitable hold. The pull should be straight down with steady pressure to reduce the possibility of the pick pivoting off. An in-cut hold is the most secure placement and small, flat or rounded holds need more concentration to maintain the pull on the axe as you move up. A hook can also be used on a vertical hold as a layaway, such as on the edge of a crack or arête where the load is maintained on the pick at 90° to the hold. Hooking with the adze is possible on large holds or in wide cracks and works best with an inclined adze.

Wedging
This is where the tool is swung and driven into a crack with force to obtain a placement, sometimes further back in the crack that placing normally cannot reach. It has to be done with care to avoid rock damage and stuck tools. The width of the crack determines which part of the tool is used: the pick, adze or hammer head. In narrow chimneys or off-widths, the whole tool can be wedged across and pulled or twisted down so that the head and spike jam. A constriction below a wedge placement is doubly secure but wedging can work in parallel-sided cracks that are exactly the correct size. Stuck or over-driven tools may be released similar to an ice placement.

Torquing
Torquing is used in cracks or features that are too wide for a wedge placement. They can be used in horizontal, vertical or, most naturally of all, diagonal cracks. Depending on the width and depth of the crack, all parts of the tool are used including the shaft and head which is usually

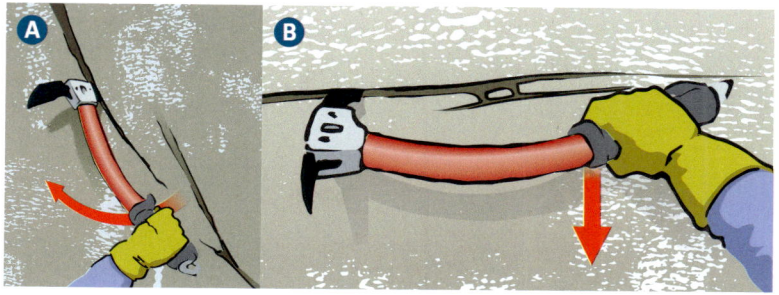

FIGURE 14.17 TORQUING: (A) PICK TORQUED IN A DIAGONAL CRACK BY TWISTING THE SHAFT TO THE VERTICAL **(B)** PICK TORQUED IN A HORIZONTAL CRACK BY PULLING DOWN ON THE SHAFT

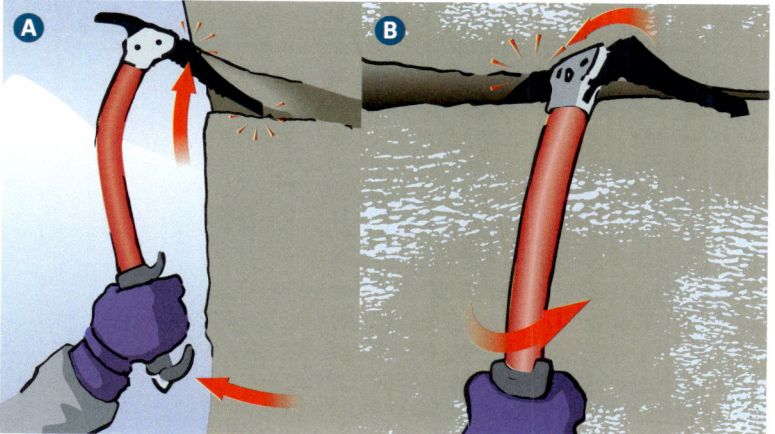

FIGURE 14.18 CAMMING: (A) PICK AND AXE HEAD AND **(B)** ADZE AND AXE HEAD CAMMED ACROSS A WIDE CRACK AND HELD IN POSITION BY PULLING OUT ON THE SHAFT

a size between the pick and hammer head. The nuts and bolts of modular tools can also be used, carefully! Torquing relies on a torsional or twisting force applied and maintained by pulling on the shaft (sideways for a vertical crack, down for a diagonal or horizontal crack) to lock the placement *(see Figure 14.17)*. The amount of torque can be adjusted by moving the grip along the shaft. Small edges and rugosities in the crack can help to hold the placement. High moves and long reaches are possible from a torque used as a layaway in a vertical crack, or undercling (pull up) in a horizontal Placements can even be found in downward facing cracks where the pick is placed so the shaft is vertical and pulled down and out – a stein pull. Outward pressure must be maintained to keep the pick in place *(see Figure 14.17 A)*.

Camming

This is where the head of the axe is levered against the rock surface from a secure pick placement such as behind a flake, and is another form of torquing, but not in a crack. Maintaining the two opposing forces will keep the tool in place *(see Figure 14.18)*.

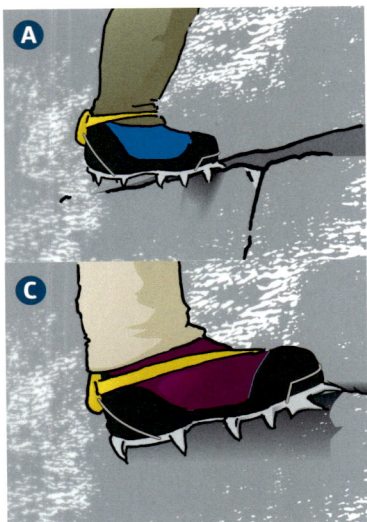
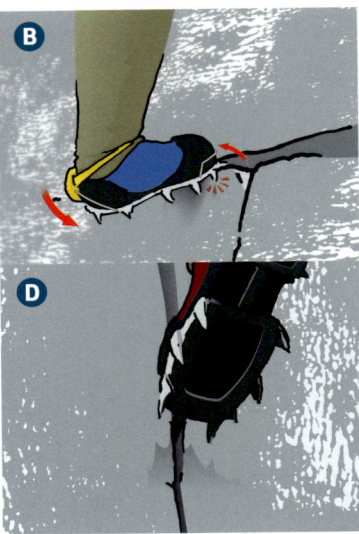

FIGURE 14.19 **CRAMPONS ON ROCK: (A)** MAINTAIN A STEADY AND LEVEL FOOT WHEN USING DUAL FRONT POINTS ON A SMALL HOLD. ON VERTICAL ROCK, THE SECOND POINTS ARE NOT IN CONTACT WITH THE ROCK **(B)** EXCESSIVE DROPPING THE HEELS MAY ALLOW THE SECOND POINTS TO CONTACT THE ROCK AND LEVER THE FRONT POINTS OFF A HOLD **(C)** A MONOPOINT WILL ALLOW A DEGREE OF MOVEMENT ON A HOLD **(D)** A MONOPOINT IS IDEAL FOR THIN VERTICAL CRACK PLACEMENTS

FIGURE 14.20 SLAB TECHNIQUE REQUIRES THAT A PLATFORM IS CREATED BY FOUR POINTS OF CONTACT – THE FRONT POINTS AND THE SECOND SET OF POINTS. WHEN THE POINTS ARE SET, FOOT MOVEMENT MUST BE KEPT TO AN ABSOLUTE MINIMUM

14.3.2 Crampons on rock

A steady foot is required to keep crampon points on a rock hold. Dual front points are the most stable although a mono point will allow more foot movement and can also be wedged in vertical and corner cracks *(see Figure 14.19)*. On the smallest of holds, only the tips of the front points are used. On slightly bigger holds the front points with the secondary points braced below are employed. On large holds a greater number of points can be placed on the hold and sloping holds require slab technique *(see Figure 14.20)*. Small horizontal cracks can be used with front points or foot jamming used in wide vertical cracks. While precise placement is almost always the key to good crampon work, if all else fails, 'bicycling' crampons on the rock may provide enough purchase to make some sort of upwards movement.

14.3.3 Vegetation (turf)

Vegetation or soil, when frozen, can offer a pick or crampon placement similar to ice. The best placements are in areas with equal amounts of soil and vegetation. Using turf placements will damage the vegetation so treat

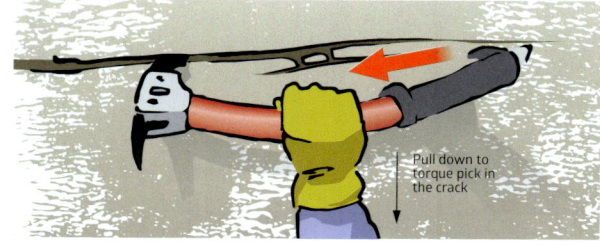

FIGURE 14.21 CHOKING THE AXE – TORQUING

FIGURE 14.22A USING HANDHOLDS
PHOTO // GILES TRUSSEL

FIGURE 14.22B USING KNEES TO GET ESTABLISHED ON A LEDGE *PHOTO // IAIN SMALL*

each one with respect. Do not climb routes that rely on turf when it is not frozen as it will be severely damaged. This can be during periods of thaw or when snow has insulated the turf and stopped it from freezing, particularly early season.

Small pieces of turf readily freeze compared with more aerated carpets of vegetation, especially those with longer stems which trap more air so delaying the freezing process. With larger pieces of vegetation such as on ledges, aim for the outer edge for better placements as this is more likely to be frozen. Deeply frozen or brittle, gravelly turf may require one or more gentle pick hits in the same place to get a secure placement. Some vegetation such as moss can shatter like ice if hit too hard or in the wrong place as can frozen waterlogged soil.

14.3.4 Other considerations

Choking-up on the axe shaft (sliding your hand up the shaft to a higher grip position) can alter the amount of torsion on the tool thus reducing the strain on the placement *(see Figure 14.21)*. Choking can also be used to gain more height from a placement, but be careful not to pull outwards on hook moves. Tools with a high finger rest will support the higher grip. Many technical tools have not only a handle but a good grip above this for a choice of holds.

Stacking tools make good use of limited placements and allow dynamic moves but are catastrophic if the placement fails! Clean potential

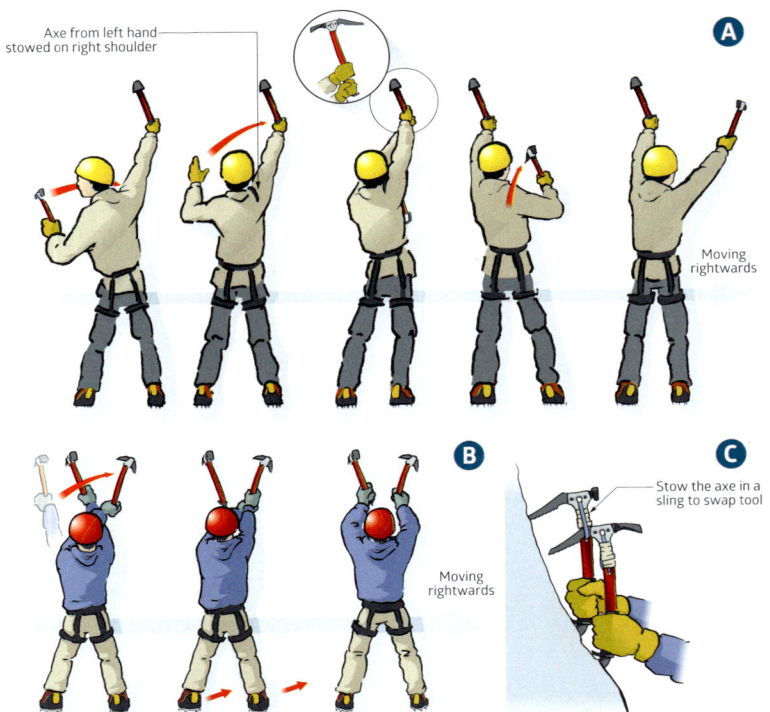

FIGURE 14.23 LEASHLESS CLIMBING – STOWING TOOLS: (A) USING A SHOULDER FOR STOWING AND HAND STACK TO SWAP TOOLS **(B)** STOWING A TOOL IN THE SNOW OR ICE AND USING A CROSSOVER AND HAND STACK TO SWAP TOOLS **(C)** A SLING ATTACHED TO THE TOOL CAN BE USED AS A LEASH ATTACHMENT OR STOWING POINT. A LENGTH OF TAPE IS SECURED THROUGH THE HOLES IN THE SHAFT AND HEAD. USE A TAPE KNOT IF THE SLING IS TO BE LOAD-BEARING. ONE SIDE OF THE SLING IS TAPED TO THE SHAFT, LEAVING THE OTHER SIDE SITTING PROUD.

foot-holds with the adze or hands as you pass them so they are obvious from above. If necessary, use your hands on large holds such as blocks, chockstones or flakes *(Figure 14.22 A)*; you can also hand jam. Knees can be used, for example when mantleshelfing onto a ledge, but it can be difficult regaining a standing position *(Figure 14.22B)*. Bear in mind that there is poor friction between clothing and snow or ice.

Tapping a pick home with the other tool can further strengthen a wedge or turf placement. However, an over-driven placement can be difficult to release once you have moved up. Enhancing a hook placement on a small edge by pecking (gentle tapping with the pick) may help to seat the point. As this damages both rock and pick, and with over-zealous pecking may render the hold less useful, it should only be used as an absolute last resort.

Know your rock type and its climbing nuances so that you have a 'feel' for the rock. The quartzite of north-west Scotland has small edges and shattered cracks which are perfect for hooking, torquing and crampons. However, the sandstone in the same area is less accommodating, with rounded and blind cracks, but offers more in the way of turf and ice. Granite typically weathers into horizontal and vertical cracks which offer good protection and placements. Mixed routes tend to be well protected but there is a fine line between spending too long looking for gear and tiring, and climbing efficiently. Mixed and buttress climbing is generally slower climbing than snow or ice, so be prepared for the cold.

Mixed climbing puts a great deal of strain on your tools and crampons. Treat them with respect and check regularly for wear and tear. Crampons can feel like stilts on bare rock. Flex your ankle to get as many points in contact with the rock as possible on large sloping holds, like French technique on ice. They will hold better than you imagine, but keep them steady!

Overhanging rock can be climbed comfortably in winter given suitable holds and cracks, but smooth slab, even moderate ones, can stop you dead! Small delicate moves are necessary using tiny rugosities and even single crystals for crampon and pick 'placements'. Sticking large wet snow blobs onto the slab and flattening off the top may give enough purchase for a handhold or a pick or crampon to balance up!

14.4 Leashless climbing

Climbing with totally leashless tools can be fast and efficient on all grades of climbs. Initially, most climbers feel uncomfortable with the concept, particularly the thought of dropping a tool. There is also a tendency to over-grip the shaft. However, with practice, the advantages of leashless climbing become apparent and dropped tools, uncommon.

Most technical tools are ergonomically designed with strength-saving pommels, finger rests and moulded grips which take some of the strain from your hands and arms. The main advantage of leashless climbing is being able to release from a tool easily to perform other tasks, such as placing gear or swapping axes without having to unclip a leash or extract from a wrist loop or let the tool 'dangle and tangle'. Swapping over hands on the same tool saves some moves, particularly when traversing or going diagonally, crossing through and matching all, allows faster climbing and helps in recovery (shaking out when pumped) during strenuous moves. Leashless tools also allow more technical moves, such as undercutting, to be performed more easily.

There are various ways of stowing the tools. The most secure method is with a good placement in the snow, ice or turf or with a solid hook on rock or wedged in a crack *(see Figure 14.23)*. With reverse curved or drooped picks and bent shafts, hooking the tool over a shoulder is quick and convenient or over the thumb grip of the other tool. Holsters, either on the rucksack or harness, are also an option but are more awkward and time-consuming to use, particularly for tools with pommels. Whatever method is used it should suit the situation.

Dropping a tool may be mildly inconvenient if it lands on an easily accessible ledge or more serious if the climbing is difficult with scant protection! If the tool is recoverable, then down climbing or lowering from a good runner (backed up if necessary) are options. If it is impossible to collect the tool, using your partner's is another option. Once you are safe, drop a rope loop if the belay is close, or pull a rope end up and throw it back to a distant belay to enable a tool to be sent up. Arranging anchors and abseiling off would be the final option.

When using lanyard leashes, tangles are not uncommon, even with ones fitted with swivels. From a secure stance and placements, unclip from one tool and untangle the leashes. Tools can also be stowed securely at stances by unclipping them from the leashes. The leashes may then be clipped together and draped around your shoulders for convenience.

14.5 Dry tooling

Leashless tools, lightweight boots, bolt-on cram-pons, heel spurs and a sport climbing approach have produced some extreme winter routes and technically the hardest winter climbs in the UK. Short and accessible summer E2s to E8s have now been climbed in winter conditions on mountain crags in the UK. It is typically a unique UK form of dry tooling, where the conditions are wintry, and dry tooling equipment and techniques are applied to traditional buttress climbing venues. The other form of dry tooling is practised on bolted and sometimes manufactured routes, very technical and on low-level crags not used for rock climbing. The techniques and equipment used for dry tooling are not within the scope of this book.

14.6 Falling off

Falling off in winter is usually more serious than falling from a rock climb. Even with a short fall, crampons can catch and result in serious injury. The frequency and quality of runners make long leader falls more of a possibility as there are normally fewer of them and they are less easy to access. Even hard winter routes will have ledges to hit during a leader fall compared with a hard rock climb. With long pitches common in winter, rope stretch is a consideration when falling off seconding, as the second may drop a considerable distance. Also, be aware of the possibility of falling onto your belayer – this is not recommended, particularly in winter!

In winter, a rucksack is often worn which raises your centre of gravity and makes head-first falls more likely and gear, such as axes and screws, can inflict stab wounds. Most falls are unexpected, usually caused by tools breaking out so there is no time to prepare for the fall. If there is time, shout to your belayer and jump for a snow ledge if appropriate. Keep axes clear of your body and the rope from behind your legs to stop flipping over. When ice or mixed bouldering, jump rather than fall off. Practise ice axe breaking with your climbing tools so that you are proficient in arresting in the event of a slip. Falling off using lanyard leashes can be potentially dangerous, particularly when a tool is flailing about. Falling onto a tool in a solid placement may mean you are hanging from the fully extended leash, which can prove difficult to pull back up. Some leashes have a loop to clip in a karabiner or sling to aid in pulling up *(see Figure 13.4.1)*. The snap link used to attach the leashes to your tools, although not fall rated, should be at least rated to the same strength as the leash – using light-weight mini karabiners may break under loading.

14.7 Training for winter climbing

Winter climbing uses a broader range of muscle groups than rock climbing. A fit climber will arrive fresh at the start of the climbing, climb faster, appreciate the walk-out and altogether have a more enjoyable day out.

The general principles apply to training for climbing at any time of the year and the subject is covered by articles, books and online instruction and videos. There are however, several areas of training that can be specific to winter climbing: improving technique, overall fitness and specific exercises. Remember two important rules: always warm up before training and it must be fun!

FIGURE 14.24 TRAINING WITH ADAPTED TOOLS ON AN INDOOR CLIMBING WALL // PETE HILL

General 'mountain fitness' is important for the approach and the return. Traditionally, winter climbers enjoyed a period of hill walking in the autumn, a great way to get used to walking with a large pack and start leg conditioning, particularly the calves. Biking and running will also improve your cardiovascular endurance and work the legs.

Focus on winter climbing specific muscle groups at the indoor wall or gym, for instance your antagonist muscles (opposing muscles need to be trained as well to prevent imbalances and injuries) which are needed for lifting and swinging your tools. Bench press or press-ups work the chest muscles and Military press or dips will work the shoulders and triceps. For endurance, use high repetitions at low intensity and for power use low reps at high intensity.

A winter specific exercise is the axe pull-up. Make up a set of hanging axe shafts or equivalent sized diameter vertical bars. These can either be free-hanging as in a doorway or tape up your picks and use your tools on a pull-up bar or in front of a wall where footholds can be used. Taking a bit of the strain off your arms permits more repetitions. Alternatively, a loop of bungee to stand in or clipped into your harness can be used for this. Train without a leash and also train locking off and hanging on one tool as if placing gear. In the gym, work the calves with calf raises. On the indoor wall, work climbs that have moves specific to winter such as steep juggy routes that work the arms and shoulders, lock-off moves, work body tension positions and abdominal muscles. Bouldering is especially good.

The best training for climbing is more climbing! Indoor and outside dry tooling walls are becoming more common for training purposes and are either commercial or homemade 'woodies'. Stone walls or roadside outcrops not used for rock climbing can also be used, providing realistic training where you can explore the limitations of tools and crampons on marginal placements. Boulder problems will work power and traverses or circuits will improve endurance. However, any falling or jumping off when wearing crampons carries a degree of risk. Bottom-roping systems can be rigged for longer sections in ascent. A helmet and face-guard are recommended. Indoor ice climbing venues are good for specific training and practising techniques for ice climbing.

Stretching is important for overall performance, being supple can add one or two grades to your climbing! Winter climbing, particularly with long approaches and heavy packs, encourages tightening of muscle groups in the legs, hips and shoulders. Stretch these areas particularly before and after a day's climbing.

Mental training for winter is the same as for rock climbing. In particular, coping with anxiety about falling off, finding good runner placements, objective dangers and the doubt about finishing the route before dark or the storm arrives!

IAIN MURRAY ON BELAY AT THE TOP OF THE FIRST PITCH OF VULCAN, V,4, GARBH CHOIRE *MOR*
PHOTO // GILES TRUSSEL

Winter anchors and belays

The traditional progression through climbing is snow, ice and mixed, therefore anchors and belays are described in this order.

The order of preference for winter anchors is rock, ice then snow and the same principles apply whether the belay is direct, indirect or semi-direct:

- The belay must be secure and solid.
- There will normally be one bombproof single-point natural anchor or at least two 'hand-placed' anchor points.
- The load is shared equally between all anchors.
- Account is taken of the direction of any possible load.
- The stance is an integral part of the whole system.

FIGURE 15.1 (A) DIRECT BELAY – THE ANCHORS ARE DIRECTLY LOADED

15.1 Snow anchors and belays

On a winter climb, rock is the first choice for anchors. On a snow route this usually means climbing to the side of a gully or, on a more open line, moving to a rocky outcrop. If rock anchors are unavailable, the decision to use a snow anchor is based on the need for speed, the type of terrain, and snow conditions. Snow anchors are not normally used as runners except when negotiating a difficult cornice or on long open slopes.

Snow anchors are likely to be less secure than those on rock or ice and constructed primarily to take a downward load. To reduce shock-loading the snow anchor and compromising the belay, a waist belay is used so a fall can be arrested dynamically – progressively by gradually applying a braking force *(see Figure 15.1 (B) and Figure 11.3 on page 145)*. Using a belay device in a snow belay will not provide sufficient dynamism in arresting a sliding fall and is not recommended.

When wearing a harness, the rope is tied into the front. To brake for a downward force, the live rope must be on the same side of the body as the rope to the anchor, otherwise the rope can be pulled from around the belayer's back as they are twisted towards the load. When a leader is climbing above a waist belay and with a good runner, an upward pull is probable, then the live rope runs on the opposite side from the anchor rope. To keep the live rope in contact with the belayer's body, it is run through a karabiner clipped into the belayer's tie-on loop (see Snow Anchors and Belays A–E overleaf).

A snow belay should be sited out of the line of falling debris and the leader should they fall without a runner, who must pass the side of the belayer that closes the waist belay. If on the opposite side, the rope will be unwrapped from the body leaving little chance of holding the fall *(see Snow Anchors and Belays F–K overleaf)*. It is important that both climbers

FIGURE 15.1 (B) INDIRECT BELAY – THE BELAYER TAKES MOST OF THE LOAD WITH A WAIST BELAY

FIGURE 15.1 (C) SEMI-DIRECT BELAY – THE BELAYER HAS THE OPTION TO TAKE MORE OR LESS LOAD BY ADJUSTING HER POSITION ON THE STANCE

are aware of this so that the waist belay can be swapped over if necessary. Keep the rope arranged for a downward pull if runners are unlikely.

15.1.1 Changeovers at snow belays

When alternate leading, the belayer may have to change the waist belay side after the second (new leader) arrives at the stance and is made secure. The second can assist by feeding the rope around the belayer's rucksack. If runners are unlikely, the belayer can set up the waist belay to anticipate the side the leader will be on, so no change of sides is necessary.

If not alternate or leading through, there has to be a change of positions at the belay but both climbers must still be secured. When the second arrives at the stance, their rope is tied to the anchor (spare screwgate karabiner in place) on the side that allows efficient changeover and positions are swapped in the bucket seat. The leader moves out of the seat in the direction of the next pitch. The anchor rope is tightened, the rope back-coiled, the waist belay taken and then the leader can untie from the anchor taking the screwgate karabiner with them *(see Figure 15.2)*. When using a buried axe, the leader takes the belayer's axe. If a snow bollard is used the second's rope has to be run around the bollard under the belayer's anchor rope.

15.2 Ice anchors

While natural ice features can be used for anchors the most common ice protection is the ice screw.

15.2.1 Ice screws

These are lightweight metal tubes made from aluminium alloy, chrome-moly or titanium. They have an external thread, a number of sharp cutting teeth and come in various lengths and diameters with different types of

Snow anchors and belays

Waist belay & harness
(A) Using a waist belay and harness

Labels: Brake hand; Anchor rope on same side as live rope; Live rope

Waist belay & harness
(B) Tying off the anchor rope to the correct length when wearing a harness

Label: Lean backward when tying off an anchor rope on a harness

(F) Set for an upward pull through a runner
(G) Anchor rope on the opposite side from live rope to reduce belayer rotation. **Note:** It would be better if the belay was nearer the rock and not in the middle of the gully, so belayer is protected from anything falling from above, including the leader!

hangers *(see Ice screws and their placement on page 223)*. Most have some form of handle to facilitate placement and removal. However, most important for the strength of the placement is the quality of the ice.

Generally, in good ice, the longer the screw the stronger the placement. Length ranges from about 10 to 20cm and larger screws, commonly about 20mm in diameter, have greater holding power. Good screws generally have at least four sharp cutting teeth and must be placed fully

Snow belay continued
(C) Anchor and live ropes on correct side
(D) Belayer has anticipated the direction of the next pitch and set for a downward load
(E) An attentive belayer with live rope diverted through a screwgate for an upward load

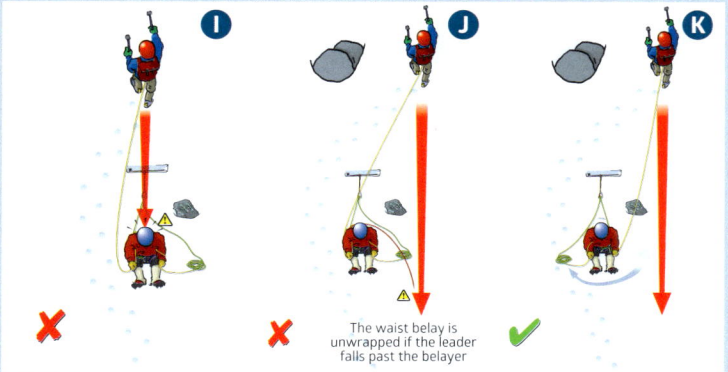

(H-J) Anticipate the direction of loading on the belay should the leader fall, so that maximum control is achieved
(K) The leader is made safe before the belay is swapped over

for optimum holding power. A selection of lengths is advisable, particularly the short ('stubbies') to mid-range for UK conditions. A long ice screw is handy for constructing 'V' threads. More teeth mean easier penetration and an aggressive, high-relief thread increases its holding power. Ideally, the thread should run to the head assuming the screw is fully inserted.

FIGURE 15.2 CHANGEOVER AT SNOW BELAY: (1) DEAD ROPE IS FLAKED BESIDE THE BELAYER SO THAT IT DOES NOT IMPEDE THE SECOND AS MAY HAPPEN IF IT IS HANGING DOWN THE SLOPE **(2)** THE SECOND ANCHORS WHILE REMAINING ON BELAY **(3)** THE LEADER TAKES THE BELAYER'S AXE (WHEN USING A BURIED AXE ANCHOR) AND HAS A FINAL CHECK OF THE BELAY BEFORE UNTYING FROM THE ANCHOR **(4)** DEAD ROPE MAY HANG DOWN THE SLOPE IF IT IS UNLIKELY TO SNAG

Placing an ice screw

In solid cold ice, the strongest placement is at 10°–15° below perpendicular (positive angle) to the ice. This also assumes the ice screws have well-spaced external high-relief threads that will resist pullout. If there is a difficulty in attaining the ideal angle, or any doubt about the quality of the ice screw threads, placing perpendicular to the ice is acceptable. However, if the ice is not ideal, or there is a possibility of melt-out, the preferred angle is 10°–15° above right angles (negative angle) to the ice surface *(see Ice screws and their placement)*. In the UK, with its very variable ice conditions, the latter is a fairly common option.

If necessary, clean off any rotten or unconsolidated surface ice and snow to get to solid ice. Smooth off the area so that the screw goes in up to the head without the hanger catching. While sharp screws can be started with no preparation, a small chipped starting hole will aid the first turn by allowing it to bite quickly. The holes created by previous pick placements may also be used if there is no evidence of fractured ice. Select the appropriate length screw and start by holding it with your palm over the end of the tube and the hanger between your thumb and forefinger. Cock your wrist anti-clockwise so that your thumb is pointing down and punch the teeth into the ice and push and turn simultaneously at the correct angle. You can achieve ¾ turn this way, enough for the screw to seat. Continue turning, initially using a little pressure from your hand, until the hanger is flush with the ice surface. If the screw has a crank handle, use this once it feels secure, normally about two turns.

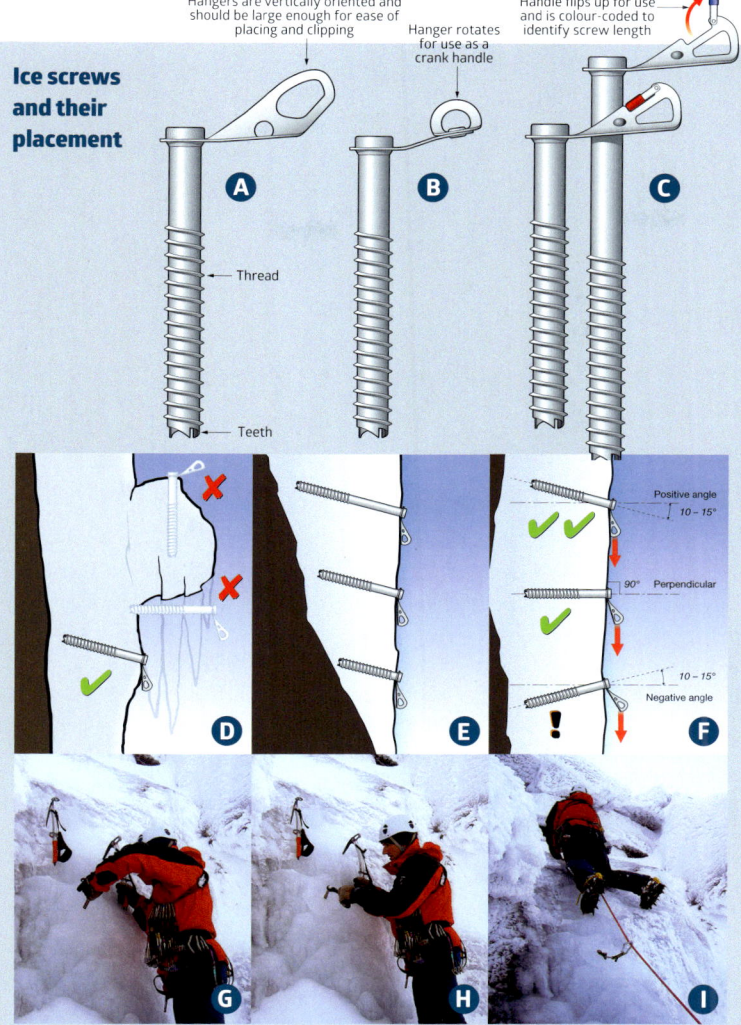

Ice screws and their placement

Ice screws:
- **(A)** Without crank handle
- **(B&C)** With crank handle

Placing an ice screw:
- **(D)** Be aware of less secure formations and if necessary clear to reach solid ice. Concave areas give more secure placements than convexities and ice bulges
- **(E)** Use the appropriate length of screw and place it at the correct angle to the ice surface
- **(F)** In good solid ice, the best angle is 10°–15° positive. Perpendicular is acceptable, a negative angle is **only** used in less than ideal ice
- **(G&H)** Place a screw from a comfortable stance, preferably hands-free or secured with a solid ice axe placement. Check the quality of the extruded ice core
- **(I)** An ice screw runner is best placed before a steepening and extended with a quick-draw of appropriate length

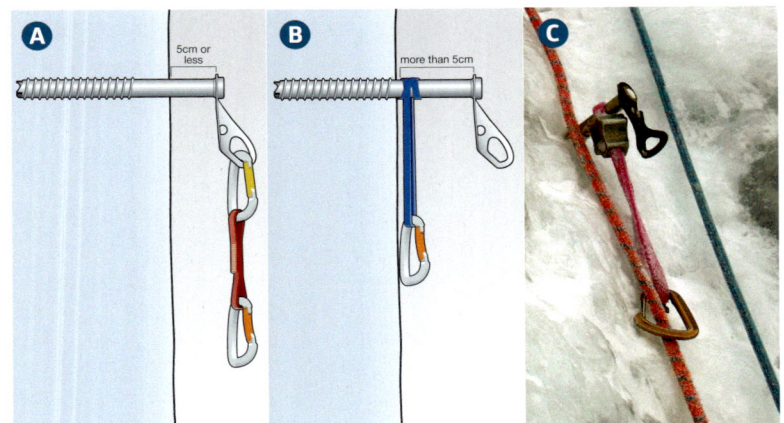

FIGURE 15.3 TYING OFF AN ICE SCREW: (A) CLIP AS NORMAL **(B)** TIE OFF WITH AN INVERTED CLOVE HITCH HARD AGAINST THE ICE SURFACE **(C)** IMPROVISED TIE-OFF – A WIRED NUT MAY ALSO BE USED

There should be a continual smooth resistance as it goes in and a core of ice should start to extrude after about half-way. Flip crank handles into the closed position before clipping the screw. For less sharp screws that have no crank or extension handle it may be necessary to use a pick through the hanger eye to get enough leverage to fully place it *(see Figure 15.7 on page 227)*. Gently tapping the hanger round with the hammer can also work.

If the screw loses resistance and turns very easily with no ice core extruding, it has hit an air pocket and if the core is broken, crumbly and resistance minimal, it has penetrated rotten ice. Either way, remove it, clear the tube and find more solid ice if possible. If it comes to a sudden halt, particularly with a change in the feel of the teeth cutting, then stop immediately. It has bottomed out onto rock or soil and extra pressure will damage the teeth. At the very least the teeth will blunt and at worst, will bend inwards. A screw may still be usable when blunt but not with bent teeth!

Tie off ice screws that have more than 5cm protruding using a clove-hitched sling, otherwise clip the hanger directly if less than 5cm protruding *(see Figure 15.3)*. Most screws (except stubbies) do not have a full-length thread which can cut the sling when loaded. Also, if the sling on a tied-off screw slides to the hanger, which is possible with screws normally placed at a positive angle, it can cut on sharp edges around the hanger if loaded. Using the correct length of screw is much preferable to tying them off. If the screw could melt out in direct sunlight or a thaw, place it in shade or cover with snow to prevent this happening. Large screws work better in these conditions.

Placing an ice screw on the lead
It is necessary to be ambidextrous when placing screws though most will try to arrange placing the screw with their dominant hand. Try to place screws from a comfortable, hands-free position such as on a ledge below a steepening as this is less strenuous and more efficient. Otherwise, from

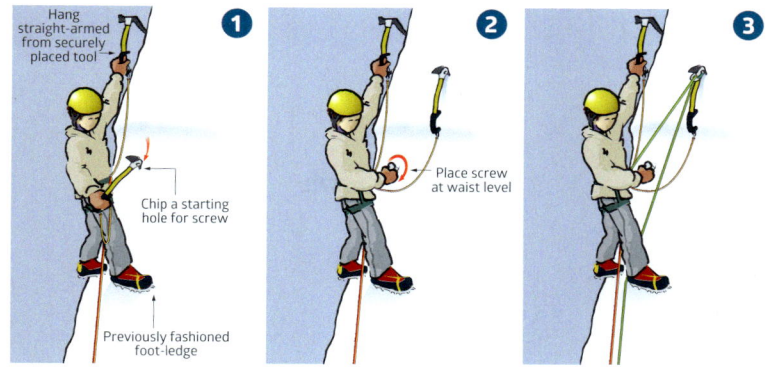

FIGURE 15.4 PLACING A SCREW ON STEEP ICE: (1) USE THE ICE FEATURES TO YOUR ADVANTAGE. FOR EXAMPLE, USE NATURAL FOOT LEDGES TO TAKE THE STRAIN FROM THE LEGS, OR CHIP A FOOT LEDGE WITH THE PICK BEFORE MOVING UP. GETTING THE HEEL ONTO THE LEDGE IS VITAL TO RELAX THE CALVES **(2)** RELEASE FROM THE SECOND TOOL, OR ALLOW IT TO HANG FROM YOUR HAND, AND PLACE THE SCREW **(3)** BEWARE OF THE CONSEQUENCES OF A TOOL FAILING WHEN USING IT AS A RESTING POINT

a stable stance, place one secure ice tool (treat this tool as your belay anchor) and hang straight-armed so the intended placement is around waist level and slightly off to the side. Place the second tool to the side and below the level of the anchor tool. If using a wrist loop leash, unclip or release your hand from the leash, or let it hang by the leash from your wrist *(see Figure 15.4)*. The distance between placements should mean no chance of ice fracturing between the picks and them breaking out.

Placing an ice screw on vertical ice is strenuous and should be avoided by taking advantage of less steep areas and resting positions such as a bridging stance. Cutting a resting foot ledge is also an option. As a last resort, if strength is waning and a fall is a possibility, security may be gained by clipping a rope into the high secure tool and using it as an overhead runner, or attaching yourself directly with a sling 'cow's tail'. Some tools have a groove in the head to run the rope into. However, these methods are regarded as rest points if the climber's weight is held.

Using an old ice screw hole (re-bored hole) is a possibility for a quick placement and handy when in a strenuous position or if there is no suitable ice available in the surrounding area. Importantly, ensure that the ice is solid around the hole. Any other holes, air pockets or fractured ice close to the pre-existing hole could potentially compromise the placement. Whilst placing the screw in the pre-existing hole, if you feel a constant resistance then that would suggest the threads are firmly biting into the ice. Also ensure that the hole is at the correct angle.

Removing ice screws
First, unclip hardware and unscrew it, being careful during the last few centimetres not to drop it. The ice core must be removed before it can be re-used. If this cannot be done immediately, then do so at the first opportunity. Most screws are easy to clean and some even have an internal taper to aid this. If the core does not remove easily, then warm the screw either with your hands, your breath or by putting it close to your body. Tapping the screw or trying to push the core out (with a 'turfie' for

example) may damage the interior or the threads, making it less efficient to place. Blowing down the tube to eject the last pieces of ice core may help, but be careful in the cold as the metal may freeze to your lips. A coating of light oil (or silicone spray) will also facilitate ice core removal and protect screws during storage.

Maintenance of ice screws

Ice screws are expensive and should be looked after. Check them regularly for damage, mainly to the teeth. Scratches to the internal surfaces made when clearing the core will encourage ice to freeze inside. The cutting edge of the teeth may be sharpened with a hand file. Bent teeth must be straightened very carefully with pliers beforehand. Protectors for ice screw teeth and threads are available, but are fiddly to use on the hill. Store screws clean and dry and remove protectors.

FIGURE 15.5 IF USING WRIST LOOP LEASHES, THIS IS A USEFUL METHOD TO SEAT LESS SHARP ICE SCREWS OR DRIVE-INS, BUT IT BECOMES A STRENUOUS POSITION TO HOLD ON VERTICAL ICE

15.2.2 Ice drive-ins

These are now less popular but are useful as a quick overhead placement. They are tubular metal with a fine thread to aid removal, a cutting leading edge, an eye to clip into and a slot for cleaning the ice core *(see Figure 15.5)*. The basic principles of length and where to place are similar to ice screws.

To place, chip a starting hole and forcefully stab or punch the snarg into it to seat. Give a single, accurate blow to seat it further and continue hammering, gently at first to reduce shattering, until it is fully home with the eye facing down. Snargs are placed at 90° to the ice surface in hard, cold ice or at 10°–15° above in softer ice. On steep ice, if it is difficult to set the snarg without the risk of dropping it, if you're using wrist loop leashes, chip a starting hole within reach of your hand in the leash of your anchor tool. The snarg can then be held until it is securely seated *(see Figure 15.5)*.

Snargs can be unscrewed by hand. If it is stuck initially, tap it round or hammer it further in to break the seal and perhaps clear ice from around the eye. Stubborn snargs can be unscrewed by using a pick through the eye as a lever, though excessive force may twist them *(see Figure 15.7)*. They may be gently re-sharpened by hand using a cone grinder.

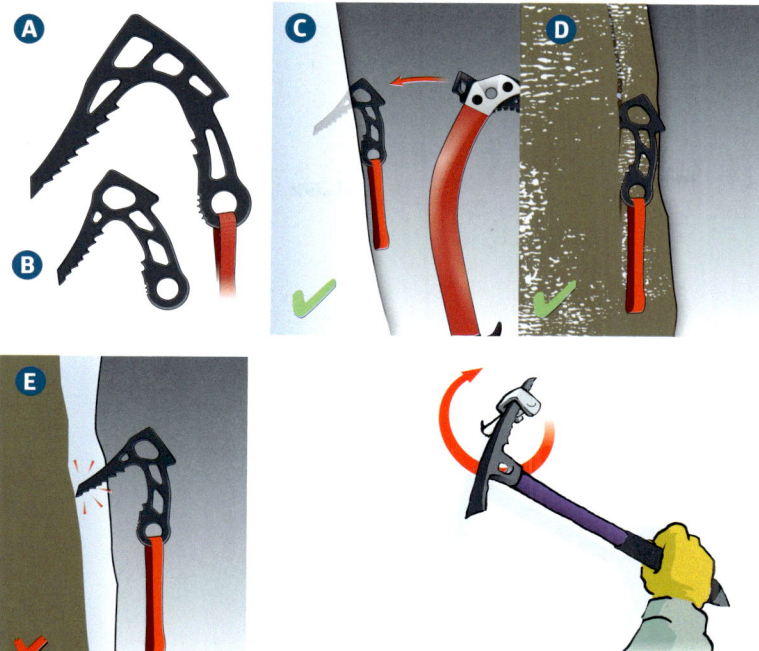

FIGURE 15.6 (A) BULLDOG® ICE HOOK **(B)** THE SMALLER TERRIER® **(C)** PLACEMENT ON ICE **(D)** PLACEMENT IN A CRACK **(E)** BEWARE ON THIN ICE

FIGURE 15.7 USING THE PICK AS A LEVER. STUBBORN SNARGS AND WARTHOGS CAN BE REMOVED AND LESS SHARP ICE SCREWS CAN BE PLACED USING THIS TECHNIQUE

15.2.3 Ice hook (Bulldog®)

This is a thin, hook-shaped steel blade with a sharp point, teeth on the lower edge, a short sewn sling at the base and a karabiner hole at the top. It is very similar in overall shape and action to an ice axe pick. However, they are awkward, heavy and snag irritatingly on other gear. They are hammered into ice but are not as secure as screws and are useful for quick placements in marginal conditions such as thin or hollow ice. They may hold a short fall or be used as a rest point. First, make a starting hole with your pick then hammer the hook home. They may be placed quickly by using previously made pick holes then tapped in. On mixed routes they can be used in turf or iced-up cracks *(Figure 15.6)*. Remove in the same manner as a rock piton. If used in rock such as in place of a rock peg, they can be very awkward to remove and may be impossible to retrieve if placed in corners.

15.2.4 Ice threads ('V' threads or Abalakov threads)

Ice threads are quick to create and very strong provided the ice is solid and they are constructed correctly. They are ideal for abseil anchors, one of the belay anchors or as a runner if short of screws and on a comfortable stance. A long ice screw (around 20 – 22cm) is needed to make the holes deep enough so they connect at least 15cm below the surface. The more ice you have in front of the two connected holes, the better the anchor

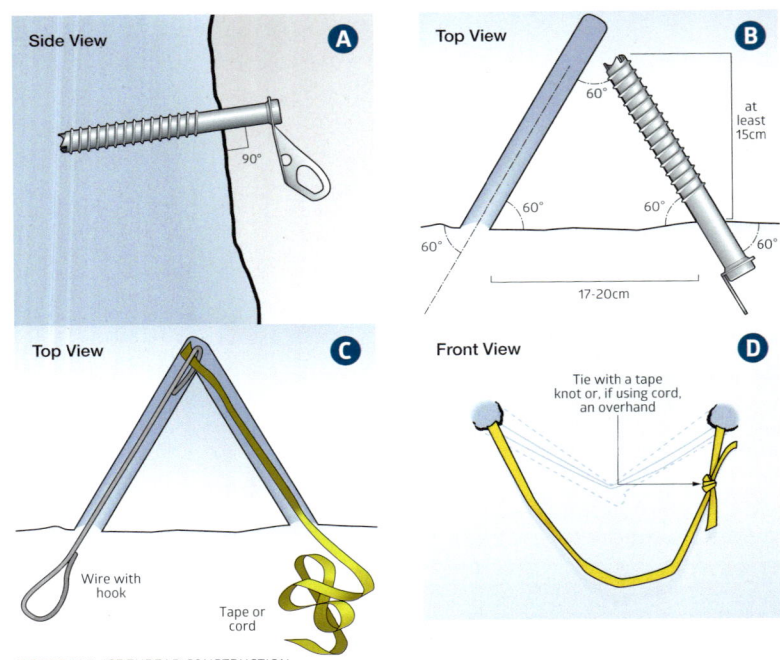

FIGURE 15.8 ICE THREAD CONSTRUCTION

will be. Choose ice that you consider would hold a good runner, is on uniform-angled ice or behind convexities in the ice.

Start the first hole with the screw at about 60° horizontally to the ice surface and screw it all the way in. Check that the ice core is of good quality then remove the screw. Start the next hole 18cm – 20cm away (just less than the length of the screw) and horizontally in line. A starting hole for the second main hole may be chipped with a pick to prevent the screw skating across the surface ice. Make the second hole at 60° from the ice in a line that will cut the first hole near its base. Placing a second ice screw in the first hole will give you a reference for the correct angle. If the holes connect at less than three quarters down the initial hole, start again in another piece of ice *(see Figure 15.8)*. Thread these interconnected holes with either cord (7mm) or tape using a tool to push and pull it through. This can be a commercial tool or improvised from wire (insulated electrical wire) hooked at one end. The wire loops of two small sized nuts can be threaded through each other and used to feed and pull through the cord or tape. It is even possible to thread a rope end through as in an abseil situation to avoid leaving an abseil sling but this can be more awkward, necessitates untying from the rope and the rope may freeze in place in exceptionally cold temperatures. Ensure that the rope is going to run smoothly before the last person leaves the stance.

15.2.5 Accessories

There are several handy accessories available for winter climbing:

Ice screw holder (Ice-flute). Plastic tubes in which screws are carried vertically and can be accessed with one hand. They also protect the screws

FIGURE 15.9 ICE SCREW BELAYS: (A&B) BELAYS USING A SINGLE ROPE. IF USING DOUBLE ROPES, CLIP EACH ROPE INTO A SEPARATE ANCHOR **(C)** A SLING IS USED TO CENTRALISE AND EQUALISE THE ANCHORS
PHOTO // GILES TRUSSELL

and threads from knocks.

Crank handle. Some screws which lack a crank handle can be placed by a separate crank. This can be carried on an adjustable elastic bandolier and links into the screw's hanger. With practice, it allows quick placements.

Multihook. A long-stemmed flat steel rod with a hook on the end which can be used as a nut key and for clearing ice from inside an ice screw. The hook is convenient when making a 'V' thread and for hooking over the trigger to remove stubborn cams.

Combined template and hook tool for 'V' threads to give accurate angles and distances.

Tool holder (Caritool). A large, lightweight plastic karabiner with a wide-opening wired gate that attaches vertically to the harness waistbelt. The gate faces out and opens down and is useful for carrying ice screws or rock pitons which can be removed single-handedly. An alternative is to carry gear on a wide-gate opening karabiner.

15.3 Ice belays

In the absence of rock anchors, use at least two good screws for the belay, including at least one long one, but the number will depend on the ice quality. Any natural ice feature such as a thread can also be incorporated into the belay. A 'V' thread can be quick to arrange as an anchor and it is not uncommon to have a mixture of rock and ice anchors. Place anchors

FIGURE 15.10 FINDING ROCK ANCHORS: (A) A CONVENIENT WIND SCOOP ALLOWS EFFICIENT CLEARING OF LIKELY AREAS **(B)** A CRACK IS CLEARED WITH THE PICK AND REVEALS GOOD NUT AND CAM PLACEMENTS

in the appropriate place, with all the usual considerations of direction of loading, belayer position and direction of the next pitch.

Ice screw anchors are placed at the appropriate angle to the surface *(see Ice screws and their placement on page 223)*, at least 60cm apart and should be offset vertically rather than side by side where horizontal fractures are more likely *(see Figure 15.9)*. If the screws are weighted, as in a hanging or semi-hanging stance, beware of pressure melting (melt-out) occurring. This is more prevalent in sunny or thawing conditions. The higher screw is placed on the side of the next pitch. If there is no alternative, it may be clipped as a runner if the start of the next pitch is poorly protected, otherwise place a runner as soon as possible to eliminate the chance of a factor two fall.

In the absence of a further ice screw or possibility of an ice thread, tools may be used as additional back-up anchors. One or both can be hammered into the ice and should be offset, vertically staggered and about 30cm apart *(see Figure 15.10)*. Tie into the most secure point of the tool and one that will exert the least twisting or outward pull such as the hole in the head or shaft. The spike hole should not be used as this is usually not load-bearing. In less brittle ice, another method is to place tools so they form an 'X'. A sling is clove-hitched around the shaft crossover point and tightened. This should be considered a last resort.

At the stance, do not allow the rope to drop down below where it could become snagged. If necessary, lap ropes over the anchor ropes or round your ankle to prevent them from sliding off.

15.4 Rock anchors

The same types of rock anchor are used as in summer, but there are several additional winter considerations. Anchors can be natural rock features such as spikes or chockstones, nuts and camming devices and rock pegs. This is also the order of preference in which anchor points are selected.

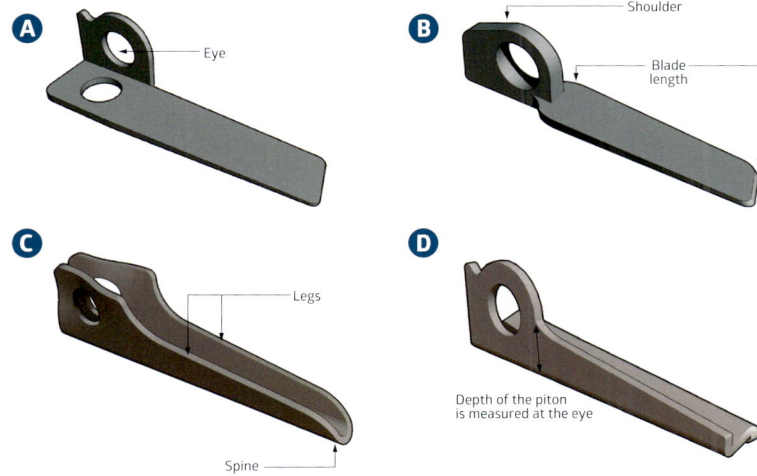

FIGURE 15.11 A SELECTION OF PITONS: THERE ARE VARIOUS LENGTHS AND DEPTHS (THICKNESSES) OF PITON WITHIN EACH CATEGORY **(A)** A KNIFEBLADE **(B)** A KINGPIN **(C)** AN ANGLE **(D)** A LEEPER

15.4.1 Finding anchors

The main difference in winter is the difficulty of locating rock anchors if they are covered with snow and ice. Knowing where to look, and how long to search in any situation, is important. Familiarity with the rock type can help and signs of others having belayed at a particular point such as old stances, areas of cleared rock or scars, can be good indicators. Otherwise, look for likely areas such as blocky ground, rock with visible cracks or features such as corners or roofs which may harbour cracks. If there is nothing obvious, then cracks need to be uncovered.

The effort involved in clearing the rock to find anchors depends on the depth and consistency of the snow. Soft powder can be brushed off with the hand but using the whole forearm allows greater areas to be cleared with one sweep. With firm snow the axe is employed. The shaft may sometimes be used but usually the adze is required. This is time-consuming so ensure you are in a productive area. Clear a wide area, not only in front of you, and select areas where the snow is softest if much clearing is required. If necessary, clear out cracks up to arms length and down to foot level. Natural rock anchors are the first choice but if there is no obvious anchor that can be used quickly then resort to hand-placed gear such as nuts, camming devices and rock pitons. At least two good hand-placed anchors are necessary for the belay *(see Figure 15.11)*.

15.4.2 Chocks

Nuts and hexes are used as in summer. They are placed above a constriction in the crack with as much metal in contact with bare rock as possible. If there is any snow, ice or grit on the sides of the crack this must be removed. Clearing can be done with the pick but beware of blunting the point. This preparation is important as a nut seated against ice may appear secure to normal testing but fail under load. This applies to both wedge-shaped and hexagonal nuts.

> **Placing and removing pitons**
>
> Pitons are placed with the eye down in horizontal cracks, angle pitons with the legs cutting into the bottom of the crack. In vertical cracks, place with the eye facing either side, whichever way enables a secure placement, but with one exception: the Leeper is placed with the eye uppermost, so when loaded, the piton's legs will torque into the crack.
>
> Use a positive swing to hammer the piton home by standing to the side with a secure stance. Do not overdrive the piton, as it may prove difficult to remove. If the piton is tied off, a second karabiner may be clipped from the sling to the eye to retain it in the event of it pulling out.
>
> Remove a piton using the same positive swing and stance, and hitting it along the crack in both directions until it loosens. Loosen it further by delicately tapping it around its middle position by using a higher grip position on the hammer. Finally, lift it out by hand. Remove all hardware from the piton before hitting it.

Test in the normal way by giving the chock a few sharp tugs in the direction of expected loading before removing it from the carrying karabiner. Use the appropriate part of the axe to tap the nut into place if necessary, taking care to avoid hitting and damaging the cord or wire. Removing stubborn placements may require careful tapping with the axe pick or spike. It is not usual to carry a nut key in winter.

15.4.3 Spring-loaded camming devices: Cams

SLCDs are less usable in winter as snow or ice between the cams and the rock can cause them to fail, but if placed with care they are still useful. If the rock is dry, clean and free of snow, ice or verglas, they are used normally and best placed between one-quarter and three-quarters open with the stem aligned in the direction of pull. If the crack is not dry, then clear the sides before placing the cam. Ensure that the cams are against bare rock and not in a position to walk. Rock type influences the usefulness of cams and the rougher the rock, the more secure they are. Granite and sandstone may give better placements than rocks such as rhyolite or mica-schist. Test placements by giving a sharp tug in the anticipated direction of load.

15.4.4 Pitons

While the use of pegs or pitons is considered unethical on UK rock climbs, they are still sometimes needed in winter for secure runners and belay anchors, but their use should be limited to essential situations. Pegs come in a variety of sizes from those that fit narrow cracks such as knife-blades or kingpins to 'U' shaped angles or 'Z' shaped Leepers which are designed for wider cracks *(see Figure 15.12)*. Most commonly used are those that fit narrow cracks as wider ones are more likely to accept nuts.

Pegs are all placed the same way. Find an area of crack where there is a slight widening, select the appropriate peg which should fit one-half to two-thirds the blade length into the crack and hammer it into place *(see Placing and removing pitons)*. When hammered, the peg should produce a rising, ringing tone. To test, with a light grip drop the hammer head a short distance onto the eye. A good placement should produce a ringing note and the hammer should bounce back. A poor peg may give a dull note and any movement indicates an unsound placement. The eye should be as close to the rock as possible to minimise leverage. If not, it should be tied off with a clove hitch in a sling, as illustrated in *Figure 15.3B* on page 224.

FIGURE 15.12 AWKWARD PITON PLACEMENT - THIS PITON CANNOT BE REMOVED BECAUSE THE CAPPED CRACK INHIBITS THE HAMMER SWING FROM ABOVE

Pegs can be placed in any crack orientation but a peg in a horizontal crack is more mechanically secure. With icy or dirty cracks, leepers or angles are best as the edges cut through any snow, ice or grit and grip on the rock below. Blade pegs may give the appearance of being secure but be held in place by ice. If a blade is used, it is possible to clear ice by hammering in the peg that appears to fit then removing it. The removal cleans ice from the crack and a larger size can then be placed securely. There are many forms of improvisation by stacking pegs to fit a crack that you do not have the correct size for.

Unless in extremis, place pegs with consideration to their removal *(see Figure 15.12)*. To remove a peg, hammer it as far as possible in one direction then back as far as it will go the opposite way. Repeat this process until it loosens enough to lift out. Hit the peg on the shoulder to minimise damage. A karabiner chain can be clipped into the top hole of a tool and shock-loaded outwards to remove stubborn pegs that have been loosened as much as possible beforehand.

15.4.5 Warthog (Turfie)

Originally used as a type of ice peg, this is useful for mixed climbing placed in vegetation or frozen soil as an emergency belay anchor or runner. This is a drive-in screw-out solid metal rod with a spiral sequence of lumps ('warts') down its length to aid removal. It is placed by hammering into the turf at 90° and fully driven in with the eye facing down. It may rotate clockwise slightly when placing because of the warts so this should be taken into consideration when initially hammering it. Tying off is not recommended as the rod tapers and is weaker lower down although this may be necessary if not fully in to the eye. To remove, put a pick through the eye and use this as a lever to unscrew, usually

Tying to anchors and linking anchors

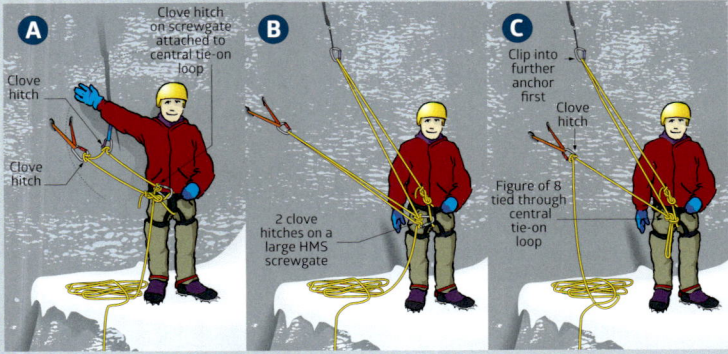

There are numerous ways of tying direct to one or more anchors with a single rope or double ropes.

(A) Generally, if anchors are within reach of the belayer, a clove hitch at the anchor is used.

(B) If the anchor is out of reach, clip in to the anchor and tie off at the harness.

(C) In practice, this is the most common: one anchor within reach and the other not.

(D&E) Beware of angles and the resulting load on anchors and slings.

(F–L) Use a long or an extra long sling to centralise and equalise anchors to save on rope and facilitate quick belays changeovers

(M) Slings used to equalise three ice screw anchors

(N&O) There are various methods of equalising anchors using two or more slings.

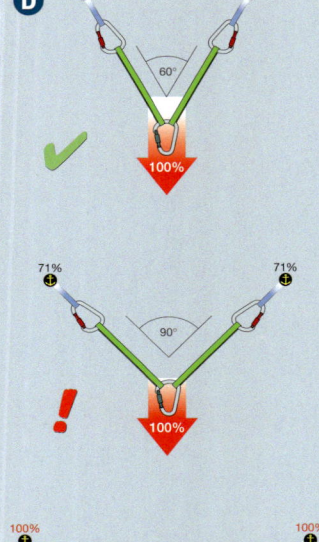

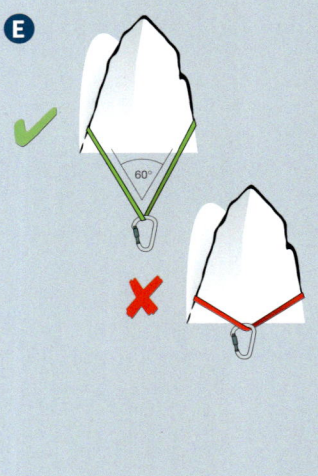

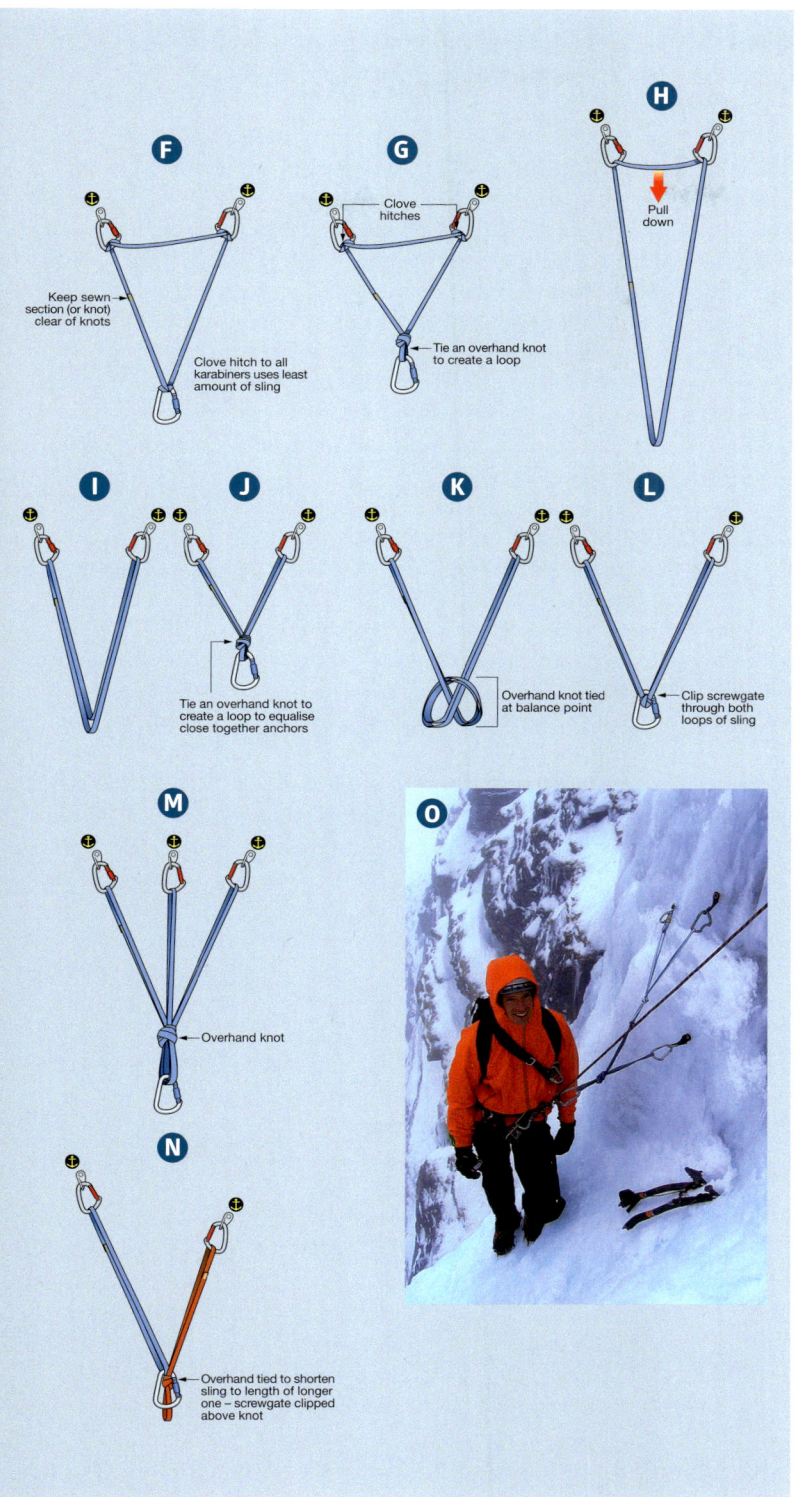

difficult in turf and sometimes they bend *(see Figure 15.7 on page 227)*. Careful thought is necessary concerning where to place the turfie bearing in mind the method of removal.

15.5 In-situ anchors

These are commonly pegs and slings used on natural anchors. Cams and nuts are usually in-situ because they could not be removed and so left. Anchors found in place should be cleared of snow and ice and tested as if you had placed them yourself.

Never assume that in-situ equipment is sound. Always check it visually, test as appropriate and, if part of a belay, back it up with more anchor points. Look – test – feel – understand. Sometimes it is difficult to make a judgement on the security of an in-situ placement because it is too heavily iced into the crack. Use it cautiously and if a runner, place a good one as soon as practicable.

15.6 Linking anchors

Although it is recommended to tie directly to belay anchors using the rope, when appropriate they are linked and equalised as on a rock climb *(see Tying to anchors and linking anchors on pages 234 and 235)*. This can be with the rope, slings or a combination of the two but in general, the fewer the links the better.

15.7 Stance construction

In winter, the size, position and comfort of the stance is often the leader's decision, particularly when a stance is cut in snow. On snow, when first arriving at a likely place for anchors, cut or stamp a small ledge to work from. When the first anchor is placed, clip a rope as a runner to protect the search for and placement of the next anchor. When that is in place, decide how you are going to tie in and where the stance is to be. On soft snow, stamping a suitable stance may suffice. On hard snow, with the rope (or ropes) through the anchors, move down so that the stance site is at chest or waist height. Protected by the rope, fashion a good stance which should be comfortably large and angled into the slope to give a positive footing *(see Figure 15.13)*. The size will depend on the hardness of the snow and the difficulty of cutting. When finished, move up onto the stance and tie tight into the anchors. If belaying standing, it is possible to lower the stance by kicking and scraping with your feet to drop slightly to adjust your final tightness onto the anchors. With crampons this is an effective way of removing snow. Once tight onto the anchors and standing comfortably, organise things for the changeover and re-racking the gear when your partner arrives. The smaller and more constricted the stance, the more you should do before your partner arrives.

If the belay stance is not going to be large enough for both, then a stance for your partner should be cut at the same time. If the snow is very hard or on ice, then a longer ledge on which you can stand with feet sideways one behind the other is the best option. Getting your heels on a ledge to rest your legs is crucial.

FIGURE 15.13 STANCE CONSTRUCTION: (1) ON STEEP OR HARD SNOW, CHOP A SMALL STANCE TO USE WHILE SEARCHING FOR ANCHORS **(2)** CLIP ROPE INTO AN ANCHOR FOR SECURITY WHILE FASHIONING THE STANCE **(3)** WHEN THE STANCE IS THE APPROPRIATE SIZE, STOW THE AXES AND TIE INTO THE ANCHORS **(4)** THE STANCE SHOULD BE ABLE TO ACCOMMODATE THE ROPE AND THE SECOND IF NECESSARY

GREG BOSWELL ON *THE GATHERING*, XIII 9, COIRE NAN LOCHAIN, NORTHERN CAIRNGORMS
PHOTO // GARRY SMITH

Winter climbing strategies

With every aspect of winter mountaineering, time is important. Winter is not the season for slow inefficient rope work, stance and belay organisation.

The basic rope work, stance and belay organisation skills are best mastered on warm rock, particularly multi-pitch routes and should be well practised before tackling winter climbing.

Time can be saved not only whilst climbing, but also in other areas. Quick decisions must be made about how long to spend looking for anchors and when to move on. If there is an obvious belay opportunity anywhere after two-thirds rope length, it is probably better to belay there rather than run out the whole rope length and spend longer searching.

Each pitch can be mentally broken down into sections where the line of least resistance, availability of runners and anchors, gear placements and rest points are considered. If possible, do this from

FIGURE 16.1 THE EAS A' CHUAL ALUINN WATERFALL, SUTHERLAND, GIVES 200M OF ICEFALL CLIMBING. THE GREATLY FORESHORTENED ORIGINAL ROUTE CHOICE **(A)** WAS MODIFIED TO FINISH UP THE MORE STABLE LEFT-HAND ICE PILLAR **(B)**. EACH BELAY WAS PLANNED TO MAKE USE OF ROCK ANCHORS. THE SECOND PITCH ZIG-ZAGS THROUGH STEEP GROUND TO A ROCK BELAY **(2)** IN A CAVE.

a distance since from below much of the climb may be out of sight or foreshortened *(see Figure 16.1)*. Adapting your route choice whist on the route is sometimes possible, where an easier option not visible from below becomes obvious. However, climbing into cul-de-sacs and not remembering which way to exit happens! Generally, you must trust your planned route in the knowledge that it leads to easier ground. Guidebook descriptions are invaluable but do not always give detailed pitch-by-pitch descriptions.

16.1 Strategies on ice

It is rare to climb a pure ice route in the UK. Mixed media are more common, although ice may form the bulk of the climb. Rock anchors, snow slopes and vegetated ledges are normal and can provide a rest from steep sections. Winter routes change in their appearance and difficulty throughout the season as the build-up of snow and ice varies. The grade of a winter climb is for 'average conditions' which may or may not exist on the day or even during a whole season.

The line of least resistance on an ice climb may include zig-zagging up icy ramps, bridging between pillars or up grooves and other ice features. A few moves to the side of a column may be less steep where a rest and an ice screw placement await. However, there may be no option but to tackle a steepening directly, so focus on your tool and crampon placements and use the ice to your advantage.

Place runners at regular intervals even if the climbing feels well within your capabilities. Importantly, arrange a good runner as soon as possible after leaving the stance to protect the belay *(see Figure 16.2)*.

FIGURE 16.2 PROTECTING THE CLIMB: AN EARLY ROCK RUNNER PROTECTS THE BELAY   *PHOTO // GEORGE McEWAN*

A 'screamer' extension is an option to protect the first crucial runner and prevent extreme shock-loading in the event of a fall. Extend runners around bulges and icicles to reduce drag, the chance of snagging and to protect your second.

16.1.1 Stances on ice

Construct a belay out of the firing line of the next pitch. Ice slivers are notoriously sharp and chunks of ice are sharp and heavy and can cause serious injury. As a leader, you have a responsibility for the safety of your belayer (they also have your life in their hands!) particularly if they are exposed to falling debris. Be aware of your position on the climb in relation to your partner and that debris can be deflected from the side. If a chunk of ice must be dropped, alert your belayer to the situation so that they can protect themselves and break the ice into smaller, lighter pieces before it falls. If you cannot belay out of the firing line where debris is channelled, as in gullies, look for stances protected by overhangs and in small caves. When belaying, make yourself as small as possible. Let your rucksack and helmet take the impact by facing away from debris and crouch over to protect your head.

Fashioning a stance on steep ice is a valuable skill. Even a small ledge allows you to take some strain off your calves and arms by resting your foot sideways. It can also ease the strain whilst placing an ice screw *(see Figure 16.3)*. Use any natural steps in the ice as a start to your stance. If there is no natural step, then use the pick or adze by chopping a horizontal line in the ice at least the length of your boot, working away from your leg at each successive chop. Move up so that it is at foot level and plant a tool solidly overhead for protection. Place the second tool a bit lower and to the side. Enhance the step by stamping and scraping with your crampons to shatter and loosen the ice. Scrape off the debris with your crampons and continue stamping and scraping until the stance is adequate.

All the considerations about ice climbs are relevant to mixed climbing.

16.2 General strategies

16.2.1 Preparation

Time can be saved with good organisation and preparation. Gather as much information about your route as possible, particularly the crux sections, likely conditions, protection, avalanche risks and descents. Guidebooks, websites and internet blogs and forums are good sources of information. Choose a route within your capabilities and bear in mind that grades are for average conditions. During periods of unstable wind slab formation, buttress routes may generally be safer than gully climbs.

Your equipment should be useable whilst wearing gloves. Gear should be checked beforehand, but carry a small crampon repair kit and spares. Spare equipment such as crampons, axes, small rack, and rope, stowed in your vehicle for the winter season is a sensible precaution against forgotten gear. You can copy your route descriptions (and alternative routes) and laminate if possible, instead of carrying a heavy guidebook or relying on smart phone apps, but this can limit your options. Do not become fixated on a particular route but be prepared to adapt to the conditions. Accidents occur when teams decide their chosen route is the only objective, in spite of it being in poor condition or if there are people on it already. Being struck by a chunk of ice or rock from above can cause serious injury and even the most conscientious leader will dislodge debris. It is also disconcerting for the party ahead forced to consider others below.

There should be a process of continual assessment of conditions, weather, etc. A degree of flexibility in decision-making is always advisable and be prepared to retreat if necessary.

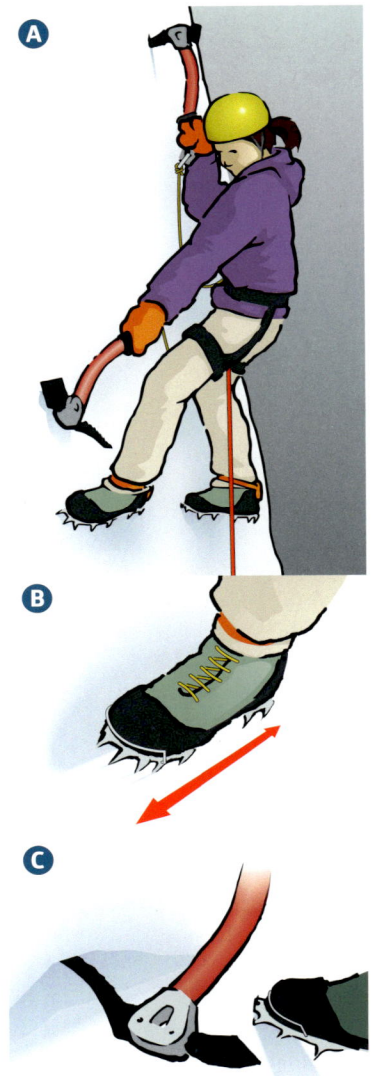

FIGURE 16.3 FASHIONING A FOOT LEDGE ON STEEP ICE: **(A)** USE A COMBINATION OF CRAMPONS AND PICK TO CREATE A RESTING FOOT LEDGE **(B)** STAMP AND SCRAPE THE FOOT BACK AND FORTH TO FASHION A FOOT LEDGE OF AT LEAST BOOT-LENGTH **(C)** USE THE PICK TO CHOP A HORIZONTAL, BOOT-LENGTH LINE AND CHOP ABOVE THE LINE WITH PICK AND ADZE

16.2.2 Approaching the climb

Reduce your equipment to an acceptable minimum. Share personal and emergency gear (first aid, repair kits and spare clothing) and adjust the rack so it is appropriate for the route – ice screws may not be required on buttress routes! For popular venues, be first on your climb so not delayed or bombarded with debris from parties above. Consider setting off in the dark and arriving at your climb at first light. In certain conditions it may be safer to approach from above. If there is an avalanche risk on the approach slopes, then abseiling in is an option. Abseiling down the line of the route enables gear left as abseil anchors to be collected on the ascent but ensure there is no one on the climb before starting down.

FIGURE 16.4 A WIND SCOOP OFFERS A COMFORTABLE PLACE TO GEAR UP *PHOTO // GEORGE McEWAN*

16.2.3 Gearing up

On short, accessible routes and in settled weather, climbing without a rucksack is an option. It can be left in a convenient place to collect on descent. Protect it from being dislodged by digging it into the snow or weighting down with a rock. Mark the location (a walking pole is a convenient marker) if there is a possibility of drifting or fresh snow. Gear up at a suitable location (safe, sheltered and preferably flat) sooner rather than at a higher, more awkward stance, although occasionally, a convenient gearing-up place and stance can be found in a windscoop at the base of the cliff.

Pack the rucksack with gear that is needed soonest at the top, particularly the ropes. Having the ropes flaked in a bag in your rucksack will save time. Eat and drink when gearing up and put on your helmet when there is any chance of a slip or if there are climbers above. Do not put it down on a slope where it can roll off. If there are no flat areas, then cut a stance and another above for the rucksack. It can be held in place with a tool through a loop or strap *(see Figure 16.4)*. Most climbs require a belay at the start. Decide early who is leading and belaying on the first pitch. The belayer carries the rope/s to the start and the leader takes the gear. The belayer flakes the rope into a stance while the leader is setting up the anchors. Tie into the rope and clip an anchor as soon as possible for security. A sling 'cow's tail' can also be used once an anchor is in place.

16.2.4 On the climb

Consider using dry-treated 55m-60m or even longer ropes. Attach karabiners to the anchors with the gate facing down and out for ease of

FIGURE 16.5 BELAY CHANGEOVERS: (A) THE STANCE IS PREPARED FOR THE CHANGEOVER **(B)** A DIRECT BELAY USING A SELF-LOCKING BELAY DEVICE AND PREPARED FOR THE CHANGEOVER

clipping. Centralise and equalise anchors that are far apart, or at a distance from the stance, with a long or super-long sling *(see Tying to anchors and linking anchors on page 234)*. If using double ropes and the next pitch is long with a possibility of running out of rope, tie into the centralised anchor point with just one of the two ropes; the other can then be used to tie into the centralised anchor on the next belay. However, it is better to tie into a single point with both ropes, using two separate knots rather than one knot in two ropes.

On long routes an option is to climb in blocks, where one person leads several pitches at a time. This is useful if one climber is stronger or fitter than the other or on a very strenuous route where the second arrives at the stance tired and the leader is rested. Centralise the anchors for a quick belay changeover. Have a spare screwgate karabiner on the anchor for the second to tie into. With good anchors, it may be quicker using a direct belay with a manual device with assisted braking for second (guide mode) *(see Figure 16.5)*.

If the ropes are icing up and difficult to use with the belay device, consider a waist belay. Prusiks, knives and emergency hardware can get iced up on your harness. Carry them in your pocket or accessible in your rucksack.

A familiar and practised racking system saves time. Generally, large and less used pieces are carried towards the back of the rack and graded to smaller, shorter and often used gear at the front. Always re-rack at the belays and operate the same system as your partner. Bandoliers can quickly be swapped and made ready by hanging on a securely placed axe or clipped into an anchor. They are easier to exchange than using harness gear loops when each karabiner has to be swapped over individually with more chance of being dropped. Before leaving the belay, remove gear (such as the belay device) attached to the rope tie-on loop, or harness central loop, to allow a clear view of foot placements.

Eat and drink on the route, particularly a long one. Rehydration is probably more important than eating, as without fluids the absorption rate of food is low and dehydration is debilitating both physically and mentally.

Have an accessible pocket full of sweets.

If you use poles, they are best stowed inside your rucksack. Protruding poles snag too easily. If you climb without a rucksack, wear a headtorch if there is a possibility of being caught in the dark.

Consider moving together on easier sections as are found on some routes. However, this must be done with full appreciation of the dangers involved and always with an adequate amount of protection (runners) on the rope between the leader and second (referred to as 'simul-climbing').

Position the stance with communication in mind. However, communications can be difficult so decide on a system of non-verbal communication. About four definite and unmistakable tugs on the rope from above for 'Climb when Ready' is usually all that is required. This may mean that the belayer takes more of the rope in through the belay device rather than hand over hand, but the second is protected at all times. As a belayer, try to imagine the process of the climb and use the rope movements to confirm this. When belaying a second, feel for any movement by putting a little tension on the rope by using overgrip and cocking the live hand wrist (known as 'snapping' the rope) – as if playing a fish!

Mobile phones and radios can also make communication easier although having a back-up system to this technology is always a good idea in case of failure or dropping.

16.2.5 Stance management

Stances are managed the same way for all summer and winter climbing.

Be aware that debris will be dislodged as snow stances are fashioned. Stow tools out of the way, particularly of moving ropes, and have them clipped in securely if necessary. On small stances, leave an attachment point at the belay for the second and prepare an alternative stance where they can stand safely when gear and ropes are being sorted. On constricted stances, ensure that the belayer's braking hand is not obstructed and remember that the belay device has to be operated correctly for both leader and second *(see Figure 16.6)*.

When belaying a second and preparing to put the rope through the belay device, pull up some spare rope and trap it under the boot instep. This creates some slack and unweighted rope which will feed through the device more easily. Ropes should be neatly flaked at the stance and not dropped with the potential for snagging, particularly in windy conditions. On large stances, make a place in the snow for the rope. On small stances, drape it in laps around a secured axe, your legs or feet or over the ropes to the anchor.

If the stance is spacious, the second may be safeguarded by simply tying a knot in the dead rope behind the belay device, otherwise attach the second to a secure point of the belay with the rope or sling. This allows the belayer to assist hands-free and if necessary, when the leader is safe, change the belay device to orientate for an upward pull. When not leading through, the second back-coils the rope while the belayer (new leader) re-racks the gear.

FIGURE 16.6 BELAY DEVICE ORIENTATION – BELAYING A SECOND: THE BRAKING HAND IS ON THE SAME SIDE AS THE ANCHOR ROPE. FOR EFFECTIVE BRAKING, THE ROPE IS ORIENTED 180° THROUGH THE BELAY DEVICE WITH NO CROSSOVERS OR TWISTS, AND **(A)** ASSISTED BY STANDING SIDE ON. **(B)** BRAKING WITH THE WRONG HAND WILL COMPROMISE THE EFFICIENCY OF THE BELAY DEVICE WHEN THE ROPE IS LOADED DUE TO THE BELAYER TWISTING AND BLOCKING THE BRAKING ROPE. **(C)** THE BELAY DEVICE IS CHANGED OVER AND THE BELAYER POSITIONED AND BRAKING CORRECTLY FOR AN UPWARD PULL. THE BELAY DEVICE IS INEFFECTIVE FOR A DOWNWARD LOAD AND A RUNNER MUST BE PLACED (PROTECT THE BELAY) TO PRODUCE AN UPWARD PULL SHOULD THE LEADER FALL. **(D)** ANTICIPATION: THE BELAYER MAY BE PULLED TOWARDS THE ROCK AND RESTRICT THE MOVEMENT OF THE BRAKING HAND.

16.2.6 Planning

Planning is perhaps the greatest help in speeding things up. Decide where the next pitch goes, who is leading and if there needs to be a change-over of the belay device from a downward to an upward load, how the leader is to be secured at the stance when the ropes are being changed over in the device. If it appears there are no runners for some way above the stance, a bomb-proof anchor point from the belay can be used as the first runner. However, if this is not appropriate, there are several options. Initially belay

FIGURE 16.7 THE ROPE BOMB: AN EFFECTIVE WAY OF THROWING ROPES. THE ABSEIL ANCHOR IS AN ICE THREAD BACKED UP WITH AN ICE SCREW CLIPPED INTO THE ABSEIL ROPE VIA A QUICKDRAW AND SHOCK-ABSORBING EXTENSION. THE CLIMBERS ARE SECURED TO A SEPARATE SCREW USING A SLING COW'S TAIL.

for a downward load until a good runner is placed, and once the leader is secure, change the belay device for an upward pull. Alternatively, belay for an upward pull and put a knot some way down the rope to jam in the belay device in the event of a fall past the stance not being held.

Continually question and anticipate. Where does the next pitch go? Is there room on the stance to sort the rack comfortably? Will the second need to be secured at the stance or do they need another stance fashioned below? Where will the ropes and tools be secured? Is there a danger from falling debris and am I protected? Am I securely positioned and my braking hand free to operate the belay device effectively?

16.3 Descent

Know where your descent is from the top of the climb and how to navigate in the dark. Have the map and compass handy and note on the map where the route finishes. Concentration is required for difficult descents especially when tiredness is a factor. If using a GPS to aid navigation, a previously stored waypoint marking the descent would help in location.

16.3.1 Abseiling in winter

Abseiling is the same as in summer with the following considerations:

- The ropes may be snowed or iced up affecting the abseil device, and back-up Prusiks may not be as effective. Multiple abseils are common and usually down more broken ground, encouraging tangles on ledges and a stop-start action. Carry plenty of spare abseil material: 2-3m of 7mm cord is ample and a knife to cut it or even an end of the main rope in an emergency.
- Anchors must be secure and the ropes retrievable. Natural anchors such as blocks, ice bollards, ice threads or snow bollards are favoured

since little gear is left. Centralised and equalised two-point anchors are used otherwise. With less friction over snowed or iced-up rock, it may be possible to retrieve the rope from direct around a natural rock anchor.

- Throwing the ropes can be difficult in windy conditions. Back-coil the ropes and flake them out close to the edge of the stance so they run freely. Throw with enough coils for weight and allow for the wind direction. Another technique is the 'rope bomb' where the ropes are wound around themselves from the ends to form a ball *(see Figure 16.7)*. When thrown, this will roll and bounce down the crag, be less affected by the wind and less likely to get caught on ledges.
- Anticipate likely problems and thoroughly check for free-running ropes. The first down double-checks by pulling from below. To release a stuck abseil rope *(see 11.8 The leader's safety on page 148)* on a restricted stance, one method is to tie into the rope and use full body weight to pull. The other end must be anchored (or belayed) for an upward pull in the event of a sudden release. Over-weighting a jammed rope can damage it. Ascending the ropes to re-arrange the abseil anchor is a last resort!
- When abseiling use a back-up if possible, have the heaviest person abseil first then remove the back-up. If abseiling from an ice thread, back it up with the ice screw, clipping the back-up into the abseil rope, not the thread. If the thread is solid then the last person removes the back-up *(see Figure 16.8)*. Alternatively, with enough abseil material, use two equalised ice threads, particularly if the ice is less than perfect!
- Retrievable ice screw and axe anchors require much practice, are not 100% reliable and therefore not recommended.

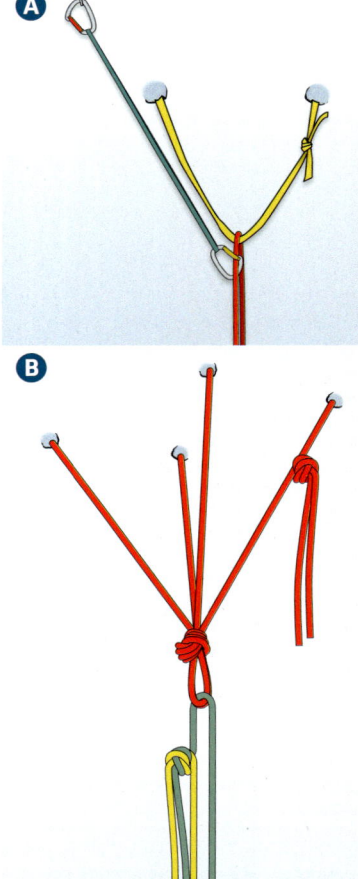

FIGURE 16.8 ICE THREAD ABSEIL: (A) THE ICE SCREW BACK-UP SHOULD NOT TAKE ANY LOAD. **(B)** IN LESS THAN IDEAL ICE, TWO ICE THREADS MAY BE USED AND EQUALISED WITH LENGTHS OF ABSEIL MATERIAL

16.4 Soloing

Soloing is arguably the purest form of climbing and is carried out more in winter than in summer. It should only be done with the full appreciation of the hazards involved, on climbs in good condition, well within the climber's capabilities and in a mental state of supreme confidence! Be familiar with the climb (or at least have the latest 'beta'), always let someone know of your intentions, wear a helmet and never solo behind other parties. Some solo climbers wear a harness and carry a minimum of appropriate technical gear and a short rope to aid retreat in the event of unforeseen circumstances. Remember that it may not be the technical difficulty of the route that presents the biggest danger but factors such as snow and avalanche conditions, cornices and weather problems.

16.5 Multi-pitch problem-solving (Improvised rescue)

Although you can never practise for every eventuality, familiarity with the basic techniques of improvised rescue is important. They are best learned and practised in summer.

In winter there are the added problems of weather and conditions, and the chance of injury from a fall or being hit by debris is greater. Cold injuries and hypothermia add complications, equipment may not operate efficiently because it is wet or icy and locations are often isolated with no immediate assistance or mobile phone reception. The main priority is to look after yourself and not put others at greater risk by using inappropriate techniques. A knowledge of outdoor emergency first aid is vital in the event of an injury. As part of the planning process, note any areas of shelter, best escape or descent routes, nearest point of contact for emergency services and finally, carry appropriate emergency clothing and equipment.

Although most problems have a simple solution there are a few basic considerations for any problem-solving process:

Look for the easiest option, shout for help and get other people involved. Do not have anyone hanging on a rope longer than necessary. Think before you act and take time to gather your thoughts and work through systems to solve the problem. Go with gravity and escape down rather than hoisting. Back-up prusiks that are used to hold a load, in case they slip. Use releasable systems such as a tied-off Italian hitch so decisions can be changed if a technique is not working. If possible, use screwgate karabiners or two back-to-back karabiners in all main anchors and connectors.

16.6 Nutrition – Food and Drink

There is actually good sense behind the traditional Scottish hill food breakfast of a 'large fry'; fat and protein are great for energy reserves! For energy-sapping long and strenuous winter trips, we need to be fed and hydrated. Climbers normally need more energy than winter walkers of around 4–5,000 calories per day, to generate heat, combat fatigue, for clear thought and endurance at the end of the day. Fill up on appropriate food the day or night before and have a good, high-calorie breakfast. Throughout the day, it is better to eat steadily rather than have one big meal: little and often is the rule. Sweets or high-energy bars can be eaten on the move. Take food that has a high energy-to-weight ratio and, above all, food you enjoy eating. Carry similar emergency food for those extra long days and replace it when used. In general, it is better to consume food that has a low to medium Glycaemic Index (GI) where blood sugar levels remain relatively stable for slow, steady fuelling. Food containing some fat and protein along with the carbohydrate usually has a lower GI.

Dehydration has a debilitating effect on performance. Drink lots of fluid the night before (water not beer!) and first thing in the morning before going out, and water or equivalent amounts of drink should be taken regularly throughout the day. A simple rehydration pack that supplies fluids on demand works well. Although a 2-litre pack adds another 5lb to your gear plus the bulk, the weight is offset by the gains made in starting the climb hydrated. Freezing-up of the tube can be a problem with rehydration systems. Using an insulating cover for the tube and nozzle, filling the bag with hot drinks and blowing the fluid in the feeder tube back into the bag stops it freezing up. Drink the first litre on the walk in, leaving one litre to drink on the climb. Urinating frequently, copiously and clearly are signs of being hydrated and any yellow colouration means that you are starting to dehydrate.

Y GRIBIN *PHOTO // KARL MIDLANE*

Winter ridges: Rope techniques

Memorable days can be had on the great ridges in the UK, moving fast and efficiently over Grade I/II ground.

The more competent may enjoy the experience solo, but for many, roped protection is necessary. Several techniques can be used, and choosing the appropriate one depends on such factors as terrain, snow and weather conditions and the competence of the party. Although soloing is fast, the consequences of a slip are serious. Conversely, pitched climbing is safer with regard to falling, but is time-consuming. Moving together roped requires good judgement, organisation and communication to be safe and enjoyable.

A variety of techniques may be employed on a single route, used in ascent, traversing and descent *(see Definitions on page 257)*. Apart from the party's experience, the most variable factor affecting decisions will be conditions. A soft snow arête one day may be an exposed, windy knife-edge of névé on another. To make informed decisions, it helps to have climbed the route in summer and be able to predict conditions for a winter ascent.

Ultimately, the rope is used because the consequence of a slip is serious and it offers protection against a fall. It is the planned use of the rope for physical support, and although there is a confidence-boosting role, the group moves faster because of this security.

All members must be practised at whichever rope technique is used, the most experienced person being the leader. With more than two climbers, the least experienced is next on the rope and the second most experienced at the end. Three is the maximum manageable number using short-roping techniques and four for moving together. There must be constant questioning by the leader about the likelihood of a slip and could this be prevented from becoming a fall using the technique employed? If no, then either the technique must be changed, or the risk is accepted but only for a very short distance.

17.1 General considerations

The closer together individuals are on the rope, the more control there is. The rope must be kept firm to prevent a slip or stumble developing into a fall and shock-loading the system. Good communications are essential for efficient movement. Technical equipment required in addition to axe and crampons includes: single 50m rope, helmet, harness, personal gear and half basic winter rack *(see Basic personal equipment on page 189 and Basic winter rack on page 190)*. The amount of equipment is modified according to the route, conditions and group experience. There will be changes in technique along the route appropriate for each section.

17.2 Moving together: Long roping

This is probably the most difficult to manage effectively since the group is spread apart. Protection is arranged by clipping into runners and/or weaving the rope behind natural anchors such as spikes and blocks *(see Figure 17.1)*. There should be at least one good point between each person. Every runner is unclipped then re-clipped behind each climber and removed by the last. If the leader runs out of gear, the group must stop in a convenient, safe location so the leader can collect it from the group.

FIGURE 17.1 MOVING TOGETHER – LONG ROPING: GOOD JUDGEMENT AND CONSTANT ALERTNESS IS VITAL FOR MOVING TOGETHER SAFELY

On easy, non-serious sections, the party can move closer together carrying hand coils to shorten the rope *(see Taking chest coils on page 255)*. These coils (or laps, as coiling kinks the rope) are only a means of transporting the rope. They should hang no lower than about knee level when in the hand. On technical ground, where moving together is inappropriate,

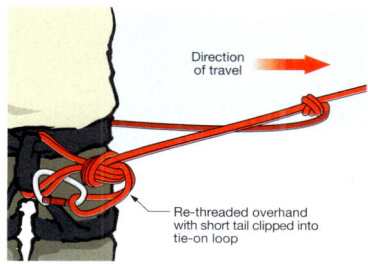

FIGURE 17.2 ISOLATION LOOP

a change is made to a more secure technique. Extra rope may be required to pitch a difficulty and with three or four on a rope, positions may be adjusted to free it up. Belays will be chosen to suit the situation, ranging from a standing or sitting braced stance, or a direct or indirect belay. Good judgement is vital for safe moving together. The option of turning back must always be open and the decision to back off should be made sooner rather than later.

17.2.1 Tying on

The last person is tied directly on to the rope. Each person thereafter is attached 10m – 15m apart. A loop is made with an overhand knot and tied into the harness with a re-threaded overhand knot, the tail of which is clipped back into the tie-on loop with a screwgate karabiner *(see Figure 17.2)*. This isolation loop gives a degree of independence whilst still providing support. It should not hang below knee level as it may snag on rocks or crampons. Tying directly to the rope for the middle persons is more secure than using a screwgate, especially in weight-bearing situations. This prevents inadvertent unclipping or cross-loading the karabiner. The leader takes any excess rope in tied-off chest coils, leaving the rope accessible should it be necessary to change techniques.

17.2.2 Descent
Moving together is only used on easy descents. The front person must be able to arrange protection. On difficult ground, non-moving together techniques include rope-protected down climbing, lowering and abseiling.

17.2.3 Traversing
Horizontal traversing is not uncommon on winter ridges, either below or along the crest. Protection must be arranged and this is normally easiest done when traversing below the crest. On exposed edges with no protection, belay one at a time. Otherwise, if someone falls unexpectedly, another must jump down the opposite side to counterbalance the fall. This is an emergency technique and requires quick reactions!

17.3 Short-roping
This is a technique used by a leader to protect one or two clients with a shortened rope. The party is as close as is manageable and the rope used to prevent a slip developing into a fall. However, it is not a fall-arresting system.

17.3.1 Tying on
The same method is used to tie on two persons as moving together, except that the distance between them is less. Tie on the last person and take 2m–3m of rope (depending on the steepness of the ground) and tie the second person on with a re-threaded overhand isolation loop. However, the isolation loop may be clipped into a screwgate karabiner, attached to the harness central tie-in point with an overhand bight if the rope is not planned to be loaded such as in climbing and lowering.

The distance between people is adjusted to suit the terrain. On steeper ground, clients are positioned further apart so there is no possibility of cramponing each other. On variable terrain, the rope may be tied to give a degree of flexibility in the distance between clients. Clip an overhand bight in the rope close to the end person into a screwgate karabiner on their tie-on loop to shorten the distance between the two. Alternatively, taking the rope over their shoulder as a chest coil and clove-hitching into the screwgate karabiner shortens the distance further. The initial distance between the two clients has to be judged to allow for the tie-offs *(see Figure 17.3)*.

The leader can carry extra rope in locked-off chest coils (secondary reservoir of rope), or stowed in a rope bag in the rucksack. Hand coils (primary reservoir of rope) may also be carried to extend the rope, for example when negotiating a step. These are locked off by taking the main rope around the back of the coils, back through the hand and pulled tight to secure *(see Figure 17.4)*. Alternatively, when carrying laps, a grip on the

Taking chest coils

The main rope from the tie-on is run up the chest, around the shoulder and under the arm to form a coil to waist-belt level. Continue coiling in the same fashion until the required length of rope remains. Alternatively, make appropriate-sized coils around your neck then slip one arm through them. To secure the coils, slide a hand between them and the body ('Lord Nelson' style) and pull a bight of rope back through; wrap it around the coils and main rope and tie-off with an overhand knot. The short tail of the knot should just clip tight into a screwgate in the main tie-on loop. Should a load come onto the leader, it will be shared between the harness and chest coils, keeping a lower centre of gravity to better resist the pull.

There are several methods of securing coils, but they must not tighten up around the body if loaded, and must allow quick access for extra rope. Test by pulling on the main rope to check that the securing knot does not slide.

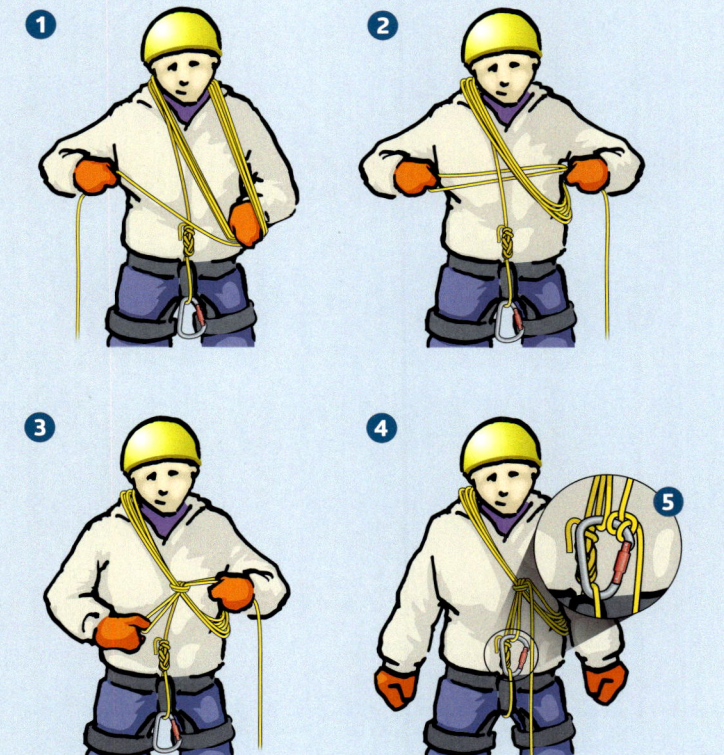

(1) Take coils to correct length, then place under arm and tighten up tie-on loop **(2–3)** Tie off coils **(4)** Clip short loop into screwgate
(5) Lower the centre of gravity by tying a clove hitch to the karabiner

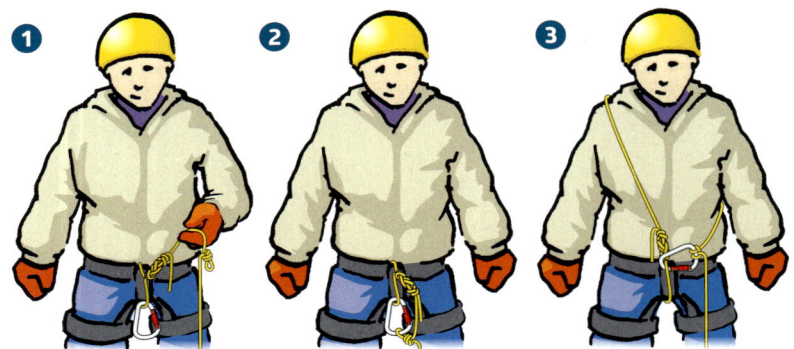

FIGURE 17.3 SHORTENING THE DISTANCE BETWEEN CLIENTS: (1–2) OVERHAND ON A BIGHT CLIPPED INTO TIE-ON LOOP OF END PERSON **(3)** END PERSON TAKES A CHEST COIL

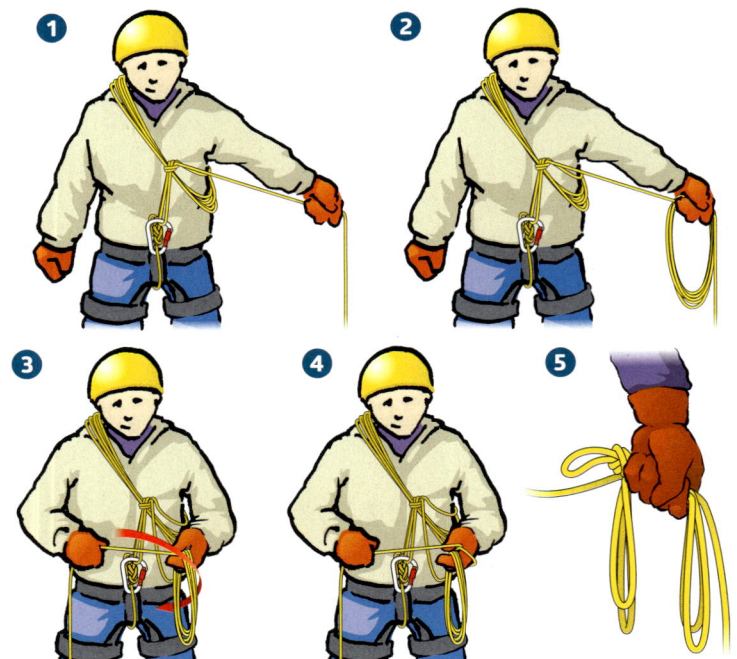

FIGURE 17.4 TAKING HAND COILS: (1–2) START FROM AN ARM'S LENGTH DISTANCE AND TAKE THE DESIRED LENGTH OF ROPE IN COILS OF ABOUT 30CM IN LENGTH **(3–4)** LOCKING OFF THE COILS **(5)** TAKING LAPS OF ROPE AND HELD BY AN OVERHAND KNOT. BEWARE OF THE KNOT SNAGGING WHEN TAKING IN

rope is achieved by tying a knot (overhand on a bight) which rests behind the hand. The amount of hand coiled rope depends on the length of the difficulty but should not overfill the hand. Hand-coils need not be carried on uniform ground such as snow slopes where a knot in the rope can be used to hold against.

General techniques for short-roping are similar to confidence-roping *(see 11.10 Confidence-roping page 150)*. It is important that the leader stays directly above the clients and the rope is kept firm by using a well-braced arm *(see Figure 17.5)*. When two people are short-roped, the rope between

Definitions

Confidence-Roping
This is used to safeguard an individual, sometimes within a group, to boost confidence in an apparently exposed situation. The individual is tied to a sling or short length of rope that is held by the instructor or leader. The leader may not even tie in to the rope. Both will usually move at the same time, thereby not impeding the progress of the group. The use of the rope is unplanned. Confidence-roping is for use in situations where a slip can be prevented from becoming a fall.

Short-Roping
This is the use of the rope to safeguard one or two individuals on terrain that is exposed and where a slip could have serious consequences. The terrain is not continuous climbing or scrambling but may have short sections of technical difficulty up to Grade II/III. Sections that require safeguarding will generally be very short but could be anything from a few metres to 20m or more, depending on where anchors can be found. The instructor or leader will generally climb the section first leaving the clients secure, possibly belayed, on a ledge. Normally, clients will move over the difficult ground at the same time, tied a few metres apart. The leader will safeguard them using appropriate belay methods. The whole party will move at the same time between sections of difficulty and in less-exposed situations. Occasionally in descent it may be appropriate to lower the clients either together or individually (see Lowering two clients). Leaders will not normally place running belays for their own safety but place them for the safety of the clients and for directional stability when safeguarding the clients.

Moving Together
The party will travel at the same time over terrain that presents a combination of exposure and technical difficulty or extreme exposure alone. Most commonly this technique is linked with moving along Alpine-type ridges or mixed climbs where speed, with a degree of safety, is important. A competent and compatible party will move together, arranging running belays between each climber. On arriving at anything of greater difficulty the party will stop and initiate 'normal' climbing procedures.

them may be held to provide security on easy ground. At a difficulty where the clients cannot be safely protected by short-roping, they can be anchored if necessary and protected by the leader above using an appropriate belay. A standing braced stance, 'snapping' the rope when taking in, would be inappropriate in all but the easiest sections *(see Figure 17.6)*.

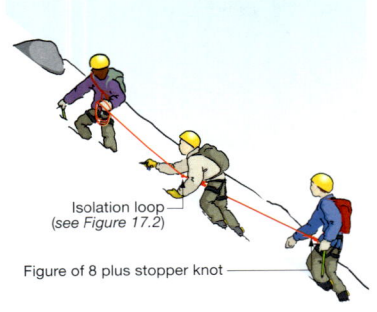

FIGURE 17.5 SHORT ROPING TWO CLIENTS: AN ATTENTIVE LEADER USES DYNAMIC BODY POSITIONING AND A WELL-BRACED ARM TO PROVIDE SUPPORT

FIGURE 17.6 A BRACED STANCE

Lowering two clients

On steep ground, lowering from a restricted stance can be problematical to start. The end person is initially protected by arranging an Italian hitch on a secondary anchor. This can be a screwgate karabiner attached to the isolation loop or clipped through the isolation loop overhand knot, which allows the clients more independent movement. The screwgate karabiner will remain in place for the lower.

BETH WILSON ON THE EAST RIDGE OF THE DOUGLAS BOULDER, BEN NEVIS   *PHOTO // DAVE EVANS*

Teaching winter climbing

Teaching winter climbing is a rewarding experience for both instructor and student, made more special by the winter mountain environment.

Teaching winter climbing involves the whole day, the instructor's role changing from leader on the walk-in, to guide and instructor on the climb and coach on the ice-bouldering session at day's end.

18.1 Base

The key to a successful day starts at the base. Gather information about the clients' aspirations, experience, confidence, attitude, learning style, fitness and personal equipment. Design a lesson plan and a structure that will be relevant, safe, enjoyable and educational, and the route choice must allow the aims and objectives to be carried out. The more time available, the easier the plan can be developed through consultation and discussion. The clients should also be aware of the nature of risk involved in the activity *(see BMC Participation Statement below)*. An informal contract is entered into and changes to the agreed plan should be by mutual agreement unless there are safety concerns. More thought is required to structure a relevant day with two clients of differing abilities.

The plan should include the overall aim for the day, the venue, route, weather forecast, prediction of conditions and avalanche hazard evaluation. Appropriate clothing and personal equipment should be physically checked and not just discussed. Technical equipment, rope and rack need to be sorted, and transport and timings checked as there may be reasons to return for a specific time.

There should be a structured progression throughout the day but ultimately it must be flexible enough to cope with unforeseen situations such as poor conditions, inaccurate weather forecasts or crowded routes. It is advantageous to have climbed the intended route or at least have information about it.

18.2 Approach

Use the approach to assess the clients' fitness, organisation, movement skills and their observational abilities. Educate them about the environment, weather, snow, navigation, climbing conditions and subjects that may impact on the day, and relate observations to the information gathered at base. If the climbs are in view, discuss the routes, conditions, tactics, approach and descent routes.

Decide whether it is appropriate to teach snow craft skills such as self-arrest, cramponing or winter belaying before climbing. This may be part of the overall plan or based on observations made on the approach relating to the clients' abilities. However, the most constructive time is spent climbing and there may be an opportunity to develop other skills

> **BMC Participation Statement**
> Climbing, hill walking and mountaineering are activities with a danger of personal injury or death. Participants in these activities should be aware of and accept these risks and be responsible for their own actions and involvement.

after the climb. If the clients' movement skills are weak, then adapt the rope-work to provide security. Unfortunately there may be no option but re-structuring the day due to factors such as bad weather, poor conditions, or lack of fitness.

When gearing up, discuss matters such as racking equipment or using a guidebook. Occasionally it may be possible to leave the clients' rucksacks below. However, this option is rarely open to an instructor who needs gear such as navigational and emergency equipment, first aid kit, repairs and spares, food, drink and extra clothing. Approaching the base of the route may be straightforward but is usually more complex, commonly up steepening snow. Other options may include abseiling or lowering in from above, traversing below the crag, or descending an easy line.

FIGURE 18.1 GUIDING TWO CLIENTS: TEACHING OPPORTUNITIES EXIST AT THE BELAYS, SUCH AS TYING TO ANCHORS AND BELAYING

There are several strategies for approaching the start of the route. Only solo with competent clients who are confident and practised at self-arrest. Soloing is fast and many approach slopes can be tackled this way, but it is also dependent on snow conditions and the run-out. What may be safe with soft snow and good steps may be dangerous when hard and icy. Stay close by to offer direction and encouragement. If the snow conditions are helpful and the clients are comfortable, then continue to the base of the route.

Consider the option to stop, make secure (self-belayed in a comfortable stance or tied to an anchor), tie on and ascend short-roping. In a non-climbing short-roping situation, the first, normally less experienced client may be attached to the rope with a screwgate karabiner. If there is a convenient spot below the crag, such as a wind-scoop or old stance, it may be possible to short-rope all the way *(see Figure 16.4 on page 243)*. However, if the ground below the climb is steep and exposed where short-roping is inappropriate and/or the first belay not obvious, then stop, normally within a rope length, secure the clients, run the rope out to the start and construct the first stance and belay. If stopping after more than a rope length, pitching may be necessary. The clients are then brought up to this stance using a direct or indirect belay. The stance is prepared for the proposed climbing system which is based on the aim for the day, the difficulty of the climb and time available. Alternatively, if the aim is for clients to lead, an option on a difficult snow slope approach is to belay below the start of the route and climb from there.

FIGURE 18.2 CLIMBING IN SERIES

FIGURE 18.3 CLIMBING IN PARALLEL. SECONDS CAN CLIMB ONE AT A TIME OR SIMULTANEOUSLY AT A SAFE DISTANCE APART

18.3 Teaching strategies

Generally, there should be a progressive teaching strategy where information is simple, consistent, drip-fed rather than an overload and the clients have hands-on learning and can react to constructive feedback. It is difficult to learn in poor weather where there is more emphasis on moving fast rather than teaching. Instructors are viewed as 'role models' and as such, safe best-practice skills and techniques are demonstrated and taught.

There are several techniques for teaching whilst on a route.

18.4 Guiding

When guiding, where clients are led up the climb, teaching opportunities exist mainly at the stances, although some instruction in the use of runners is possible when close to the belay. Coaching is difficult when guiding. The rope system used depends on the number and experience of the clients, the difficulty of the climb and the conditions. Belays are single point or equalised to assist in the changeovers, *(see Tying to anchors and linking anchors on page 234)* although teaching tying into two separate anchors is still possible *(see Figure 18.1)*. Stances are often more spacious and comfortable than in summer and on snow they can be cut to suit the anchor location.

Skills that can be explored at the belay include placing and tying into anchors, fashioning a stance, organising and managing the stance and ropes, correct use of the belay device (orientation in relation to the braking hand and belaying a second or a leader) and positioning on the stance *(see Figure 16.5 on page 244)*. There are more teaching opportunities using an indirect belay rather than an auto-blocking device with a direct

FIGURE 18.4 CLIMBING IN PARALLEL – CLIPPING RUNNERS: (A) CLIP THE ROPES INTO SEPARATE EXTENSIONS. A FALL WHEN LEADING AND CLIPPING TWO SINGLE ROPES INTO ONE EXTENSION CAN OVERLOAD THE PLACEMENT AND KARABINER AND IF ONE ROPE RUNS OVER ANOTHER, MAY CAUSE FRICTION MELTING DUE TO UNEVEN AMOUNTS OF ROPE STRETCH. **(B)** EACH SECOND REMOVES RUNNERS ON THEIR ROPE AND THE LAST PERSON REMOVES RUNNERS THAT HAVE BEEN USED FOR BOTH ROPES **(C)** ONE QUICKDRAW WITH TWO ROPES
PHOTO // BRENDAN WHELAN

belay. It is good practice to use indirect belays with novices as direct belays require more judgement and are usually inappropriate for belaying a leader. The choice of rack is dependent on the route and the aims of the day but each client should have some personal equipment, such as long slings and screwgate karabiners, for use at belays *(see Basic personal equipment on page 189)*.

18.4.1 Rope systems

The simplest rope management system for guiding on multi-pitch climbs uses a single rope and basic rack with one client. It may also be used with two clients with one tied on an isolation loop *(see Figure 17.2 on page 253)*. This is quick, particularly when using a direct belay, but usually limited to easier routes where the objective is an introduction to winter climbing. Up to four clients can be managed this way although the length of usable rope is reduced by each isolation loop. Clients can also get in each other's way, the distance between them is difficult to manage and having them climb at the same time can detract from the experience. Harder climbs using a single rope is limited to one-to-one guiding, although two half-ropes may be used to introduce double-rope technique and are useful for abseiling. Guiding two clients and climbing as a three requires thoughtful rope management (using two lightweight single ropes), efficient stance organisation and careful runner placements. There are two options, either climbing in series *(see Figure 18.2)* or in parallel *(see Figure 18.3)*. Each has its own advantages and disadvantages.

18.4.2 Climbing in series

Climbing in series is simpler to manage, both on the route and at the stance, but progress is slower. For teaching the use of the belay device, both clients still have an opportunity to belay the leader but will need to change positions on the ropes for each to have the opportunity to belay a second. It can be awkward to abseil retreat if the leader backs off a route and there is more than half the rope run out when using in-series technique as usually only one rope is immediately available. A notable disadvantage of climbing in series is that the leader will have no direct control of the last client and if they prematurely unclip from the anchors, there will be up to a full rope length of slack rope at the stance. This would not be the case when climbing in parallel if the leader takes in and secures both ropes before either client starts to climb.

18.4.3 Climbing in parallel

When climbing in parallel, the clients climb simultaneously (quick and efficient on easy ground), or one at a time, depending on the pitch. Either way, there must be good rope, runner and client management to prevent complications, particularly at the stance. Using contrasting coloured ropes and slings, and coloured markings on screwgate karabiners, helps. The leader must be proficient in belaying two seconds climbing together. However, it can be distracting if one climbs faster and has to keep stopping to wait for the other. With rope stretch a slip can land one client on the other if they are not far enough apart. Runners are either clipped separately into each rope, two extenders of differing length are used in the same runner or an overhand knot tied in a sling to create two loops – one for a karabiner for each rope. It is not good practice to clip two ropes, which will move at different rates, into a single karabiner and can lead to rope twists if they are removed incorrectly *(see Figure 18.4)*. The leader can be belayed on both ropes, by one client (difficult with full ropes), or by both clients with a rope each (runners on each rope) or on one rope, trailing the other but still putting both ropes into the runners. Runners on the trailing rope will be used for route indication, directional stability or for instructional purposes.

18.4.4 Stance management

Stance organisation with two seconds, and teaching at the stance, need not be complicated with a bit of thought and good management *(see Figure 16.5 on page 244)*. Explain procedures before leaving the stance. When in parallel, decide who is climbing first (usually the one on the outside of the stance), how far apart, which rope the runners will be on and who collects them. Recap on climbing calls and non-verbal communications. Explain who is to belay and consequently where they must be positioned on the stance *(see Stance management overleaf)*. If more than one stance is required (staggered stances), decide who goes where and where the rope is flaked. If a client is out of reach of the anchor, tie them in so there is no possibility of a fall before they reach the anchor to untie. This could be a figure of eight tie-back or clove hitch on a screwgate karabiner at their harness but not a clove hitch at the anchor unless it can be untied by the other client who is within reach of the anchor.

On arrival at the belay, identify the line of the next pitch and position the stance accordingly. When climbing in parallel, take in both clients' ropes even if they are seconding one at a time and tie off the rope of the client who remains at the lower belay. For clients arriving at the stance, it is easier to supervise them into the anchors in front of you rather than behind; belay with your back to the start of the next pitch *(see Stance management overleaf)*. Explain where and how to store the ropes and tools so that they are safe. For teaching using two anchors, have spare karabiners on the anchors, or make sure that it is possible for the client to clip karabiners directly into the anchors *(see Figure 18.1 on page 261)*. Working with several ropes in winter in poor weather means tangles are possible. A simple method for sorting tangles, after making everyone secure, is to untie an end, untangle the ropes and tie back on.

18.5 Teaching leading in winter

This is perhaps the most demanding aspect of mountaineering instruction due to the large number of factors involved when making judgements to allow clients to develop skills in a safe manner. Foremost, clients must have the desire and competence to lead and understand the risks involved. Familiarity with belaying, placing runners and anchors and knowing how to operate a belay device is essential. Sometimes aspiring leaders have rock climbing experience and have led in summer which simplifies the task. The climb should be in good condition and at an appropriate level of difficulty for the client. If too hard, exposed or strenuous, the clients will not be able to concentrate on learning. If too easy it may become boring and cause lapses in concentration which can be dangerous.

18.5.1 General

The instructor should be in a position to safeguard the clients and discuss and check runners and anchor placements. Clients may lead the whole or part of a route depending on the objectives, their abilities and time available, the instructor adapting teaching techniques as appropriate. When using the in-series guiding method, an aspirant leader can climb on a slack top rope and belayed on the other rope from below for a feeling of leading, especially if the client places separate runners. The instructor must be in a position to see to be able to judge the amount of slack rope correctly.

18.5.2 Soloing

Soloing alongside or above a novice leader is a common and effective technique on easier routes. The instructor needs complete confidence in their ability and to be able to quickly set up a belay if necessary. Being fully aware of the client's ability and confidence is important so that you know when to intervene. There are inherent dangers when soloing such as being knocked off, hit by falling debris or caught in an avalanche or cornice collapse. Avoid soloing below other climbers and never solo below the client or put yourself in a position where they can grab you should they panic. There is also little immediate physical assistance for the leader although the instructor should be able to get into a position to

Stance management
Positioning of the clients

(A) Instructor using 'in series' rope system. Clients are positioned one above the other on a restricted stance and out of the line of fire of falling debris. **Client 2** is belaying (must have unrestricted braking with the belay device) and **Client 1** is climbing first.

(B) Two groups instructing on the same route using 'in series' rope system, but climbing opposite sides of the ice to avoid falling debris. Both groups have spacious stances, which allow convenient positioning of the clients. The red-helmeted second of **Group 2** could also be positioned on the ledge below the belay.

(C) Instructor using 'in parallel' rope system. The belayer, **Client 1**, will be first to climb, leaving **Client 2** to dismantle the belay.

Positioning of the Instructor

(D) Both instructors are positioned with their backs to the direction of the next pitch. **Group 1** Instructor has extended the belay forward to enable a clear view of the clients.

(E) The Instructor has fashioned a large ledge and has moved to allow the client to position correctly at the belay. A second client would be positioned below the belay on this restricted stance

(F) The rope is back-coiled before the instructor moves off. A runner is placed as soon as possible.

give a top rope if the client feels uncomfortable. Self-protection can be by means of a cow's tail set up to clip into anchors when required. A half rack and a half rope (uncoiled in a bag for quick access) can be used to lead, construct a belay, place runners and, if necessary, set up a top rope and a small mechanical ascender is useful although 'occasional' ascenders and Prusiks may be ineffective on icy ropes.

18.5.3 Fixed rope

Climbing alongside on a fixed rope using an ascending device is more secure and safer for the instructor, and physical assistance can be offered from the fixed rope. However, it is time-consuming, needs a direct line and is usually not possible to set up for a multi-pitch route. The instructor can fix the rope by climbing an easy route to the top or solo the pitch or one nearby. Another option is for the instructor to lead the pitch, fix a belay and pull their rope up to the belay (the rope end must be left free) where it is ready for assistance, or abseil down to ascend alongside the leader *(see Figure 18.5)*. The client can clip the instructor's runners and/or place their own. The fixed rope may be knotted below the instructor with overhand loops to provide the leader with a runner if necessary. Asking the client to assess the quality of runner placements using a 'score' system from 1 (poor) to 5 (excellent) develops judgement skills which can positively affect their confidence in leading. Instructor feedback is necessary.

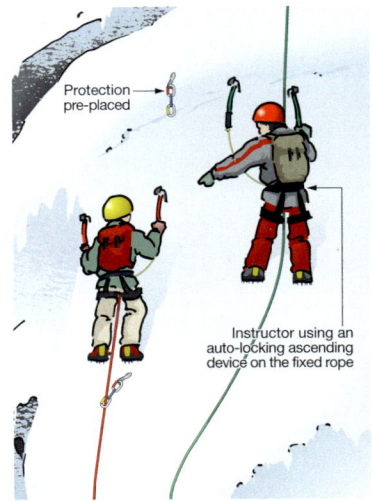

FIGURE 18.5 TEACHING LEADING USING FIXED ROPE. THE INSTRUCTOR SHOULD HAVE THE MEANS TO ASCEND AND DESCEND THE FIXED ROPE TO OFFER ASSISTANCE

18.6 Descents

The usual descent from a climb is to walk off. Steeper descents can be short-roped. Abseiling is an option for short routes to descend to the base of the crag although winter is not the best time to teach novices to abseil. Otherwise, the usual techniques for abseiling with clients apply. Be aware of heavy packs, iced ropes, cold hands and falling debris in winter. However, there are normally bigger ledges and stances to operate from. Usually the instructor will stack the clients on the rope and then abseil first to prepare the next belay, particularly in bad weather or where the next stance is out of sight *(see Abseiling with clients overleaf)*. Lowering clients can be an option if easy ground is within reach.

Once on easy ground, use some of the remaining time on the return to base to review the day and provide honest and constructive feedback.

FIGURE 18.6 COACHING CLIMBING: PRE-PLACED AXES ALLOW CLIENTS TO FOCUS ON FOOT PLACEMENTS
PHOTO // BRENDAN WHELAN

18.7 Technique training

18.7.1 Ice and mixed bouldering, bottom-roping and indoor walls

These are constructive methods of coaching the finer points of tool and crampon placements and using gear in a challenging but relatively safe environment. The clients should be given the freedom to develop a climbing style that suits their abilities and equipment. Experience in placing runners can be gained by practising on a rope, simulating placing protection on the lead. Normally, a bottom-roping system is used and several ropes can be set up on routes of varying difficulty. This allows a higher client-to-instructor ratio and is easier for group supervision. If the belay uses ice screw anchors, beware of pressure-melting or melt-out on warm days. Using a 'V' thread anchor backed up with an ice screw would be better in this situation.

Easy access to the anchors is important, as is a short set-up time, best done during a food break or when the group is practising other skills. With clients who are competent belayers, the instructor can be alongside the climber on a fixed rope coaching. If the venue is exposed or has an awkward run-out, an anchored handrail rope can be used to safeguard the movement along the base of the outcrop. Use intermediate anchors for long sections of rope and make good stances or even a walkway for ease of moving around. Caution the group about walking below climbs, particularly ice, as falling debris can cause injury. Belayers should be out of the line of fire and anchored if appropriate.

Numerous movement skills and exercises can be practised on a rope, but bear in mind that novices will tire. For ice these include: staggering tools versus classic front-pointing; straight arm hangs to conserve

Abseiling with clients

A — Knotted long sling attached to harness with lark's foot

B — Attach abseil device to lower loop; Instructor

C — A french prussik may be attached for additional security

D — Screwgate on sling ready to attach to anchor; Instructor; Rope threaded through anchor; Ice axes secured

strength (monkey hangs); climbing bulges; hooking (only after a few holes have developed); standing on footholds rather than kicking in; climbing with no tools or one tool only; speed climbing (make sure the belayer takes in fast enough); reducing the number of tool placements; climbing with a rucksack; swapping tools to try different designs; placing ice screws on steep ice; cutting stances on moderately steep ice or foot ledges on steep ice; climbing leashless; trying techniques such as back-stepping, laying-away on icicles and stacking tools; practise down climbing and traversing *(see Figure 18.6)*.

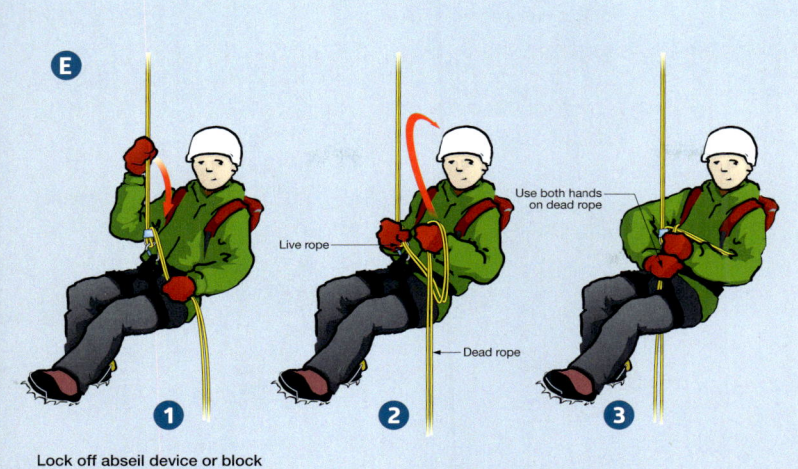

(A) Attached to the anchor while rigging the abseil
(B) Clients are stacked on the abseil rope and the instructor descends first. The clients are trapped while the tension is maintained on the abseil rope
(C) Disconnect from the anchor and allow the sling to hang free or clip it to the harness on the opposite side from the braking hand
(D) Clients arrive at a stance prepared for another abseil. The instructor maintains a controlling grip of the ropes
(E) **Increasing friction during an abseil**
If it is difficult to control an abseil descent, a simple temporary method to increase the friction uses a twist of rope around the body.
1 If possible, take some weight off the rope, otherwise lock off the abseil device.
2 Take a twist of rope, making sure the dead rope lies over the live rope and feed it over head and rucksack.
3 Move the rope to waist level and between legs.

Bouldering (limited height above the ground) should not be done on outcrops with dangerous run-outs. The group should be organised so that no one stands below a climber or uses spotting techniques. Ice bouldering can include traverses, circuits, and short problems if there is an easy descent from the top. Be aware of the landings although jumping into deep soft snow is comparatively safe. Landing on hard snow or on slopes when wearing crampons can easily cause injuries.

Venues for mixed climbing bottom-rope sessions should have a variety of tool and crampon placements. Ideally there should also be rock protection placements along the bottom of the crag and on the climb. Mixed training would include: use of crampons only or tools only; climbing the same route twice but trying different methods of climbing – hooking only, torquing and wedging only, no tools, no crampons; experimenting with turf placements; placing protection as on the lead; placing and removing pitons and other exercises as for ice.

Indoor dry tooling walls and specialised indoor ice climbing walls offer a great opportunity to practise skills in a teaching-friendly environment particularly if time is a constraint.

See also *14.7 Training for winter climbing on page 215*.

ON BEN NEVIS AT DUSK AND HEADING TOWARDS THE SAFETY OF THE RED BURN DESCENT ROUTE
PHOTO // GARRY SMITH

part 6

Winter incidents

DIGGING SNOW HOLES IN THE WHITE CORRIES, GLEN COE   PHOTO // DAVE EVANS

Winter shelters

The ability to construct a snow shelter is important for anyone venturing into the mountains in winter. Primarily, being able to efficiently create some form of shelter in an emergency could save your life by providing protection from the elements.

The difference between being outside in a winter storm compared with the protection provided by even the most rudimentary of shelters is very significant. A shelter may not be a haven of luxury but it could see you through a night out with little more than discomfort rather than developing hypothermia or cold injury.

Snow shelters are not the only possible shelters in winter but the alternatives of camping or using bothies have their limitations. While bothies can be secure, safe and comfortable, their valley locations are often of limited use and those that are better situated can be very popular and crowded at certain times. Camping in winter can also be problematic with difficulties in pitching tents due to frozen or snow-covered ground. More importantly the wind speeds frequently reached in the mountains can make camping fraught or even impractical with the scattered remnants of tent material attesting to this fact.

FIGURE 19.1 DIGGING IN NEAR THE TOP OF A STEEP BANK OF SNOW

Snow shelters can be divided into two main categories: emergency shelters, those that are made in an emergency situation, and planned snow shelters or snow holes, for which the appropriate equipment is carried, both for construction and habitation. While there is probably little requirement to use a snow hole in the UK, this can provide a unique experience of living in the mountains in winter. A snow hole can provide a secure base, be very comfortable and, unlike a tent, cannot blow down. Unfortunately it may take two to three hours of hard work to construct and it is susceptible to thaw, covering by drifting snow and even avalanches. However, they do teach a lot about living in snow and much of this relates directly to the construction of emergency shelters. How and where to dig, how to organise equipment and how to exist for a night out in an emergency situation are all enhanced by having made and lived in a specifically constructed snow hole.

19.1 Tools

In an emergency, something that can be used to dig and cut snow with is required. This is normally the ice axe, anything flat such as a deadman, or even your own hands and feet. A collapsible shovel is invaluable in these situations and as a piece of group or personal equipment can dramatically reduce the time and effort required to construct a shelter. The more robust, the better, as digging in some snow types can put a lot of strain on equipment. Also useful, particularly if the snow is firm, is a snow saw

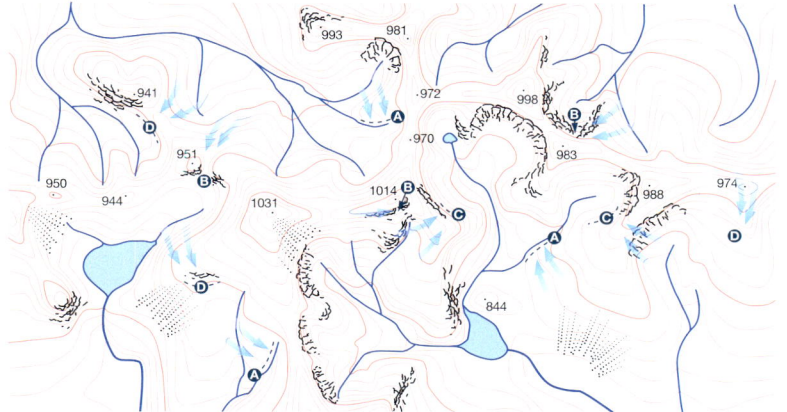

FIGURE 19.2 MAP SHOWING SNOW SHELTER SITES: (LOCATION NOT SPECIFIED TO REDUCE ENVIRONMENTAL IMPACT) **(A)** STREAM BEDS – CONTOURS 'SHARP' ENOUGH TO INDICATE DEEP, OBVIOUS STREAM BANKS, THEREFORE A GOOD CHANCE OF SNOW DRIFTING IN LEE OF STREAM BANK SLOPE CHANGE **(B)** PROMINENT 'SLOTS' IN A RIDGE (NARROW BEALACHS, CHANNELS) FUNNELS WIND AND SNOW THROUGH UNTIL LEE SLOPE CHANGE **(C)** SAFE SITES (AS INDICATED BY CONTOURS) AT THE END OF A CORNICE **(D)** OPEN SLOPE DRIFT SITES USUALLY IN THE LEE OF A RIDGE/SPUR AND ON A STEEPENING IN THE SLOPE AS INDICATED BY A FEW CONTOURS CLOSER TOGETHER THAN THE PRECEDING AND FOLLOWING SLOPE.

which can be of steel or aluminium. This should have large teeth and importantly, a practical and comfortable handle.

19.2 Location and material

The first consideration for any snow shelter is the site but this may be closely linked to the type of snow. A flat site will dictate a different method of construction compared with a moderately angled or a steep slope. Also, a large open steep slope may be more susceptible to avalanches. In basic terms the softer the snow the easier it is to dig into, while harder snow is more easily fashioned into blocks. Soft, deep snow means digging; hard, shallow snow means building is the easier option. However, conditions often fall between the two with the choices of both excavation and construction available. All things being equal, digging in will be quicker than building.

If the snow is fairly soft, the best place is a short, steep lee slope where it is possible to dig in as directly as possible. This may also have the advantage that shelter from the elements may be available once digging is started. Dig near the top of the slope where gravity assists removal of the spoil and reduces the effort *(see Figure 19.1)*. Concave slopes, although more likely to be corniced, are better than convex as they tend to be less avalanche-prone and more likely to offer greater headroom than convex slopes.

Using the map is the first step in locating a good site *(see Figure 19.2)*. Try to locate a slope such as in a stream-bed, below an edge or behind a ridge or large boulder. The problem here is that you are selecting an accumulation zone and in certain conditions of winds and drifting snow there is the danger of being buried. On a large slope the avalanche danger could also be very real. As with most things in winter, knowing the past weather and snow history and the layering within the snow pack is invaluable for making reasoned choices about where to look.

> **19 Locating snow shelter sites**
>
> Pre-trip planning noting any possible emergency shelter sites is useful, but observation on the hill is probably more important. For instance, are your assumptions of snow deposition and drifting confirmed or have drifts formed on other aspects? Take note of any old snow holes that may still provide good shelter. Be open-minded as to the possibilities of snow shelter sites, for example snow creep fracture lines, particularly above steep-sided stream-beds, may offer shelter with a minimum of work to modify.
>
> Wind scoops below cliffs or outcrops can offer short steep snow slopes for digging into. Any short sharp change of slope angle, even on moderate terrain, that has an aspect away from the prevailing winds may offer a good site.
>
> Assuming no avalanche risk, where cornices peter out at the sides of a corrie edge or a steep slope, it may be possible to drop down and dig in at the cornice edge. Checking out from above may be done with the security of a rope.
>
> Some cornices may 'roll over' forming a tunnel. If it is safe from collapse, digging an entrance into the tunnel and widening can provide quick shelter.

If the snow is firm and can be cut into good blocks, a steep slope is still the better option as the slope itself can form a part of the construction and blocks can be manoeuvred into place from above, using gravity. If there is an avalanche risk or the risk of avalanche is likely to increase because of drifting snow, it will be better to avoid any steep lee slopes, choose a safe location and spend more time and effort constructing your shelter. Always be prepared to adapt your ideas and design to the conditions that you find. Sometimes hard or soft snow layers dictate the easiest way to dig. Natural hollows such as below cornices may give shelter with little alteration. A hard or icy layer may mean that you have to dig along rather than in.

19.3 Cutting blocks

The ability to cut snow blocks effectively is a must for making a snow shelter. They may be used simply to close up an entrance or be necessary for the whole construction. First, find the most suitable snow which hopefully will be the top layer, often wind-slab, but it may be deeper down which means more work. Take blocks from a quarry located above and to the side of the shelter site so they can be slid down rather than carried into place.

Blocks are easily cut with a snow saw but can be effectively produced with an ice axe and can vary in size and consistency from too big to carry to frustratingly fragile. Select an undisturbed snow site and dig a horizontal step across the slope a bit longer than the required block size

FIGURE 19.3 LIFTING OUT A SNOW BLOCK

and cut up the sides and then along the back of the block. The side cuts should be slightly angled so that the block can slide out. Lastly, cut underneath the block to isolate it then slide it forward and out. This is the danger time for breaking the block: make sure that it is detached all the way around as you undermine it and be ready to support it on both arms as it comes free *(see Figure 19.3)*. Depending on the hardness of the snow, a bit of leverage may be needed to finally break it free.

When quarrying, the length of the cutting tool determines the size of the block, particularly when cutting underneath. If using a saw, cutting is easy. When using an axe the pick is usually too short to give reasonable-sized blocks. The axe shaft can be more effective or, if the snow is not too hard, then a strong avalanche probe or walking pole with the basket removed can be a useful alternative. Sometimes it is best to start cutting with the adze or the pick then use the axe shaft to finish off. When the first block is removed, the second is taken out the same way using the newly exposed face to start. Blocks that break should be set to the side; they may be useful later and so reduce the amount of quarrying needed.

19.4 Other considerations

When making any type of snow shelter, there are some general principles worth observing. The more you know about the snow pack before starting, the better choices you can make. Probe the snow with whatever you have: avalanche probe, walking pole or even the ice axe as this can tell you something about the depth and layering of the snow.

As digging in may create a weakness in the snowpack which could trigger an avalanche, dig at the top of the slope – it is better to be on the top rather than buried from above. If the site is susceptible to drifting there may be less accumulation higher up the slope so less chance of being completely buried. If in doubt, go elsewhere!

19.5 Personal preparation

Making a snow shelter is hard work so it may be worth removing some clothing before starting to avoid becoming soaked in sweat and melting snow. Dig a ledge to the side of site and leave rucksacks and other equipment secured so that they cannot be blown away or covered with debris. Before settling down for the night, brush snow off your clothing and get as dry as possible. Try to get as much insulation below you as possible as this is where most cold comes from. Try to have as little of your body in contact with the snow, so sitting in a foetal position is better than lying down. Even in an emergency shelter, body heat can raise the temperature above freezing.

19.6 Finishing off

Mark the site of the shelter with something, such as an avalanche probe, walking pole or rope. This does two things: it makes it easier to find if someone such as a rescue team is out looking for you and it can stop others falling through the roof. It would be ironic to survive the night then be injured by someone's cramponed foot! If there are several snow holes in the same area, link the entrances with a rope so they can all be found in case of drifting over. If possible, attach the end of the rope to the marker where it can be followed back to the shelters, in the event of a search and rescue. Always take your digging tools, be it axe or shovel, into the shelter with you in case you have to tunnel out.

Make sure there is sufficient ventilation and check this regularly, ensuring that the entrance does not become totally blocked with snow. Generally it is best to have the entrance lower than the main area as this allows cold air to drain out, it will not collect so much snow and be less liable to drift closed. As getting out of the weather is often the first concern, shelters can be joined up from inside if they are close together. This is a great morale booster in any emergency situation.

19.7 Bivouac bags

Personal bivouac bags are useful in an emergency situation. If made of a breathable material then getting inside is the best option. If not, such as is the case with heavy-duty polythene bags, the question is more complex as going into the bag will produce condensation and hence wet clothes. Whether to stay warmer and wetter or colder and drier will depend on what is likely to happen afterwards and weather conditions at the time. Will you get out of the shelter to be soaked by wet snow, sleet or even rain or will you face freezing conditions, where everything will freeze solid? Will there be a rescue team looking for you, how much spare clothing is available, and so on? Every situation will be unique and demand its own individual answer.

19.8 Environmental considerations

Old snow holes can be unsightly after melting out, so make sure that all litter is removed. It is easy to lose things in the snow, so it is necessary to be very organised about food, candle wax, matches and the like. As a number of groups may use the same areas, the cumulative effect of even minor carelessness can be very noticeable. If making practice emergency shelters, destroy them before you go. They can be a danger if hidden by further snow and someone falls through the roof.

Sanitation is as important in winter as any other time of the year although the signs of your passing may not be visible until spring. As at any time of the year, best practice should be followed. Ideally, all solid waste should be removed and disposed of hygienically back in civilisation.

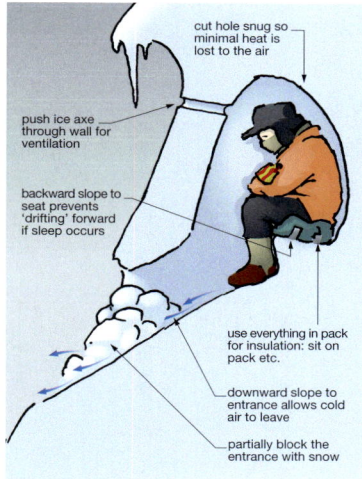

FIGURE 19.4 A BIVVI SHELTER

FIGURE 19.5 A BLOCKED HOLE SHELTER, MAKING USE OF A HARD SNOW LAYER. ALWAYS MOVE AS LITTLE SNOW AS POSSIBLE. IF A HARD LAYER OF SNOW MAKES IT DIFFICULT TO DIG THROUGH, USE IT TO MAKE A SMALL ENTRANCE AND CLEAR A LARGER VOID BEHIND

Failing that, faeces should be buried at least 10cm in the soil at least 50m from any water supply and any toilet paper should be wrapped and sealed in a plastic bag and carried out with the rest of the litter. Burying can be difficult in winter when there may be no open ground showing and/or the ground is frozen solid. If there is no option, try to defecate away from popular areas such as at the foot of climbing routes, where people are liable to be active. Consider what will happen in the spring when the snow melts and the impact it will have on the environment and water sources at that time. The question of whether to have a discrete area that everyone uses as a toilet, such as a pit, or to have it spread about more thinly over a greater area will depend on the specific situation.

19.9 Constructing emergency snow shelters

19.9.1 Bivvy shelter

Going straight into a steep bank of soft snow makes the easiest type of emergency shelter. Dig straight in, making a tunnel about shoulder width for about 1m then dig upwards. The height of the initial tunnel/slot will depend on the ease with which the slot can be blocked up. The less you need to bend down to dig, the more efficient and less painful on the back the digging will be. The narrower the entrance, the easier it is to reduce in size should that be necessary. Although digging upwards means that snow will land on you, it is easier working with gravity than lifting snow out. The hole should eventually be egg-shaped as this will accommodate a sitting person *(see Figure 19.4)* and, for a small amount of extra work, the chamber can be widened to accommodate others. If the entrance is sufficiently low and below your feet then drifting snow entering should

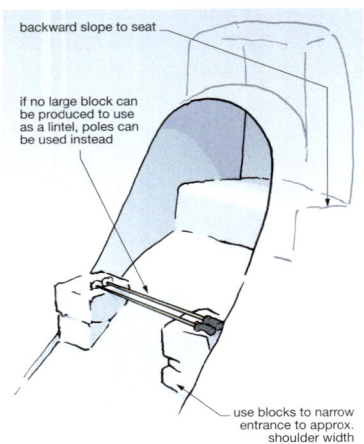 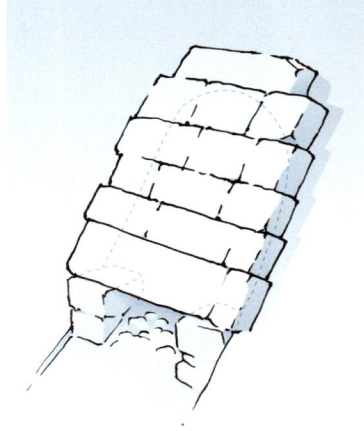

FIGURE 19.6 BLOCKED HOLE USING POLES AS A LINTEL

not be too great a problem. The entrance can often be improved by kicking down with your feet. Sometimes, it is easier to totally close up the entrance and re-dig a small tunnel up into the shelter.

Cut a seat which slopes back as this will last better. If the seat slopes outwards then you will have to brace to prevent sliding forward thus making it less comfortable. Make an air hole with the shaft of the axe at about face level, sit on as much insulation as possible and link a rope to any other shelters. If your feet are cold, slackening laces and putting your feet in an empty rucksack may be warmer. In soft snow and with practice, it should be possible to get out of the elements in less than half an hour.

19.9.2 Blocked hole

If the snow is firm and makes good blocks or if the slope is easy-angled, the easiest type of shelter is made by digging and building. Cut into the slope to form a slot a little more than shoulder width and a bit higher than you are when sitting upright. Make a seat sloping back into the slope. If the hardest part of the snow is the top layer it may be possible to cut a smaller hole then tunnel up in the roof to create more headroom with little extra effort *(see Figure 19.5)*. There is usually a balance between the ease of digging and the difficulty of blocking in a hole.

When the digging is finished, the front must be blocked in. Leave a hole just big enough to crawl into then cut a ledge on either side of the hole at this level. Next cut a block large enough to span this gap. This lintel is the most important block and if you cannot cut a block big enough to bridge a gap, walking poles or similar (which may be carefully removed later) can provide a good starting point and smaller blocks built on top as you would with bricks, *(see Figure 19.6)*. Alternatively use a block or two to reduce the width and place the lintel on these. When finished, any gaps in the building can be filled with snow to seal it totally. Snow dug from lower down can be good for this if it is slightly damp as then it may freeze in place. Be careful when doing this, as over-enthusiastic patting can collapse the whole thing!

20 Unplanned bivouac

The decision to spend a night or any significant length of time out on a mountain in winter should never be taken lightly. Every effort should be made to get down off the tops to a more sheltered area, even if it means a lengthy walk through the night so long as the group remains relatively warm and fit. There are a few situations where the decision is obvious: a physical injury, exhaustion, hypothermia or hopelessly lost in severe weather in the region of serious ground. It may even be an individual or member of another group who needs assistance. The type of emergency will dictate the distance that the group can travel, and the nature of the terrain, snow pack and weather conditions will also have an influence in choosing the site. Once the decision to make a shelter is taken, then the following should be considered:

- Discuss the situation with the group and in particular, the procedures for constructing the shelter.
- The leader's group shelter may be used to good effect, initially as temporary shelter for an injured person and if necessary as shelter during any group briefing. Depending on weather conditions, the group shelter may be used as part of the main emergency shelter (see below).
- Keep the group members as busy as is practical in order to maintain warmth during the shelter construction.
- If there is an injured person, the leader will normally take care of that person and at the same time, organise the rest in constructing their shelter. The injured person should be in the same shelter as the leader so that they can be monitored and treated if necessary.
- Morale may be maintained and boosted if the group can work together and if there is communication between members whilst in the shelter. The leader should keep contact with the rest of the party during the period of shelter. If individual shelters are close together, a small hole may be made between each shelter to allow communication.

PHOTO // GILES TRUSSELL

Snow graves

(A) Snow grave with a person in it
(B) The completed snow grave
(C) Snow grave on a slope with a wall on the lower side
(D) Snow grave using a hard snow layer
(E) Snow grave with tented blocks
(F) Completed snow grave with tented blocks.

19.9.3 Snow graves

If you need to construct a shelter on flat ground and/or there is a shallow snow pack, then a snow grave or a version of it may be the only option. Again this requires a combination of digging and building. Find a suitable spot with at least 0.5m of snow and mark out a shape a bit wider and longer than yourself. Then dig down so that the grave is deeper than the body. If possible try to remove the snow in good blocks to be used later *(see Snow graves B)*. When this is big enough to lie down in, roof over the grave with blocks, either from the initial digging or cut elsewhere and moved into place. Fill any gaps with loose snow. Leave two good big

FIGURE 19.7 A SHOVEL-UP   PHOTO // LIBBY PETER

FIGURE 19.8 SHOVEL-UP: (A) PILE OF RUCKSACKS TO PILE SNOW ON FOR SHOVEL-UP **(B)** COVER SACKS WITH FABRIC, SUCH AS OUTER SHELL, AND COMPACT SNOW ON TOP **(C)** DIG OUT PACKS FROM THE SIDE TO MAKE AN ENTRANCE AND ENLARGE INTERIOR TO SUIT

blocks by the head end where there should be enough room to crawl in feet first and pull these blocks over to seal the entrance *(see Snow graves C)*.

If the snow has a hard surface it may be worthwhile scraping out snow from under the edges to increase the size of the chamber without increasing the size of the top hole *(see Snow graves D)*. If on a slope, then snow taken out from the grave can be piled up on the downhill side to form a wall to bring both sides to the same level before roofing over. This cuts down the amount of digging required. If the snow does not cut into blocks large enough to roof over the grave or is too shallow to get deep enough into then smaller blocks can be leant against each other tent-fashion to form the cover *(see Snow graves E and F)*.

This snow shelter is the least attractive of emergency shelters. It has been said that snow graves are just that! It generally takes longer to construct as more digging is needed, the hole can fill up as you dig if there is spindrift blowing and it is difficult to seal the head end once inside. Lying down means much more of the body is in contact with the snow and so is colder. As much insulation below you as possible helps, as does lying with your knees drawn up to your chest in the foetal position.

19.9.4 Shovel-ups or snow mounds

This type of shelter depends on having soft snow and, if it is dry and fresh, fairly light winds. It can be created on flat ground and where there is not enough depth of snow to dig in. To construct this type of shelter, a mound of snow is piled up and then hollowed out. The act of piling up the snow produces changes in it so that it consolidates rapidly *(see Figure 19.7)*. To make both shovelling up and hollowing out easier, a pile of rucksacks or similar can be the starting point for the mound the size of which will depend on the number of people it must hold. Covering the sacks with bivvy bags, shelters or similar is a help.

Mark out a circle in the snow about a metre radius more than the internal size required. Lay the rucksacks in this and pile snow on top, patting down regularly. When the mound is large enough to hollow out and leave walls about 0.3 to 0.5 metres thick, then burrow in on the lee side and pull out the sacks. Then hollow out the mound from the inside until it is large enough *(see Figure 19.8)*. The eventual thickness of the walls will depend on how well the snow has consolidated and how near the temperature is to freezing. You can also continue carefully piling the already disturbed snow from the inside of the shelter onto the roof to increase the mound size and to continue to enlarge it from inside. Once complete, the interior walls can be smoothed off and some type of entrance tunnel constructed or doorway fashioned from a rucksack or the like. These shelters are vulnerable in thaw conditions.

19.10 Constructing planned snow shelters

19.10.1 Snow holes and caves

Purpose-built snow holes can provide a good, secure base in the mountains. In the UK the main problem with living in a snow hole is not the cold, but rather thawing conditions. For this reason snow holes in this country are best constructed to stay as cool as possible compared to those used in Arctic conditions where the design is to limit the space to be heated and have a sink for cold air. In a snow hole personal equipment and insulation should provide the warmth although with two or three occupants it is easy to raise the temperature to above zero.

While there can be several different shapes and designs, the way they are dug depends on a number of factors, such as the size of the site, depth and hardness of the snow, availability and type of equipment and the number in the group. The first task is to find a suitable site and then probe to ensure there is sufficient depth of snow; a minimum of two metres probing horizontally is best. Establishing how easy or difficult it is to make blocks can also influence the type of hole.

The most efficient type of shelter is usually one dug with two entrances which are parallel and at the same level. These are cut into a steep part of the slope near its top and should be at shoulder width and height and about 1.5 metres apart *(see Figure 19.9)*. If the snow is firm then cutting blocks and removing them is more efficient than digging and the blocks can be set aside and used later. Working on the upper part of the slope means that gravity assists in clearing the snow. If not, then excavated snow may need to be moved two or even three times. Once these doorways are well into the slope they are joined up. This is the most awkward time for digging when space is restricted. Once a U-shape has been formed, the required space is hollowed out.

If unsure of how big to make it, then get the occupants to lie down and see if there is enough room. There should be enough space so no one is touching the sides and there is enough height to stand up comfortably.

FIGURE 19.9 SNOW HOLES SHOWING ONE-DOOR AND TWO-DOOR CONSTRUCTION

The final shape may well be dictated by the consistency and layers in the snow but the most economic, in terms of effort and space, is a half a sphere.

The walls, ceiling and floor should all be smoothed off. If there are protrusions on the roof and there is any melting, then these points become saturated and the source of drips. A good way of smoothing off is to use the back edge of a snow saw. Hold the handle and the tip and flex it into a slight curve then use this to skim the roof and walls. Finally, cut ledges at lying down head height all round the walls to store equipment and provide places to put candles or other lights. If the shelter cannot easily be made high enough to stand up comfortably, then dig a hole in the floor so each person can stand up in turn, for example, when getting organised to go outside.

Once the interior digging has been done one of the doors must be closed and the other entrance adapted for use. Choose the door which would be less convenient for prolonged use to close. This is best done with blocks which, if not already cut when digging, should be cut from a quarry up and to the side and slid into place. Blocking up can either be a vertical wall or one which follows the slope and gives more space inside. If it is difficult to make big blocks then pile up snow and pat it firm. The extra disturbance of the snow will make it easier to work with *(see Figure 19.10)*.

All rucksacks and tools should be taken inside at this stage and the remaining entrance reduced in size and blocked off in the usual manner as for blocked hole shelters. When there is drifting snow, lengthening the entrance tunnel outwards will reduce the chance of being completely buried. Ensure that the entrance is lower than the main floor as this will reduce drifting inside. If there is drifting and the entrance is too high, snow will pile in with remarkable speed.

FIGURE 19.10 A TWO-DOOR SHELTER WHERE BLOCKS WILL BE USED TO CLOSE OFF ONE ENTRANCE. THE WIDE DOOR SPACING WOULD MAKE A SNOW HOLE FOR MORE THAN TWO PEOPLE.
PHOTO // MATT HAWKINS

FIGURE 19.11 INSIDE A SNOW SHELTER WITH PLENTY OF HEIGHT AND SMOOTH WALLS

This type of snow hole can be cut with only one door, sometimes a good option with very soft, easy-digging snow, if there is only one shovel or if there could be a problem closing the door. The disadvantage is that only one person can work at a time so others can get cold when waiting.

Finally, mark the site with an avalanche probe or similar and if there are several holes link them with a rope which is taken inside each entrance. Note where the thinnest part of the roof is in case you need to dig your way out through that point and keep the shovels inside the hole in case of severe drifting. Alternatively, if you are leaving the hole and returning later, shovels should be left outside in a position where they can be easily found and not drift over. If avalanche transceivers are carried, then one can be left in a hole to aid location if they do become buried.

In these snow holes, the roof is likely to sag after a fairly short time so if the shelter is too small initially it may be unusable in a short time as the roof descends, especially if the temperatures are above freezing. If this happens, all the gear may need to be packed up and more digging or roof enlarging may be required. Old shelters of this type may have very icy floors and roofs after a few cycles of freeze and thaw. This can make enlarging them harder work than actually digging a new shelter.

19.10.2 Living in a snow hole

While a snow hole can give good comfortable accommodation, making the best of it requires good personal organisation. Make sure the floor is flat and level, the roof is not going to drip and there are plenty of storage shelves round the walls *(see Figure 19.11)*.

FIGURE 19.12 PERSONAL ORGANISATION INSIDE A GOOD SHELTER WITH A FLAT FLOOR AND STORAGE SHELVES
PHOTO // BILL STRACHAN

Sleeping

A four-season synthetic filled sleeping bag or at least a good three-season one works best in the potentially damp conditions in a snow hole. Down-filled bags, whilst they have advantages, will lose loft and insulation if they become damp and are better in cold, dry conditions. A full-length self-inflating mat provides the best insulation with closed-cell foam mats being second choice. Shorter mats will need further insulation of the legs and feet although your rucksack can be used for this. For snow hole luxury, a breathable and waterproof bivvy bag can be used to enclose both sleeping bag and mat *(see Figure 19.12)*.

Cooking

The most convenient stoves are resealable propane/butane mix canister gas stoves and there are several efficient gas burners available. If the gas canister is also the base for the stove, it should be insulated to reduce cooling of the gas which makes it less efficient. A piece of closed-cell foam mat will suffice. If the canister has cooled or runs low on fuel, then warming it in your sleeping bag or sitting it in a pan filled with a few centimetres of warm water can restore pressure. Liquid fuel or, multi-fuel stoves are also an option. However, meths-burning (methylated spirits) stoves do not work efficiently as a flow of air is required over the burner. Hanging and tower stoves can also work well in a snow hole.

One stove and two pots for three people as a minimum is a good combination. Stainless steel pots with tight-fitting lids to prevent heat loss work well. Although steel is heavier than aluminium, it offers a better heat exchange and is more robust. Use the pan lid while boiling water to increase the stove's efficiency and prevent steam overwhelming the shelter and creating drips. Snow for melting for water can be scraped from the roof or sliced from a snow block, but if there is a source of water nearby then this will save on fuel.

Meals
Almost all living and cooking can be done from the comfort of your sleeping bag. Foodstuffs that require the minimum of cooking are recommended. Dehydrated foods that are made ready by just adding boiling water and 'boil-in-the-bag' meals are fuel-efficient and also better for the local environment as there will be less likelihood to have to dispose of food waste from a pot. Depending on the number of people in the shelter, it is better if one or two volunteer to prepare a specific meal, rather than trying to share the work of every meal between the group.

Lighting
Using candles for lighting will save headtorch battery life. Candles give lots of reflected light if placed in niches around the walls. The small 'night-light' candles need to be insulated from the snow to work efficiently. Always pack out used candles as rubbish.

Clothing
Before settling down, change into any spare dry clothes that you have. Dry socks in particular can make the difference between a pleasant night and little sleep with cold feet! Slightly damp clothing may be worn in the sleeping bag and can dry out overnight. Boots and inner boots should be protected from the dampness and can be brought into your sleeping bag to re-warm.

Drifting snow
Keep a careful watch on the entrance and do not allow it to become completely covered. A severely drifted-over entrance can reduce the amount of oxygen available. Indications of this happening can be candles dimming, stoves not burning properly which may produce poisonous combustion gases, and general tiredness, headaches and, in extreme situations, difficulty in breathing. Drifting will require someone getting up at regular intervals to check and clear snow from the entrance. It is too easy to become warm and comfortable, isolated from the outside and not realise that snow can be burying the whole area. In the worst of conditions drifting snow can be piling in at over 1m per hour!

ⓘ 21 Briefing notes for snow shelters

If instructing any aspect of the use of snow holes or shelters, clear briefings are essential. If going on a planned snow hole trip, a talk with good visuals is a great help. Explain and illustrate in a comfortable environment how snow shelters are made - trying to explain how to construct a snow hole on-site in poor weather conditions is undesirable! Recap on the previous weather pattern, weather forecast and avalanche forecast if available and how this relates to looking for the mostly likely locations and finding the most suitable sites. In light of the forecasts, examine likely dangers such as avalanche risk, drifting show and rising temperatures. The use of maps to illustrate wider principles is helpful.

Ensure that you have the appropriate equipment. At least one shovel in the group is probably standard for normal winter walking. For a planned snow hole trip, snow shovels, saws and avalanche probes will be required. Avalanche transceivers are recommended to mark the snow hole and aid in locating the site in difficult conditions. If practising emergency shelters then a good demonstration is needed. The aim should be to get out of the weather in less than half an hour. It is worthwhile if everyone can try digging with only an axe but also try with a shovel to experience the difference this makes. When completed, safety precautions such as marking and roping the shelters must be made clear.

Whether in a snow hole or shelter the greatest danger is probably drifting in. Every person must be aware of their responsibility for keeping their entrance clear and the signs of lack of air and knowing where the thinnest part of the roof is in case they need to dig out. How the rope is used to find other snow holes must also be made clear.

It must be stressed during winter training courses, particularly the training of mountain leaders, that if faced with an emergency when snow shelters must be used, a thorough appraisal of the situation and the alternatives is required before deciding to dig in. What is the physical and mental state of the group, the condition of the snow and the weather, what are the alternatives and what is the situation with torches and emergency equipment are all issues to be questioned before looking for a site.

WATERLOGGED SNOW LYING OVER STREAM

Water hazards

Water hazards can be a considerable problem in winter. While it would be nice to think that bogs and marshes are frozen solid and streams are covered by bridges of solid snow, the reality is usually very different.

FIGURE 20.1 CROSSING A SNOW BRIDGE

The normal techniques of dealing with water hazards are applicable but with some additional winter problems.

Ice not strong enough to support your weight over bogs and marshes can be a problem, as can crossing streams. Good winter boots and gaiters, however, should keep the water out from short immersions. More serious is crossing substantial streams when the banks and boulders are covered in snow and ice. Using boulders to cross may be hazardous with a high risk of slipping on icy rocks. It is often better to stand on ice-free rocks which lie below the surface of the water. This may be wetter but safer and can be appropriate when rocks are covered by verglas or snow. Poles are a great help and aid to balance when crossing streams.

Crossing streams should be easier as they freeze over and become covered with snow and ice but before this happens they can be difficult and dangerous as deep, soft snow can hide usable boulders, make the footing treacherous, the edges ill-defined and steep banking difficult and strenuous to negotiate. Falling through snow bridges into streams can be extremely dangerous with freezing water and the difficulty of escaping. If this is a danger, then using a rope to belay each person over may be required.

Larger bodies of water such as lakes should be treated with extreme caution if frozen over. Only venture onto large ice-covered expanses of water if totally convinced the ice is thick enough to hold your weight. Be aware that ice is often weaker near the shore and especially where streams enter and leave.

In a strong thaw, river and stream crossing can be serious with ice-cold water and the danger of being swept under snow banks. Often these thaws raise the water level for longer periods of time so waiting for the water level to drop may not be the option that it is in summer. Signs of weakening snow above streams can include sagging and cracking. While the methods of river crossing either with or without a rope are the same at any time of the year, the problems of wetting, cold and hypothermia need to be considered.

GOOD CONDITIONS ON THE FINAL ICY PITCH OF 'PSYCHEDELIC WALL' (VI 6), BEN NEVIS
PHOTO // MURDOCH JAMIESON

Cold injuries

In winter, the cold air temperatures and the difficulty of drying clothing after immersion bring a greater susceptibility to cold injuries. By contrast, the glare of sunlight on snow also brings its own problems.

21.1 Hypothermia

Hypothermia is the condition where the body core temperature drops below 37°C and is clinically described as a core temperature of 35°C or below. The core is the major organs of the body such as the heart, lungs, liver, kidney and brain. If the body is unable to maintain its 37°C through the normal processes of metabolism and movement and is insufficiently insulated from the elements, it will first reduce the blood supply to the periphery and extremities to try to maintain the core temperature. If heat loss is not halted and the body continues to cool then shivering results: an involuntary muscle activity that produces heat. Further heat loss worsens the condition and is characterised by feeling cold and tired, becoming uncommunicative, showing uncharacteristic behaviour, clumsiness and disorientation. Further cooling can lead to unconsciousness and eventually death.

In the mountains the onset of hypothermia is generally slow although hypothermia caused by immersion in cold water can be extremely rapid. Since hypothermia affects the brain, the thought process and decision-making, it is difficult for victims to recognise the condition in themselves.

The factors affecting heat loss are convection, particularly from wind chill, and conduction through direct contact with cold surroundings such as wet clothing or snow, and radiation, where the body loses heat to its surroundings with moisture evaporating from the skin and in breathing. Cold, wet and windy conditions and lack of food, insufficient or ineffective clothing, poor morale, exhaustion or injury are all contributory factors. In the case of benightment, accident or incapacitating injury, hypothermia is very likely to be an additional complication. Exhaustion and hypothermia are very closely linked as the body becomes unable to produce enough energy to maintain itself at the correct temperature.

If someone is suspected of being hypothermic then further heat loss must be stopped. Get the casualty into shelter and insulate them from the ground and further heat loss. If possible, remove wet clothing and replace with dry. If this is impractical then put extra clothing on top of the wet layers. Warm drinks and food are beneficial but never give a casualty alcohol or tobacco.

In the case of an unconscious or injured casualty then the basic first aid provisions of airway, breathing and circulation take priority. Do not

> **22 Prevention of hypothermia**
>
> Prevention is better than cure. The better you know the group, the easier it is to spot any unusual behaviour which could be early signs of hypothermia. Make sure everyone has sufficient clothing and food, and look out for signs of poor eating or excess alcohol the previous night. In harsh conditions, institute a buddy system to help spot signs of hypothermia. The classic mental test of counting down from one hundred in sevens is a useful test. If there are any long delays, accidents or injuries, then keep the danger of hypothermia in mind.

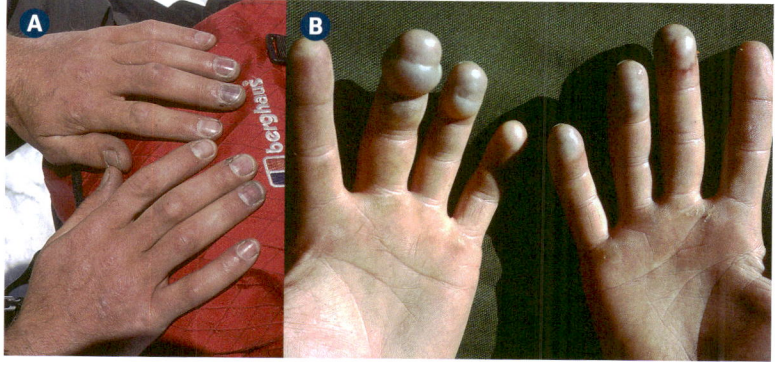

FIGURE 21.1 FROSTBITE: **(A)** FINGERS SHOWING BOTH DEEP AND SUPERFICIAL FROSTBITE TAKEN ABOUT 15 HOURS AFTER BEING AFFECTED. IN THIS CASE, THE TOP OF THE THIRD FINGER ON THE RIGHT HAND WAS LOST TO DEEP FROSTBITE **(B)** THE DEVELOPMENT OF BLISTERS SOME TIME LATER   *PHOTO // DAVE HOLLINGER*

attempt re-warming of a deeply hypothermic casualty. Put them in the recovery position if appropriate and avoid unnecessary movement as this could precipitate heart problems.

21.2 Frostbite

Frostbite is a localised cold injury, usually in the body's periphery. The body tries to protect itself from the cold by shutting down the circulation to the extremities in an attempt to maintain the core temperature. These extremities, the toes, fingers, nose, ears and cheeks, are the commonest places to suffer frostbite damage. Here, tissue freezes as ice crystals form between the cells and grow by extracting water from them causing dehydration in the cells. Damage is also caused by obstruction to the blood supply. There are two degrees of frostbite: superficial, which is known as frostnip, or deep frostbite. Both initially look similar but frostnip can be treated on the hill and frostbite cannot *(see Figure 21.1)*.

At the onset of both, the extremities can first feel painful but as the tissue freezes, feeling is lost. The area becomes white and waxy and can be firm to the touch. In more severe cases blisters may appear, though this may be at a later stage. Because frostbite is associated with the body cooling down, it is often combined with hypothermia and so may be part of a more serious, larger picture. In any case, the quality of an individual's circulation will play an important part in their susceptibility to frostbite.

21.2.1 Superficial frostbite

Frostnip is treatable in the field by re-warming the affected area, usually by the direct application of body heat. This can be your own or someone else's, with the armpit, groin and mouth being best to provide heating. Re-warming fingers, ears and nose is fairly straightforward: simply press the cold part against a warm one. With frostnip to the face, a buddy system can be used where partners keep watch on each other's face for white patches, especially in windy conditions. Re-warming toes however, is more problematic and it may take some discipline to heat up cold feet. The danger sign of feet which are cold and painful suddenly appearing to improve should not be ignored as this could be due to them becoming

FIGURE 21.2 HIGH-QUALITY GOGGLES CAN PREVENT SNOW BLINDNESS   *PHOTO // OLLY SANDERS*

frostbitten. Stop, take off boots and socks and re-warm the toes on a companion's body. Once feeling has returned and the affected area re-warmed, the sensible course of action would be a return to the valley.

21.2.2 Deep frostbite

In frostbite, the tissues are frozen and the blood supply to the affected area severely impaired or even absent. This can affect muscle, tendon, nerves and bone and can lead to tissue loss. Deep frostbite is more likely found after exposure to very low temperatures but can occur in less cold conditions as a result of prolonged exposure. This can be exacerbated by factors such as wet gloves or socks.

Frostbite is initially treated the same way as frostnip. However, it is vital that a re-warmed area is protected from further freezing or physical damage. It is less damaging to return with a frozen foot than to do so on one which has been thawed. Any blisters should not be burst but covered with a sterile dressing. In the UK, it is unlikely that frostbite would need to be treated by anyone other than a medical professional. The strongest advice is to leave deep frozen tissue until skilled help is available.

There are more things not to do to a frostbitten area than there is treatment. These include:

- Do not rub with anything at all
- Do not warm with direct heat
- Do not give cigarettes or alcohol
- Do not burst any blisters
- Do not allow re-warmed tissue to get cold again

21.3 Immersion foot

Although not directly a cold injury and unlikely to be encountered, this is not unlike frostbite and is caused by prolonged exposure of the extremities to wet and cold. This could develop through having continually wet feet for more than a couple of days, so could be seen on a long cross-country expedition. Contributory factors are similar to those leading to hypothermia and are generally cooling, exhaustion, dehydration and lack of proper nutrition. The symptoms include numbness, pins and needles and slight swelling. Other symptoms such as blisters, burning and shooting pains may develop later.

21.4 Snow blindness

Snow blindness is caused by excessive exposure to ultra violet light. Normally most of the UV light is absorbed by the atmosphere, water vapour and pollutants in the air. What does reach us does not normally present a problem as our eyes are shielded from these damaging rays by our eyebrows and eyelashes. However, on snow this UV can be reflected into the eyes from below. Fresh snow can reflect about 90% of this light and this can be as bad on days when the sky is overcast as the UV is also reflected from the clouds. The result is that these rays are trapped between the snow and the cloud with an increase in power.

This over-exposure to UV light can be harmful and painful. Eyes feel irritated and dry and as if they are full of sand. Moving the eyes and blinking can be very sore, they can become red and water excessively and the eyelids may swell. Temporary blindness may even result. Fortunately, the damage is not permanent and eyes heal themselves in a few days. A dark environment and cold compresses may ease the discomfort.

The best prevention is to use good quality goggles or sunglasses. These should not allow light to enter from the sides, above or below, and have high quality lenses (*see Figure 21.2*).

21.5 Sunburn

Because of the way UV light is bounced from the snow surface, it is easy to get badly burned on sunny days, especially in the spring. Sun creams or blocks with a high factor sunscreen should eliminate this problem but remember to put it on below the chin and under the ears and nose. These are areas which receive much of this reflected light. A salve or bloc to protect the lips is also worthwhile.

21.6 Prevention

With all cold injuries, prevention is definitely better than the cure. Frostbite and immersion foot are all exacerbated by poor footwear, insufficient insulation, poor nutrition, dehydration and lack of appropriate preparation. Any restriction of the circulation, such as too tight boots or gloves or crampon straps, can increase the likelihood of developing frostbite. Individuals who suffer from circulation disorders are even more susceptible.

23 Prevention of cold injuries

The main aids to avoiding cold injury are knowledge, preparation and vigilance. Ensure the group is suitably equipped, that boots and crampons fit well and do not restrict circulation. Make sure everyone has sufficient food, drink and extra clothing, especially gloves and/or mitts. Brief everyone about the dangers of cold injury and what to look for. If particularly cold and windy, institute a buddy system, watch for frostnip on cheeks, noses and ears. Give the group plenty of opportunity to say how they are feeling and take action early on if there are signs of cold damage. If one person in the group is showing signs of frostnip, it is likely that others are experiencing similar problems. The better you know the group, the easier it is to make appropriate judgements. When in really bad conditions, try to talk to people individually, and look at them when doing this. One of the early signs of hypothermia may be being uncommunicative and withdrawn and this could easily be overlooked in a group situation.

Reynaud's Syndrome is a condition affecting the circulation in which the digits rapidly turn white then blue, become cool to the touch and feel numb. This is brought on by cold although emotion and stress can also trigger its onset. It is not uncommon and the majority of those affected appear to be women. Prior knowledge of anyone suffering from Reynaud's Syndrome, circulatory problems or taking medication which could affect circulation is important in winter.

It is easier to keep extremities warm rather than re-warm them after they have become cold, so appropriate clothing is vital. Having enough insulation on the legs is important for the feet, and ensuring there are no gaps at the wrist helps keep the hands warm. Avoid becoming dehydrated as then the blood becomes thicker and peripheral circulation decreases. Although not so obvious in cold conditions, it is still necessary to keep drinking and remember that by the time you are thirsty it is becoming too late. If your urine is yellow you are becoming dehydrated. Using a hydration system with a drinking hose is a good idea to ensure sufficient fluid intake. Besides spare clothing, having spare sunglasses or goggles and sun cream and lip salve can also be handy in certain conditions.

HEADING FOR CASTLEGATES GULLY IN THE LOCH AVON BASIN, NORTHERN CAIRNGORMS
PHOTO // GARRY SMITH

A1 Access legislation

A.1.1 Current legislation on access

	Recent legislation	Code	Access	Natural Heritage
Scotland	Land Reform (Scotland) Act 2003	Scottish Outdoor Access Code	Scottish Natural Heritage	Scottish Natural Heritage
Northern Ireland	The Access to the Countryside (Northern Ireland) Order 1983	Northern Ireland Country Code	Northern Ireland Countryside Access and Activities Network (CAAN)	Environment and Heritage Service
Wales	Wales Countryside and Rights of Way Act 2000	Country Code	Cyfoeth Naturiol Cymru/Natural Resources Wales	Cyfoeth Naturiol Cymru/Natural Resources Wales
England	Countryside and Rights of Way Act 2000	Country Code	Natural England	Natural England
Republic of Ireland	Occupiers Liability Act 1995. This is not a specific act regarding access, but includes access issues	Mountaineering Ireland 'Good Practice Guide for Walkers and Climbers'	Mountaineering Ireland	The Heritage Council

You can find out more by visiting the following websites:

Legislation for the UK, Scotland, Wales and Northern Ireland
www.legislation.gov.uk/

Scotland

Scottish Natural Heritage
www.snh.gov.uk

Scottish Outdoor Access Code
www.outdooraccess-scotland.com

England

Natural England
www.naturalengland.org.uk

Wales

Cyfoeth Naturiol Cymru/ Natural Resources Wales
www.naturalresourceswales.gov.uk

Northern Ireland

Department of Agriculture, Environment and Rural Affairs
www.daera-ni.gov.uk/

Countryside Access and Activities Network
www.countrysiderecreation.com

Republic of Ireland

The Heritage Council
www.heritagecouncil.ie

Legislation for the Republic of Ireland
www.oireachtas.ie/parliament

UK

Dept of Environment, Food and Rural Affairs
www.defra.gov.uk/wildlife-countryside

Joint Nature Conservation Committee
www.jncc.gov.uk

Her Majesty's Stationery Office
www.opsi.gov.uk

A2 Mountain Training

Mountain Training's qualifications and skills courses are nationally recognised and have been developed to educate and train people in walking, climbing and mountaineering.

Our courses are run by approved providers who are scattered all around the UK and Ireland. When you book onto a course, they're the ones who will train and assess you, teach you how to climb, navigate, lead etc.

On a day to day basis, Mountain Training is run by a small staff team in the UK and Ireland. There are also quite a few volunteers who represent the interests of outdoor and educational organisations and help to steer Mountain Training at a strategic level.

When we're not busy creating and refining our schemes and ensuring the quality of our courses, Mountain Training also provide:
- advice on safety in the outdoor industry
- a range of publications to support the awards
- opportunities for Continued Personal Development through the Mountain Training Association

A.2.1 Mountain Training's winter qualifications
Three of our qualifications involve training and assessment in winter.
- Winter Mountain Leader
- International Mountain Leader
- Winter Mountaineering and Climbing Instructor

More information about each qualification can be found on our website: *www.mountain-training.org*.

A.2.2 Who uses the qualifications?
The users of our qualifications come from a variety of places including organisations within the public sector, such as local authority education establishments, and voluntary youth organisations. In recent years there has been a rapid increase in the provision of mountain-related activities by the private and voluntary sector. Specific users include teachers, Duke of Edinburgh's Award assessors, Scout leaders and a wide range of independent operators.

A.2.3 What is involved?
Although the details of each scheme vary there are a number of common elements.

Registration
Before attending any course candidates must create an account on our Candidate Management System (CMS), or log in if they already have one, and register for the appropriate scheme.

Training courses
All the qualifications involve practical training delivered by specially approved training staff. The relevant awarding body monitors the standards of training. Some schemes have the facility to recognise relevant prior experience and training by granting exemptions from training.

Consolidation period
In pursuit of a leadership qualification, training courses alone cannot turn people into effective leaders and it is important that candidates use the time between training and assessment to practise your skills, paying particular attention to any weaknesses identified during the training course.

Assessment
All of our walking leadership qualifications have mandatory practical assessments conducted by specially approved assessors.

Continuing personal and professional development
Having gained a qualification, candidates are expected to maintain and record their involvement in the activities as both an individual and as a leader. Opportunities for development are available through the Mountain Training Association (MTA), British Association of International Mountain Leaders (BAIML) and the Association of Mountaineering Instructors (AMI).

A.2.4 The mountaineering councils

The British Mountaineering Council (BMC), Mountaineering Scotland and Mountaineering Ireland are the representative bodies for hill walkers, climbers and mountaineers in the UK and Ireland. They lobby and advise government on a range of important issues such as access, risk and responsibility and changes in legislation.

Mountain Training and the mountaineering councils work closely together in a number of areas concerned with mountaineering good practice for individuals, leaders and groups. On a broad level, Mountain Training administers formal training schemes and the mountaineering councils dispense advice and expertise in more informal areas of activity such as student clubs, mountaineering clubs and youth participation.

A3 Useful contacts

A3.1 Climbing sites

www.ukclimbing.com
www.ukbouldering.com/board/index.php

Irish Climbing
www.climbing.ie
www.irishclimbing.com

A3.2 Weather sites

www.metoffice.gov.uk
www.metcheck.com
www.mwis.org.uk
www.sais.gov.uk

A3.3 Books and Maps

Cordee
T 0116 254 3579
www.cordee.co.uk

Cicerone Press
T 01539 562 069
www.cicerone.co.uk

Stanfords Ltd
www.stanfords.co.uk

A3.4 Rescue

Mountain Rescue Committee of England and Wales
www.mountain.rescue.org.uk

Irish Mountain Rescue Association
www.mountainrescue.ie

Mountain Rescue Committee of Scotland
www.mrcofs.org

National Search and Rescue Dogs Association
www.nsarda.org.uk

A3.5 Environment

RSPB
www.rspb.org.uk

Cyfoeth Naturiol Cymru/ Natural Resources Wales
www.naturalresourceswales.gov.uk

Natural England
www.naturalengland.org.uk

Scottish Natural Heritage
www.snh.gov.uk

A3.6 Mountain Training

Mountain Training
Siabod Cottage
Capel Curig
Conwy LL24 0ES
T 01690 720 272
info@mountain-training.org
www.mountain-training.org

A3.7 Mountaineering councils

British Mountaineering Council
BMC, 177–179 Burton Road,
Manchester M20 2BB
T 0161 445 6111
F 0161 445 4500
office@thebmc.co.uk
www.thebmc.co.uk

Mountaineering Ireland
Sport HQ, 13 Joyce Way,
Park West Business Park,
Dublin 12, Ireland
T 00 3531 625 1115
info@mountaineering.ie
www.mountaineering.ie

Mountaineering Scotland
MC of S, The Old Granary,
West Mill Street,
Perth PH1 5QP
T 01738 638 227
info@mountaineering.scot
www.mountaineering.scot

A3.8 Professional associations and government agencies

Adventure Activities Licensing Authority
17 Lambourne Crescent,
Llanishen, Cardiff CF4 5GG
T 02920 755 715
info@aala.org
www.hse.gov.uk/aala

Association of Mountaineering Instructors (AMI)
www.ami.org

Health and Safety Executive
Rose Court, 2 Southwark Bridge,
London SE1 9HS
hseinformationservices@natbrit.com
www.hse.gov.uk

Mountain Training Association (MTA)
www.mountain-training.org/mta

British Association of International Mountain Leaders (BAIML)
www.baiml.org

A4 Index

A

Abalakov threads *227*
anchors *153*
    abseil anchor *160*, *168*, *247*
    bollard *154*, *158*
        ice *168*
        snow *158*
    bucket seat *156*
    buried axe *160*
        reinforced *163*
        T axe *163*
    centralised *234*, *244*
    deadman *163*
    ice *167*, *219*
    natural *168*, *236*
    in-situ *236*
    linking *234*
    rock *169*, *230*
        chocks *231*
        finding *231*
    snow *154-167*
        improvised *167*
    stomper *157*
    tying to *139-144*
    vertical axe *167*
avalanche *109*
    action if caught *126*
    avoidance *124*
    axe test *123*
    compression test *123*
    crystal size *122*
    hardness tests *(see also Snow)* *121*
    hazard evaluation *124*
    rescue *128*
    route selection *124*
    searches *128*
    slope assessment *119*
    sastrugi *104*
    slope angles *119*
        wind slab *106*
    snow pits *120*
    Scottish Avalanche Information Service *114*
    survival *127*
    terrain traps *120*
    types of *110*
        loose snow *110*
        slab *111*
        wet snow *114*
    wetness test *(see also Snow)* *122*
    safety *92*
    transceivers *129*, *290*

B

Be Avalanche Aware *115*
belays and belaying *134*, *153*
    belay device *188*
    dead rope *157*, *158*
    foot brake *166*
    ice *229*
        ice screw anchors *219*
    indirect belay *154*
    live rope *156*, *158*
    shoulder belay *141*, *158*
    snow *154*, *218*
    changeovers at *219*
    stomper *157*
    waist belay *141*, *157*
bivvy bag *(see Equipment)*
boots *7*, *176*
bottom-roping *269*
bouldering *269*

C

cams *232*
climbing techniques *194*
    accessories *228*
    bouldering *214*, *269*
    cornice *198*
        scarp slope *198*
        tunnelling *199*
    down climbing *203*
    dry tooling *214*

falling off *214*
grades *195*
ice climbing *199*
  'eggshell' *201*
  'staggering' *202*
  axe swing *199*
  crampon techniques *201*
  dinner-plating *201*
  front-pointing *202*
  ice bulges *205*
  ice formations *204*
  névé *201*
  reading the ice *201*
  remove the pick *200*
  snow-ice *201*
  starring *201*
  steep ice, moving on *202*
  thin ice *205*
leashless climbing *213*
mixed climbing *207*
  axe techniques *207*
  camming *209*
  choking *211*
  crampons on rock *210*
  hooking *208*
  stacking *211*
  torquing *208*
  turf *211*
  vegetation *210*
  wedging *208*
resting *198*
snow climbing *194*
  'choking' the axe *194*
  daggering *194*
  French technique *91, 194*
  front-pointing *93, 194, 196*
  hybrid technique *94, 194*
traversing *203*
clothing *4, 35, 176*
  balaclava *178*
  base layer *4*

belay jacket *7, 176*
gaiters *9, 176*
  supergaiters *10*
gloves *10, 178*
  mitts *10, 178*
hat *11, 178*
  balaclava *9*
helmet *11, 73, 187*
jacket *6, 7*
layering system *4, 7*
mid layer *5*
outer shell *4, 6*
over-trouser *6*
salopettes *6*
shell jacket *176*
shell trousers *176*
soft shell *5, 176*
wicking *4*
compass *(see Navigation)*
cold injuries *249, 297*
  frostbite *299*
    deep *300*
    superficial *299*
  hypothermia *298*
  immersion foot *300*
  prevention *301*
  snow blindness *301*
  sunburn *301*
crampons *83, 185*
  anti-balling plates *91*
  attachment of *87, 186*
  balling-up *91*
  care and maintenance of *88*
  carrying *88*
  clip-on *9, 87*
  emergency repairs *89*
  fit *87, 187*
  mono point *186*
  putting on *89*
  technical *185*
  techniques *91*

American *94*
flat-footing *91*
French *91*
front-pointing *93*
hybrid *94*
mixed *94*
types *84*
   articulated *84*
   flexible *84*
   rigid *86*

D

daggering *(see Climbing techniques)* *194*
descent *247, 268*
   'rope bomb' *148, 247*
   angel's wings *142, 147*
   classic *142, 147*
   lowering two clients *258*
   South African *142, 147*
   throwing ropes *247*
   while moving together *254*
   with clients *268, 270*
dry tooling *(see Climbing techniques)* *214*

E

environmental issues *17*
   erosion *18*
   litter *20*
   path widening *18*
   sanitation *19*
   vegetation *20*
   winter climbs *20*
equipment *3*
   bivvy bag *12*
   gloves *10*
   goggles *12*
   group shelter *13*
   headtorch *12*
   rucksack *11, 177*
      technical *137*
   personal *189*

walking poles *13-15*
snow saw *278*
winter rack *190*
erosion *(see Environmental issues)* *18*

F

frostbite *(see Cold injuries)*

G

gaiters *(see Clothing)*
glissading *80*
gloves *(see Clothing)*
goggles *(see Equipment)*
GPS *(see also Snow)* *49*
graupel *(see also Navigation)* *101*
group shelter *(see Equipment)*
guiding *262*
   climbing in parallel *264*
   climbing in series *263*
   rope systems *263*
   stance management *264*

H

harness *188*
   improvised *141, 139*
headtorch *(see Equipment)*
helmet *(see Clothing)*
hypothermia *(see Cold injuries)*

I

ice axe *55, 178*
   'choking' *194*
   adze *56*
   camming *209*
   care and maintenance of *182*
   carrying the *58*
   finger rest *182*
   hammer *56*
   head, the *56*
   hooking *208*
   lanyard leashes *183*

leashes *57, 184*
pick *56, 180*
pommel *182*
shaft *57, 179*
spike *57*
stowing the *58*
technical *178*
torquing *208*
wedging *208*
length *58*
ice drive-ins *226*
ice screws *219*
'V' threads *227*
maintenance of *226*
placement *222*
on the lead *224*
removing *225*
tied-off *224*
ice threads *227*
improvised rescue *(see Rescue)*
indoor walls *269*

K

karabiner *189*
care and maintenance of *189*
kicking steps *(see Steps)*
knots *135-139*
bowline *136*
clove hitch *137*
figure of eight *136*
friction hitch *141*
half hitch *139*
Italian hitch *138*
lark's foot *139*
overhand *135*
stopper knot *137*
stoppered slipknot *137*
tape knot *135*

L

litter *(see Environmental Issues)*

M

map *(see Navigation)*
mixed climbing *207*

N

Naismith's Rule *38*
navigation *31*
aiming-off *43*
altimeter *35*
attack point *43, 46*
bearing *38*
back *35*
following a *37*
taking a *37*
boxing *45*
compass *34*
contour *42, 43*
dead-reckoning *39*
distance *37, 41*
dog-legs *44*
GPS *49*
handrail *44*
leapfrogging *40*
map *33*
map reading *42*
pacing *38*
problem winter conditions *32*
relocation *35*
route choice *42*
sighting *39*
slope aspect *45*
sweep search *48, 49*
tick-off features *44*
timing *38*
using footprints *40*
whiteout *33*
wristwatch *34*
strategies *38*
nutrition *148, 249*

P

pitons *232*
    placing and removing *232*

Q

quickdraw *189*
    energy-absorbing *190*

R

rescue *249*
rime ice *(see also Snow)* *100*
rock anchors *(see Anchors)*
rope *187*
    'rope bomb' *148, 247*
    attaching to *139*
    controlling the *141*
    double-rope *187*
    fixed rope *268*
    half ropes *187*
    live *(see Belays and belaying)*
    single rope *187*
    throwing *247*
    systems *263*
    rope techniques *251*
      confidence-roping *257*
      descent *254*
      general considerations *252*
      long roping *252*
      lowering two clients *258*
      moving together *252*
      short-roping *254, 257*
      taking chest coils *255*
      traversing *254*
      tying on *254*

S

safety standards *(see Equipment)* *177*
sanitation *(see Environmental Issues)*
screamer *(see Quickdraw)*
security *133*
    attaching to the rope *139*

controlling the rope *141*
cutting steps *(see also Steps)* *65*
emergency equipment *137*
knots *(see separate entry)* *135*
shoulder belay *141, 158*
spotting *134*
tying to anchors *140-144*
using a rope *134*
waist belay *141*
    without a rope *134*
self-arrest *71*
    basic position, the *74*
    feet first *75*
    head first *76*
    preparation *73*
    rolling *79*
    self-belay *72*
    slope selection *72*
    tumbling *79*
    without the axe *79*
self-belay *(see Self-Arrest)*
shelters *277*
    bivvy shelter *283*
    blocked hole *284*
    cutting blocks *280*
    emergency snow shelter *283*
    environmental considerations *282*
      litter *282*
      sanitation *282*
    finishing off *282*
    location *279, 280*
    preparation *281*
    shovel-up *287*
    snow cave *288*
    snow grave *286*
    snow hole *288*
    tools *278*
    unplanned bivouac *285*
shovel *278*
sling *191*
    sit sling *139, 141*

snow *99*
  cornice *107*
  depth hoar *103*
  dry loose snow *106*
  faceting *102*
  firn *102*
  formations *105*
  graupel *101*
  kinetic growth *102*
  melt-freeze cycle *103*
  névé *103*
  rime ice – difference between and snow *100*
  rounding *100*
  sastrugi *104*, *105*
  scarp slope *107*
  solar radiation *104*
  stability checks *(see also Avalanche)* *122*
  structure of *99*
  surface hoar *103*
  temperature gradient *102*, *103*
  types of *105*
  wet *107*
  wind slab *106*
  wind effects on *104*
  wind features *104*
soloing *249*, *265*
Scottish Avalanche Information Service *114*
stance construction *236*
stance management *245*, *262*, *266*
steps *62*
  ascent *63*
  bucket *68*
  cutting *65*
  descending *64*
  kicking *62*
  letterbox *68*
  pigeonhole *69*
  plunge *64*
  side *68*
  slab *68*
  slash *66*
  traversing *64*
  type of *66*
  in descent *64*
  patterns *66*
sweep search *(see Navigation)*

T

teaching winter climbing *259*
  approach *260*
  climbing in parallel *264*
  climbing in series *263*
  fixed rope *268*
  guiding *262*
  rope systems *263*
  stance management *264*
  strategies for *262*
  leading in winter *210*
technical equipment *(see Equipment)*
technique training *269*
training for winter climbing *215*
turfie *233*

V

verglas *100*

W

walking poles *(see Equipment)*
warthog *233*
water hazards *295*
snow bridges *296*
winter climbing strategies *239*
  approaching the climb *243*
  descent *247*
  gearing up *243*
  preparation *242*
  stance management *245*, *264*, *266*
  stances on ice *241*
winter grades *195*

FOUND THIS BOOK USEFUL?

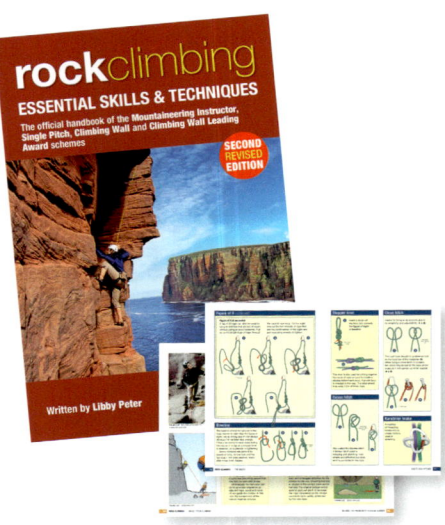 

ROCK CLIMBING
LIBBY PETER
ISBN 978 0954 151164
Essential skills and techniques for all aspects of single-pitch, multi-pitch and indoor climbing.

NAVIGATION IN THE MOUNTAINS
CARLO FORTE
ISBN 978 0954 151157
Tools and techniques for navigating in the hills and mountains including winter, overseas and GPS.

Available in all good bookshops and online

You will find the other essential Mountain Training publications helpful too

INTERNATIONAL MOUNTAIN TREKKING
PLAS Y BRENIN INSTRUCTIONAL TEAM
ISBN 978 0954 151171
A practical manual for trekkers and leaders covering all elements of international trekking.

HILLWALKING
STEVE LONG
ISBN 978 0954 151195
The official handbook of the Mountain Training walking schemes.

www.mountain-training.org